Human Rights Activism and the End of the Cold War

Two of the most pressing questions facing international historians today are how and why the Cold War ended. *Human Rights Activism and the End of the Cold War* explores how, in the aftermath of the signing of the Helsinki Final Act in 1975, a transnational network of activists committed to human rights in the Soviet Union and Eastern Europe made the topic a central element in East–West diplomacy. As a result, human rights eventually became an important element of Cold War diplomacy and a central component of détente. Sarah B. Snyder demonstrates how this network influenced both Western and Eastern governments to pursue policies that fostered the rise of organized dissent in Eastern Europe, freedom of movement for East Germans, and improved human rights practices in the Soviet Union – all factors in the end of the Cold War.

Sarah B. Snyder is a Lecturer in International History at University College London. She has published a number of scholarly articles in journals such as *Cold War History, Diplomacy and Statecraft, Journal of Transatlantic Studies*, and *Journal of American Studies*, as well as multiple book chapters. Dr. Snyder specializes in transnational, international, and diplomatic history.

To Danny

Human Rights in History

Edited by

Stefan-Ludwig Hoffmann, *Zentrum für Zeithistorische Forschung*
Samuel Moyn, *Columbia University*

This series showcases new scholarship exploring the backgrounds of human rights today. With an open-ended chronology and international perspective, the series seeks works attentive to the surprises and contingencies in the historical origins and legacies of human rights ideals and interventions. Books in the series will focus not only on the intellectual antecedents and foundations of human rights, but also on the incorporation of the concept by movements, nation-states, international governance, and transnational law.

Other books in the series:

Stefan-Ludwig Hoffmann, editor, *Human Rights in the Twentieth Century*

Human Rights Activism and the End of the Cold War

A Transnational History of the Helsinki Network

SARAH B. SNYDER

University College London

CAMBRIDGE
UNIVERSITY PRESS

CAMBRIDGE UNIVERSITY PRESS
Cambridge, New York, Melbourne, Madrid, Cape Town,
Singapore, São Paulo, Delhi, Mexico City

Cambridge University Press
32 Avenue of the Americas, New York NY 10013-2473, USA

Published in the United States of America by Cambridge University Press, New York

www.cambridge.org
Information on this title: www.cambridge.org/9781107645103

First published 2011
First paperback edition 2013

A catalogue record for this publication is available from the British Library

Library of Congress Cataloging in Publication data
Snyder, Sarah B., 1977–
Human rights activism and the end of the cold war : a transnational
history of the Helsinki network / Sarah B. Snyder.
p. cm. – (Human rights in history)
Includes bibliographical references and index.
ISBN 978-1-107-00105-3 (hardback)
1. Human rights. 2. Human rights advocacy. 3. Cold War. I. Title.
JC571.S688 2011
323.09'047–dc22   2010052776

ISBN 978-1-107-00105-3 Hardback
ISBN 978-1-107-64510-3 Paperback

Contents

Acknowledgments

Writing this book has been a thoroughly enjoyable experience, in large part due to the people and institutions that have supported me throughout this process.

A number of institutions generously granted funds necessary to facilitate my research travel in Europe and the United States, including the Department of History and the Graduate School of Arts and Sciences at Georgetown University, the Organization of Security and Cooperation in Europe, the Gerald R. Ford Foundation, the Open Society Archives, the Robert J. Dole Institute of Politics at the University of Kansas, the Scowcroft Institute of International Affairs at Texas A & M University, and the Whitney and Betty MacMillan Center for International and Area Studies, the Department of History, and International Security Studies at Yale University.

I have benefited from the wise counsel and insightful criticism of many readers as I revised this manuscript. My undergraduate and graduate advisers, Abbott Gleason and Nancy Bernkopf Tucker, both deserve particular mention not only for their careful attention over the years but also as they have served as important role models for the type of scholar and teacher I aspire to be. Like many first books, mine began as a dissertation, and Michael Kazin, David Painter, and Mark von Hagen offered useful suggestions on how best to revise it for publication. In subsequent years, Jan Eckel, Mark Lawrence, Mark Bradley, Sam Moyn, Will Hitchcock, John Gaddis, and an anonymous reader for Cambridge University Press provided further advice. In addition, I have benefited greatly from the support of friends and colleagues, in particular Amy Sheridan, Allison Higgins, Meredith Oyen, Craig Daigle, Paul Rubinson, Hang Nguyen,

Amanda Moniz, Katie Darnton, Ryan Irwin, and Greg Domber. The Department of History at University College London has recently become my new professional home, and I appreciate their warm welcome as I put the finishing touches on this manuscript.

I would also like to acknowledge the support and encouragement my immediate and extended family has offered me in the different phases of writing this book. In addition, I would like to express my appreciation to those who housed and fed me in my research travels, including Allison Higgins, George and Sue Schreck, Stephen and Jaynie Lilley, Meredith Oyen, Craig Daigle, Josh Pollack, Brian and Anne Bennett, Paul Rubinson and Kristin Hay, and Duane and Ann Oyen. Furthermore, Eric Crahan and his colleagues at Cambridge University Press have expertly shepherded my manuscript through the editorial and production process.

Lastly, a special thank you to my husband, Danny Fine, to whom I have dedicated this book. It is fitting that our relationship began as editor and writer on a student newspaper many years ago, as he has remained an insightful and good-spirited editor of my writing, always making it more accessible and concise. More importantly, he has been unwavering in his support of my vocation regardless of where it has taken me, and us.

Introduction

The rapid demise of communism in Eastern Europe, the reunification of a long-divided Germany, and finally the disintegration of the Soviet Union stunned almost all observers. These three developments, all within a few years of each other, represent for many the end of the Cold War. Understanding how and why the Cold War concluded is one of the most pressing questions historians face today. Thus far, scholars have considered a range of factors in assessing the end of the Cold War, with the predominant explanations focusing on Soviet economic stagnation, the arms race, the influence of ideas, the power of personality, Eastern European agency, and overextension abroad.[1] Historians generally have

[1] See for example, Archie Brown, *The Gorbachev Factor* (New York: Oxford University Press, 1996); John Lewis Gaddis, "Hanging Tough Paid Off," *Bulletin of American Scientists* (January/February 1989): 11–4; Stephen G. Brooks and William C. Wohlforth, "Economic Constraints and the End of the Cold War," in William Wohlforth, ed., *Cold War Endgame: Oral History, Analysis, Debates* (University Park: Pennsylvania State University Press, 2003); T. Ivan Berend, *From the Soviet Bloc to the European Union: The Economic and Social Transformation of Central and Eastern Europe since 1973* (New York: Cambridge University Press, 2009), 6, 20; Jeffrey T. Checkel, *Ideas and International Political Change: Soviet/Russian Behavior and the End of the Cold War* (New Haven: Yale University Press, 1997); Andrew Bennett, "The Guns That Didn't Smoke: Ideas and the Soviet Non-Use of Force in 1989," *Journal of Cold War Studies* 7:2 (Spring 2005): 81–109; Thomas Risse-Kappen, "Ideas Do Not Float Freely: Transnational Coalitions, Domestic Structures, and the End of the Cold War," *International Organization* (Spring 1994): 185–214; Daniel C. Thomas, "Human Rights Ideas, the Demise of Communism, and the End of the Cold War," *Journal of Cold War Studies* 7:2 (Spring 2005): 110–41; Robert D. English, *Russia and the Idea of the West: Gorbachev, Intellectuals and the End of the Cold War* (New York: Columbia University Press, 2000); Gregory F. Domber, *Supporting the Revolution: America, Democracy, and the End of the Cold War in Poland, 1981–1989* (Ph. D. Dissertation, George Washington University,

I

underestimated the role of human rights advocacy and the influence of the 1975 Helsinki Final Act, which was the culmination of three years of negotiations at the Conference on Security and Cooperation in Europe (CSCE) and contained principles to govern East–West interactions in Europe.[2] The Helsinki Final Act, however, spurred the development of a transnational network that significantly contributed to the end of the Cold War.

Examining the end of the Cold War through the lens of the CSCE also suggests a less traditional endpoint to the half-century superpower rivalry – January 19, 1989. On that date, the CSCE Vienna Review Meeting ended, representing a substantive end to the divide that had previously characterized Europe and East–West relations. The significance of the close of the Vienna Meeting lay first in its concluding document, which had been under negotiation since November 1986. The agreement contained provisions supporting religious freedom, protecting civil liberties, and easing international travel as well as most importantly, a mandate to meet in Moscow in 1991 to discuss what was termed the "human dimension," namely human rights and human contacts. Second, unlike previous meetings that were characterized by disingenuous claims by Eastern European governments, the Vienna Meeting was notable for the concrete progress made on human rights during the course of the negotiations. Under internal and external pressure, communist leaders eased restrictions on emigration, freed political prisoners, and allowed greater access to independent information. Such changes signaled a dramatically different approach to East–West relations as well as to the relationship between state and society in Eastern Europe, which suggested the Cold War had ended or that, at least, its framework had been meaningfully altered.

From the CSCE's opening negotiations in 1972 to the first session of the Vienna Review Meeting in November 1986, attitudes toward the conference evolved considerably. As will be shown in the chapters that follow, the Soviet Union was the principal proponent of holding the CSCE,

---

2008); Constantine Pleshakov, *There Is No Freedom Without Bread!: 1989 and the Civil War That Brought Down Communism* (New York: Farrar, Straus and Giroux, 2009); Victor Sebestyen, *Revolution 1989: The Fall of the Soviet Empire* (New York: Pantheon Books, 2009); and Charles S. Maier, *Dissolution: The Crisis of Communism and the End of East Germany* (Princeton: Princeton University Press, 1997).

[2] Others have taken a broader view of the CSCE but without the benefit of multiarchival sources. See for example, William Korey, *The Promises We Keep: Human Rights, the Helsinki Process and American Foreign Policy* (New York: St. Martin's Press, 1993).

but once the Helsinki Final Act was signed, Soviet leaders feared possible damaging consequences from the subsequent negotiations. The United States, on the other hand, resisted the initial CSCE discussions and was skeptical of the value of the Helsinki Final Act but came to see the agreement as a valuable tool in its competition with the USSR. Over time, the Western and neutral and nonaligned participants in the CSCE were able to ensure that it became a forum that facilitated political change and eventually led to improved human rights practices.

My work makes a number of important contributions to the historical literature, including highlighting the Commission on Security and Cooperation in Europe as an essential advocate for and collaborator with the emerging transnational network of Helsinki activists; demonstrating its central role in transforming the United States attitude toward and position in the CSCE; examining how the Moscow Helsinki Group's decision to monitor Soviet compliance with the Helsinki Final Act reframed the content and significance of the Helsinki Final Act; explaining how United States President Jimmy Carter's focus on human rights, and more specifically on the CSCE, integrated the issue permanently into United States foreign policy toward Eastern Europe; demonstrating how the formation of Helsinki Watch and the International Helsinki Federation for Human Rights strengthened and formalized diffuse Helsinki monitoring activities, heightening their effectiveness; establishing that the selection of Mikhail Gorbachev to lead the Soviet Union offered Helsinki activists and their government supporters an opportunity to achieve their objectives because he recognized that progress on human rights had become a prerequisite for his reforms; and revealing how Helsinki activism ultimately contributed to the peaceful end of the Cold War in Europe. Finally, my research adds to the growing body of literature on the history of global human rights politics.

My research on the influence of the Helsinki process on the end of the Cold War builds upon the work of scholars such as Daniel C. Thomas, who has examined the influence and acceptance of human rights norms in the wake of the signing of the Helsinki Final Act. Like Thomas's scholarship, my findings indicate Mikhail Gorbachev and other Eastern European leaders may have moderated their personal attitudes toward and thinking about human rights in the late 1980s, but the evidence currently available is only suggestive. What can be shown is that a number of Soviet officials came to see changing their country's human rights practices as in their national interests, given that their records had become tied to progress on trade, arms control, and political support. My work presents a more complex account, emphasizing that collective and individual human rights advocacy influenced the end of the Cold War rather than concentrating solely on human rights norms.

In the following chapters, I examine how what began as a Soviet effort to secure its post–World War II borders ultimately played a meaningful role in the end of the Cold War. Since 1954, the Soviets had pursued what they termed a European Security Conference in order to secure formal recognition of the frontiers in Central and Eastern Europe. Their proposal, however, did not gain any Western support until the late 1960s and early 1970s, when it was considered in the context of a broader effort at reducing East–West tension. Neutral states, Western European governments, and even the United States eventually saw advantages to considering and later accepting the Soviet proposal. The negotiations that followed, officially called the CSCE, were long and contentious, spanning almost three years in their first phase. They were characterized by competing ideas on the goals of the talks, as the Soviet Union and its satellites primarily focused on security concerns and expanding trade, while the North Atlantic Treaty Organization (NATO) allies sought to open the Iron Curtain through human contacts provisions, to enable the future peaceful reunification of the two Germanys, to prevent military interventions, and to achieve greater Eastern respect for human rights.[3] As the talks dragged on, negotiations became bogged down in arcane details such as the placement of punctuation in agreed texts. The final result, however, produced a new framework for East–West relations and offered citizens of CSCE states the opportunity to move beyond the division of Europe. The conference may have seemed to outside observers akin to the nineteenth century Congress of Vienna, but its potential to transform individual lives was more far-reaching.[4]

Throughout this work, my use of the term "human rights" is guided by the definition outlined in the thirty articles of the 1948 United Nations Universal Declaration of Human Rights and upon which the Helsinki Final Act was based. The Universal Declaration addresses three broad classes of rights: the integrity of the human being, or freedom from

---

[3] Human contacts provisions covered a range of educational and cultural exchanges as well as family visits, marriages between citizens of different states, tourism, and professional travel.

[4] Many have likened the CSCE negotiations that produce the Helsinki Final Act to the 1814–5 Congress of Vienna, in terms of its historical importance and geographical scope. See for example, Iuri Vladimirovich Dubinin, "Khel'sinki 1975: Detali Istorii," *Voprosy Istorii* 11–2 (1995): 101.

governmental intervention against the person; political and civil liberties; and social and economic rights.[5] Given that the Helsinki Final Act directly referenced the Universal Declaration, the states participating in the CSCE theoretically should have had a common understanding of what was meant by human rights. In actuality, differing conceptions of human rights complicated the CSCE, as Western states tended to emphasize the first two classes of rights outlined in the Universal Declaration whereas Eastern states focused on the third.

The Helsinki Final Act was an international agreement to which countries were not bound legally.[6] Instead, it was a declaration of intention, and therefore the obligations therein were only moral and political. As it was not binding in international law, the leaders' signatures were supposed to imbue the document with its strength.[7] That the Helsinki Final Act so shaped East–West relations and the end of the Cold War despite this inherent structural weakness is a testament to those who campaigned for years for its implementation and to the eventual influence of the "Helsinki effect" on policymakers.[8]

The CSCE negotiations from 1972 to 1975, and the Helsinki Final Act that resulted, were structured around four groupings of issues, which were called "baskets" in CSCE terminology. The first basket outlined ten principles to guide East–West relations:

  I. Sovereign equality, respect for the rights inherent in sovereignty
 II. Refraining from the threat or use of force
III. Inviolability of frontiers
 IV. Territorial integrity of states
  V. Peaceful settlement of disputes
 VI. Nonintervention in internal affairs

---

[5] Universal Declaration of Human Rights, www.un.org/Overview/rights.html (accessed April 6, 2006).

[6] One observer declared the Helsinki Final Act was "a new kind of animal. It has the body of a treaty, the legs of a resolution and the head of a declaration of intent." Angela Romano, *From Détente in Europe to European Détente: How the West Shaped the Helsinki CSCE* (New York: P. I. E. Peter Lang, 2009), 29.

[7] A. H. Robertson, "The Helsinki Agreement and Human Rights," *Notre Dame Lawyer* 53:34 (October 1977): 34; and William Korey, "The Legacy of Helsinki," *Reform Judaism* (Spring 1988): 9.

[8] Daniel Thomas argues that "the Helsinki Final Act's formal commitment to respect human rights contributed significantly to the demise of Communism and the end of the Cold War," a phenomenon he labels the "Helsinki effect." Daniel C. Thomas, *The Helsinki Effect: International Norms, Human Rights, and the Demise of Communism* (Princeton: Princeton University Press, 2001), 4.

VII. Respect for human rights and fundamental freedoms, including the freedom of thought, conscience, religion or belief

VIII. Equal rights and self-determination of peoples

IX. Cooperation among states

X. Fulfillment in good faith of obligations under international
law[9]

Basket One also included confidence-building measures (CBMs) such as
advanced notification of troop maneuvers, prior notification of military
movements, and provisions for the exchange of observers and disarmament. For the East, the principle regarding the inviolability of frontiers
was the "cornerstone of security in Europe" because it meant the recognition of long-sought Eastern European borders.[10] In contrast, the West
heralded Principle Seven, which addressed respect for human rights and
fundamental freedoms, and Principle Six, regarded by Western states as a
renunciation of the Brezhnev Doctrine, the Soviet justification for intervention in socialist, satellite states. In the years after the Act's signing,
CSCE diplomats, human rights activists, and political leaders repeatedly
pointed to Principle Seven as marking a commitment by Eastern bloc
leaders to respect human rights. Faced with Western criticism, Soviet
leaders strived to claim Principle Six exempted them from criticism of
their internal affairs, including their human rights practices; their argument, however, was never given serious credence internationally.

The second basket outlined how to make economic, scientific, technological, and environmental cooperation possible across the East-West
divide. The agreed text discussed facilitating business contacts and industrial co-operation, encouraging tourism, and expanding transportation
networks. In addition, it focused on the exchange of economic and com-
mercial information.[11] The second basket did not play a significant role
in the subsequent years in part because almost all CSCE states were also
members of the United Nations Economic Commission for Europe, which
already addressed East–West cooperation in this area.[12]

---

[9] The Helsinki Final Act, www.osce.org/documents/mcs/1975/08/4044_en.pdf (accessed
May 17, 2006).

[10] V. Yaroslavtsev, "Basis of European Security," *International Affairs* (USSR) 5 (May
1976): 16.

[11] There also was a brief statement between the second and third baskets on issues relating
to security and cooperation in the Mediterranean, a concession to Malta.

[12] Stefan Lehne, *The Vienna Meeting of the Conference on Security and Cooperation in
Europe, 1986–1989* (Boulder: Westview Press, 1991), 8–9.

Western negotiators had pushed aggressively for the Basket Three provisions, which they hoped would ease Eastern European isolation.[13] Agreed measures included increasing contacts related to family reunifications, bi-national marriages, and travel. In addition, Basket Three addressed humanitarian issues such as improved working conditions for journalists, educational cooperation, and the free flow of information. In the immediate aftermath of the Helsinki Final Act, Western European CSCE delegates initially focused on using the human contacts provisions in Basket Three as a means to pressure Eastern Europe to open itself to the West, as it was easy to point to specific provisions unfulfilled by the East. Over time, however, the respect for human rights and fundamental freedoms outlined in Basket One became a more effective tool to advocate liberalization in Eastern Europe.

The fourth basket addressed follow-up procedures, continuing the CSCE by stipulating that a review meeting would take place in Belgrade, Yugoslavia, in 1977 to assess the progress countries had made in fulfilling the terms of the Helsinki Final Act. Although initially expected to have little significance, the CSCE meetings subsequent to the signing of the Helsinki Final Act and known collectively as the "Helsinki process" were instrumental to increasing compliance with the agreement. These meetings presented repeated opportunities for those committed to implementation of the agreement to influence Eastern European states. Held in Belgrade (1977–8), Madrid (1980–3), and Vienna (1986–9), they shaped the course of the CSCE and the Cold War.

Given that the content of the Helsinki Final Act's commitment to human rights derived from the Universal Declaration of Human Rights, why was the Helsinki Final Act far more influential on the observance of human rights and the Cold War? Unlike the Universal Declaration and other international attempts to elevate the importance of human rights, the Helsinki Final Act was uniquely formulated to give rise to a transnational network because the terms of the agreement established that CSCE states could exchange views on implementation of the Helsinki Final Act, meaning human rights abuses would now be subject to international diplomacy.[14] The key difference was the follow-up meeting agreed

---

[13] Peter Wallensteen, "American Soviet Détente: What Went Wrong?" *Journal of Peace Research* 22:1 (March 1985): 5; and Julian Critchley, "East-West Diplomacy and the European Interest: CSCE, MFR and SALT II," *Round Table* 255 (1974): 306.

[14] Elizabeth Borgwardt has argued that the 1941 Atlantic Charter should be considered the first international declaration on human rights but as its purpose was conceived differently, its successor the Universal Declaration is a more appropriate point of comparison.

to in Basket Four and the resulting development of a Helsinki process. The promise to evaluate Helsinki implementation provided the rationale for establishing a United States congressional commission and human rights groups to monitor adherence to the agreement. Importantly, the first review meeting led to a second; a whole series of meetings followed that fostered links among Helsinki advocates and cemented the CSCE and human rights advocacy onto the international diplomatic agenda.

The signing of the Helsinki Final Act by thirty-five European and North American parties, and in particular the document's publication in Eastern Europe, spurred the development of a network devoted to ensuring its implementation.[15] Over the years, what I consider a transnational Helsinki network came to include a range of groups and individuals, including politicians, diplomats, human rights activists, Jewish refuseniks, ethnic nationalists, international NGOs, journalists, human rights experts, and ethnic interest groups.[16] Together, and across national borders, they pressed for adherence to the human rights and human contacts provisions of the Helsinki Final Act. The range of transnational contacts inspired by the Helsinki process was broad and unprecedented. It became commonplace for an Eastern European dissident to write to an American diplomat asking that his plight be addressed in upcoming talks or for an American-Polish activist to press the Polish Ambassador to the United States to free a trade union organizer.

＊In the chapters that follow, I explore how the Helsinki Final Act came to play an influential role in East–West relations and analyze the essential

---

Elizabeth Borgwardt, *A New Deal for the World* (Cambridge, MA: Harvard University Press, 2005), 1–11.

[15] Transnational advocacy networks, like the Helsinki network, are bound together by a commitment to shared values. Margaret Keck and Kathryn Sikkink, *Activists Beyond Borders: Advocacy Networks in International Politics* (Ithaca: Cornell University Press: 1998), 1.

[16] Those engaged in human rights advocacy were inspired by diverse motives. Some were drawn to Helsinki activism by their own ethnic or religious affinity with those oppressed in the Soviet Union and Eastern Europe. Others became involved based on a broader commitment to respect for human rights. Finally, some supporters felt compelled to get involved after moving personal encounters. Varied actors, spread across the CSCE-signatory states, changed the place of human rights in East–West diplomacy and pressured Eastern states to moderate their treatment of their citizens. Here I draw upon a previously published examination of the emergence of the transnational Helsinki network: Sarah B. Snyder: "The Rise of the Helsinki Network: 'A Sort of Lifeline' for Eastern Europe," in Poul Villaume and Odd Arne Westad eds., *Perforating the Iron Curtain: European Détente, Transatlantic Relations, and the Cold War, 1965–1985* (Copenhagen: Museum Tusculanum Press, 2010), 179–193, which is reprinted here in revised form with permission from Museum Tusculanum Press.

components of the transnational network: the establishment of the United States Commission on Security and Cooperation in Europe, the formation of international human rights groups, and an increasing American role in the CSCE follow-up meetings. In August 1975, Representative Millicent Fenwick (R-NJ) was so moved by her interactions with dissidents in the USSR that she proposed a joint legislative and executive committee to monitor compliance with the Helsinki Final Act, especially Basket Three, and to advocate greater international implementation. The result of these efforts, the Commission on Security and Cooperation in Europe, became a strong advocate for United States activism on human rights and an essential part of the transnational Helsinki network.

At the same time Fenwick established the Commission, human rights activists in the Soviet Union, prompted by publication of the Helsinki Final Act in Soviet newspapers, proceeded to form their own group dedicated to compliance with the agreement. Popularly known in the West as the Moscow Helsinki Group, it included activists with a range of agendas but a common goal of monitoring Helsinki implementation. The establishment of the Moscow Helsinki Group and the Commission within a month of each other raised the international profile of the Helsinki agreement and garnered greater attention for Helsinki issues in East–West relations. As important, the Moscow Helsinki Group inspired the formation of many other monitoring groups in the East and the West, which collectively exerted influence on international diplomacy.

The effectiveness of nongovernmental human rights activism more broadly was heightened through partnerships with key governments committed to Helsinki compliance, none of which was more crucial than the United States. Although Ford signed the Helsinki Final Act, it was the 1976 presidential election of Jimmy Carter that brought high-level attention to human rights and a strong government commitment to the Helsinki process. Unlike his predecessors, Carter made human rights an important component of United States foreign policy, one he valued personally and spoke out on vocally. His focus on human rights, and more specifically the CSCE, put the issue permanently on the agenda of United States foreign policy toward Eastern Europe. Carter raised the American profile within the CSCE such that the United States was the most forthright advocate of Helsinki compliance at the 1977–8 Belgrade Follow-up Meeting. Without Carter's leadership, the Belgrade Meeting could have offered Eastern states the opportunity to tout their efforts at Helsinki implementation with little dissent. Instead, Carter appointed an outspoken jurist, Arthur J. Goldberg, to head the United States delegation.

Goldberg's brash negotiating style was unique to the traditionally staid and deferential multilateral forums such as the CSCE. He arrived in Belgrade armed with detailed statistics and narratives of Eastern abuses compiled by the Commission, the Moscow Helsinki Group, and other interested nongovernmental organizations (NGOs), and he challenged Eastern European states to adhere to their international commitments. Goldberg's style infuriated many, but he and Carter successfully established a standard whereby those who flouted their Helsinki obligations would be publicly humiliated in an international forum. Given the unique Soviet–American relationship, United States adoption of the network's agenda and pursuit of Helsinki implementation in bilateral and multilateral relations were essential to later progress on Helsinki compliance in the Soviet Union and Eastern Europe.

Because Goldberg's diplomacy required heavily documented briefs to support his charges of Eastern human rights abuses, his tenure as ambassador strengthened links among Eastern-monitoring groups, United States diplomats, and the Commission, which acted as an international clearinghouse for Helsinki information. To this end, Goldberg suggested in the aftermath of Belgrade that the burgeoning transnational Helsinki network would benefit from a United States–based monitoring group made up of private citizens. His idea became Helsinki Watch, the most prominent Western NGO devoted to Helsinki monitoring. Helsinki Watch's establishment proved critical because as Eastern repression of Helsinki activists escalated, Western NGOs were needed to lead the monitoring effort. Helsinki Watch later initiated more formal links among Helsinki monitoring groups throughout the CSCE, transforming the informal Helsinki community into a more formal Helsinki coalition.

✷ My work studies how the network operated, examining the intertwined efforts by dissidents, human rights activists, and Western politicians and diplomats to champion human rights in the Soviet Union and Eastern Europe.[17] The Helsinki network began as disparate monitoring groups committed to similar ideals but with little means to coordinate strategy or influence international diplomacy. Over time, transnational activism related to the Helsinki Final Act gave rise to a more formal

---

[17] Claus Jäger, a member of the West German parliament, argued at a European conference on human rights that human rights activists should not be termed "dissidents," which he argued "belittles and minimizes the decisive role of the groups." Instead, he suggested they be called "human rights fighters" or "freedom fighters." Claus Jäger, "Human Rights in Enslaved Europe," 1979, Folder 44, Box 35, Accession 3560–006, Henry M. Jackson Papers, University of Washington, Seattle, Washington (hereafter Jackson Papers).

transnational "coalition" led by an international nongovernmental organization, the International Helsinki Federation for Human Rights (IHF), to pursue the network's agenda more effectively. The creation of the IHF enabled Helsinki advocates to pursue joint strategies and tactics, heightening their effectiveness.[18]

The Helsinki network developed transnationally due to what scholars of social movements and transnational activism have called a "boomerang" pattern. The "boomerang" describes the method by which domestic actors, confronted with obstacles to influencing their own governments as was the case in the Soviet Union and Eastern Europe, identify external actors who can raise their concerns internationally and exert pressure more effectively.[19] Helsinki advocacy developed in a number of ways, in particular by acquiring what social movements scholars call "moral authority" or enhanced power beyond their means, by engaging in "verbal sanctioning" or public shaming, and by "framing" or "shaping grievances into broader and more resonant claims."[20] Members of the transnational Helsinki network used each of these methods at varying points as they advocated for greater observance of human rights.

What seemed to be an increasingly effective network of Eastern activists, Western NGOs, and United States policymakers was threatened by Carter's defeat in the 1980 presidential election by Ronald Reagan, an avowed opponent of the Helsinki Final Act. Reagan, who had established a long record of disagreement with the CSCE prior to his inauguration, took office in 1981 and, surprising nearly all human rights activists, pursued a CSCE policy that was unexpectedly consistent with

---

[18] Sanjeev Khagram, James V. Riker, and Kathryn Sikkink define a transnational coalition as "sets of actors linked across country boundaries who coordinate shared strategies of sets of tactics to publicly influence social change." Sanjeev Khagram, James V. Riker, and Kathryn Sikkink, "From Santiago to Seattle: Transnational Advocacy Groups Restructuring World Politics," in Sanjeev Khagram, James V. Riker, and Kathryn Sikkink, eds., *Restructuring World Politics: Transnational Social Movements, Networks, and Norms* (Minneapolis: University of Minnesota Press, 2002), 7.

[19] Keck and Sikkink, *Activists Beyond Borders*, 12; and Daniel C. Thomas, "Boomerangs and Superpowers: International Norms, Transnational Networks and US Foreign Policy," *Cambridge Review of International Affairs* 15:1 (2002): 26.

[20] Kathryn Sikkink, "Restructuring World Politics: The Limits and Asymmetries of Soft Power," in Khagram, Riker, and Sikkink, eds., *Restructuring World Politics*, 312; Rosemary Foot, *Rights Beyond Borders: The Global Community and the Struggle over Human Rights in China* (New York: Oxford University Press, 2000), 8–9; Sidney Tarrow, *Power in Movement: Social Movements and Contentious Politics*, 2nd ed. (New York: Cambridge University Press, 1998), 21; and Martha Finnemore and Kathryn Sikkink, "International Norm Dynamics and Political Change," *International Organization* 52 (1998): 899.

and more effective than Carter's policy. Moreover, the Reagan administration's efforts to improve NATO coordination on CSCE strategy strengthened the Western position at the Madrid Review Meeting (1980–3) and the meetings that followed. Despite Reagan's opposition to the CSCE before entering office, his administration ultimately recognized the CSCE as a useful forum initially to embarrass and later to influence Soviet and Eastern European leaders. As a result, he continued Carter's ardent defense of human rights during the many CSCE meetings held during his presidency as well as in bilateral sessions with Soviet leaders.

Nevertheless, the effectiveness of American support for the Helsinki network was highly dependent on the willingness of the Soviet Union to engage in genuine negotiations, and through 1984 Soviet leaders were extremely reluctant to concede that the international community had a right to influence domestic policies. Gorbachev, however, initiated a new era of Soviet thinking that required new international relationships. Upon taking office, Gorbachev faced a myriad of domestic problems including a stagnating economy, decaying infrastructure, and environmental degradation. Abroad, he was locked in an expensive arms race with the United States, was bogged down in an exhausting war in Afghanistan, was suffering strained relations with Europe and China, and was overextended in Eastern Europe and the Third World. Influenced by exposure to Western ideas, advice from like-minded aides, and the circumstances of his generation, Gorbachev believed the appropriate response was fundamental reform of the Soviet system. He chose to pursue *glasnost'* (or openness), *perestroika* (or restructuring), and new political thinking, which significantly altered Soviet diplomacy and the domestic system. Transnational activism had made Soviet human rights practices an obstacle to improving East–West relations, and Reagan, in his summit meetings with Gorbachev at Geneva, Reykjavik, Washington, and Moscow, repeatedly pressed the issue. This high-level advocacy, together with individual and collective nongovernmental efforts, influenced Gorbachev and Soviet Foreign Minister Eduard Shevardnadze to affect change, enabling more productive CSCE meetings, improvement in East–West relationship, and the gradual lessening of Cold War tensions.[21]

---

[21] Human rights norms as advocated by the Helsinki network also resonated with Gorbachev and his aides to a far greater extent than with his predecessors. The influence of these norms on reform-minded Soviet leaders is important, but their power in explaining the transformation of Eastern Europe has at times been overemphasized. In my view, human agency, much of which was not directly inspired by international norms, was central to

As Gorbachev recognized that changing the Soviet role in the CSCE was important to normalizing relations with the West, he slowly undertook both episodic and systemic measures to do so. A number of the steps taken by Gorbachev, such as reducing curbs on the free flow of information, releasing political prisoners, easing restrictions on free speech, and signaling that the Soviet Union would no longer intervene militarily in Eastern Europe, contributed to the fall of communism in Eastern Europe, which in turn precipitated German reunification and ultimately influenced the collapse of the Soviet state.

Soviet and other Eastern European reforms demonstrate the effectiveness of the Helsinki network's agenda. They had succeeded in first framing the debate on human rights abuses and drawing increased international attention to the issue. Second, they capitalized on the commitments made in the Helsinki Final Act and subsequent CSCE agreements to respect human rights, facilitate human contacts, and periodically assess implementation. Third, they worked to secure and retain the commitment of high-level political leaders to the cause. Their advocacy was instrumental in influencing changes in Eastern European practices as they shaped Gorbachev's thinking about Soviet interests, which facilitated reform.[22] The Helsinki Final Act and the process that followed played an important role in the end of the Cold War by unifying Soviet domestic opposition, offering incentives for change in Eastern Europe, creating a means for human rights activists to advance their agenda on an international stage, and facilitating the transition to a new Europe.

Note on Sources

Drawing upon records in the United States, the Czech Republic, Hungary, the United Kingdom, and Canada, my manuscript is the first comprehensive scholarly treatment of the evolution and impact of the Helsinki process. Nevertheless, in the course of my research, I faced a number of challenges. The first was that many government documents were unavailable, which is a problem for all scholars trying to push the boundaries of

the development and effectiveness of the transnational Helsinki network. Daniel Thomas writes, "International norms enable transnational networks to mobilize and achieve influence beyond their command of traditional power resources because world politics is as much about authority and legitimacy as it is about material resources." Daniel C. Thomas, "Human Rights in U.S. Foreign Policy," in Khagram, Riker, and Sikkink, eds. *Restructuring World Politics*, 72.

[22] Keck and Sikkink, *Activists Beyond Borders*, 201, 203.

contemporary history. I attempted to surmount this obstacle by consulting the papers of members of Congress and CSCE ambassadors as well as the collections of ethnic and human rights groups. In the case of the United States, I also filed copious Mandatory Review and Freedom of Information Act requests, many of which have been acted upon positively. Despite difficulties in gaining access to Soviet records for this period, considerable official and nongovernmental documents are available. I utilized a range of Russian-language sources, including oral histories on deposit at the Hoover Institution, Radio Free Europe/Radio Liberty's *Samizdat* Archive at the Open Society Archives, the Russian and Eastern European Archive Document Database – Russian Archives Document Database (REEADD-RADD) Collection at the National Security Archive, the Andrei Sakharov Archives, and the Archives of the Soviet Party and Soviet State microfilm collection. Furthermore, I am fortunate to have been able to supplement my own research with the growing body of international history on the CSCE produced by scholars such as Gottfried Niedhart, Oliver Bange, Angela Romano, Thomas Fischer, and Wanda Jarzabek. The second challenge was presented by the nature of human rights activism in Eastern Europe. Given the threat of harassment, arrest, and imprisonment, the practice of maintaining archives endangered human rights activists. As such, the absence of official archives of Eastern European monitoring groups has led me to rely extensively upon Radio Free Europe/Radio Liberty's *Samizdat* Archive, the Andrei Sakharov Archives, interviews, memoirs, and published collections.

Bridging the East–West Divide

The Helsinki Final Act Negotiations

The official CSCE negotiations began in November 1972, and for two and a half years, thirty-five European and North American states debated what became known as the Helsinki Final Act. By the time the agreement was signed on August 1, 1975, the content bore little resemblance to early Soviet proposals. Instead, the text included a number of unique elements advocated by Western and neutral and nonaligned (NNA) states that led to the CSCE's surprising influence on East–West relations. The agreement's follow-up mechanism, commitment to respect human rights, and provisions for human contacts all fostered the development of a transnational network that played an important role in shaping political and social change in Europe in the late 1980s.

A number of earlier works, predominantly written by diplomats engaged in the CSCE negotiations, have addressed the years of talks that produced the Helsinki Final Act and examined the process by which thirty-five delegations finally reached a consensus. This chapter builds upon their accounts and other more recent scholarship. It begins by explaining why the Soviets lobbied for the conference beginning in 1954, and why Western states ultimately agreed to participate. My discussion, however, focuses more closely on how the NATO caucus succeeded in transforming the CSCE agenda and reshaping it to the West's long-term advantage despite many internal disagreements and an overall lack of foresight as to the significance of the Helsinki Final Act. Most significant to the development and influence of a transnational Helsinki network was Eastern agreement to Principle Seven, committing them to respect human rights, and to the human contacts provisions in Basket Three. Soviet diplomats' concessions on these points had surprising and unintended consequences, heightening human rights activism in the USSR and elsewhere in the Soviet bloc. Western diplomatic efforts ensured that the CSCE concluded with a final document far different from that initially conceived by the Soviets. The negotiations in Finland and Switzerland in the early 1970s laid the foundation for the transnational Helsinki activism that followed.

Securing the participation of thirty-four other European and North American countries in the CSCE negotiations and their ultimate agreement to the Helsinki Final Act was initially seen as a great diplomatic coup by the Soviets. The conference had long been sought by the Soviets, who hoped for formal recognition of the post-World War II borders in Central and Eastern Europe. The Soviet Union first proposed a treaty on "collective security in Europe" at the 1954 Foreign Ministers Meeting. The Soviet proposal, designed to replace NATO and diminish United States influence in Europe, was rebuffed immediately.[1] The Soviet Union and its allies were persistent on the issue, however, because they believed it would fulfill various objectives, most significant of which was the opportunity to secure international recognition for Eastern European borders, as there had been no formal treaty ending World War II. Offering protection to the German Democratic Republic (GDR), Poland, and Czechoslovakia from future Federal Republic of Germany (FRG) revanchism would increase communist legitimacy in Eastern Europe; in addition, it would protect the Soviet Union's own territorial gains. Thus, from the Soviet perspective, the proposed conference was about securing the postwar order, territorial expansion, as well as European and international legitimacy. The concept gained little traction, however, for a number of years.

The late 1960s and early 1970s were marked by increasing efforts to diminish East–West tension in Europe, and, as such, proposals to hold a European security conference began to garner more serious attention than they had previously. Western European governments, responsive to citizens who had grown tired of living in a divided Europe dominated by the tension of the Cold War, felt compelled to engage in dialogue with the East. The Netherlands, for example, wanted to use a conference to challenge the status quo and alter East–West relations.[2] Moreover, the

---

[1] Proposal, February 10, 1954, United States Department of State, *The Conference on Security and Cooperation in Europe: Public Statements and Documents, 1954–1986* (Washington: U.S. Department of State, Bureau of Public Affairs, Office of the Historian, 1986); and Statement, February 10, 1954, ibid. Canada and the United States were not part of the original 1954 Soviet proposal.

[2] Floribert Baudet, "'It Was Cold War and We Wanted to Win': Human Rights, Détente, and the CSCE," in Andreas Wenger et al., eds., *Origins of the European Security System: The*

United Kingdom and others saw potentially positive implications for Eastern European autonomy and warned against dismissing such proposals.[3] Canada viewed participation as offering a significant advantage to Canadian and Western interests.[4] Italy, on the other hand, was one of a number of countries concerned it could weaken Western European unity and integration.[5] The United States had opposed Soviet calls for a European Security Conference, as it was first known, for many reasons, but most basic was the Soviets' exclusion of the United States from the potential proceedings.[6] As there was general agreement among the NATO allies that the United States and Canada must be included, the Soviet Union eventually eased its opposition on the issue.[7]

Helsinki Process Revisited, 1965–75 (New York: Routledge, 2008), 184–6. Angela Romano sees the Dutch as the most concerned about the possible consequences of a CSCE, leading to their divergence from the other members of the European Community. Romano, *From Détente in Europe to European Détente*, 154–5.

[3] REU 25, "Current West European Attitudes Toward a European Security Conference," April 3, 1969, Folder 1, Box 709, Country Files: Europe, NSC Files, Nixon Presidential Materials Project, National Archives, College Park, Maryland (hereafter NPMP); and Romano, *From Détente in Europe to European Détente*, 151. Oliver Bange, however, argues that British diplomats were slow to see the CSCE as having a possible positive impact on Eastern Europe in the long term, and that it wasn't until 1974 that they shifted their view of the CSCE. Oliver Bange, "*Ostpolitik* as a Source of Intrabloc Tensions," in Mary Ann Heiss and S. Victor Papcosma, eds., *NATO and the Warsaw Pact: Intrabloc Conflicts* (Kent: The Kent State University Press, 2008), 115. Additional recent scholarship has portrayed Britain as cautious about the proposed ESC (European Security Conference), seeing it possible as "a trap rather than an opportunity." In the end, seeing the conference as inevitable, Britain turned toward maintaining Western unity and making sure concessions that favored Western interests were secured from the East. Luca Ratti, "Britain, the German Question and the Transformation of Europe: From *Ostpolitik* to the Helsinki Conference, 1963–1975," in Oliver Bange and Gottfried Niedhart, eds., *Helsinki 1975 and the Transformation of Europe* (New York: Berghahn Books, 2008), 91.

[4] Michael Cotey Morgan, "North America, Atlanticism, and the Making of the Helsinki Final Act," in Wenger et al., eds., *Origins of the European Security System*, 26.

[5] Romano, *From Détente in Europe to European Détente*, 152.

[6] East German analysis of support for an ESC identified the United States as its "main opponent." Factor Analysis, September 25, 1971, CSCE Negotiation Process, Cold War International History Project Virtual Archive.

[7] For greater discussion of the challenges the United States faced as it tried to balance its bilateral relationship with the Soviets and its relations with its NATO allies over these issues, see Sarah B. Snyder, "The United States, Western Europe, and the Conference on Security and Cooperation in Europe, 1972–1975," in Matthias Schulz and Thomas A. Schwartz, eds., *The Strained Alliance: U.S.–European Relations from Nixon to Carter* (New York: Cambridge University Press, 2009), 257–75. Copyright © 2010 The German Historical Institute. Parts of that chapter are reprinted here in revised form with permission from Cambridge University Press. Csaba Békés argues that the Warsaw Pact states had

Among the Western states, representatives of the six countries that made up the European Community (EC) worked to develop a common position for the proposed conference while the fifteen NATO countries simultaneously attempted to develop a joint stance.[8] In some ways, the EC was preferable over NATO as the principal forum in which Western CSCE policy would be formulated given France's lack of interest in working within NATO and the poor human rights records of Greece, Turkey, and Portugal at the time.[9] Indeed, several scholars have recently focused on successful EC diplomacy within the CSCE, arguing it was able to gain Soviet agreement to an expansive notion of security, one that addressed people as well as states.[10] The NATO allies, however, also played a key role given the size of the alliance and the outsize influence of the United States with the Soviets.

By 1971 NATO members had also entered into discussions about how best to achieve allied objectives in a European Security Conference and moved beyond initial Soviet hopes for a short, narrowly defined conference to envision one that would be as advantageous as possible to Western European goals. The Warsaw Pact countries had originally proposed an agenda addressing only the renunciation of force and economic and technological exchange. To strengthen the substance of the agenda, NATO focused on including governing principles for relations between CSCE states; free movement of people, ideas, and information; environmental cooperation; and human rights. The NATO countries wanted the conference to consider measures that would materially reduce the tension in Europe and genuinely increase security.[11] NATO leaders also recognized

always assumed the United States and Canada would participate in the conference but did not include them in the initial proposals to ensure GDR participation. Csaba Békés, "The Warsaw Pact, the German Question and the Birth of the CSCE Process, 1961–1970," in Bange and Niedhart, eds., *Helsinki 1975 and the Transformation of Europe*, 124.

[8] In one effort, the six EC countries – France, the FRG, Italy, the Netherlands, Luxembourg, and Belgium – formulated an articulation of Western European foreign policy, the Davignon Report. The October 1970 Davignon Report called for a foreign policy in line with Europe's "tradition and its mission" and said, "United Europe must be founded on a common patrimony of respect for liberty and human rights." One observer has argued the emphasis on human rights in the CSCE negotiations was a Western European initiative that grew out of the development of the Davignon Report. Jeremi Suri, "Détente and Human Rights: American and West European Perspectives on International Change," *Cold War History* 8:4 (November 2008): 536, 538.

[9] Daniel Möckli, *European Foreign Policy During the Cold War: Heath, Brandt, Pompidou and the Dream of Political Unity* (New York: I. B. Tauris, 2009), 61, 63, 123, 138.

[10] See for example, ibid., 99, 113, 115.

[11] Final Communiqué, December 9–10, 1971, www.nato.int/docu/comm/49–95/c711209a. htm (accessed May 17, 2006); and "NATO and Détente: Facing East at Brussels,"

the opportunity to exhibit the "superiority" of life in the West to that under the Soviets, and their desired agenda reflected that goal.[12] The State Department identified a conference as important to achieving long-term American objectives of expanding the "influence of the Western community ... eastward."[13]

Although allied and American thinking was largely in agreement on overall NATO objectives, a coherent strategy and agreement were not reached for some time. Many American administration officials wanted to put the Soviets "on the tactical defensive" by including force reductions and supporting a permanent institution to which East European states could appeal if threatened militarily.[14] The United States supported a more aggressive agenda than some of its allies, in part to demonstrate that significant differences remained between the East and the West, which would imply that the continuation of the Atlantic alliance and the presence of American troops in Europe were necessary.[15]

Despite repeated efforts to maintain allied unity, a State Department report characterized NATO allies as "more divided, perhaps, than ever" over progress on CSCE as they began their NATO ministerial meeting in December 1971.[16] Some of these divisions centered on what subjects should be addressed at the conference and the degree to which the West should take adversarial positions. For example, some American policymakers identified the potential for propaganda victories and even some Soviet concessions during the negotiations on freer movement, although there were hesitations about pursuing such an assertive approach on a

December 15, 1971, DEF 1 EUR, 12/1/71, Box 1707, Subject and Numeric Files, 1970–73, Political and Defense, General Records of the Department of State, Record Group 59, National Archives, College Park, Maryland (hereafter RG 59).

[12] Memorandum, Livingston to Kissinger, July 19, 1972, Folder 1, Box 830, Name File, NSC Files, NPMP.

[13] Political Counselor to the United States Ambassador to NATO James Goodby depicts the United States, or at least the U.S. Mission to NATO, as much more active than other observers have. James E. Goodby, "The Origins of the Human Rights Provisions in the Helsinki Final Act," unpublished manuscript, in the possession of the author, 18.

[14] NSSM 138: A Conference on European Security (Analytical Summary), October 2, 1971, Folder 1, Box H-63, Institutional NSC Files, NPMP; NSSM 138: Conference on European Security: Talking Points, October 2, 1971, ibid.

[15] CSCE Task Force Second Interim Report, May 15, 1972, Folder 7, Box 103, Executive Secretary's Briefing Book, RG 59. Senator Mike Mansfield's (D-MT) repeated introduction of an amendment calling for a significant reduction of American forces in Europe raised concerns among the NATO allies.

[16] "NATO and CSCE: The Road to Helsinki," DEF 1 EUR, 2/17/72, Box 1708, Subject and Numeric Files, 1970–73, Political and Defense, RG 59.

controversial subject; State Department official George Vest warned that the issue of freer movement was a "card" that "should be used for what it was worth and not over-played."[17] France and the FRG worried that such discussions might be too confrontational for the Soviets, whereas others, such as the Dutch and the British, focused on the potential positive effects from such negotiations.

Extensive advanced consultations eventually led the NATO position to be more far-reaching than initially considered, with lasting importance to the significance of the Helsinki Final Act. James Goodby, who was posted to the United States mission to NATO for much of this period, sees the State Department as having had an "aim of changing the status quo in Eastern Europe, using the issue of human rights as a means of challenging Soviet dominion over that area" in its thinking about the CSCE in the early 1970s.[18] Goodby argues that before the fall of 1970, the NATO allies were focused only on securing agreement that would prevent further Soviet action under the guise of the Brezhnev Doctrine. In his view, State Department prodding fundamentally changed Western European thinking about a security conference and convinced the NATO allies that the proposed conference also could be used to influence how a state treated its citizens, which marked an important reconception of the potential for the concluding agreement.[19] Some on the United States CSCE Inter-Agency Task Force thought that if the NATO allies could maintain a uniform position, they could exact concessions on human rights provisions due to Soviet emphasis on a "successful" conference.[20]

Despite such discussions, the United States was less focused on developing the form and substance of the conference, and the European allies ultimately led the efforts to protect Western interests in the conference

[17] Reply to NSSM 138, October 2, 1971, Folder 1, Box H-063, Institutional "H" Files, NSC Files, NPMP; and Telegram, U.S. Mission NATO to SecState, March 1, 1972, DEF 1 EUR, 3/1/72, Box 1708, Subject Numeric Files, 1970–73, Political and Defense, RG 59.

[18] James E. Goodby, *Europe Undivided: The New Logic of Peace in U.S.–Russian Relations* (Washington: United States Institute of Peace, 1998), 52–3.

[19] Goodby argues that despite a more reticent role by the State Department during the CSCE negotiations, it had a significant impact due to these early efforts. His account may overemphasize the influence of American diplomats on Western European CSCE policy. Goodby, "The Origins of the Human Rights Provisions in the Helsinki Final Act," 13; and Goodby, *Europe Undivided*, 54.

[20] Secretary of State William Rogers sent the report to David Kennedy, U.S. Permanent Representative to the North Atlantic Council for use in NATO negotiations. Rogers to Kennedy, March 20, 1972, DEF 1 EUR, 3/20/72, Box 1708, Subject Numeric Files, 1970–73, Political and Defense, RG 59; and Attachment to Memorandum, March 20, 1972, Folder NSDM 162, Box H – 233, Institutional "H" Files, NSC Files, NPMP.

preparations. Although the United States was less involved in the planning than its allies, its position was of particular importance given attempts to maintain harmony within the Atlantic alliance. British head of the Foreign and Commonwealth Office's Western Organizations Department, Crispin Tickell, wrote, "We do indeed want to avoid any European/American row about CSCE, and we agree that the avoidance of such a row is more important than abstract arguments about how a hypothetical conference might be prepared."[21]

The Consultations stage to establish the agenda for the CSCE, also known as the Multilateral Preparatory Talks (MPT), began on November 22, 1972, in Dipoli, Finland, not far from Helsinki. As the agenda would determine the substance of the negotiations and the outline of the final agreement, the MPT was a critical component of the CSCE and presented an opportunity for the Western powers to seize control. The meetings lasted seven months and were shaped by a number of factors: Western emphasis on enhancing the substance of the agreement, lack of interest by American foreign policymakers, Western European concern about public reaction, and increased pressure by the Soviets on the United States and others to accommodate their objectives.

The Helsinki Consultations were used to develop an outline of the final CSCE agreement; the detailed language would be worked out in the subsequent negotiations in Geneva that would begin in August 1973. Allied objectives for the CSCE, all of which the NATO states pursued in the MPT in Dipoli, included diminishing East–West divisions in Europe, in part by lessening the isolation of Eastern European states. The allies worked to strengthen their CSCE proposals by supporting provisions related to human rights and formulating confidence-building measures (CBMs) in order to balance Eastern European proposals at the talks.[22] Many of the wide-ranging objectives to which NATO was committed necessitated securing consensus of the Warsaw Pact and NNA states as well as managing any intra-alliance differences over priorities and

---

[21] Letter, Tickell to Butler, March 27, 1972, in G. Bennett and K. A. Hamilton, eds., *Documents on British Policy Overseas: The Conference on Security and Cooperation in Europe, 1972–1975 Series III: Volume II* (London: The Stationery Office, 1997) (hereafter DBPO). The Western Organizations Department was the primary group working on CSCE issues for the British government.

[22] Telegram, U.S. Mission NATO to SecState, April 8, 1972, MBFR-CSCE Backup Book, Part 3, Box 482, President's Trip Files, NSC Files, NPMP. A British document suggested that NATO had decided to withhold judgment until after the MPT, implying if the results were not satisfactory they would not yet be committed to the conference. Draft Brief, November 13, 1972, *DBPO III:II.*

strategy. Overall, the Western states were organizing to achieve maximum gains at the talks without succumbing to any of their long-held fears about Soviet maneuvering and manipulations. Although NATO members were in general agreement about their defensive goals, countries disagreed as to the balance between extracting concessions and threatening European détente with confrontational negotiations, which was a question that would plague allied relations throughout the years under consideration here.

The relative lack of United States interest in the CSCE continued during the MPT in Dipoli. In Ferraris's view, the American "attitude of detachment" was "ostentatiously" displayed there. He rightly notes that Kissinger regarded the CSCE "as an exercise, at best significant for public opinion, but certainly not as an essential component of the substantial make-up of the process of détente."[23] To United States CSCE delegate John J. Maresca, the speaking order at the foreign ministers meeting in Helsinki following the Dipoli Consultations most clearly illustrated American lack of interest in the conference preparations; according to him, all the other thirty-four states asked for special placement on the speakers list, whereas the United States made no such request. This led Secretary of State William Rogers to be listed last, an embarrassment only partially lessened after his arrival in Helsinki, when the Finnish hosts switched places with the United States, moving Rogers up to the twenty-first position. The Soviets, who had designated a diplomat to wait outside the Finnish foreign ministry overnight to secure their spot on the list, spoke first.[24] American apathy, it seems, was principally a result of skepticism about the conference's impact.

The Helsinki Consultations ended on June 8, 1973, with an agreement on Final Recommendations that delineated the timing of the formal conference and the four baskets of issues to be discussed in the Geneva phase. By the end of Dipoli, the negotiators had already defined the elements of each of the baskets, indicating that delegates at Geneva would consider proposals on freedom of movement, dissemination of information, and different types of exchanges. In addition, the negotiations had outlined what would be the ten principles of Basket One, including the respect for human rights and fundamental freedoms. Success in broadening the

---

[23] Luigi Vittorio Ferraris, ed., *Report on a Negotiation: Helsinki-Geneva-Helsinki, 1972–1975* Marie-Claire Barber, trans. (Alphen ann den Rijn: Sijthoff & Noordhoff, 1979), 66.

[24] John J. Maresca, *To Helsinki: The Conference on Security and Cooperation in Europe, 1973–1975* (Durham: Duke University Press, 1985), 39–40.

agenda to include issues such as family reunification and working conditions for journalists, not part of early Soviet proposals, led to positive
appraisals in the West.[25] Nevertheless, fundamental disagreements within
the NATO alliance and between East and West on the agreements guiding
principles and human contacts provisions remained and would characterize much of the negotiations in Geneva.[26]

The Soviets initially had hoped for a short conference with a brief,
superficial, political declaration on postwar borders, territorial integrity,
and nonuse of force; they wanted to stymie Western efforts to infuse more
content into the agreement.[27] In order to gain Western participation, however, the Soviets had agreed in Dipoli to broaden the agenda to humanitarian issues and others of interest to the Western Europeans. The Soviet
strategy during the Geneva stage was to push the negotiations toward a
summit finale as quickly as possible while reserving the flexibility to make
certain strategic concessions in order to reach a successful conclusion to
the conference, which for them meant a document addressing principles
of détente and economic cooperation.[28] To this end, the Soviets pursued
a range of tactics, including public statements and bilateral pressure. In
American characterizations, Soviet pressure tactics included blackmail
and "abusive comments."[29] Furthermore, the Soviets attempted to breed
dissention among the NATO allies by informing some countries of their

---

[25] Final Recommendations of the Helsinki Consultations (Helsinki 1973), Ottawa 1985,
Organization for Security and Cooperation in Europe Archives, Prague, Czech Republic
(hereafter OSCE Archives). Representative Dante Fascell (D-FL) later described the
transformation of the conference agenda as "a remarkable turning of the tables." Dante
Fascell, "Human Rights: The United States at Belgrade," *Department of State Bulletin*
(May 1978): 40.

[26] Final Communiqué, June 14–15, 1973, http://www.nato.int/docu/comm/49–95/
c730614a.htm (accessed May 17, 2006). A five-day foreign minister-level meeting officially launched the CSCE on July 3, 1973.

[27] Ferraris, ed., *Report on a Negotiation*, 101.

[28] Minute, Tickell, January 18, 1974, *DBPO III: II*; and *Central Intelligence Bulletin*,
August 21, 1974, CIA Records Search Tool, National Archives, College Park, Maryland;
February 18, 1974, Folder CSCE LOG Washington-Geneva, Box 4, Albert William
Sherer, Jr., Papers, Yale University, New Haven, Connecticut (hereafter Sherer Papers);
and Letter, Brezhnev to Ford, March 8, 1975, Folder 1, Box 8, Office Of The Counselor,
Records Of Helmut Sonnenfeldt, 1955–1977, RG 59; Memorandum, Sonnenfeldt to
Kissinger, March 10, 1975, ibid.; and Letter, Ford to Brezhnev, March 18, 1975, ibid.
(hereafter Sonnenfeldt Collection). The *Central Intelligence Bulletin* was a daily intelligence brief intended for senior officials.

[29] Memorandum, Clift to Kissinger, April 19, 1975, Folder CSCE, 1975 (2) White House,
National Security Council Europe, Canada and Ocean Affairs Staff Files, National
Security Adviser, Gerald R. Ford Library, Ann Arbor, Michigan (hereafter NSA, GRFL).

own bilateral negotiations with the United States in Washington before the United States had communicated this to its allies.[30]

There was a growing belief among the allied delegations, however, that Soviet conduct demonstrated their strong commitment to the conference and meant they must be near to yielding on some issues in order to achieve a summit before August 1975; according to the United States delegation in Geneva, the Soviets "pretend nonchalance, but their behavior showed that they were quite evidently under growing time pressure."[31] Indeed, a Soviet diplomat later reported that Brezhnev said, "If Helsinki is held, then I can die."[32] In the United States delegation's view, some Western countries preferred waiting to seize the advantage while others were more concerned with simply ensuring the conference would be over.[33] However, the perception that the Soviets were becoming increasingly vulnerable with the passage of time was supported as they finally displayed greater flexibility in negotiations at Geneva at the end of May 1975.[34] The Soviets were more willing to bargain on Basket Three than on the CBMs at the time, but in Kissinger's words, the concessions began "dribbling out."[35] This was in contrast to the first years of negotiations, in which the Soviets conceded only minor points at highly opportunistic moments. Siegfried Bock, who headed the GDR's delegation at Dipoli, has argued the Warsaw Pact delegations made a tactical mistake by putting such great emphasis on ending the CSCE negotiations swiftly as that left them open to pressure from the West: "The more discernibly the Soviet Union showed that it wanted the conference to become an early success, the more vigorously did the West present demands of their own in regard to the humanitarian issues."[36]

---

[30] Briefing Item, April or May 1975, Folder CSCE, 1975 (2) White House, Box 44, National Security Council Europe, Canada and Ocean Affairs Staff Files, NSA, GRFL.

[31] Telegram, US Mission Geneva to SecState, May 3, 1975, Folder 11, Box 7, Sonnenfeldt Collection.

[32] A. Kovalev, *Azbuka Diplomatim* (Moscow: Interpraks, 1993), 188. Even if such a quote is apocryphal, it indicates the extent to which Brezhnev was perceived to be attached to a CSCE summit.

[33] Telegram, US Mission Geneva to SecState, April 29, 1975, Folder Switzerland – State Department Telegrams – To SECSTATE – NODIS (4), Box 13, President's Country Files for Europe and Canada, NSA, GRFL.

[34] Briefing Memorandum, May 29, 1975, Folder CSCE 1975 (3) White House, Box 44, National Security Council Europe, Canada, and Ocean Affairs Staff Files, NSA, GRFL.

[35] Memorandum of Conversation, May 30, 1975, Folder Britain 1975, Box 4, Sonnenfeldt Collection.

[36] Siegfried Bock, "The CSCE – An Era of Dissent *and* Consensus," http://www.wilsoncenter.org/topics/docs/2007–09–15BockPaperFinal.pdf (accessed August 25, 2009).

An important element in the Soviet CSCE strategy was utilizing ongoing bilateral talks with the United States to influence American negotiating positions and convince the United States to pressure its allies to relent on proposals opposed by the USSR. At times this succeeded, as the United States was motivated by broader concerns about Soviet–American détente and thus engaged in CSCE-related negotiations outside the CSCE framework; for example, during Nixon's July 1974 trip to Moscow, the United States enhanced its support for the Soviet Union's plan for a final stage summit, articulating an "assumption" that the negotiations would warrant such a meeting.[37] Similarly, Kissinger worked closely and clandestinely with the Soviets to forge compromises at Geneva. For instance, the United States and the Soviet Union reached an agreement on Basket Three language, but in order to avoid raising Western European suspicions, they developed a plan whereby "Country X," later decided to be Finland, would introduce the language. The United States would comment favorably on the "new" language once other countries, including the USSR, had reacted.[38] This instance was part of a larger ongoing Soviet–American dialogue about how to reach agreements without appearing to circumvent the multilateral proceedings.[39] For the most part, although, the bilateral discussions involved Soviet diplomats pushing for commitments from the United States that it would not make.[40]

At the root of the Soviet frustration with the proceedings were delays they attributed to overly aggressive proposals from Western Europe, a complaint with which some United States policymakers agreed. Kissinger, when confronted by Soviet Foreign Minister Andrei Gromyko, blamed the slow speed on the Europeans, whom he described as "crazy on the subject of human contacts."[41] Indeed, some Western European countries, taking advantage of strong Soviet desires for a successful conclusion of the

---

[37] Joint Communiqué, July 3, 1974, United States Department of State, *The Conference on Security and Cooperation in Europe.*

[38] Memorandum of Conversation, May 7, 1974, Folder 4, Box 71, HAK Office Files, NPMP; and Memorandum, Stabler to Kissinger, June 6, 1974, Folder 8, Box 8, Sonnenfeldt Collection.

[39] Telegram, SecState to AmEmbassy Moscow, April 4, 1974, Folder 1, Box 723, Country Files: Europe, NSC Files, NPMP; Telegram, AmEmbassy Moscow to SecState, April 19, 1974, ibid.; and Kovalev, *Azbuka Diplomatim,* 189.

[40] Telegram, AmEmbassy Rome to SecState, October 25, 1973, Folder 1, Box 696, Country Files: Europe, NSC Files, NPMP. See also February 7, 1974, Folder CSCE LOG Washington-Geneva, Box 4, Sherer Papers.

[41] Memorandum of Conversation, December 22, 1973, Folder 2, Box 69, *The Road to Helsinki,* Cold War International History Project Conference Volume. At times, however, this was a strategy to camouflage American intransigence. For example, when Gromyko

conference, had pushed confrontational issues such as freer movement of people.[42] CSCE negotiations dragged in the fall of 1974 due to Western European unwillingness to compromise, as some states were quite zealous, including the Netherlands, which pursued an aggressive campaign for the sanctity of private correspondence.[43] The Dutch approach to the negotiations frustrated the Soviets and at times even their allies.[44] Prince Henri of Lichtenstein depicted the Dutch as the most ardent of the Western negotiators, saying, "We all throw stones at the Soviets, but the Dutch throw entire blocks of concrete."[45] The Soviets certainly had the Dutch in mind when they referred to some Western Basket Three proposals as "excessive and obnoxious."[46]

The Warsaw Pact states, at times, also disagreed among themselves about how to approach the conference. The Soviet Union attempted to speak for the entire Eastern bloc, but its interests frequently were not aligned with its satellites. Eastern European states hoped to use the CSCE to address their specific interests in East–West relations while enhancing

---

advocated ending the Conference before the upcoming American summit in Moscow, Kissinger deflected blame onto the Western European allies although he was privately working against such a timetable. Memorandum of Conversation, April 28, 1974, Folder 4, Box 71, HAK Office Files, NSC Files, NPMP. The dismissive attitude with which Kissinger regarded these proposals likely emboldened the Soviets in their unwillingness to compromise.

[42] Historian Daniel Möckli describes the EC states as "the fortress of Western interests" that worked to rebuff "Eastern attempts to water down" Basket Three provisions. Möckli, *European Foreign Policy During the Cold War*, 116.

[43] Telegram, US Mission Geneva to SecState, September 25, 1974, Switzerland –SDT-To SecState – EXDIS (1), Box 13, President's Country Files for Europe and Canada, NSA, GRFL; and Telegram, US Mission Geneva to SecState, November 19, 1974, State Department FOIA Reading Room, http://aad.archives.gov/aad/createpdf?rid=173345 &dt=1572&dl=823 (accessed on May 8, 2006); and Ljubivoje Acimovic, *Problems of Security and Cooperation in Europe* (Rockville: Sijthoff and Noordhoff, 1981), 112. The Canadians described the Dutch as taking the "hardest and most Calvinistically righteous line of all in Western caucus in dealing with the Soviets and Eastern Europeans." Telegram, GENEV to EXTOTT, July 23, 1975, Volume 9093, 20–4-CSCE, Volume 58, RG 25, National Archives, Ottawa, Ontario, Canada (hereafter National Archives, Canada).

[44] Baudet, "'It Was Cold War and We Wanted to Win'" in Wenger et al., eds., *Origins of the European Security System*, 187.

[45] Ibid., 192.

[46] Record of Conversation, March 18, 1975, *The Moscow Helsinki Group 30th Anniversary: From the Secret Files* National Security Archive Electronic Briefing Book No. 191 (Washington: National Security Archive, 2006), www.nsarchive.org (accessed June 1, 2006). For further discussion of the Dutch negotiating strategy, see Baudet, "'It Was Cold War and We Wanted to Win'" in Wenger et al., eds., *Origins of the European Security System*.

their position with respect to the Soviet Union, which at times created a divergence from Soviet positions.[47] Romania, the most prominent example, saw CSCE provisions on noninterference in internal affairs and the renunciation of the use of force as providing some security protection from a potential Soviet invasion.[48] Nonetheless, Eastern European diplomats largely followed the Soviet lead and did not exercise independent authority in these negotiations that would later prove so significant to the future of the region.

The Western European strategy for the Geneva stage, like its approach to Dipoli, was focused on gaining Soviet concessions on human contacts, which the NATO allies achieved by capitalizing on the Soviet desire for a short conference that ended at the summit level. According to Goodby, there was hope among diplomats negotiating the NATO position on Basket Three that the CSCE could "unfreeze the situation" in Eastern Europe by exposing people there to new influences, although there was less optimism about the Soviet Union.[49] France and Britain both hoped provisions on human contacts could slowly improve the situation in Eastern Europe.[50] Throughout the negotiations in Geneva, the delegates debated if the final stage would be a summit with heads of state or if the meeting would conclude at a lower level. As the Soviets showed their desperation for a summit conclusion, Western and neutral states maintained that their level of participation was dependent on the substance agreed to at Geneva and thus pressed for more Eastern concessions. Soviet attempts to preserve some of their original vision of the CSCE as a large European conference, presided over by Brezhnev, at which heads of

---

[47] Karl E. Birnbaum, "The Member States of the Warsaw Treaty Organization and the Conference on Security and Cooperation in Europe: Current Preoccupations and Expectations," *Cooperation and Conflict* 9:1 (1974): 29; Hermann Wentker, "Pursuing Specific Interests Within the Warsaw Pact: The German Democratic Republic and the CSCE-Process," in Carla Meneguzzi Rostagni, ed., *The Helsinki Process: A Historical Reappraisal* (Padua: CEDAM, 2005), 45; and Constantin Vlad, "Romania and the CSCE Process, 1960–1975," in Rostagni, ed., *The Helsinki Process*, 97.

[48] Telegram, SecState to AmEmbassy Bucharest, August 28, 1974, Folder Romania-State Department Telegrams From SecState – EXDIS, Box 11, President's Country Files for Europe and Canada, NSA, GRFL; Memorandum of Conversation, June 11, 1975, Folder June 11, 1975 – Ford, Kissinger, Romanian President Nicolae Ceausescu, Box 12, Memcons, ibid.; and Vlad, "Romania and the CSCE Process, 1960–1975," in Rostagni, ed., *The Helsinki Process*, 103.

[49] James Goodby Interview, April 1, 2005; and Romano, *From Détente in Europe to European Détente*, 115.

[50] Romano, *From Détente in Europe to European Détente*, 127; and Marie-Pierre Rey, "France and the German Question in the Context of *Ostpolitik* and the CSCE, 1969–1974," in Bange and Niedhart, eds., *Helsinki 1975 and the Transformation of Europe*, 59.

state all signed an agreement recognizing the postwar borders ultimately enabled the Western Europeans to gain acquiescence on Basket Three elements opposed by the East.

Western European diplomats had taken the lead in Geneva because Kissinger remained uninterested in the CSCE. Guy Coriden, who was a member of the United States delegation, remembers, "Nobody really cared about [the CSCE]. We really felt that we were out there alone. We didn't have much instruction from Washington."[51] George Vest, who was one of the heads of the United States delegation, suggests the lack of instructions might be due to the contradictory positions of the secretary of state and national security adviser. According to Vest, Rogers supported "strong human rights activity," whereas Kissinger felt, "You should forget all this business about human rights."[52] Kissinger and advisers such as Sonnenfeldt, however, were cautious about the CSCE before the talks began and believed confrontational debate had limited positive potential. He did not ascribe much significance to the human contacts provisions being negotiated, such as an Italian proposal on free access to foreign printed information.[53] At one point, Kissinger remarked: "What is it that suddenly possesses the West to believe that it can affect the domestic structure of the Soviet Union through a treaty signed in Geneva of peripheral significance?"[54] In addition, he did not want to risk unnecessary disagreements with the Soviet Union.[55] Prophesying about negotiations with the Soviets, Sonnenfeldt wrote, "The West will press for freer

---

[51] Guy E. Coriden, Jr., Interview, November 18, 1992, *The Foreign Affairs Oral History Collection of the Association for Diplomatic Studies and Training*, Library of Congress, http://memory.loc.gov/ammem/collections/diplomacy/ (accessed March 6, 2010).

[52] George S. Vest Interview, July 6, 1990, *The Foreign Affairs Oral History Collection of the Association for Diplomatic Studies and Training*, Library of Congress, http://memory.loc. gov/ammem/collections/diplomacy/ (accessed March 6, 2010). For more on Kissinger's approach to human rights, see Daniel Jonathan Sargent, *From Internationalism to Globalism: The United States and the Transformation of International Politics in the 1970s* (PhD Dissertation, Harvard University, 2008), 419–25.

[53] CSCE/II/J/3, October 4, 1973, CSCE II/vol. 18, OSCE Archives.

[54] Secretary's Staff Meeting Report, October 29, 1973, National Security Archive, Washington, District of Columbia. See also Jeffrey D. Merritt, "Unilateral Human Rights Intercession: American Practice under Nixon, Ford, and Carter" in David D. Newsom, ed., *The Diplomacy of Human Rights* (Lanham: University Press of American for Institute for the Study of Diplomacy, Georgetown University, 1986), 44, 51.

[55] Thomas Delworth, a Canadian diplomat involved in many of the early CSCE negotiations, told me that Kissinger dismissed the value of Basket Three provisions such as the free flow of information by noting the wide variety of international newspapers available in Berlin in the 1930s had not prevented Hitler's rise to power. Thomas Delworth Interview, December 7, 2005; and Thomas, *The Helsinki Effect*, 78.

movement of people and information. The East will parry with a general promise not to interfere with movement of people and information. This will be hailed as an important beginning. Nothing much will change." In his view, "some debating points may be scored" but an agreement on freer movement would not significantly affect Europe.[56] Sonnenfeldt's assessment was quite accurate as the agreement's language itself would not change the communist system in Eastern Europe; not until Eastern European states began to implement their CSCE commitments on freedom of movement was European stability affected. With the benefit of hindsight, Kissinger later suggested that he had identified a "long-term opportunity" in the CSCE, but he only wanted to use American participation in the conference as a tool to restrain Soviet behavior and did not have a prophetic understanding of the negotiations' long-term significance.[57]

As the Geneva stage wore on, Italian diplomat Luigi Ferraris wrote there was "the risk of transforming the CSCE into a permanent inter-European debating forum."[58] In order to avoid such a fate, some states began to moderate their positions.[59] By early May 1975, State Department Counselor Helmut Sonnenfeldt reported to Kissinger that there was a "virtually unanimous desire" among those in Geneva to end the conference by swiftly moving to the final stage.[60] Yet, tension within the NATO caucus had increased due to frustration with the lack of Soviet movement and allegations that the United States might settle for a weaker Basket Three. United States Ambassador to the Geneva negotiations Albert J. Sherer, Jr., reported that his delegation was working hard to soothe disagreements among the allies, but trust between many of the countries had waned.[61] After a final flurry of negotiations,

[56] Memorandum, Sonnenfeldt to Kissinger, August 19, 1972, *NATO, the Warsaw Pact and Détente, 1965–1973*, Cold War International History Project Conference Volume.

[57] Henry Kissinger, *Diplomacy* (New York: Simon and Schuster, 1994), 758. According to Soviet diplomat Anatoly Kovalev, in Helsinki Kissinger told him that the United States had made a mistake and underestimated the significance of Vienna and Helsinki. Kovalev, *Azbuka Diplomatim*, 197–8.

[58] Ferraris, *Report on a Negotiation*, 402.

[59] Telegram, U.S. Mission Geneva to SecState, September 25, 1974, Switzerland – SDT-To SecState – EXDIS (1), Box 13, President's Country Files for Europe and Canada, NSA, GRFL.

[60] Memorandum, Sonnenfeldt to Kissinger, Folder 11, Box 7, Sonnenfeldt Collection.

[61] Briefing Item, May 27, 1975, Folder CSCE 1975 (3) White House, Box 44, National Security Council Europe, Canada, and Ocean Affairs Staff Files, NSA, GRFL; April 22, 1975, Folder CSCE LOG Washington-Geneva, Box 4, Sherer Papers; and April 23, 1975, ibid.

the negotiation of the four baskets of the Helsinki Final Act finally ended on July 21, 1975.[62]

The representatives of thirty-five European and North American states signed the Helsinki Final Act on August 1, 1975, in Helsinki. The agreement has often been described as the "high point of détente" and contained far-reaching agreements on East–West interactions, political borders, military confidence-building measures, trade, and human contacts. It was a key diplomatic turning point in the Cold War, as over time the agreement spurred the development of a transnational network committed to Helsinki implementation and inspired popular movements against the communist regimes.[63]

The Helsinki Final Act was a consensus document signed by thirty-five nations, whose delegates had starkly different understandings of the meaning and obligations of the agreement. Much as the United States and the Soviet Union had differing conceptions of détente, the two superpowers had divergent interpretations of the act, in particular related to the binding nature of the signatories' commitments and the degree to which each side intended to fulfill its obligations.[64] It also was quickly apparent that Eastern and Western states were determined to emphasize different

[62] As discussed at greater length in the introduction, the first basket outlined ten principles guiding relations in Europe, including inviolability of frontiers, respect for human rights and fundamental freedoms, territorial integrity of states, and peaceful settlement of disputes. It also incorporated confidence-building measures such as advanced notification of troop maneuvers.

[63] Ford and Brezhnev signed the Helsinki Final Act along with representatives of Austria, Belgium, Bulgaria, Canada, Cyprus, Czechoslovakia, Denmark, Finland, France, the Federal Republic of Germany, the German Democratic Republic, Greece, the Holy See, Hungary, Iceland, Ireland, Italy, Liechtenstein, Luxembourg, Malta, Monaco, the Netherlands, Norway, Poland Portugal, Romania, San Marino, Spain, Sweden, Switzerland, Turkey, the United Kingdom, and Yugoslavia. To characterize the scale of the CSCE, there were 4,700 proposals, drafts, and papers; 2,500 formal sessions; and 1,000s of informal meetings. Yuri Kashlev, "The CSCE in the Soviet Union's Politics," *International Affairs* (USSR) 7 (1992): 66–7; Y. B. Kashlev, "SBSE v 1975–1990," in Y. B. Kashlev, ed., *Khel'sinskii Protsess v Sovetskoi/Rossiiskoi Vneshnei Politike: 1975–2000* (Moscow: Diplomaticheskaia Akademiia MID RF, 2000), 14; Mike Bowker and Phil Williams, *Superpower Détente: A Reappraisal* (Newbury Park: SAGE Publications, 1988), 63; Wallensteen, "American Soviet Détente: What Went Wrong?," 1; Gregory A. Flynn, "The Content of European Detente," *Orbis* 20 (Summer 1976): 402–3; and William G. Hyland, *Mortal Rivals: Superpower Relations from Nixon to Reagan* (New York: Random House, 1987), 10.

[64] Douglas G. Scrivner, "The Conference on Security and Cooperation in Europe: Implications for Soviet-American Détente," *Denver Journal of International Law and Policy* 6:1 (1976): 142–3: and Bowker and Williams, *Superpower Détente*, 93.

FIGURE 1. President Gerald R. Ford signs the Final Act of the Conference on Security and Cooperation in Europe on August 1, 1975. Courtesy Gerald R. Ford Library.

elements of the Helsinki agreement. The Soviet Union and its allies, for example, trumpeted principles such as the inviolability of frontiers and noninterference in internal affairs, whereas Western states focused on provisions for freedom of movement and other human contacts provisions.[65]

Although the United States would later fight with the Soviets over lack of compliance in the East for many years, Kissinger can be considered complicit in establishing nonimplementation as acceptable. Throughout their bilateral talks on the CSCE, the Soviets gave early signals that, not unsurprisingly, they did not intend to implement all provisions of the agreement fully. Kissinger seems to have implicitly accepted Soviet plans for partial compliance given the issue's low priority for him. For example, in September 1974 talks in Washington, Kissinger and Gromyko discussed the nature of obligation to the CBM provisions of the agreement, with the Soviet foreign minister noting it was a "moral commitment." Kissinger asked if a "moral obligation" was more or less binding than a legal commitment, to which Gromyko responded that "as a rule it will be carried out." Gromyko's answer and Kissinger's failure to address Gromyko's

[65] Memorandum, Ingersoll to Ford, January 15, 1976, Conference on Security and Cooperation in Europe, 1976 (1) NSC, Box 45, National Security Council Europe, Canada and Ocean Affairs Staff, NSA, GRFL.

qualification "as a rule" implied there was some sense between the two that the Helsinki agreement would be less than completely obligatory.[66] This interpretation is further supported by Kissinger's repeated references to the Helsinki Final Act as "unenforceable" or even "meaningless."[67] Kissinger and Gromyko also jointly mocked the third basket and its provisions for cultural contacts, deriving the most amusement from the idea that they might allow a country to open a "cabaret" in Moscow.[68] At one point, Kissinger said to Gromyko, "I don't think you'll change your system as a result of Basket III" and implied that he did not expect the Soviets to adhere completely to Basket Three provisions.[69] Similarly, Nixon had earlier pressured Brezhnev to make concessions on the third basket because the language was theoretical and not a "fact."[70] The available record is echoed in the memories of Soviet translator Viktor Sukhodrev, who has said the Soviets "had been conditioned by Henry Kissinger to treat the whole thing as something of no practical importance." He recalls Kissinger telling Gromyko, "Mr. Minister, why are we quibbling over these forms of words? No matter what goes into the final act, I don't believe that the Soviet Union will ever do anything it doesn't want to."[71]

Not surprisingly, there also were divergent views on which side benefited most from the agreement. Former American diplomat to the Soviet Union Marshall Brement notes that the Soviets thought they had secured a great diplomatic achievement in the Helsinki Final Act, one for which Gromyko had worked for twenty years.[72] And, indeed, that was

---

[66] Memorandum of Conversation, September 20, 1974, Soviet Union August–September 1974, Box 8, Sonnenfeldt Collection.

[67] Memorandum of Conversation, May 30, 1975, Britain 1975, Box 4, Sonnenfeldt Collection; and Memorandum of Conversation, August 15, 1974, August 15, 1974–Ford, Kissinger, Box 5, Memcons, NSA, GRFL.

[68] Memorandum of Conversation, April 28, 1974, Folder 4, Box 71, NSC, HAK Office Files, NPMP; and Memorandum of Conversation, June 29, 1974, Folder 3, Box 77, Country Files: Europe, NSC, ibid.

[69] Memorandum of Conversation, May 19, 1975, Folder 7, Box 11, Sonnenfeldt Collection.

[70] Memorandum of Conversation, June 29, 1974, Folder 3, Box 77, Country Files: Europe, NSC, HAK Office Files, NPMP.

[71] Viktor Sukhodrev in "'SALT II and the Growth of Mistrust': Conference #2 of the Carter-Brezhnev Project (A Conference of U.S. and Russian Policymakers and Scholars Held at Musgrove Plantation, St. Simon's Island, Georgia, May 6–9, 1994), on file at the National Security Archive.

[72] Marshall Brement Interview, April 11, 1990, *The Foreign Affairs Oral History Collection of the Association for Diplomatic Studies and Training*, Library of Congress, http://memory.loc.gov/ammem/collections/diplomacy/ (accessed August 5, 2010).

also the dominant interpretation among those in the American press and politics. Critics of the Helsinki Final Act saw the principle on the inviolability of frontiers and others as signaling official Western acceptance of Soviet territorial acquisitions during World War II.[73] These criticisms dovetailed with those who had always asserted that the Soviet Union's goal with the CSCE was the expansion of its influence in Europe.[74] Principle Six, which disavowed intervention into internal affairs, was the most controversial part of the first basket as the two sides interpreted it in starkly different lights.[75] For the West, Principle Six was a rebuke to the Brezhnev Doctrine, ensuring that the Soviets could not again intervene militarily in Eastern European countries as they had in the past. In contrast, the Soviets were minimally concerned about Principle Six's impact on their influence in Eastern Europe, and instead interpreted Principle Six as a way to prevent the West from interfering with internal policies, including human rights.[76] This viewpoint, however, neglected to focus on many of the onerous commitments to which the Soviets agreed.

Explaining how the Soviets could have signed a document so potentially disadvantageous to them and ultimately threatening to their system, one observer has suggested Gromyko made numerous concessions he regarded as meaningless in the final negotiations because he could not allow the conference to fall apart due to the national and personal prestige associated with it.[77]

---

[73] Lev E. Dobriansky, "CSCE and the Captive Nations," *The Ukrainian Quarterly* 31 (Autumn 1975): 253. In an April 14, 1975, opinion piece, William Safire wrote, "World War II will soon be coming to its official end. The Russians won." Robert Kennedy Eichhorn, *The Helsinki Accords and Their Effect on the Cold War* (M.A. Thesis, California State University, Fullerton, 1995), 180.

[74] Vojtech Mastny, *Helsinki, Human Rights, and European Security: Analysis and Documentation* (Durham: Duke University Press, 1986), 46.

[75] Eichhorn, *The Helsinki Accords and Their Effect on the Cold War*, 25; and Michael Howard, "Helsinki Reconsidered: East–West Relations Two Years After the Final Act," *Round Table* 267 (1977): 241–8.

[76] The second and least controversial basket addressed economic, scientific, and technological cooperation between CSCE states. The third basket concentrated on humanitarian issues such as the reunification of families, the improvement of working conditions for journalists, and increased cultural exchanges. The fourth basket set up a follow-up meeting to review implementation of the Helsinki Final Act in October 1977 in Belgrade.

[77] Wilfried Loth, *Overcoming the Cold War: A History of Détente, 1950–1991* Robert F. Hogg trans. (New York: Palgrave, 2002), 131. Alexander Bovin, who was an aide to KGB head Yuri Andropov, has reportedly said that Soviet reformers "fought" for agreement with the Helsinki Final Act as a means of reform. Evidence to support this assertion, however, is lacking. Robert G. Kaiser, *Why Gorbachev Happened: His Triumphs and His Failure* (New York: Simon and Schuster, 1991), 90–1.

In addition, Soviet diplomat Yuri Kashlev suggests that Brezhnev signed the Helsinki Final Act without carefully reviewing it.[78] Brezhnev's unfamiliarity with the terms of Basket Three likely was less to blame, however, than Soviet assumptions that they would never have to implement the accord's provisions. To this point, Gromyko is reported to have told Brezhnev in response to concerns about the Helsinki commitments: "We are masters in our own house," assuring him that the Soviet leaders could decide how to define human rights.[79] Dobrynin later acknowledged that the Soviets were interested only in the first two baskets and tried to downgrade the importance of the third basket however possible.[80] Soviet ideologist Mikhail Suslov, however, understood the significance of what the Soviets had agreed to and blamed Anatoly Kovalev, who had headed the Soviet delegation.[81] Other Soviet leaders also were concerned, particularly President Nikolai Podgorny, Premier Alexei Kosygin, and KGB head Yuri Andropov, but Gromyko sold it as a victory.[82]

---

[78] Kashlev, "The CSCE in the Soviet Union's Politics," 68; and Kashlev, "SBSE v 1975–1990," in Kashlev, ed., *Khel'sinskii Protsess v Sovetskoi/Rossiiskoi Vneshnei Politike*, 17. Zubok alleges Brezhnev "was in a semi-coma" at Helsinki and "barely managed to affix his signature to the Final Act." Vladislav Zubok, *A Failed Empire: The Soviet Union and the Cold War from Stalin to Gorbachev* (Chapel Hill: University of North Carolina Press, 2007), 246.

[79] Christopher Andrew and Vasili Mitrokhin, *The Sword and the Shield: The Mitrokhin Archive and the Secret History of the KGB* (New York: Basic Books, 1999), 322; and John Lewis Gaddis, *The Cold War: A New History* (New York: Penguin Press, 2005), 188. Indeed, as discussed in an earlier chapter, Nixon and Kissinger may have led the Soviets to believe the United States would not insist on compliance.

[80] William Korey, "The Unanticipated Consequences of Helsinki," *OSCE ODHR Bulletin* 3:3 (Fall 1995): 8–14; and Anatoly Dobrynin, *In Confidence: Moscow's Ambassador to America's Six Cold War Presidents* (New York: Random House, 1995), 345–6. According to Soviet diplomat Anatoly Kovalev, Gromyko said, "It would be good to cut out the bottom from under this Third Basket." Svetlana Savranskaya, "Unintended Consequences: Soviet Interests, Expectations and Reactions to the Helsinki Final Act," in Bange and Niedhart, eds., *Helsinki 1975 and the Transformation of Europe*, 181.

[81] Kashlev, "The CSCE in the Soviet Union's Politics," 68; Korey, *The Promises We Keep*, xxi; and Savranskaya, "Unintended Consequences," in Bange and Niedhart, eds., *Helsinki 1975 and the Transformation of Europe*, 179.

[82] Loth, *Overcoming the Cold War*, 131. One scholar has suggested the Soviets involved in negotiating the Helsinki Final Act might not have been concerned about the content of the agreement because they had been so successful in suppressing human rights activism up to that point. Svetlana Savranskaya, "The Battles for the Final Act: the Soviet Government and Dissidents' Efforts to Define the Substance and the Implementation of the Helsinki Final Act," paper presented at the conference "European and Transatlantic Strategies in the Late Cold War Period to Overcome the East–West Division of Europe," Copenhagen, Denmark, November 30–December 1, 2007.

Soviet claims of triumph at Helsinki complicated American public interpretation of the agreement, which was decidedly negative. A range of groups and individuals, including a number of prominent politicians, opposed the Helsinki Final Act, arguing that it served Soviet, not American objectives; many believed it formally recognized the Soviet annexation of Estonia, Latvia, and Lithuania and acquiesced in Soviet domination of Eastern Europe.[83] A *Wall Street Journal* editorial urged Ford not to sign the agreement, pleading, "Jerry, don't go."[84] The principal line of American criticism was that the United States had given away too much in the negotiations and had required little of the Soviets in return; many believed Kissinger had focused on minimizing human rights in order to defuse confrontation with the Soviet Union and preserve détente.[85] In the United States, there were concerns that the agreement represented a diplomatic defeat for the West, or in the words of one commentator, "a new edition of Munich."[86]

Western European views generally were more optimistic than those in the United States, which was consistent with their divergent ideas about détente as well as the value of the conference, and their different roles in negotiations. A European Council declaration on the content of the Helsinki Final Act, approved at a July 17, 1975, meeting, stated, "The Final Act represents a step toward détente whose real importance can be measured only by effective application by all participating states of all the principles reaffirmed and measures approved."[87] The FRG and France may have expressed the most enthusiasm about the CSCE, as the FRG was pursuing improved relations with the East, and France wanted to introduce more multipolarity to the Cold War.[88]

Remarks by the leaders assembled in Helsinki reflected the different interpretations of the Helsinki Final Act that would plague the CSCE for many subsequent years. Speaking first, Finnish President Urho Kekkonen, who had marshaled the ESC initiative to fruition, told the assembled leaders, "This is a day of joy and hope for Europe. We have every reason

---

[83] For further discussion, see Sarah B. Snyder, "'Jerry, Don't Go': Domestic Opposition to the 1975 Helsinki Final Act," *Journal of American Studies* 44:1 (February 2010): 67–81.

[84] Editorial, "Jerry, Don't Go," *Wall Street Journal*, July 23, 1975, 14.

[85] Flynn, "The Content of European Détente," 411; and Korey, *The Promises We Keep*, xxii.

[86] Dubinin, "Khel'sinki 1975," 101.

[87] Telegram, USMission EC Brussels to SecState, July 18, 1975, Belgium-State Dept. Telegrams to SECSTATE-EXDIS, Box 1, Presidential Country Files for Europe and Canada, NSA, GRFL.

[88] Loth, *Overcoming the Cold War*, 148.

to believe that a new era in our mutual relations is dawning and that we have set out on a journey through détente to stability and enduring peace."[89] Brezhnev was similarly positive about the conference, sounding familiar Soviet themes that the Helsinki Final Act represented an end to the Second World War: "The Soviet Union regards the results of the Conference not merely as a necessary summing up of the political outcome of the Second World War ... Possibilities for co-operation extend now also to areas where it was unthinkable in the years of the cold war." At the same time he indicated Soviet resistance to discussing internal policies, cautioning, "no one should try to dictate to other peoples on the basis of foreign policy considerations of one kind or another the manner in which they ought to manage their internal affairs."[90] British Prime Minister Harold Wilson, in contrast, highlighted the issues of human rights and human contacts by criticizing restrictions in the Soviet Union and Eastern Europe, saying, "There is no reason why in 1975 Europeans should not be allowed to marry whom they want; hear and read what they want, travel abroad where and when they want, and meet whom they want."[91]

In his speech to the collected heads of state, Ford suggested that the CSCE offered an opportunity for Europe to overcome its divisive past and reestablish positive intra-European relations. Ford had asked his speechwriters to emphasize "hope" in his speech, and against Kissinger's advice, strengthen the rhetoric.[92] He also referenced the long-standing connections between the American and European people, including the ancestral links to Europe that many Americans felt. In his most famous remarks in Helsinki, Ford emphasized implementation of the agreement: "History will judge this Conference not by what we say here today, but by what we do tomorrow – not by the promises we make, but by the promises we

---

[89] Urho Kekkonen (Finland), July 30, 1975, CSCE/III/vol. 24, OSCE Archives.

[90] Leonid Brezhnev (USSR), July 31, 1975, CSCE/III/vol. 24, OSCE Archives. A CIA report prepared shortly before the signing of the Helsinki Final Act predicted "the long-term effects of the conference are not likely to be discernible for many years." The CIA analysis notes that as the conference progressed, the Soviets became increasingly concerned about the potential impact of monitoring the agreement's implementation. Memorandum, "The CSCE and Western Europe – Pluses and Minuses," July 18, 1975, CSCE, 1975 (1) National Security Council, Box 44, National Security Council Europe, Canada and Ocean Affairs Staff, NSA, GRFL.

[91] Elliott to Callaghan, August 12, 1975, *DBPO III: II.*

[92] AP, "Ford Overruled Kissinger, Toughened Helsinki Speech," *Richmond Times-Dispatch*, August 9, 1975, A–3, Press Clipping Helsinki, 1975, OSCE Archives; and Note, July 3, 1975, Speeches (3), Box 43, Presidential Handwriting File, GRFL.

keep."[93] Ford's strong stand at Helsinki was intended to impress Eastern leaders and to quiet domestic critics of his trip but had little resonance at home.[94]

Upon his return on August 4, 1975, Ford announced he was glad he had traveled to Helsinki because it reinforced American support for liberty and peace in Eastern Europe.[95] However prescient Ford's remarks may have been, at the time few recognized the future consequences of the Helsinki Final Act.[96] The summit in Helsinki marked the beginning of an ongoing process in which the CSCE states gathered periodically in follow-up meetings, as stipulated by Basket Four, to review the implementation of the Act and pursue further efforts to decrease East–West tension. These meetings established a framework within which Helsinki compliance was monitored carefully and also offered the opportunity for those active on Helsinki issues to press for greater adherence to the terms of the act.

The content of the final agreement was essential to the CSCE's long-term prospects. Over time Soviet assent to respect human rights and fundamental freedoms, to adhere to provisions governing East–West contacts, and to review progress toward Helsinki implementation in two years' time, all had far-reaching influence on politics and society in Eastern Europe. Kissinger's lack of interest may have diminished the agreement's impact in the early years of the Helsinki process by implying the Soviets would not need to adhere to the terms of the agreement. Numerous challenges, however, in the form of Eastern dissidence and activist politicians challenged Soviet assumptions, transforming the Helsinki process into a force for change in Europe.

[93] Address, August 1, 1975, United States Department of State, *The Conference on Security and Cooperation in Europe.*

[94] The *Los Angeles Times* regarded it as "probably Mr. Ford's most impressive speech." Amy Schapiro, *Millicent Fenwick: Her Way* (New Brunswick: Rutgers University Press, 2003), 167.

[95] Statement, August 4, 1975, 8/1/75 CSCE (4), Box 176, Robert T. Hartmann Papers, GRFL.

[96] More skeptical observers suggested that the conference might be more appropriately compared to the notoriously ineffective Kellogg-Briand Pact of the 1920s. Editorial, *Philadelphia Inquirer*, August 6, 1975, Judith Buncher, ed., *Human Rights and American Diplomacy: 1975–77* (New York: Facts on File, 1977), 20; and Editorial, *Washington Star*, July 29, 1975, ibid., 23.

2

"A Sort of Lifeline"

The Helsinki Commission

The Helsinki Final Act's fourth basket set a follow-up meeting to assess compliance in Belgrade in 1977, giving countries more than two years to begin putting the provisions agreed to at Helsinki into practice. In the intervening years, the agreement inspired a range of people inside and outside government to develop formal and informal mechanisms to monitor Helsinki implementation. The myriad of international responses represented the beginning of the development of a transnational Helsinki network. In the United States, legislative involvement in the CSCE process dramatically heightened in the immediate aftermath of Ford's trip to Helsinki, beginning with a congressional delegation to Moscow and culminating with the creation of a joint legislative–executive commission to monitor implementation of the agreement. Officially known as the Commission on Security and Cooperation in Europe, it also was called the Helsinki Commission and the Fascell Commission for its long-time chair, Representative Dante Fascell (D-FL). This chapter maps the development of the Commission, including executive branch opposition to its creation; analyzes the Commission's early efforts at monitoring; and evaluates its significance to the broader Helsinki process. As will be illustrated later, the Commission enhanced United States monitoring of compliance with the Helsinki Final Act and facilitated the development of a network of groups and individuals committed to its implementation, heightening the influence of the Helsinki process over time by buttressing nongovernmental human rights activism abroad.

The impetus to create the Commission should be viewed as part of a larger pattern of congressional activism in foreign policy in these years, which began with Congress's desire to reassert itself against the embattled Nixon administration and the president's "imperial" style of conducting foreign policy.[1] More specifically, it should be seen in the context of two significant developments in American domestic and international politics that emboldened congressional activism: the Vietnam War and the Watergate scandal. The factors driving the creation of the Helsinki Commission closely mirrored some of the issues surrounding the Jackson–Vanik Amendment, which linked Soviet most-favored-nation trading status to the removal of excessive obstacles to Jewish emigration, in that both were congressional initiatives to press human rights concerns in relations with the Soviet Union.[2] In both instances, the executive branch opposed the legislation as an unwanted intrusion into the realm of foreign affairs as well as a misguided attempt to prioritize respect for human rights above Soviet–American détente.

There were signs of congressional interest in Helsinki monitoring even before Ford signed the agreement but little indication of the important role members of Congress would eventually play. In May 1975 hearings on the CSCE, Fascell indicated that he saw a monitoring mechanism as logical, saying to Assistant Secretary of State for European Affairs Arthur A. Hartman, "it seems reasonable that you would at least want a measure of Soviet actions or Eastern bloc actions after the culmination of stage III to see how they handled it and to get some measure of where they are going in terms of propaganda and political effort."[3] Other members

---

[1] The House Foreign Affairs Subcommittee of International Organizations and Movements, under the leadership of Representative Donald Fraser (D-MN), began hearings on human rights in 1973 and influenced the push for increased attention to human rights in United States foreign policy. David P. Forsythe, "Human Rights in U.S. Foreign Policy: Retrospect and Prospect," *Political Science Quarterly* 105:3 (Autumn 1990): 439; and Arthur M. Schlesinger, Jr., *The Imperial Presidency* (Boston: Houghton Mifflin, 1973).

[2] In this period, Senator Henry M. Jackson (D-WA) and others actively supported Jewish emigration. See for example, Jackson to Dobrynin, January 19, 1973, Folder 10, Box 1, Accession 3560–028, Jackson Papers; and Press Release, April 13, 1975, Folder 16, Box 245, Accession 3560–005, ibid. Other examples include the introduction of more congressional oversight of the intelligence community and the passage of the War Powers Resolution as the Congress attempted to restrict presidential activism abroad. John Sinclair Petifer Robson, *Henry Jackson, The Jackson–Vanik Amendment and Détente: Ideology, Ideas, and United States Foreign Policy in the Nixon Era* (PhD Dissertation, The University of Texas at Austin, 1989), 63.

[3] "Conference on Security and Cooperation in Europe," May 6, 1975, CSCE, 1975 (1) NSC, Box 44, National Security Council Europe, Canada and Ocean Affairs Staff: Files, NSA, GRFL. As early as January 1973, Senator Henry Bellmon (R-OK) had proposed a congressional ad hoc committee to keep Congress "abreast of developments at the Conference on Security and Cooperation in Europe." Bellmon to Proxmire, January 4, 1973, Folder 13, Box 135, William Proxmire Papers, Wisconsin Historical Society, Madison, Wisconsin. In

of Congress, such as Representative Robert F. Drinan (D-MA), similarly identified monitoring as useful for American foreign policy objectives and interest groups, seeing potential to use the Helsinki Final Act against the Soviet Union on the issue of Jewish emigration.[4] More substantive measures – namely the formation of the Commission – would be triggered by the August 1975 trip that Representative Millicent Fenwick (R-NJ) and other members of the House of Representatives took to the USSR in the aftermath of the CSCE as part of a United States–Soviet Union Interparliamentary Exchange.

Nineteen members of Congress embarked upon a twenty-five-day trip through Eastern Europe three days after Ford signed the Helsinki Final Act. In their talks with Soviet officials in Moscow, differences emerged as to the extent to which the agreement was binding on its signatories. In an effort to characterize compliance as compulsory and gain Soviet acceptance of that interpretation, Fenwick appealed to the Soviets to honor Brezhnev's signature by implementing the provisions of the act.[5] Fenwick's argument seemed to be a salient point with some Soviet officials.[6] Yet, in a meeting with the congressional delegation, Brezhnev himself suggested some elements of the Final Act would necessitate further negotiations between states; an American official reported Brezhnev implied "the Soviets may not be prepared to implement on an equal basis all the principles agreed to in Helsinki."[7] Although the United States delegation struggled to gain a clear understanding of Soviet intentions, they believed that Principle Seven and the third basket nonetheless provided justification for foreigners to question the Soviet Union on its human rights

---

his resolution proposing the committee, Bellmon suggested the CSCE could be the "most significant diplomatic event of this decade."

[4] Judy Siegel, "U.S. Congressman: 'Pressure Soviets to Observe Helsinki Pact,'" *Jerusalem Post*, August 28, 1975, Folder 1: Helsinki Accord, Box 5, Subject Files: Soviet Jewry, Robert F. Drinan Papers, Boston College, Chestnut Hill, Massachusetts (hereafter Drinan Papers).

[5] United States–Soviet Interparliamentary Exchange, August 11, 1975, Folder 3, Box 8, Travel Series, Carl Albert Collection, Carl Albert Center Congressional Archives, University of Oklahoma, Norman, Oklahoma (hereafter Albert Collection).

[6] United States–Soviet Interparliamentary Exchange, August 12, 1975, Folder 3, Box 8, Travel Series, Albert Collection; and Memcon, August 12, 1975, 10 AM, Folder 27, Box 7, ibid.

[7] Soviet attitudes toward Helsinki implementation during these meetings reflect assumptions made at the end of the Geneva phase that the government would not comply with elements that interfered with its internal affairs, as it defined them. AmEmbassy Moscow to SecState, August 15, 1975, Folder 5, Box 8, Travel Series, Albert Collection; and General Statement of Impressions, Folder 27, Box 7, ibid.

practices. As such, in addition to the high-level discussion on Helsinki progress, Representatives Fenwick and Sidney R. Yates (D-IL) raised a number of individual cases with Soviet leaders during the trip.[8] For years, however, the Soviets and their allies rejected this interpretation, arguing Principle Six prevented interference in internal affairs, thereby trumping other provisions that might permit the United States to question domestic human rights abuses.

It was Fenwick's visits with Soviet citizens while in Moscow that led her to initiate the creation of a new organization within the United States government to protect their human rights. Importantly, Fenwick met Soviet scientist Yuri Orlov, who would later lead grass roots efforts to ensure Helsinki compliance and with whom she discussed Soviet human rights abuses as well as attempts to induce Soviet fulfillment of the terms of the agreement.[9] Fenwick later described meeting Soviet dissidents and refuseniks "in heartbreaking meetings, in small shabby flats and hotel rooms" and hearing "the cries of all these desperate people."[10] Yet, she viewed Soviet citizens as "hopeful" that the Helsinki Final Act would improve their political and social rights.[11] In her view, Soviet dissidents viewed international recognition as "a sort of lifeline."[12] Orlov says that he suggested to Fenwick that "the West should use the Helsinki Accords to pressure the Soviet government to honor its human rights obligations, and monitor how well it honored them" and returned to the United States committed to the cause.[13]

Fenwick was inspired by her encounters in the Soviet Union to take action, describing her trip as "a somewhat distant and theoretical exercise in international diplomacy" that "became a dramatically present

---

[8] Transcript attached to Dexheimer to English, August 29, 1975, Folder 4, Box 8, Travel Series, Albert Collection.

[9] Fenwick also talks about being inspired to propose the Commission after meeting a woman with a "desperate expression" as a result of her husband's detention. News Release, "Impressions of the Trip to Russia," September 11, 1975, Folder 33, Box 7, Travel Series, Albert Collection; and Millicent Fenwick, *Speaking Up* (New York: Harper and Row, 1982), 161.

[10] The term *refusenik* referred to those, usually Jewish, who had been denied permission to emigrate. Schapiro, *Millicent Fenwick*, 169; and Reminiscences of Millicent Fenwick (1988), on pages 404–11 in the Columbia University Oral History Research Office, Butler Library, Columbia University, New York, New York.

[11] Testimony, May 4, 1976, Folder 1, Box 181, Millicent Fenwick Papers, Rutgers University, New Brunswick, New Jersey (hereafter Fenwick Papers).

[12] Fenwick, *Speaking Up*, 161.

[13] Yuri Orlov Interview, March 27–8, 2008; and Korey, *The Promises We Keep*, 47.

and personal issue."[14] She returned to the United States convinced of the importance of creating a formal mechanism to monitor Helsinki implementation: "The trip made a lasting impression on many of us who realized, after talking for many hours with dissidents and Soviet citizens wanting to emigrate, that the hopes of these people had been pinned to the implementation of the Helsinki Accord which had been signed just before our arrival."[15] Shortly thereafter, Fenwick announced her intention to create a legislative–executive commission to oversee Helsinki implementation.[16]

Fenwick's emergence on the national stage as a champion of human rights surprised many political observers given her age and junior status. Fenwick, who was sixty-four, appeared to be a stately grandmother complete with ever-present strands of pearls and had little in her background foretelling her later leadership on this issue. She had been raised in considerable wealth and unique circumstances, including three years in Spain while her father served as the United States ambassador.[17] A brief, failed marriage left her with two children to support, which she did by writing for *Vogue* for fourteen years, rising to become associate editor. After retiring from *Vogue*, Fenwick became increasingly involved in New Jersey politics and philanthropy, focusing on prison reform, civil rights, gender discrimination, child abuse, the plight of migrant farm workers, consumer protection, and New Jersey Senator Clifford Case's campaigns. Fenwick later described herself as having an "obsession about justice" that she could not explain.[18] She became known as a feisty, pipe-smoking legislator, serving in the New Jersey state legislature and as the director of the New Jersey Division of Consumer Affairs. Her work in New Jersey fostered an interest in human rights and equality that she brought with her to Washington after her election to the House of Representatives in 1974.[19]

---

[14] Fenwick, *Speaking Up*, 161.

[15] Millicent Fenwick, May 17, 1976, *Congressional Record*, Folder 1, Box 181, Fenwick Papers; and R. Spencer Oliver Interview, February 26, 2008.

[16] Newsletter, "Impressions of the Trip to Russia," September 11, 1975, Folder 33, Box 7, Travel Series, Albert Collection. Her emphasis on human rights throughout her legislative career led some to term her the "Republican Roosevelt," clearly referencing Eleanor, not Franklin or Teddy. Schapiro, *Millicent Fenwick*, 169.

[17] Schapiro, Millicent Fenwick, 47–59.

[18] Millicent Fenwick Interview, December 17, 1985, *The Foreign Affairs Oral History Collection of the Association for Diplomatic Studies and Training*, Library of Congress, http://memory.loc.gov/ammem/collections/diplomacy/ (accessed March 8, 2010).

[19] Schapiro, *Millicent Fenwick*, 104–31.

On September 9, 1975, Fenwick introduced House Resolution 9466 to establish a Commission on Security and Cooperation in Europe, which she envisioned as a body composed of six senators, six members of the House of Representatives, and three members of the executive branch—one each from the Departments of Commerce, State, and Defense. She intended the legislative members to be split equally along party lines.[20] Fenwick, a first-term representative, turned to her more senior New Jersey colleague to help push her bill through the Senate, and Senator Clifford Case (R-NJ) introduced S. 2679 on November 17, 1975. Upon doing so, Case made a statement declaring that "Congress should be able to play an important role in the all-important area of human rights which all too often appear to be of only secondary concern to the executive branch."[21]

As Fenwick and Case's bills moved forward, there were early signs that the executive branch did not support creating such a Commission, with administration officials suggesting that it would infringe upon and needlessly replicate their foreign policy responsibilities. In Fenwick's view, although, the establishment of a Commission would strengthen the State Department's efforts, not duplicate them.[22] Furthermore, members of Congress saw the Commission's establishment as necessary given the broader pattern of indifference toward human rights under Kissinger and Ford.[23] In Case's testimony at Congressional hearings, he noted that the executive branch had not exhibited sufficient concern in monitoring Helsinki compliance.[24] Representative Joshua Eilberg (D-PA) testified that without the Commission, the significance of Helsinki would diminish: "There should be no doubt that unless there is a constant public monitoring of how the various signatories to the Helsinki Declaration live up to the promises of the section on

---

[20] Ibid., 171.

[21] "Establishing a Commission on Security and Cooperation in Europe," April 23, 1976, Folder 6, Box 274, Fenwick Papers. Fenwick was a long-time supporter of Case. In his 1960 campaign for the Senate, Fenwick had served as co-chair of the Citizens for Senator Case Committee. Schapiro, *Millicent Fenwick*, 110.

[22] Press Release, April 27, 1976, Press Releases: Jan.–June 1976, Box 284, Fenwick Papers. The State Department, however, disagreed claiming that the Commission proposed by Fenwick and Case's bills would not "add to the efforts and procedures already established." "Establishing a Commission on Security and Cooperation in Europe," April 23, 1976, Folder 6, Box 274, Fenwick Papers.

[23] Madeleine K. Albright and Alfred Friendly, Jr., "Helsinki and Human Rights," in Edmund S. Muskie, Kenneth Rush, and Kenneth W. Thompson, eds., *The President, The Congress and Foreign Policy* (Lanham: University Press of America, 1986), 294–5.

[24] Statement, May 4, 1976, Helsinki Commission, Box 66, Clifford Case Papers, Rutgers University, New Brunswick, New Jersey (hereafter Case Papers).

human rights they will be ignored by the Soviet Union and, quite probably, other East European countries."[25] Eilberg's analysis undoubtedly was correct, as even with the Commission and other active advocacy groups, the Soviet Union ignored elements of the Helsinki Final Act for many years to come.

Domestic political considerations cannot be dismissed as factors in congressional support for the initiative. The Czechoslovak National Council, Polish American Congress, and other politically important Eastern European ethnic groups supported creating the Commission.[26] Former Commission staffer Alfred Friendly, Jr. suggests the body's formation in an election year was politically motivated, indicating Fascell's eventual support of Fenwick's initiative may have been due to his sense that the Commission could be used to the advantage of the Democratic Party. Friendly argues Fascell was also motivated by the interest of Jewish groups, a key constituency in his Florida district, in the establishment of a Commission.[27]

The bill ultimately gained bipartisan support, passing in the House by a vote of 240–95 and in the Senate shortly thereafter.[28] Speaking on the floor in support of the bill before the House vote, Fascell summarized the argument in support of the Commission:

When I first learned of Mrs. Fenwick's proposal I was skeptical about the wisdom of setting up yet another government entity for such a specific purpose ... I am now convinced that such an entity would not only be useful but could play a vital role in the promotion of human rights and in making certain that détente will be a two-way street and will mean substantive progress on fundamental

---

[25] Statement of Joshua Eilberg, May 4, 1976, Folder 1, Box 181, Fenwick Papers; and Memorandum, Kraft to Case, May 4, 1976, Helsinki Commission, Box 66, Case Papers.

[26] The Commission was also supported by the Veterans of Foreign Wars, Federation of American Scientists, National Conference on Soviet Jewry, and National Confederation of American Ethnic Groups. Albright and Friendly, "Helsinki and Human Rights," in Edmund S. Muskie, Kenneth Rush, and Kenneth W. Thompson, eds., *The President, The Congress and Foreign Policy*, 294–5; Lukomski to Members of the Polish American Congress Board of Directors, November 25, 1975, Folder 2, Box 138, Aloysius A. Mazewski Papers, Immigration History Research Center, University of Minnesota, Minneapolis, Minnesota (hereafter Mazewski Papers); Pell to Ferjencik, January 26, 1976; and Chalupa et al. to Pell, December 22, 1975, Russia, Box 5, 94th Congress, 1975–1976, Claiborne Pell Papers, University of Rhode Island, Kingston, Rhode Island (hereafter Pell Papers); and Rugienius and Urbonas to Ford, 31 January 1976, FG 431 Commission on Security and Cooperation in Europe, Box 216, WHCF, GRFL.

[27] Alfred Friendly, Jr., Interview, May 6, 2008.

[28] Press Release, May 17, 1976, Press Releases: Jan.–June 1976, Box 284, Fenwick Papers.

humanitarian issues of concern to the people of the United States and other western nations.[29]

The creation of the Commission corresponded with changing public opinion, as many people who had opposed Ford's signature of the Helsinki Final Act, including prominent ethnic leaders and members of Congress, now supported the Commission and its work, hopeful that its emphasis on monitoring compliance could improve conditions in Eastern Europe.

Once the bill had passed Congress, the Ford administration faced a delicate decision as to how it should handle the legislation. Noting the significant congressional support for the bill juxtaposed with considerable executive branch reservations, one State Department official suggested the president allow it to become law without his formal signature.[30] The root issue was the White House's unwillingness to concede elements of foreign policymaking to the legislative branch.[31] The State Department had written that such a Commission "would not be the most practical or effective means for coordinating" implementation efforts and that the State Department's "CSCE action office" within the Department's European Bureau was sufficient to monitor implementation.[32] As evidence of State Department opposition, Secretary of State Kissinger later said had he known Ford would sign the bill he "would have fought it to the death" and suggested in a meeting with his staff that the executive branch not be "helpful" to the Commission.[33] The National Security Council (NSC) also was firm in its opposition.[34] When wider public opinion was considered, however, a Commerce Department official noted that a veto of the legislation could be understood by the public

[29] May 17, 1976, *Congressional Record*, Folder 1, Box 181, Fenwick Papers.

[30] Memorandum for the President, May 28, 1976, FG 431 Commission on Security and Cooperation in Europe, 8/9/74–6/30/76, Box 216, WHCF, GRFL.

[31] Albright and Friendly, "Helsinki and Human Rights," in Edmund S. Muskie, Kenneth Rush, and Kenneth W. Thompson, eds., *The President, The Congress and Foreign Policy*, 285.

[32] McCloskey to Fenwick, September 1975, FG 431 Commission on Security and Cooperation in Europe, 8/9/74–6/30/76, Box 216, WHCF, GRFL; and McCloskey to Morgan, November 1975, ibid.

[33] Memcon, July 26, 1976, CSCE, 1976 (2) WH, Box 44, National Security Council Europe, Canada and Ocean Affairs Staff Files, NSA, GRFL. Kissinger's repeated claims to have been unaware of the bill, its passage, and the president's plan to sign it are surprising given his involvement in and animosity toward the Helsinki negotiations, but may reflect his role as head of the State Department rather than National Security Adviser.

[34] Davis to Baroody and attachments, April 5, 1976, FG 31 4/1/76–6/30/76, Box 118, WHCF, GRFL; and Leo P. Ribuffo, "Is Poland a Soviet Satellite?: Gerald Ford, the Sonnenfeldt Doctrine, and the Election of 1976," *Diplomatic History* 14 (Summer 1990): 391.

as lack of interest in human rights.[35] White House staffers considering the implications of Ford's options in the context of his contest with former California governor Ronald Reagan for the Republican nomination came to a similar conclusion: supporting the Commission would highlight a tougher stance with the Soviets, which was politically advantageous.[36]

Having listened to his advisers' divergent opinions, Ford decided to endorse the legislation. Ford signed the bill on June 3, 1976 in the Oval Office with only Fenwick, Case, and Fenwick's legislative aide Bill Canis present, limiting the fanfare at the behest of Scowcroft and the NSC.[37] Explaining his decision, Ford would later cite a genuine commitment to the Helsinki Final Act as opposed to political opportunism: "Having signed the accord I felt it was absolutely essential to proceed with the review process. If we were going to implement the Helsinki Accords we were going to have to monitor it."[38] It is difficult to know if Ford was revising history given the positive record of the Commission in the subsequent years, but the evidence suggests this to be the case.

Congressional posturing for a spot on the Commission began almost immediately, with numerous members lobbying for a position. Speaker of the House Carl Albert designated the four Democratic members from the House: Jonathan B. Bingham (D-NY), Paul Simon (D-IL), Dante Fascell (D-FL) and Sidney Yates.[39] Minority Leader John J. Rhodes (R-AZ) nominated Fenwick and Representative John Buchanan, Jr. (R-AL) as the two

[35] Smith to Lynn, May 27, 1976, FG 431 Commission on Security and Cooperation in Europe, 8/9/74–6/30/76, Box 216, WHCF, GRFL.

[36] Kuropas to Baroody, March 24, 1976, SPS/FG 11 6/1/75–5/31/76, Box 83, WHCF, GRFL; and Memorandum, Calkins to Scowcroft and Friedersdorf, October 24, 1975, FG 431 Commission on Security and Cooperation in Europe, 8/9/74–6/30/76, Box 216, ibid.

[37] Press Release, June 4, 1976, Press Releases: Jan.–June 1976, Box 284, Fenwick Papers. Despite their exclusion from the ceremony, numerous ethnic leaders wrote to Ford to express their support for the Commission. Schapiro, *Millicent Fenwick*, 175. For example, see Rogaway to Ford, June 11, 1976, Conference on Security and Cooperation in Europe, 1976 WH (2), Box 44, National Security Council Europe, Canada and Ocean Affairs Staff: Files, National Security Adviser, GRFL. Scowcroft argued against a public ceremony for the bill due to the administration's stated opposition to it and its resistance to increasing congressional assertiveness in executive matters. Special Assistant for Ethnic Affairs in the Office of Public Liaison Myron Kuropas, concerned more about domestic politics, argued at least to include a number of ethnic leaders, but the NSC plan to limit the participants prevailed. Scowcroft to Friedersdorf, May 29, 1976, FG 431 Commission on Security and Cooperation in Europe, 8/9/74–6/30/76, Box 216, WHCF, GRFL; and Wolthuis to Nicholson, June 2, 1976, ibid.

[38] Schapiro, *Millicent Fenwick*, 175–6.

[39] *Fascell to Albert*, May 18, 1976, Folder 42, Box 215, Legislative Series, Albert Collection.

FIGURE 2. President Gerald R. Ford signs legislation creating the Commission on Security and Cooperation in Europe as Representative Millicent Fenwick and Senator Clifford Case, the bill's sponsors, observe. Courtesy Gerald R. Ford Library.

Republican House members.[40] Senate leadership named Richard Stone (D-FL), Claiborne Pell (D-RI), Patrick Leahy (D-VT), Case, James Buckley (Conservative-NY), and Dick Clark (D-IA) as Commissioners.[41]

Fascell, a long-time representative from South Florida, was appointed Chair of the Commission and shaped the Commission to such an extent that it was often referred to as the Fascell Commission. He had served

---

[40] Fenwick to Rhodes, June 10, 1976, Folder 10, Box 56, Minority Leader Files-Legislative, MSS-2, John J. Rhodes Minority Leader Papers, Arizona State University, Tempe, Arizona; Buchanan to Rhodes, May 27, 1976, ibid.; Gilman to Rhodes, June 10, 1976, ibid.; Rhodes to Albert, June 11, 1976, ibid.; Rhodes to Albert, June 11, 1976, Folder 42, Box 215, Legislative Series, Albert Collection; and Press Release, June 11, 1976, Box 2443, Dante Fascell Papers, University of Miami, Coral Gables, Florida (hereafter Fascell Papers).

[41] The Commission gained valuable resources from the State Department and USIA officers assigned to its staff, including one Foreign Service officer, Guy Coriden, who had served on the CSCE negotiating team. Albright and Friendly, "Helsinki and Human Rights," in Edmund S. Muskie, Kenneth Rush, and Kenneth W. Thompson, eds., *The President, The Congress and Foreign Policy*, 301. Case and Buckley co-sponsored an amendment to begin funding the Commission as of July 1. Letter to Ford, June 24, 1976, Helsinki Commission, Box 66, Case Papers.

in World War II as a member of the Florida National Guard and later pointed to his experience in the African and Italian campaigns as motivating his desire to enter public service, saying, "If Americans are going to be sent to war, I want to know why and be part of the process that decides whether they should go."[42] In his nineteen terms in Congress, Fascell served on the House Foreign Affairs Committee for thirty-six years and was its committee chair for nine years.

One of the Commission's most pressing issues in its early days was securing executive branch representation, as the signed bill called for one member to be appointed to the Commission by each of the Departments of Commerce, State, and Defense. Fascell repeatedly sparred with the White House over the executive branch members given its continued opposition to the Commission. The solution, agreed to in an exchange of letters between Ford and Fascell, delineated the parameters of executive branch participation in the Commission. The executive branch members would fill observer roles that would avoid voting or questioning witnesses as well as necessitate recusal from certain discussions and limit responsibility for the Commission's decisions.[43]

Once composition of the Commission was set, Fascell and others began to consider the body's mission. Among those Fascell consulted was R. Spencer Oliver, who would later become the Commission's chief of staff. Oliver reports he recognized the Commission could be very important in winning the ideological struggle of the Cold War and that he advised Fascell to "hold the Soviets' feet to the fire." Oliver further told Fascell the Commission could "be the voice of the dissidents" and needed to work to influence United States policy in this regard.[44] Not surprisingly, the Soviets opposed the Commission, arguing its emphasis on the third basket was not in line with the CSCE principle that all baskets were equally important and alleging the body was interfering in internal Soviet affairs.[45]

As the Commission began its work, staff members met with a range of religious, ethnic and human rights groups and activists to assess efforts to implement the Helsinki Final Act. There were limits to the Commission's

[42] "A Tribute to Dante B. Fascell," www.library.miami.edu/archives/fascell/tribute/df3.html (accessed July 7, 2008).

[43] Memorandum, Hartman et al. to Kissinger, September 1, 1976, CSCE, 1976 (5) NSC, Box 45, National Security Council Europe, Canada and Ocean Affairs Staff: Files, NSA, GRFL.

[44] R. Spencer Oliver Interview, February 26, 2008.

[45] Robinson to Ford, October 27, 1976, CSCE, 1976 (7) WH, Box 45, National Security Council Europe, Canada and Ocean Affairs Staff: Files, NSA, GRFL.

authority, however; although it could try to influence United States policy, the members of the Commission were acting outside the State Department, which formulated official American CSCE policy. Over time, Commissioners nonetheless would create meaningful roles for the Commission and the Eastern monitoring groups they championed in the Helsinki process.

The Commission's most prominent undertaking in its first year was a research trip to Europe, which enabled Commissioners to evaluate Helsinki monitoring there, establish contacts with other CSCE states, and explain the Commission's mission. Commissioners Fascell, Pell, Bingham, Fenwick, and Simon traveled to eighteen states, although the Soviets blocked the Commission's entry to Warsaw Pact countries. In addition, they met with representatives from NATO, the European Community, and other international organizations, as well as many private individuals and interested groups.[46] Kissinger barred executive branch participation in the trip, but it was nevertheless successful, as the tour heightened connections among different groups and activists involved in Helsinki monitoring.[47] The Commission's trip offers an important example of early efforts to coordinate Helsinki monitoring transnationally.

One of the Commission's main tasks was to draw attention to violations of the Helsinki Final Act in the hope that publicity would lead states to improve their records.[48] The Commission focused primarily on the plight of political prisoners, refuseniks, and those suffering human

[46] Report of the Study Mission to Europe to the Commission on security and Cooperation in Europe, February 11, 1977, CSCE Folder 2, Box 2443, Fascell Papers; Albright and Friendly, "Helsinki and Human Rights," in Edmund S. Muskie, Kenneth Rush, and Kenneth W. Thompson, eds., *The President, The Congress and Foreign Policy*, 302–3; and Briefing Book, CSCE European Trip, November 5–23, 1976, CSCE, 1977–1976, Box 30, Pell Papers.

[47] Pell further criticized the State Department action by saying, "Kissinger's decision now calls into question what, despite the president's action in signing the law establishing the commission, the administration's real intentions are regarding it." News Release, November 1, 1976, Box 2443, Fascell Papers; "3 on Helsinki Panel Curbed by Kissinger," *New York Times*, November 2, 1976, Folder 14, Box 274, Fenwick Papers; Leigh et al. to Kissinger, October 26, 1976, Folder 5, Box 11, Sonnenfeldt Collection; Henry S. Bradsher, "Kissinger, Hill Spar Over Europe Trip of Helsinki Commission," *Washington Star*, November 2, 1976, CSCE Folder 2, Box 2443, Fascell Papers. Fascell described Kissinger's action as "deeply regrettable." New Release, Commission on Security and Cooperation in Europe, November 1, 1976, Folder 15, Box 274, Fenwick Papers. Oliver has suggested that Kissinger and Dobrynin colluded to deny Commission members visas to Eastern European countries, but I could find no evidence to support that charge. Schapiro, *Millicent Fenwick*, 181; and Mastny, ed., *Helsinki, Human Rights, and European Security*, 12, 118.

[48] Catherine Cosman Interview, April 8, 2008.

rights violations.[49] It was able to gain influence and advance its agenda by holding hearings on Helsinki compliance, undertaking a considerable, broad-based study of adherence to the Helsinki Final Act, and serving as a clearinghouse for information.[50] For many years, the Commission was the most comprehensive source on Helsinki compliance in the United States. Much of the information arriving at the Commission was unsolicited, and often tragic; Alfred Friendly, Jr., wrote to Fascell about reports arriving about family reunification cases: "They come, in pathetic detail, unsolicited in every mail delivery."[51] Evaluating the influence of the Commission, long-time Commission staffer Catherine Cosman argues that its authority was "not just rhetorical." In her view, the Commission succeeded in "humanizing" activists, which enhanced sympathy for their plight.[52]

The establishment of the Commission offered an outlet for the Eastern monitoring groups, which would emerge shortly thereafter, and their research on violations of the Helsinki Final Act. The Commission fostered a transnational network of Helsinki activists and gave a voice to their grievances through its hearings, reports, and advocacy. It relied heavily on documents and reports from Eastern Europe, at times invited exiled dissidents to testify, and championed Helsinki monitors. The Commission received and translated many *samizdat* documents and forwarded them to other CSCE states and interested groups.[53] As such, it played a critical role, connecting different activists and policymakers across interests and national lines.[54] The significance of the Commission rests in its

---

[49] John Finerty, written communication with the author, June 24, 2008.

[50] As part of its effort, the Commission conducted fourteen hearings with fifty-six witnesses and surveyed 1,035 recent Soviet émigrés. "Report to the Congress of the United States on Implementation of the Final Act of the Conference on Security and Cooperation in Europe: Findings and Recommendations Two Years After Helsinki," August 1, 1977, Box 2443, Fascell Papers; and Korey, *The Promises We Keep*, 40–1.

[51] Friendly, Jr., to Fascell, January 21, 1977, document is in the author's possession.

[52] Catherine Cosman Interview, April 8, 2008. The highly positive assessments given by former Commission staff members are borne out in the historical record.

[53] *Samizdat* can be translated as "self-published" and refers documents such as banned literature or reports of abuses that were produced and distributed clandestinely. Commission on Security and Cooperation in Europe, "A Thematic Survey of the Documents of the Moscow Helsinki Groups," May 12, 1981.

[54] The Commission offers an example of what Kenneth Cmiel has called the effect of "third-party influence," which he describes as a tactic through which human rights activists influence sympathetic government figures, such as a member of Congress who in turns uses their influence to press for increased observance of human rights by a repressive government. Kenneth Cmiel, "The Emergence of Human Rights Politics in the United States," *The Journal of American History* 86:3 (December 1999): 1242.

connections with a broader Helsinki community, and the influence it was able to bear on the implementation of Helsinki obligations and the broader protection of human rights.[55] For example, Commission staff worked closely with Western NGOs such as Helsinki Watch and activists such as Ludmilla Alekseeva, who represented the Moscow Helsinki Group in the West.[56] Furthermore, the religious, ethnic, and human rights groups in regular contact with the Commission provided it with information not available through embassy channels, served as witnesses at Commission hearings, and enabled personal connections with activists or victims from the Soviet Union and Eastern Europe.[57] The Commission was an essential advocate for and collaborator with the emerging transnational network of Helsinki activists, and it was at the center of the transformation of the United States attitude toward and role in the CSCE.

Importantly, the Commission also worked to focus American attention on Helsinki implementation. Through their efforts to convince United States policymakers to press Helsinki compliance, members of the Commission succeeded in making the Helsinki process a more potent international force for change. Jimmy Carter's election in 1976 changed the course of United States involvement in the Helsinki process and enabled the Commission to exert increasing influence on American policy and CSCE activities generally. Under the Carter administration, members of the Commission and its staff played an integral role in United States CSCE policy.[58] Operating between the official policymakers of the State Department and unofficial groups, the United States Helsinki Commission maintained a particularly unique position during CSCE review meetings as members of the Commission and its staff filled key roles on American delegations.

Although not regularly involved in United States diplomacy, the Commissioners used their status as members of Congress to the benefit of the broader Helsinki network, the majority of which did not have such access

---

[55] Fenwick wanted to create connections internationally among different groups interested in monitoring the Helsinki Final Act. Fenwick to Dirnecker, April 2, 1976, Folder 2-Western European Monitoring, Box 272, Fenwick Papers.

[56] Catherine Cosman Interview, April 8, 2008.

[57] John Finerty, written communication with the author, June 24, 2008.

[58] Despite efforts by Carter's political appointees to work closely with the Commission, its struggles with the State Department would not fully subside, and entrenched bureaucratic interests and substantive differences would persist throughout Carter's term. For further discussion of tension between the Commission and the State Department, see Guy E. Coriden, Jr., Interview, November 18, 1992, *The Foreign Affairs Oral History Collection of the Association for Diplomatic Studies and Training*, Library of Congress, http://memory.loc.gov/ammem/collections/diplomacy/ (accessed March 6, 2010).

or clout. In this vein, Commissioners often sought to influence Soviet and Eastern European leaders directly through correspondence and meetings in which they often raised concerns transmitted to them by human rights activists. For example, Friendly, briefing Fascell for his upcoming meeting with Dobrynin, wrote he should "try to spell out to him why Americans really do care about Basket Three ... What hurts the Soviet image just as much [as the arms race and Angola] are the restrictions on emigration and travel, the restraints on outside information, the intolerance of political and religious dissent."[59] Yet, for many years, the Commission's entreaties to Eastern European leaders seemed to have no positive effect.[60]

Nonetheless, the Commission's potential long-term significance was apparent to those who worked closely with it or who relied on it to advance their agenda more effectively on the national, or even international, stage. At the end of his term as Commerce Department Commissioner-Observer, Mansfield Sprague wrote to Ford that he had "formed the firm conviction that this Commission has within its potential a real chance to influence history ... it can bring to bear moral persuasion to influence the gradual movement of governments to achieve the high ground expressed in Basket III."[61] Over the subsequent years, the Commission used its resources and influence to press for changes in United States foreign policy and the treatment of Soviet and Eastern European citizens. Oliver, evaluating the long-term influence of the Commission, said there was "no doubt in my mind that what we did in the Helsinki Commission is that we engaged the Soviets in the ideological struggle and we won."[62] Yale Richmond, a former State Department official who worked for the Commission from 1980 to 1983, echoes Oliver's sentiment, arguing that Ford's signature of the Helsinki Final Act "did as much, if not more, to bring about the collapse of communism than Ronald Reagan did years later."[63]

---

[59] Memorandum, Friendly to Fascell, January 21, 1977, document is in the author's possession.

[60] Although Soviet attacks on the Commission indicated its influence and efficacy: "Fascell and his Commission will surely get new appropriations for continuing their slanderous activates against the Socialist countries under the hypocritical pretext of monitoring the observance of the Helsinki Accords." "Kremlin Blasts Commission," *CSCE Digest*, February 27, 1981, Folder 2, Box 152, Part I, Arthur J. Goldberg Papers, Manuscript Division, Library of Congress, Washington, District of Columbia (hereafter Goldberg Papers).

[61] Sprague to Ford, December 17, 1976, document is in the author's possession.

[62] R. Spencer Oliver Interview, February 26, 2008.

[63] Yale Richmond, *Practicing Public Diplomacy: A Cold War Odyssey* (New York: Berghahn Books, 2008), 155.

3

Even in a Yakutian Village

Helsinki Monitoring in Moscow and Beyond

The Helsinki Final Act spurred a profusion of dissident activity in Eastern Europe, which eventually created broad, domestic political implications for Soviet and Eastern European leaders. At the same time as the Commission was established in the United States, Eastern Europeans were mobilizing less formal, but equally important, elements of the transnational network. The monitoring groups that developed across Europe called upon the Soviet Union and others to uphold their Helsinki commitments and drew international attention to their reports of human rights abuses. These groups, including most prominently the Moscow Helsinki Group, became part of a larger political and social movement that influenced the end of the Cold War. This chapter explains how the monitoring groups that developed in the Soviet Union and elsewhere reframed the content and significance of the Helsinki Final Act, using it to advance human rights in Eastern Europe.

Although the Helsinki Final Act provided the impetus for the formation of new groups, many of the key figures in the Helsinki network had previously worked together to advance human rights. Activists in the Soviet Union had organized together sporadically for more than a decade; their early efforts included protests such as the December 1965 demonstration in Moscow's Pushkin Square to commemorate the anniversary of the Universal Declaration of Human Rights, which a close observer of Soviet human rights activism has argued marked the "birth" of the civil rights movement in the Soviet Union and the first movement of its kind in a socialist state.[1] In addition, the human rights movement

---

[1] Benjamin Nathans, "Soviet Dissidents and Human Rights," paper presented at "A New Global Morality?: The Politics of Human Rights and Humanitarianism in the

comprised groups such as the Initiative Group to Defend Human Rights in the USSR, the Moscow Human Rights Committee, and a Moscow chapter of Amnesty International as well as publications such as the *Chronicle of Current Events*, a prominent *samizdat* journal that played an important role in documenting Soviet abuses.[2] The groups tried collectively, with little success, to publicize widespread Soviet human rights violations. Writings such as Alexander Solzhenitsyn's *One Day in the Life of Ivan Denisovich* had exposed domestic and foreign audiences to the Soviet system of forced labor camps in which prisoners suffered from limited medical care, malnutrition, strict punishment, and exhausting work norms.[3] The plight of those unable to emigrate from the Soviet Union was also well documented. Activists sought to demonstrate the pervasive nature of Soviet violations by additionally highlighting the plight of those who wished to practice their religion, educate their children in their national language, or choose their place of residence. Efforts to alleviate Soviet conditions had not yet borne fruit when Sakharov was awarded the 1975 Nobel Peace Prize only months after the summit in Helsinki.[4] In his Nobel Peace Prize lecture, "Peace, Progress, and Human Rights," Sakharov specifically noted the lack of Soviet progress on implementation of the Helsinki Final Act, which was supported by the fact that the Soviets prohibited Sakharov from accepting the award

1970s," Freiburg Institute for Advanced Studies, Freiburg, Germany, June 2010; Benjamin Nathans, "The Dictatorship of Reason: Aleksandr Vol'Pin and the Idea of Rights under 'Developed Socialism,'" *Slavic Review* 66:4 (Winter 2007): 632; H. Gordon Skilling, *Samizdat and an Independent Society in Central and Eastern Europe* (London: Macmillan Press, 1989), 201; Edward Acton, "Revolutionaries and dissidents: The role of the Russian intellectual in the downfall of Tsarism and Communism" in Jeremy Jennings and Anthony Kemp-Welch, eds., *Intellectuals in Politics: From the Dreyfus Affair to Salman Rushdie* (New York: Routledge, 1997), 151; and Ludmilla Alexeyeva, *Soviet Dissent: Contemporary Movements for National, Religious, and Human Rights* (Middletown: Wesleyan University Press, 1985), 9. I have chosen to use the anglicized version under which she published in the United States only in the footnotes. Discussion of Alekseeva's role in the main text will use the proper transliteration of her name.

2 Valery Chalidze, *The Soviet Human Rights Movement: A Memoir* (New York: The American Jewish Committee, 1984), 23.

3 Alexander Solzhenitsyn, *One Day in the Life of Ivan Denisovich* trans. Gillon Aitken (New York: Farrar, Straus and Giroux, 1971); and Peter B. Reddaway, "Theory and Practice of Human Rights in the Soviet Union," in Donald P. Kommers and Gilburt D. Loescher, eds., *Human Rights and American Foreign Policy* (Notre Dame: University of Notre Dame Press, 1979), 126.

4 Andropov to the Central Committee, November 30, 1975, S.II.2.4.106, Box, 46, Papers of Andrei Sakharov, Andrei Sakharov Archives, Houghton Library, Harvard University, Cambridge, Massachusetts (hereafter Sakharov Papers).

in person.[5] His wife, Yelena Bonner, was traveling abroad at the time his award was announced and delivered the lecture in his place while Sakharov attended the trial of human rights activist Sergei Kovalev in Vilnius.[6] The juxtaposition of Bonner in Oslo while Sakharov observed Kovalev's trial demonstrated to many the Soviet Union's poor human rights record.[7]

Despite ongoing Soviet repression, the agreement did not go unnoticed in Moscow. Surprising observers, the Soviet government published twenty million copies of the Helsinki Final Act in the two main Moscow newspapers, *Pravda* and *Izvestia*.[8] The act also was published in national languages within the Soviet Union and later in pamphlet form.[9] Why the Soviets chose to publish an agreement with such radical commitments, by USSR standards, has never been fully explained. Likely Soviet leaders thought the act's publication would highlight its positive security measures without instigating protests. Furthermore, as the Soviet Union, and Brezhnev specifically, had long pressed for the conference, the resulting agreement, signed at a high-level international summit, was a source of pride to Soviet leaders. Recent scholarship has suggested Soviet publication of the UN Universal Declaration of Human Rights was used to celebrate socialist legality, which might have also influenced the decision to publish the 1975 agreement.[10] According to Soviet Ambassador to the United States Anatoly Dobrynin, Soviet leaders did not foresee a lasting response to the Helsinki Final Act's publication, in part because Brezhnev thought that he could minimize the impact of the third basket domestically: "But he was wrong. The condition of Soviet dissidents certainly did not change overnight, but they were definitely encouraged by this historic document. Its very publication in *Pravda* gave it the weight of an official document."[11] Former

[5] Andrei D. Sakharov, "Peace, Progress, and Human Rights," in Andrei D. Sakharov, *Alarm and Hope*, Efrem Yankelevich and Alfred Friendly, Jr., eds., (New York: Alfred A. Knopf, 1978), 13.

[6] Ibid., 18.

[7] Emma Gilligan, *Defending Human Rights in Russia: Sergei Kovalyov, Dissident and Human Rights Commissioner, 1969–2003* (New York: Routledge, 2004), 46.

[8] Victor Zora, "The Kremlin Passes the First Test," *Washington Post*, August 7, 1975.

[9] A. Adamishin et al. *From Helsinki to Belgrade: The Soviet Union and the Implementation of the Final Act of the European Conference: Documents and Material* (Moscow: Progress Publishers, 1977), 13.

[10] Jennifer Amos, "Embracing & Contesting: The Soviet Union and the Universal Declaration of Human Rights, 1948–1958," in Stefan-Ludwig Hoffmann, ed., *Human Rights in the Twentieth Century* (New York: Cambridge University Press, 2010), 157–60.

[11] Andrew and Mitrokhin, *The Sword and the Shield*, 311; and Anatoly Dobrynin, *In Confidence*, 346.

Soviet diplomat Sergei Kondrashev echoes Dobrynin's assessment of the importance of publishing the text, although he suggests Soviet leaders did expect some popular reaction:

I have to tell you that by allowing the official publication of the Helsinki Final Act in our country, we took a bold step. Naturally, we understood that it would cause a very certain reaction in the country. Indeed, very soon Helsinki groups began to emerge, the dissident movement developed.[12]

Kondrashev's remembrance fits with suggestions made by some that publication of the agreement was pressed by reformers within the leadership group who wanted to move away from the orthodoxy espoused by Ideology Secretary Mikhail Suslov and others.[13] Soviet diplomat Anatoly Kovalev claims that he understood the ideological and political subtext of the Helsinki Final Act, although not its full implications, writing that eventually it was interpreted as the "legalization of dissidence," which "loosened the ground for the human rights movement and the growth of Helsinki groups."[14]

Public knowledge of the agreement had far-reaching and clearly unintended consequences. Representative Robert Drinan, who was in Moscow at the time of the document's publication, describes Sakharov and Jewish refusenik Anatoly Shcharansky as "amazed but jubilant" to read the full text of the act in a Soviet newspaper.[15] Moscow Helsinki Group founding member Ludmilla Alekseeva reported, "Soviet citizens, reading the text of the Final Act in the papers, were stunned by the humanitarian articles; it was the first they had heard of any kind of international obligations in the human rights field of their government."[16] With the terms of the agreement as inspiration, dissidents moved to establish monitoring groups that would urge all signatories to uphold their Helsinki commitments.

---

[12] Sergei Kondrashev, "'SALT II and the Growth of Mistrust': Conference #2 of the Carter-Brezhnev Project," National Security Archive.

[13] English, *Russia and the Idea of the West*, 302.

[14] Kovalev, *Azbuka Diplomatim*, 198.

[15] Anatoly Shcharansky changed his name to Natan Sharansky upon his emigration to Israel. For purposes of clarity, I have chosen to use the original spelling of his name throughout the text. Robert F. Drinan, *The Mobilization of Shame: A World View of Human Rights* (New Haven: Yale University Press, 2001), 73. Drinan reports that Sakharov told him Soviet agreement to the Helsinki Final Act marked a new beginning in the Soviet Union. Robert F. Drinan, "Glasnost's Architect," *Boston Globe*, December 17, 1989, A17.

[16] Alexeyeva, *Soviet Dissent*, 336. Alekseeva remains a prominent human rights activist in Moscow. Ellen Barry, "Russian Dissident's Passion Endures Despite Tests," *New York Times*, January 12, 2010, A1.

By far the most influential NGO that emerged in the wake of the signing of the Helsinki Final Act was the Public Group to Promote Fulfillment of the Helsinki Accords in the USSR, which was formed on May 13, 1976, by eleven prominent Soviet dissidents and known in the West as the Moscow Helsinki Group or the Moscow Helsinki Watch Group.[17] The Group's formation was prompted by Shcharansky's idea for an international movement of seminars and discussions on human rights. In his conception, the groups would start in the West first, at Soviet activists' invitation, and then a related Soviet group would be formed in response. Instead, Yuri Orlov proposed forming a Helsinki-focused group in Moscow with well-known dissidents and then seeing if the West would follow suit. In Shcharansky's words, "This is far more risky than what I had suggested, but since I am the one who got [Orlov] thinking about it, there is nothing I can do but join."[18]

The Moscow Helsinki Group was designed to monitor the positive and negative sides of Soviet Helsinki implementation and "work in informing the population inside the country and in informing the West" of violations of civil and human rights in the Soviet Union.[19] Orlov reports he spent two months discussing the idea with other dissidents in Moscow before ultimately drafting the document that announced the creation of the Group.[20] It was intended to be "within the bounds of legality," as the Soviet government had signed the Helsinki Final Act and theoretically had asked citizens to help with the monitoring.[21] The Group hoped

[17] I have used Moscow Helsinki Group or the Group throughout.

[18] *Arkihiv Samizdata* 2542, May 1976, Box 84, Published Samizdat, Samizdat Archives, Records of Radio Free Europe/Radio Liberty Research Institute, Open Society Archives, Central European University, Budapest, Hungary (hereafter Open Society Archives); Paul Goldberg, *The Final Act: The Dramatic, Revealing Story of the Moscow Helsinki Watch Group* (New York: Morrow, 1988), 35–7, 39; and Yuri Orlov, *Dangerous Thoughts: Memoirs of a Russian Life*, trans. Thomas P. Whitney (New York: William Morrow and Company, 1991), 188–9.

[19] Petro G. Grigorenko, *Memoirs*, trans. Thomas P. Whitney (New York: W. W. Norton and Company, 1982), 434–5.

[20] Orlov, *Dangerous Thoughts*, 189. Orlov points to the long history of human rights activism in the Soviet Union that preceded the formation of the Moscow Helsinki Group, arguing those active in the Moscow Helsinki Group had thought about human rights issues in the Soviet context for many years and were already quite experienced by the time the Group formed. Yuri Orlov Interview, March 27 and 28, 2008.

[21] H. Stuart Hughes, *Sophisticated Rebels: The Political Culture of European Dissent, 1968–1987* (Cambridge: Harvard University Press, 1988), 108; Edward Bailey Hodgman, *Détente and the Dissidents: Human Rights in U.S.–Soviet Relations, 1968–1980* (PhD Dissertation, University of Rochester, 2003), 243; and Joshua Rubenstein, *Soviet Dissidents: Their Struggle for Human Rights*, 2nd ed. (Boston: Beacon Press, 1985), 312.

to break what Soviet dissident Andrei Amal'rik described as the human rights movement's cycle of "arrest–protest–arrest."[22] Furthermore, dissidents intended to build upon what they saw as "timid but nonetheless unprecedented efforts on the part of recent Western leaders" to press the Soviet Union to uphold its commitments. Orlov hoped Western support would force Soviet authorities to "moderate their repressive policy, thereby assisting the realization of democratic rights."[23] His unconventional reaction to the Helsinki Final Act was an essential impetus to the development of Eastern monitoring efforts.

The original composition of the Moscow Helsinki Group was a deliberate attempt to bring together a diverse set of leading dissidents. In Alekseeva's words, the Helsinki process enabled the "unification of the human rights movement with religious and national movements" because all were working toward rights outlined in the Helsinki Final Act, and this was reflected in the eleven founding members of the Moscow Helsinki Group – Jewish refuseniks, human rights activists, and those focused on the rights of national minorities.[24] According to Orlov, once he had drafted a statement reflecting the group's mission, he and Shcharansky went to close colleagues in Moscow, with Shcharansky contacting primarily refuseniks and Orlov reaching out to scientists. In addition to Orlov and Shcharansky, the Group's founding members were Alekseeva, Alexander Korchak, Malva Landa, Vitaly Rubin, Yelena Bonner, Alexander Ginzburg, Anatoly Marchenko, Petro Grigorenko, and Mikhail Bernshtam.[25] The Moscow Helsinki Group was intended to be a "bridge" between different activists focused on

---

[22] Andrei Amal'rik, *Notes of a Revolutionary*, trans. Guy Daniels (New York: Alfred A. Knopf, 1982), 310.

[23] Grigorenko, *Memoirs*, 434–5.

[24] Alexeyeva, *Soviet Dissent*, 345–6; and Rudolf L. Tökes, "Human Rights in Eastern Europe: An Overview, 1977–1980," Statement to the Commission on Security and Cooperation in Europe, March 25, 1980, in Mastny, *Helsinki, Human Rights, and European Security*, 143–52. Nonetheless, divisions within communities such as the Jewish refuseniks remained. Gal Beckerman, *When They Come For Us, We'll Be Gone: The Epic Struggle to Save Soviet Jewry* (New York: Houghton Mifflin Harcourt, 2010), 335.

[25] Marchenko was imprisoned at the time of the group's founding but joined nonetheless in support of the Group's mission. Marchenko's account of his time in prison was an early form of human rights monitoring. He wrote, "The main aim of these notes is to tell the truth about today's camps and prisons for political prisoners – to those who wish to hear it. I am convinced that publicity is the sole effective means of combating the evil and lawlessness that is rampant in my country today." Anatoly Marchenko, *My Testimony*, trans. Michael Scammel (New York: Dell Publishing, 1969), 2; and Walter Parchomenko, *Soviet Images of Dissidents and Nonconformists* (New York: Praeger, 1986), 117.

religious, ethnic, economic issues as well as between workers and intellectuals.[26] Members also possessed different skills and networks of value to the Group; for example, Shcharansky's fluency in English and contacts with Western reporters and diplomats were also important to the Group's mission.[27] According to Shcharansky, his English skills helped him to act as an unofficial spokesman for the Group and to send documents abroad.[28] Speaking about the Group's formation ten years later, Shcharansky noted the diverse individuals and interests Orlov had brought together:

You see, there were Zionists and monarchists, Russians and Ukrainians and Byelorussians, and even Eurocommunists, I'd say, people of absolutely different views. There were those who wanted to leave, like myself or Vitaly Rubin, and those who were concerned about the situation in Soviet prisons and camps, and those who were concerned mainly about religious freedoms. But all of us were united by the Helsinki group.
  Of course, this was Yury [sic] Orlov's great achievement, and even now I can't understand how he managed to do the job so successfully.[29]

Orlov asked Sakharov to serve as the Group's head, given his immense international and domestic stature, but anticipated refusal: "By that time I knew Sakharov quite well, and I knew how he felt about groups and group documents, so I knew he wouldn't accept ... But it would have been impolite of me not to ask him to head the group. The offer was just a matter of courtesy, but, of course, if he had agreed, it would have been wonderful, too."[30] As expected, Sakharov did not welcome such a role and therefore declined: "I preferred the freedom of speaking out as an individual ... But I had no objection to endorsing group documents when I approved their content, and did so on many occasions."[31] Instead, Sakharov's wife, Yelena Bonner, joined the Group to lend it greater credibility.[32]

After Sakharov declined to lead the Group, Orlov became its head. Orlov was a physicist by training who had struggled professionally since

[26] Amal'rik, *Notes of a Revolutionary*, 312–3.
[27] Parchomenko, *Soviet Images of Dissidents and Nonconformists*, 118.
[28] Natan Sharansky Interview, November 19, 2008.
[29] "The Tenth Year of the Watch," *New York Review of Books*, June 26, 1986.
[30] Goldberg, *The Final Act*, 39, 43.
[31] Andrei Sakharov, *Memoirs*, trans. Richard Lourie (New York: Knopf, 1990), 456; and Richard Lourie, *Sakharov: A Biography* (Hanover: Brandeis University Press, 2002), 281.
[32] Goldberg, *The Final Act*, 47; Sakharov, *Memoirs*, 457; and Amal'rik, *Notes of a Revolutionary*, 311–2.

making a perceived "anti-Party" speech in the wake of Soviet leader Nikita Khrushchev's Twentieth Party Congress speech in 1956.[33] Orlov subsequently suffered a type of exile in which he could find work as a physicist only in Armenia. After spending sixteen years there working on an electron accelerator, he returned to Moscow and became increasingly involved with dissidents, refuseniks, and human rights advocates. In particular, Orlov was active in Amnesty International and publicly defended human rights activists.[34] As a result of these activities, which included writing a letter to Brezhnev, after 1973 Orlov was prevented from working as a scientist any longer.[35]

Although the Group was designed to fall within Soviet laws and be consistent with the Helsinki Final Act's stipulation that an individual had the right "to know and act on his rights and duties in [the human rights] field," the founders anticipated the government would try to repress them.[36] Indeed, the Committee for State Security (KGB) was aware of the Group's plans even before it had announced its intentions and wasted little time in applying pressure. Sensing that it risked disbandment before inception, the Group quickly proclaimed its formation to a Western journalist at Sakharov's apartment on May 12, 1976.[37] In order to avoid overshadowing the announcement with his potential arrest, Orlov went underground for two days until he heard news of the Group's formation over Western radio.[38] Orlov had hoped the announcement would receive wide press coverage in the West, but initially it garnered little attention. For example, Reuters carried the news and it was picked up by the *New York Times* and the *Los Angeles Times*; those papers, however, did not highlight the report, running the stories on pages eight and nineteen respectively. The *Washington Post* did not publish any news of the Group's formation.[39]

---

[33] Orlov, *Dangerous Thoughts*, 118–22.

[34] Ibid., 158–62, 168, 171, 174–6.

[35] Rumyantzev to Central Committee, September 28, 1973, S.II.2.4.82, Box 46, Sakharov Papers.

[36] The Helsinki Final Act, www.osce.org/documents/mcs/1975/08/4044_en.pdf (accessed May 17, 2006); Gilligan, *Defending Human Rights in Russia*, 12; and Tony Kemp-Welch, "Afterword: East or West?" in Kevin McDermott and Matthew Stibbe, eds., *Revolution and Resistance in Eastern Europe: Challenges to Communist Rule* (New York: Berg, 2006), 199.

[37] Orlov, *Dangerous Thoughts*, 190–2.

[38] Ibid., 192–3; and Yuri Orlov Interview, March 27 and 28, 2008.

[39] Goldberg, *The Final Act*, 51–2; and Orlov, *Dangerous Thoughts*, 188–9.

The government responded to the Group's formation almost imme-diately, alleging that its activities were not allowed.[40] According to Shcharansky, the KGB believed the establishment of the United States Commission within weeks of the Moscow Helsinki Group indicated col-lusion between the two groups and threatened the regime.[41] On May 15, the KGB informed Orlov that his group was illegal and unconstitu-tional and that he did not have the right to question the Soviet govern-ment's commitment to Helsinki.[42] The KGB's warning to Orlov actually increased coverage of the Group in the West, moving it up to page three in the *New York Times*.[43]

In spite of government pressure, the Group undertook a range of mon-itoring activities and drafted a report assessing the first year of Soviet compliance with the Helsinki Final Act. According to the Group's study, international attention had led the Soviets to act more "tentatively" with respect to human rights abuses, but it outlined continuing repression and Soviet disregard for the Helsinki Final Act.[44] Due to the mistreatment they incurred for their efforts, Orlov also outlined an appeal to the CSCE signatories to defend Helsinki monitors and their efforts to assess human rights in the Soviet Union.[45]

The Group's scope was expanded by citizens across the Soviet Union who sought out members for assistance with their cases. Western radio stations such as Voice of America and Radio Liberty helped disseminate news about the creation of the Moscow Helsinki Group, leading to broad awareness throughout the Soviet Union.[46] According to Orlov, news

[40] Christopher S. Wren, "Moscow Cracks Down on a Rights Group," *International Herald Tribune*, May 17, 1976, Human Rights, 1974–1976, Box 689, Old Code Subject Files, Soviet Red Archives, Records of Radio Free Europe/Radio Liberty Research Institute, Open Society Archives.

[41] Commission on Security and Cooperation in Europe Hearing, "Natan Shcharansky to Mark the 10th Anniversary of the Moscow Helsinki Group," May 14, 1986, 99th Congress/2nd Session.

[42] Goldberg, *The Final Act*, 53.

[43] Ibid., 54.

[44] "An Evaluation of the Influence of the Helsinki Agreements as They Relate to Human Rights in the USSR," Human Rights, 1974–1976, Box 689, Old Code Subject Files, Soviet Red Archives, Records of Radio Free Europe/Radio Liberty Research Institute, Open Society Archives; and *Arkhiv Samizdata* 2605, September 20, 1976, Box 88, Published Samizdat, Samizdat Archives, Records of Radio Free Europe/Radio Liberty Research Institute, Open Society Archives.

[45] *Arkhiv Samizdata* 2617, May 27, 1976, Box 88, Published Samizdat, Samizdat Archives, Records of Radio Free Europe/Radio Liberty Research Institute, Open Society Archives.

[46] Commission on Security and Cooperation in Europe Hearing, "Repercussions of the Trials of the Helsinki Monitors in the USSR, July 11, 1978, Second Session, 95th

about the Group and its activities was so well disseminated that even women in a small Yakutian village in Siberia had heard of him and his group. Many Soviets who knew of its existence found a group member to report a firsthand case of abuse when in Moscow.[47] Orlov estimates that he had two to three visitors every day, including, for example, religious believers from the Caucasus and Ukraine and workers from the Baltic republics.[48] Shcharansky remembers people coming from as far away as Siberia to see Orlov and other members.[49] Although crucial to the Group's mission, collecting stories of repression took a toll on its members. Petro Grigorenko wrote in his memoirs about the emotional cost of human rights monitoring:

> It was the fate of those of us who were called "dissidents," "renegades," and "enemies of society" to collect human grief. We had to listen every day to heart-rending stories and to watch impotently as the bureaucratic apparatus tormented innocent people. All we could do was cry out at their pain. Many people came to us for precisely that reason – they did not even have a "voice" with which to cry out themselves.[50]

Group members also traveled extensively throughout the Soviet Union to conduct research on compliance with the Helsinki Final Act.[51] For example, Alekseeva traveled to Lithuania to investigate reports of human rights violations of young schoolboys, and Alexander Podrabinek conducted field research on exiled prisoners in Siberia and nationalist demonstrations in Lithuania.[52] Shcharansky and Jewish refusenik Vladimir Slepak, who later joined the Group, investigated the plight of Jews living in a central Siberian village; Orlov traveled to Ukraine to follow up on a former political prisoner jailed for his nationalist beliefs.[53] For most of the Group members, Helsinki monitoring consumed much of their time,

---

Congress"; and Commission on Security and Cooperation in Europe Hearing, "Soviet Helsinki Watch, Reports on Repression, June 3, 1977, First Session, 95th Congress"; and Yale Richmond, *Cultural Exchange and The Cold War: Raising the Iron Curtain* (University Park: The Pennsylvania State University Press, 2003), 184.

[47] Yuri Orlov interview, March 27 and 28, 2008; and Orlov, *Dangerous Thoughts*, 199–200.

[48] Yuri Orlov Interview, March 27 and 28, 2008. Despite the dispersed awareness of the Group's existence and regular contacts from a broad range of Soviet citizens, it remained an elite group. Acton, "Revolutionaries and dissidents," in Jennings and Kemp-Welch, eds., *Intellectuals in Politics*, 160.

[49] Natan Sharansky Interview, November 19, 2008.

[50] Grigorenko, *Memoirs*, 443.

[51] Yuri Orlov Interview, March 27 and 28, 2008.

[52] Rubenstein, *Soviet Dissidents*, 238.

[53] Yuri Orlov Interview, March 27 and 28, 2008. Before his arrest, Shcharansky also was involved in researching a number of documents on emigration. Natan Sharansky Interview, November 19, 2008.

partly due to their inability to find employment given their dissident status but also because such work required a considerable commitment.[54]

The Group utilized research gained through firsthand testimonials and fact-finding missions to publish reports of Soviet human rights abuses, which in the words of Shcharansky "prevent[ed] the Soviet Union from turning the third basket into lip service."[55] Group members compiled numbered documents detailing Soviet violations of the Helsinki Final Act, such as "Document Number 1," which discussed the trial of Mustafa Dzhemilyev, who had advocated the return of Crimean Tatars to Crimea, and "Document Number 2," which addressed the interruption of telephone service.[56] Over time, the Group's documents focused on a wide range of issues, including: national self-determination, the right to choose one's residence, emigration and the right of return, freedom of belief, the right to monitor human rights, the right to a fair trial, the rights of political prisoners, abuse of psychiatry, and human contacts; the documents' authors highlighted human rights violations that affected every layer of Soviet society.[57] They also highlighted repression of Helsinki monitoring. For example, a May 1977 document detailed arrests of members of the Ukrainian and Lithuanian Helsinki Groups.[58]

The ultimate purpose of these documents was to keep the international community focused on the Helsinki Final Act and the Soviet Union's non-compliance with the agreement. Knowing that it was unlikely to succeed in pressing the Soviets to reform, the Moscow Helsinki Group focused on building international support for its agenda. The Group's initial strategy was to make thirty-five copies of each document and send them by registered mail to the thirty-four Moscow embassies affiliated with the CSCE and directly to Brezhnev.[59] Its decision was fueled by what political

---

[54] Applying to emigrate or engaging in human rights activity could often lead to the loss of employment, which could then serve as a pretext for arrest on charges of parasitism.

[55] Natan Sharansky Interview, November 19, 2008.

[56] The Crimean Tatars, as their name suggested, were indigenous to the Crimean peninsula until Stalin deported the entire ethnic group in 1944. In the following years, they sought unsuccessfully to return to their homeland. Mosckovskai Khel'sinskai Gruppa – Obshchestvo "Memorial," *Dokumenty Moskovskoi Khel'sinskoi Gruppi, 1976–1982* (Moscow: Mosckovskai Khel'sinskai Gruppa, 2006), 24–6, 28–31.

[57] Ludmilla Alekseeva, "O Dokumentakh Moskovskoi Khel'sinskoi Gruppi," in Mosckovskai Khel'sinskai Gruppa – Obshchestvo "Memorial," *Dokumenty Moskovskoi Khel'sinskoi Gruppi, 1976–1982*; Orlov, *Dangerous Thoughts*, 196–7; and Goldberg, *The Final Act*, 85.

[58] Mosckovskai Khel'sinskai Gruppa – Obshchestvo "Memorial," *Dokumenty Moskovskoi Khel'sinskoi Gruppi, 1976–1982*, 201.

[59] Moscow Helsinki Group members demonstrated their dissatisfaction with the Soviet regime through what Albert Hirschman has called the "voice option." Albert O.

scientist Daniel Thomas has described as the "boomerang effect," or instances in which nongovernmental actors make appeals transnationally "in order to circumvent blocked domestic opportunities for protest."[60] Thomas's formulation accurately captures the pattern of many Eastern monitoring groups, as the Helsinki Final Act and the follow-up CSCE meetings enabled Eastern dissidents to petition outside observers, an important fact given how unresponsive domestic governments were.[61] As Soviet dissident Valery Chalidze wrote in 1977, "During the past few years, Soviet dissidents have almost given up appealing to their own government, preferring to try world public opinion, international human rights organizations, and other governments that have dealings with the Soviet government. We have no other recourse if Moscow is unwilling to listen to us."[62] Charter 77 similarly complained that Czechoslovak authorities had not responded to their petitions, leading to the decision to appeal to international leaders such as Kurt Waldheim, the secretary general of the UN, and leaders of CSCE states.[63]

Moscow Helsinki Group members also met with foreign correspondents to reach audiences beyond the Soviet Union. Western journalists, in particular those posted to Moscow bureaus or working for the Voice of America or Radio Liberty, were essential to the development of a broader Helsinki network through their dissemination of information from dissidents

---

Hirschman, *Exit, Voice, and Loyalty: Responses to Decline in Firms, Organizations, and States* (Cambridge: Harvard University Press, 1970), 4. Nathans notes the Moscow Helsinki Group appealed to Western governments rather than the United Nations as the earlier Initiative Group of the Committee on Human Rights had done. Nonetheless, the Moscow Helsinki Group adopted the methods of the Initiative Group. Nathans, "Soviet Dissidents and Human Rights."

[60] Thomas, "Boomerangs and Superpowers," 26. See also Sidney Tarrow, *The New Transnational Activism* (Cambridge: Cambridge University Press, 2005), 145.

[61] For example, see H. Gordon Skilling's discussion of Charter 77 in H. Gordon Skilling, *Charter 77 and Human Rights in Czechoslovakia* (Boston: George Allen & Unwin, 1981).

[62] Valery Chalidze, "Human Rights: A Policy of Honor," *Wall Street Journal*, April 8, 1977. As initial efforts proved ineffective due to governmental interference with the mail, varied methods were used to deliver Moscow Helsinki Group documents. One American diplomat reports that his wife sent such documents abroad in the embassy's personal pouch. Goldberg, *The Final Act*, 57; and Larry Napper Interview, October 1, 2009. Orlov reports he successfully passed the Group's documents to an Italian official, which is why, in his view, an Italian translation of a Moscow Helsinki Group document appeared in his KGB file. West German officials, on the other hand, would not accept the Group's documents because it had been declared an illegal group. Yuri Orlov Interview, March 27 and 28, 2008.

[63] Kubišová and Hejdánek to Waldheim et al., November 1978, Foreign Policy – Packard – Czechoslovakia, 1981, Legislative Assistants: Mike Packard, Legislative Relations, Robert

to the wider world.[64] Of the increasing international attention paid to human rights activism in the wake of the Helsinki Final Act, Shcharansky writes, "Things had changed so dramatically that I no longer had to think up ways to interest the press in the statements and letters of refuseniks or dissidents; the correspondents literally tore them out of my hands."[65] The Soviets, recognizing this connection, began expelling Western journalists they thought were facilitating public criticism of Soviet human rights practices. When Associated Press reporter George Krimsky was expelled, members of the Moscow Helsinki Group sent him a note praising him for his "meaningful dispatches on the human-rights movements in the USSR" with stories that "have become part of international *glasnost*."[66]

The Moscow Helsinki Group also developed an especially productive relationship with the Commission on Security and Cooperation in Europe, which became the basis for a wider collection of groups and individuals committed to Helsinki adherence. For example, the Commission translated all documents it received and forwarded them to other CSCE states and interested groups.[67] Fascell notes how dissidents in Eastern Europe, including the members of the Group, reshaped Western understandings of the Helsinki Final Act:

The East made undertakings to respect human rights and dignity, but without the expectation that it could be held to the promises it made. What happened, instead, was a remarkable turning of the tables. It was accomplished not by any brilliant strategists in Washington or at NATO, but by a small band of intrepid Soviet citizens who began to say out loud – so that the rest of the world could hear – that the Soviet Union must make good on its own laws and its Helsinki commitments. Their demands made us respond. It was they – members of what has come to be called the Soviet Helsinki Watch and, later, the signatories of Charter '77 in Prague – who made the West aware of the value of Helsinki.[68]

The Helsinki Final Act served as a common foundation for human rights NGOs in the USSR, producing what Alekseeva called a "collective

---

J. Dole Senate Papers, Robert J. Dole Institute of Politics, The University of Kansas, Lawrence, Kansas (hereafter Dole Senate Papers).

[64] Eichhorn, *The Helsinki Accords and Their Effect on the Cold War*, 193–4; and Korey, *The Promises We Keep*, 49.

[65] In Sharansky's view, this increased international interest prompted a concerted effort by Soviet leaders to repress the Group, leading to the arrests of Orlov, Ginzburg, and others. Natan Sharansky, *Fear No Evil* (New York: Random House, 1988), 163.

[66] Goldberg, *The Final Act*, 220.

[67] CSCE, "A Thematic Survey of the Documents of the Moscow Helsinki Groups," May 12, 1981.

[68] Dante Fascell, "Breaking the Silence Barrier," in Barry M. Rubin and Elizabeth P. Spiro, eds., *Human Rights and U.S. Foreign Policy* (Boulder: Westview Press, 1979), 179.

phenomenon of Soviet dissent."[69] A number of monitoring groups subsequently developed along the Moscow Helsinki Group's model in the Soviet Union: the Christian Committee for the Defense of Believers' Rights in the USSR, the Working Commission to Investigate the Use of Psychiatry for Political Purposes, and the Ukrainian Public Group to Promote the Implementation of the Helsinki Agreements in the USSR. Shortly thereafter, Helsinki Groups in Lithuania, Georgia, and Armenia were founded, marking the development of a Helsinki network. The activist groups that arose utilized similar tactics – nonviolent, working within the constitution, and calling on governments to honor obligations to international agreements.

The Ukrainian Helsinki Group, the next group to form, began the expansion of Helsinki monitoring beyond Moscow and offered a model for the others that followed. Mykola Rudenko founded the Ukrainian Public Group of Assistance to Implementation of the Helsinki Agreements in the USSR after hearing about the Moscow Group through foreign radio broadcasts.[70] Established on November 9, 1976, Rudenko's group explicitly declared it was responding to the Moscow Helsinki Group's call for more national groups. Shortly thereafter, the Ukrainian Group's first document arrived in Moscow, where the Moscow Helsinki Group had pledged to assist the Ukrainians in communicating its reports of violations abroad.[71] In its first memorandum, the Ukrainian Group focused on "ethnocide" against Ukrainians, the suppression of the Ukrainian language, and the plight of Ukrainian political prisoners.[72] Grigorenko, a

---

[69] Alexeyeva, *Soviet Dissent*, 345–6; and Tökes, "Human Rights in Eastern Europe: An Overview, 1977–1980," Statement to the Commission on Security and Cooperation in Europe, March 25, 1980, in Mastny, *Helsinki, Human Rights, and European Security*, 143–52.

[70] Mykola Rudenko was a member of the Moscow Amnesty International chapter before setting up the Ukrainian Helsinki Group. Goldberg, *The Final Act*, 92. Sharansky notes that he felt a degree of responsibility toward the Helsinki groups that developed in other Soviet republics, in particular when their members traveled to Moscow to meet with journalists. Natan Sharansky Interview, November 19, 2008.

[71] *Arkhiv Samizdata* 2842, November 12, 1976, Box 97, Published Samizdat, 1968–1992, Samizdat Archives, Records of Radio Free Europe/Radio Liberty Research Institute, Open Society Archives; and Lesya Verba and Bohdan Yasen, eds., *The Human Rights Movement in Ukraine: Documents of the Ukrainian Helsinki Group, 1976–1980* (Washington: Smolosky Publishers, 1980), 20–3.

[72] Declaration and Memorandum No. 1, Folder 18, Box 73, Accession 3560–005, Jackson Papers. The group was supported in the United States by the Helsinki Guarantees for Ukraine Committee, which felt that the Ukrainian Helsinki Group was largely ignored in the American press. Zwarun to Jackson, February 16, 1977, Folder 18, Box 73, Accession 3560–005, Jackson Papers.

member of both the Moscow and Ukrainian Helsinki Groups, describes the establishment of the Ukrainian Group as a "catalyst to action in the other union republics of the USSR."[73] Shortly thereafter, the Lithuanian Helsinki Group formally announced its establishment in a press conference on November 27, 1976, in Orlov's apartment.[74] The Georgian Helsinki Group was formed as well and maintained similarly close relations with the Moscow Helsinki Group.[75]

In these years, Helsinki monitoring groups extended beyond the USSR to Poland, Czechoslovakia, and elsewhere.[76] Some of the most prominent groups in Poland were the Polish Workers' Defense Committee (KOR), created in the spring of 1976; the Movement for the Defense of Human and Civil Rights (ROPCiO), which formed in March 1977 and focused on Helsinki monitoring; and the Helsinki Committee in Poland, which started at Helsinki Watch Executive Director Jeri Laber's suggestion in 1979.[77] In its initial phase, KOR was focused on securing amnesty for

[73] Grigorenko, *Memoirs*, 437. Grigorenko, a former general in the Soviet army, was active on human rights issues before he became a member of the Moscow and Ukrainian Helsinki Groups. Andropov to the Central Committee, February 12, 1976, Perechen 60, Dokument 5, Fond 89: Communist Party of the Soviet Union on Trial, Archives of the Soviet Party and Soviet State, Yale University, New Haven, Connecticut (hereafter Fond 89).

[74] Goldberg, *The Final Act*, 132. Later, there were even links among Helsinki activists in prison. Shcharansky writes about spending time in Chistopol Prison with Victoras Piatkus, leader of the Lithuanian Moscow Helsinki Group. Sharansky, *Fear No Evil*, 246.

[75] Yuri Orlov Interview, March 27 and 28, 2008.

[76] The GDR was one Eastern European state in which collective human rights activism did not develop in the 1970s. Fundamentally, there were no Helsinki monitoring groups in the GDR until the Initiative for Peace and Human Rights was established in 1985 for a number of reasons. First, as opposed to Poland, Czechoslovakia, or the Soviet Union, there was not a history of early state-citizen conflicts having produced an opposition in the GDR. Second, opposition figures in the GDR hoped to reform the system rather than make a break from communism. Third, the peace movement in the GDR drew most opposition figures. Finally, many of those opposed to the regime in the GDR emigrated, which drained the pool of possible opposition figures. Douglas Selvage, "The Struggle Against Transnational Resistance: The East German Ministry for State Security, Charta 77, and Opposition in East Germany, 1977–1980," paper presented at Society of Historians of American Foreign Relations Annual Meeting, Falls Church, Virginia, 2009.

[77] Proposed changes to the Polish Constitution also acted as an important instigator of dissent in Poland. Tenley Adams, "Charter 77 and the Workers' Defense Committee (KOR): The Struggle for Human Rights in Czechoslovakia and Poland," *East European Quarterly* 26:2 (Summer 1992): 222; and Tony Judt, "The Dilemmas of Dissidence: The Politics of Opposition in East-Central Europe," *East European Politics and Societies* 2:2 (1988): 191. See also Janusz Bugajski and Maxine Pollack, *East European Fault Lines: Dissent, Opposition, and Social Activism* (Boulder: Westview Press, 1989), 115; Daniel C. Thomas, "The Helsinki Accords and Political Change in Eastern Europe," in Thomas Risse et al., eds., *The Power of Human Rights: International Norms and Domestic Change* (New York: Cambridge University Press, 1999), 216–17, 221; and

workers arrested in the wake of 1976 protests.[78] KOR conducted what it termed "social work," assisting workers and their families, especially during their trials, providing financial, moral, and legal assistance.[79] It focused on both a humanitarian project in support of the arrested workers and a public relations campaign to increase awareness and build support for an amnesty, in part through underground publishing.[80] The Polish government and police worked against KOR, harassing its members, and in one extreme example, were likely responsible for the murder of Stanisław Pyjas, a student who was affiliated with KOR.[81]

Nevertheless, KOR's pressure on the Polish government was influential in securing the 1977 general amnesty of workers. The group then shifted its focus and name to become Social Self-Defense Committee KOR (KSS-KOR) in September 1977.[82] KOR also reached out to dissident groups in Czechoslovakia, Hungary, and the Soviet Union, meeting with Charter 77 activists on the Polish–Czechoslovakian border twice and issuing a joint statement on the occasion of the tenth anniversary of the Warsaw Pact invasion of Czechoslovakia.[83] In addition to contacts with Helsinki Watch, which will be described in the subsequent chapter, Polish activist

---

Jeri Laber, *The Courage of Strangers: Coming of Age with the Human Rights Movement* (New York: Public Affairs, 2002), 152–3. See Chapter 5 for further discussion of Laber's connections with Eastern European dissidents.

[78] Michael H. Bernhard, *The Origins of Democratization in Poland: Workers, Intellectuals, and Oppositional Politics, 1976–1980* (New York: Columbia University Press, 1993), 78–9.

[79] Barbara J. Falk, *The Dilemmas of Dissidence in East-Central Europe: Citizen Intellectuals and Philosopher Kings* (New York: Central European University Press, 2003), 36.

[80] Bernhard, *The Origins of Democratization in Poland*, 124. The formation of KOR and ROPCiO in Poland initiated a wave of *samizdat* in Poland that dwarfed the phenomenon in Czechoslovakia and the Soviet Union. Jan Józef Lipski, *KOR: A History of the Workers' Defense Committee in Poland, 1976–1981* trans. Olga Amsterdamska and Gene M. Moore (Berkeley: University of California Press, 1985), 109; and Skilling, *Samizdat and an Independent Society in Central and Eastern Europe*, 13.

[81] Jan Kubik, *The Power of Symbols Against the Symbols of Power: The Rise of Solidarity and the Fall of State Socialism in Poland* (University Park: The Pennsylvania State University Press, 1994), 157.

[82] Adams, "Charter 77 and the Workers' Defense Committee (KOR)," 227; H. Gordon Skilling, *Samizdat and an Independent Society in Central and Eastern Europe*, 179; and Kubik, *The Power of Symbols Against the Symbols of Power*, 6, 154.

[83] Robert Zuzowski, "The Origins of Open Organised Dissent in Today's Poland: KOR and Other Dissident Groups," *East European Quarterly* 25:1 (Spring 1991): 83; Skilling, *Charter 77 and Human Rights in Czechoslovakia*, 172–3; and Memo for the Record, n.d., USSR: [HW] J. Laber's Memos [on Eastern Bloc Meetings]; 1979, Box 53, Country Files, Jeri Laber Files, Record Group 7, Human Rights Watch Records, Center for Human Rights Documentation and Research, Rare Book and Manuscript Library, Columbia University Library (hereafter HRWR).

Zbigniew Romaszewski reports he was in regular contact with representatives of the Swedish and Norwegian Helsinki groups.[84]

Because KOR operated openly and survived, it inspired other groups to follow its model.[85] One of the most prominent Polish examples was ROPCiO. The group focused on the disparity between the international commitments the Polish government had made both at Helsinki and at the UN and its policies and practices towards its citizens.[86] KOR also influenced the formation of Solidarity; the trade union's leader Lech Wałęsa said, "The whole affair is based on the fact that KOR taught us this job."[87]

In Czechoslovakia, Charter 77 was launched on January 1, 1977, with a four-page document that catalogued the abuses of human rights there. The Charter said, "We welcome the fact that the Czechoslovak Socialist Republic has agreed to the Helsinki Agreements. However, their enactment is at the same time an urgent reminder that many fundamental human rights are violated in our country."[88] It was not an organization like the Moscow Helsinki Group but a grass-roots movement that drew attention to contradictions between Czechoslovak law, the government's signature of the Helsinki Final Act, and life in Czechoslovakia.[89] Nonetheless, Charter 77 organizers were cognizant of the Moscow Helsinki Group at the time, as Václav Havel told Orlov many years later, "I think that the existence of Helsinki Committees in the Soviet Union really influenced us before we established Charter '77."[90] Speaking about the connection between Charter 77 and the Helsinki Final Act, spokesperson Jan Patočka said,

Certainly Helsinki was the beginning of all of this. We were waiting to see if the Helsinki principles would be implemented here, if they would have the force of

---

[84] Zbigniew Romaszewski, written communication to the author, January 26, 2010.

[85] Zuzowski, "The Origins of Open Organised Dissent in Today's Poland," 72–3; Bernhard, *The Origins of Democratization in Poland*, 131; Lipski, *KOR*, 6; Adams, "Charter 77 and the Workers' Defense Committee (KOR)," 234; and Pleshakov, *There Is No Freedom Without Bread!*, 105.

[86] Bernhard, *The Origins of Democratization in Poland*, 140.

[87] Some view KOR as an essential precursor to Solidarity, in that it reconstituted civil society in Poland. Ibid., 202; Maryjane Osa, *Solidarity and Contention: Networks of Polish Opposition* (Minneapolis: University of Minnesota Press, 2003), 154–5; and Archie Brown, *The Rise and Fall of Communism* (New York: Harper Collins, 2009), 424.

[88] Charter '77, January 1, 1977, in Hans-Peter Risee, ed., *Since the Prague Spring: The Continuing Struggle for Human Rights in Czechoslovakia* (New York: Random House, 1979), 11.

[89] John Keane, *Václav Havel: A Political Tragedy in Six Acts* (New York: Basic Books, 2000), 244–5; and Mastny, *Helsinki, Human Rights, and European Security*, 105.

[90] Havel Day, February 22, 1990, Czechoslovakia: Havel, Vaclav: Havel Day [at Helsinki Watch], 1990, Box 17, Country Files, Jeri Laber Files, Record Group 7, HRWR.

law. One had to do something as a citizen, as a human being, to insure that these rights that were given to us would not remain a dead letter. The fundamental question now is indeed whether this action will bring about more freedom or more repression.[91]

Czechoslovak dissidents launched their initiative in January 1977 for several reasons – Prague Spring had begun in January 1968, Amnesty International had declared 1977 the Year of Political Prisoners, and the Belgrade Follow-up Meeting was to open later that year.[92] The spokespeople gathered 243 signatures for the Charter 77 declaration, which garnered considerable international press in the days after the initiative's announcement.[93] In response, the police in Czechoslovakia tried to squelch Charter 77, raiding homes, seizing records, and even working to identify the typewriters used in producing the documents. Given the diffuse nature of Charter 77, however, efforts to repress it were complicated and unsuccessful.[94] Charter 77 persisted, publishing reports, detailing the seizure of documents, and appealing for an end to the targeting of Charter 77 signatories.[95] Shortly thereafter, a number of Charter 77 signatories formed the Committee for the Defense of the Unjustly Prosecuted (VONS) in Czechoslovakia. Modeled after KOR, its mission was to offer assistance to those repressed by the state. VONS intended to offer material and moral support as well as draw public attention to such persecutions.[96]

As groups proliferated across Eastern Europe, some tried to make contact and coordinate their efforts, forming the transnational connections essential to the Helsinki network. In addition to the border meetings of Polish and Czechoslovakian human rights activists, there is evidence of other transnational connections among Helsinki monitors. For example, Sakharov, members of the Moscow Helsinki Group, and members of the

---

[91] Patrick Vaughan, "Zbigniew Brzezinski and the Helsinki Final Act," paper presented at the conference "From Helsinki to Gorbachev, 1975–1985: The Globalization of the Bipolar Confrontation," Artimino, Italy, April 27–9, 2006.

[92] The arrests, trials, and convictions of the rock band Plastic People of the Universe were also instigations for Charter 77. H. Gordon Skilling, "Charter 77 and the Musical Underground," *Canadian Slavonic Papers* 22:1 (1980): 1, 10.

[93] Keane, *Václav Havel*, 246–7, 250.

[94] Skilling, *Charter 77 and Human Rights in Czechoslovakia*, 98.

[95] Patočka, Havel, and Hájek, Charter '77 Document Number 2, January 8, 1977; and Patočka and Hájek, Charter '77 Document Number 3, January 15, 1977, in Risee, ed. *Since the Prague Spring*, 156, 159.

[96] Falk, *The Dilemmas of Dissidence in East-Central Europe*, 92; and Defense of the Unjustly Persecuted, April 1980, Foreign Policy – Packard – Czechoslovakia, 1981, Legislative Assistants: Mike Packard, Legislative Relations, Dole Senate Papers.

Working Committee to Investigate the Abuse of Psychiatry for Political Purposes wrote to both Charter 77 and KOR in August 1978, seeking to enhance contacts and cooperation among activists in Czechoslovakia, Poland, and the Soviet Union.[97]

Elsewhere in Eastern Europe, many people responded to the Helsinki Final Act individually rather than collectively. For example, in East Germany, more than 100,000 people formally applied to leave the GDR.[98] Austrian diplomat Franz Ceska later said, "I was in East Berlin by that time when [the Helsinki Final Act] was printed in the *Neues Deutschland*, which was sold out at 11 o'clock in the morning. People said 'Honecker signed, we want to go to West Germany.'"[99] Hans-Dietrich Genscher, minister of foreign affairs for the FRG, asserted the Helsinki Final Act had such a strong influence on the GDR due to easy access to information through West German television and the agreement's discussion of free movement of people.[100] In the year after the signing of the Helsinki Final Act, the number of applications for exit permits grew by 54 percent.[101] In a more local example, Karl-Heinz Nitschke, a doctor from a small Saxon town, drew up a petition pressing for the fulfillment of the GDR's

---

[97] Andrei Sakharov et al., Letter to Human Rights Defenders in Poland and Czechoslovakia, August 1978, in Skilling, *Charter 77 and Human Rights in Czechoslovakia*, 279–80.

[98] Timothy Garton Ash, *The Polish Revolution: Solidarity 1980–82* 3rd ed. (New Haven: Yale University Press, 2002), 335. East Germans sought to demonstrate their lack of support for Honecker's regime by emigrating. See Hirschman, *Exit, Voice, and Loyalty*, 4.

[99] Summary Notes Day 2, Oral History Conference in Vienna, February 22–3, 2007, "The Historical Experience of the Neutral and Non-aligned States in the CSCE," Oral History Workshop, Austrian Institute for International Affairs, Vienna Austria, available at: http://www.php.isn.ethz.ch/conferences/previous/documents/ViennaConf_Day2_000.pdf (accessed April 16, 2008). It was the first time *Neues Deutschland* had sold out in its history. Peter Grieder, "'To Learn from the Soviet Union is to Learn How to Win': The East German Revolution, 1989–90," in McDermott and Stibbe, eds., *Revolution and Resistance in Eastern Europe*, 162. According to Hermann Wentker, the GDR did not want to publish the Helsinki Final Act, but the Soviets pressured them to do so. Yet, despite East German hesitancy to publish the agreement, it was viewed in the GDR as a foreign policy achievement given that the state had gained international recognition. Wentker, "Pursuing Specific Interests Within the Warsaw Pact," in Rostagni, ed., *The Helsinki Process*, 56.

[100] Memcon, December 8, 1976, Mircea Munteanu and Kristina Terzieva, ed., *From Global Politics to Human Rights: The CSCE Follow up Meeting, Belgrade, 1977*, a CWIHP Document Reader compiled for the international conference "30 Years since the First CSCE Follow-up Meeting in Belgrade 1977," Belgrade, Sava Center, March 8–10, 2008. Available through the Cold War International History Project.

[101] Wentker, "Pursuing Specific Interests Within the Warsaw Pact," in Rostagni, ed., *The Helsinki Process*, 58.

commitment to freedom to emigrate that garnered 1,000 signatures.[102] There were also, with time, some in the GDR who pressed the government to live up to its human rights obligations, but Helsinki activism focused on issues other than emigration was not as pronounced in the GDR.[103]

In the Soviet Union, the KGB was quick to hassle the Moscow Helsinki Group, but it did not meaningfully repress the Group for nine months, giving activists a crucial window to organize themselves and establish transnational connections. Soviet authorities allowed the Moscow Helsinki Group to operate between its establishment in May 1976 and Orlov's arrest in February 1977, and the intervening months were critical to the Moscow Helsinki Group as it was able to publish eighteen documents alleging human rights violations. [104]

In the absence of definitive evidence, multiple theories abound as to why the KGB hesitated to crack down on the Group immediately, given that Soviet officials saw the establishment of the Moscow Helsinki Group in a broader pattern of propaganda and subversion by "enemy" states. Officials believed that the Moscow Helsinki Group "pursue[d] the provocative goal of questioning the sincerity of attempts by the USSR to implement the Final Act of the Conference on Security and Cooperation in Europe, and thereby to put pressure on the government of the Soviet Union on questions pertaining to the realization of the Helsinki agreements."[105] Orlov attributes the slow Soviet response to bureaucratic lethargy, seeing the KGB as taking its time to collect the adequate documents and denunciations to support its case. Yet, Andropov made a presentation to the Central Committee on the activities of the Group in November 1976, three months before the formal crackdown.[106] Orlov also suggests the

---

[102] Ned Richardson-Little, "'No Human Rights without Socialism – No Socialism without Human Rights!': Socialist Human Rights and the Helsinki Accords in East Germany," paper presented at "A New Global Morality?: The Politics of Human Rights and Humanitarianism in the 1970s," Freiburg Institute for Advanced Studies, Freiburg, Germany, June 2010.

[103] John C. Torpey, *Intellectuals, Socialism, and Dissent* (Minneapolis: University of Minnesota Press, 1995), 74–5.

[104] Yuri Orlov Interview, March 27 and 28, 2008.

[105] Andropov to Central Committee, November 15, 1976, in Joshua Rubenstein and Alexander Gribanov, ed., *The KGB File of Andrei Sakharov* (New Haven: Yale University Press, 2005), 217–8.

[106] Andropov summarized the Group's methods, including researching alleged violations and soliciting external pressure on Soviet officials; he reported that the KGB was undertaking efforts to neutralize the Group and its activities. Andropov to the Central Committee, November 15, 1976, S.II.2.6.1.18, Box 51, Sakharov Papers.

close link between the Helsinki Final Act and Brezhnev's personal prestige might have delayed Soviet action against the Group.[107] Soviet leaders paid careful attention to international attitudes toward dissidents and Helsinki implementation in the Soviet Union, which one observer argues likely contributed to the relative restraint by the Soviets with respect to the Moscow Helsinki Group.[108] The Soviets may have delayed crushing the Helsinki monitors initially because they feared endangering détente with the United States, but deteriorating Soviet–American relations during the Carter administration likely lessened Soviet conviction that there was a benefit to allowing dissent to continue.

Once repression began in February 1977, Helsinki monitors faced punishments ranging from harassment to long prison terms.[109] KGB Head Yuri Andropov had determined, "The need has thus emerged to terminate the actions of Orlov, fellow Helsinki monitor Ginzburg and others once and for all, on the basis of existing law."[110] Soviet officials decided to arrest Orlov and other dissidents to prevent their "ability to cause controversy in the West and a negative reaction in some communist parties."[111] Shcharansky now believes the KGB's crackdown on the Group was due in part to the degree of influence it has achieved abroad,

---

[107] Yuri Orlov Interview, March 27 and 28, 2008.

[108] As Svetlana Savranskaya notes, the reaction of the KGB toward the Moscow Helsinki Group's formation was "very mild treatment by Soviet standards." Svetlana Savranskaya, "The Battles for the Final Act: the Soviet Government and Dissidents' Efforts to Define the Substance and the Implementation of the Helsinki Final Act," paper presented at the conference "European and Transatlantic Strategies in the Late Cold War Period to Overcome the East–West Division of Europe," November 30–December 1, 2007; and Andropov to the Central Committee, March 29, 1977, in Munteanu and Terzieva, eds., *From Global Politics to Human Rights: The CSCE Follow up Meeting, Belgrade, 1977.* Constantine Pleshakov echoes this analysis suggesting that the 347 people who were imprisoned for political reasons between 1976 and 1980 compares favorably with the repression during Stalin's rule. Pleshakov, *There Is No Freedom Without Bread!*, 89.

[109] In December 1976, Mykola Rudenko and another Ukrainian Helsinki Group member were arrested in what some have viewed as the initiation of a campaign against Helsinki activists. Grigorenko, *Memoirs*, 438; and Goldberg, *The Final Act*, 118–20. According to Alekseeva, growing connections between different Soviet monitoring groups so concerned the Soviet authorities that they were willing to repress them, even risking Western condemnation. Alexeyeva, *Soviet Dissent*, 17.

[110] Andrew and Mitrokhin, *The Sword and the Shield*, 327–8.

[111] Proposal to the Central Committee of the Communist Party of the Soviet Union, January 20, 1977, *The Moscow Helsinki Group 30th Anniversary: From the Secret Files* (Washington: The National Security Archive, 2006) no. 191, http://www.nsarchive. org (accessed May 25, 2006); and Memorandum, January 20, 1977, in V. A. Kozlova and C. V. Mironenko, eds., *Kramola: Inakomyslie v SSSR pri Khrushcheve u Brezhneve 1953–1982 gg* (Moscow: Materik: 2005), 400–4.

in particular in the United States Congress.[112] Orlov went underground when the KGB began preparations to arrest him, returning to Moscow only when he learned that founding member Alexander Ginzburg had been arrested on February 3. Group members decided Orlov could not remain in hiding because openness and the Group's legality were important principles to preserve: in Orlov's view, "[the arrest] changed the situation. It would be immoral for the chairman of a group to stay in hiding when a member had been arrested."[113]

Orlov's arrest swiftly followed Ginzburg's, coming on February 10. The KGB then spent ten months questioning him.[114] In his interrogation, Orlov denied that his actions "had the intention of undermining or weakening the Soviet regime," but the KGB's forty-page indictment charged him with "anti-Soviet agitation and propaganda."[115] Interestingly, one piece of evidence used against Orlov by the KGB was a letter from Dante Fascell wishing Orlov's group well and saying that the Commission had wanted to meet with his group, but the United States delegation had been refused visas; the KGB characterized the letter as a "letter of instruction."[116] Orlov's trial began on May 15, 1978, lasted four days, and ended with a seven-year sentence in a hard labor camp to be followed by five years of exile.[117]

The irony of the Soviets' arrest of Orlov, which was an attempt to prevent him from causing "controversy in the West," is that his trial and long sentence became the source of considerable international condemnation of the Soviet regime. The State Department protested Orlov's conviction and sentence, arguing, "To punish as subversive activities aimed at increasing free expression of opinion and at promoting governmental observance of formal obligations solemnly undertaken is a gross distortion of internationally accepted standards of human rights."[118] Roger Baldwin, head of the International League of Human Rights, wrote to Anatoly Dobrynin to express distress about arrests of Orlov as well as Ginzburg and Rudenko.[119] Charter 77 also issued statements related to

[112] Natan Sharansky Interview, November 19, 2008.
[113] Orlov, *Dangerous Thoughts*, 211.
[114] Ibid., 217.
[115] Andrew and Mitrokhin, *The Sword and the Shield*, 334–5.
[116] Orlov, *Dangerous Thoughts*, 219; and Yuri Orlov Interview, March 27 and 28, 2008.
[117] Parchomenko, *Soviet Images of Dissidents and Nonconformists*, 127.
[118] Transcript of Daily News Briefing, May 18, 1978, Folder 6, Box 148, Part I, Goldberg Papers.
[119] Baldwin to Dobrynin, February 11, 1977, General Correspondence U.S.S.R. 1977, Box 62, International League for Human Rights Records, Manuscripts and Archives

repression of Shcharansky, Sakharov and others in the Soviet Union.[120] Even the Belgian Communist Party conveyed concern over Orlov's arrest, conviction, and sentencing.[121]

In the wake of international attention to Orlov's trial, Soviet leaders were apprehensive about the prospect that Orlov and other Moscow Helsinki Group monitors would be awarded the 1978 Nobel Peace Prize. Such a development would redirect international attention on Soviet human rights practices only three years after Sakharov had won. Andropov brought the issue before the Central Committee, and the KGB undertook a mission to undermine Orlov's candidacy.[122] When the prize was awarded to Menachem Begin and Anwar al-Sadat for the Camp David Peace Accords, the KGB regarded its efforts as a great success, claiming, "The work that we did exerted useful influence on the foreign policy leadership of Norway and, in our opinion, made it possible for the residency's task to be carried out – to prevent the award of the Nobel Peace Prize to Yuri Orlov and his Committee."[123]

The KGB's arrests of Rudenko, Orlov, and Ginzburg were only the beginning of an effort to crush the Helsinki groups. Soviet authorities employed a range of tactics with varying degrees of ruthlessness. They offered some activists the "opportunity" to emigrate, and a number of activists, many of whom had long fought to leave, did so.[124] Alekseeva was among those who left the Soviet Union, emigrating in 1977. Her departure, while weakening the Group in Moscow, failed to serve the government's broader purpose as she continued her activism as the Western representative of the Group. Moscow Helsinki Group founding members Mikhail Bernshtam, Vitaly Rubin, and Alexander Korchak emigrated as well, and Grigorenko was stripped of his Soviet citizenship while seeking medical treatment abroad.[125]

Division, Humanities and Social Sciences Library, The New York Public Library, New York, New York (hereafter International League for Human Rights).

[120] Skilling, *Samizdat and an Independent Society in Central and Eastern Europe*, 59.

[121] Central Committee Decree, May 30, 1978, Russian and Eastern European Archive Document Database–Russian Archives Document Database (REEADD-RADD) Collection, National Security Archive, Washington, District of Columbia (hereafter National Security Archive).

[122] Andropov to the Central Committee, August 1978, REEADD-RADD Collection, National Security Archive; and Andrew and Mitrokhin, *The Sword and the Shield*, 329.

[123] Andrew and Mitrokhin, *The Sword and the Shield*, 329–30.

[124] Eichhorn, *The Helsinki Accords and Their Effect on the Cold War*, 223.

[125] Grigorenko, *Memoirs*, 436; and Politburo Protocol, February 4, 1978, REEADD-RADD Collection, National Security Archive. Soviet officials were frustrated with Grigorenko's human rights activism, did not object to Grigorenko's journey to the United States for

Shcharansky was one of the KGB's next targets, and he was treated as a considerable threat to the regime. Born Jewish, Shcharansky had little knowledge of his religion and no attachment to Israel until the Six Day War in 1967, which he reports stirred his interest and pride in the country. When he finished his education in mathematics and computer science, Shcharansky applied to emigrate to Israel in 1973. After his visa was denied, Shcharansky took part in many short-lived protests to draw attention to the plight of Soviet Jews and refuseniks like himself. In this period, Shcharansky met Avital Steiglitz and married her in July 1974, the day before she emigrated to Israel, with the belief that he would soon follow. Instead, Shcharansky's visa applications were repeatedly denied, and his increased activism led to intensified KGB surveillance. Shcharansky had become involved in the Moscow Helsinki Group due to a broader commitment to human rights that led him to work with Sakharov, helping to facilitate his contacts with foreign journalists. The KGB arrested him on March 15, 1977, alleging that he had slandered the Soviet Union with Moscow Helsinki Group documents; he was charged with anti-Soviet activity and treason.[126] Shcharansky was imprisoned for sixteen months before the completion of his trial and then sentenced to thirteen years: three in prison and ten in a strict-regime labor camp.[127] Shcharansky alternated between prison and labor camps for the next eight years, repeatedly conducting hunger strikes to protest prison authorities' interference with his correspondence with his family.[128]

In his memoirs, Shcharansky recounts that immediately after his arrest he had hoped international attention would force the Soviets to change course: "And only last month they had arrested my friends Yuri Orlov and Alexander Ginsburg from the Helsinki Watch Group. This had been greeted by outrage throughout the free world, and even the White House had protested. And now my own arrest on a charge of treason was a direct challenge to Americans, so the public outcry would be even greater." Shcharansky put his faith in the connections he and others had forged with those in the West, anticipating they might be able to influence the Soviets: "With the Helsinki Review Conference coming up in Belgrade, the issue of Soviet compliance with the Helsinki Accords was sure to be

medical treatment, and then deprived him of his citizenship. Andropov to the Central Committee, November 24, 1977, Perechen 60, Dokument 12, Fond 89.
[126] Sharansky, *Fear No Evil*, 153, 157.
[127] Ibid., ix–xxii.
[128] Ironically, while in prison Shcharansky came to discover firsthand some of the inaccuracies in the Moscow Helsinki Watch Group's reporting on prison conditions: "Our

in the news. The Soviets were stuck. Maybe they'd put all three of us on a plane and ship us out of the country."[129] Indeed, those concerned with his arrest tried to attract international attention; Sakharov wrote,

Shcharansky's arrest, following the arrest of other Helsinki Watch Group members, is an act of defiance the Soviet authorities have added to their game of provocation before the Belgrade Meeting. It amounts to an attempt to blackmail the new U.S. administration before the visit of Secretary of State Vance, an attempt to force the Administration to renounce its worldwide human-rights policy and to consolidate an official license for the Soviets to wreak lawlessness.[130]

International condemnation did ensue, but Soviet authorities were undeterred. Shcharansky's account of his interrogation highlights the extent to which Soviet officials were determined to resist external pressure on human rights. After United States Secretary of State Cyrus Vance visited the Soviet Union in March 1977, Shcharansky's interrogator declared: "We won't permit any interference in our internal affairs. The Americans won't save you from *ras-s-strel* [execution]."[131] In a testament to how seriously Soviet authorities regarded the Moscow Helsinki Group and the threat it presented to the regime, the outcome of Shcharansky's trial was discussed in the Politburo. There, Andropov asserted Shcharansky's sentence would be decided by his behavior at trial, as was Orlov's.[132] Shcharansky endured nine years of imprisonment until an international campaign led by his wife, Avital, aided his liberation.

Although the international outcry had little impact on Shcharansky's case initially, over time the movement, which joined scientists, Jews, human rights activists, and many others moved by his case, may have kept him alive and eventually secured his release. Shcharansky wrote:

Later, after my release, I learned that tens of thousands of people all around the world had written to me during my imprisonment. None of these letters ever reached me, and I was never informed about their existence. In all probability they were burned.

But although I never received them, it was extremely important that these letters were sent. To the regime, they served as a constant reminder that people all over the world knew about me and cared about my fate. This was why the

---

Helsinki reports on political prisoners didn't always correspond to reality. As I would discover, reality was much worse, much harsher than we had described it." Ibid., 153.

[129] Ibid., 19.

[130] Sakharov, *Alarm and Hope*, 151, 177.

[131] Shcharansky was repeatedly threatened with execution. Sharansky, *Fear No Evil*, 39.

[132] Politburo Meeting Minutes, June 22, 1978, Perechen 42, Dokument 72, Fond 89.

authorities sometimes retreated, and it probably explains why they kept me alive during my prolonged hunger strike in 1982.[133]

In his memoirs, Shcharansky notes his KGB interrogators had dismissed protests led by his wife Avital outside the Soviet Embassy in London as "nothing more than students and housewives." Yet, after his release Shcharansky always told those who had demonstrated for him that, "in the end the army of students and housewives turned out to be mightier than the army of the KGB."[134]

Authorities in the Soviet Union, Czechoslovakia, Poland, and elsewhere who cracked down on Helsinki monitoring hoped to stem the tide of reports of violations to the West, in particular in advance of the Belgrade Follow-up Meeting. Ultimately, their repression of activists such as Orlov and Shcharansky, however, garnered considerable, negative international attention. The Moscow Helsinki Group and other monitoring groups had already made important connections with concerned people around the world by sending their reports to Western NGOs as well as CSCE signatories, and they had created international constituencies to advocate on their behalf in the wake of a crackdown.

By the mid 1970s, a transnational advocacy network devoted to Helsinki monitoring was developing. How had the efforts of dissidents in Moscow produced a wider movement? Social movements theorists Margaret Keck and Kathryn Sikkink have examined how transnational advocacy networks successively persuade others of their agenda, and their research is relevant to this case. First, in order to gain support for their platform, members of Helsinki monitoring groups employed "information politics," which includes the collection and distribution of relevant information such as reports on human rights violations. Second, the network used "symbolic politics," which means using symbols to make situations seem more immediate to distant observers. For example, through its documents, the Moscow Helsinki Group successfully translated Soviet citizens' suffering into personal, evocative stories for an international audience. The families and friends of political prisoners undertook

---

[133] Sharansky, *Fear No Evil*, 244–5.

[134] Ibid., 170. Many years later, human rights activist Cathy Fitzpatrick wrote a memorandum on the importance of writing letters to Soviet officials on dissidents' behalf: "Of course its discouraging to keep writing these letters to 'black holes in space,' never knowing who reads them. But we must persist, because we cannot imagine what situation these prisoners would be in if we didn't write. And although they may not be release altogether, their situation can improve if enough letters are written." Memorandum, n.d., Papers U.S.S.R. Orlov Yuri, Box 63, International League for Human Rights.

similar efforts, with one prominent example being the international campaign spearheaded by Avital Shcharansky on her husband's behalf. Third, the groups relied upon "leverage politics" or drawing upon an influential figure to champion the network's agenda when it has limited direct influence. As I will discuss in subsequent chapters, Helsinki activists counted on CSCE diplomats and political leaders to advance their commitment to Helsinki compliance. Fourth, "accountability politics," or holding leaders responsible for upholding policies to which they commit themselves, was a fundamental element of the Helsinki process as the Helsinki monitors and the follow-up meetings were designed to ensure commitments made in August 1975 were being fulfilled.[135] Helsinki monitors used these different tools to protest human rights abuses and capture the attention of foreign actors who could aid their cause.

As the Belgrade Follow-up Meeting approached, monitoring groups in a number of Eastern European states were documenting violations of the Helsinki Final Act and working to communicate their findings internationally, with activists realizing the meeting was a means to highlight their plight and grievances. With the exception of the Commission and ethnic and religious interest groups, Helsinki activism was most prominent in Eastern Europe at this point. Although these Eastern European groups were vital to the cause, bringing about meaningful change required allies on the other side of the Cold War divide. As I will discuss in subsequent chapters, these allies would soon emerge, and Helsinki monitors in Eastern Europe would increasingly rely upon official and nongovernmental champions in the West to advance their cause.

Historian Benjamin Nathans has suggested that dissidents should be appreciated for their contribution to intellectual history of Russia and the twentieth century without considering their political significance. In his view, they can be credited with discrediting socialist legality, and their contribution to the development of human rights discourse and ideas was important as well.[136] It is true dissidents were significant in their own right, but as my study has shown, they participated in a broader community of human rights activists beyond Moscow and the borders of the Soviet Union. And it was precisely due to these connections that their activism resonated so powerfully in the international sphere.

Monitoring groups in Eastern Europe served as an essential conduit of evidence of Eastern human rights abuses. They exposed Eastern practices,

[135] Keck and Sikkink, *Activists Beyond Borders*, 16.
[136] Nathans, "Soviet Dissidents and Human Rights."

often succeeding in focusing international attention on a particularly troubling case. In time, the broader transnational Helsinki network of which the Moscow Helsinki Group was a key party, was able to effect implementation of the Helsinki Final Act and secure improved observance of human rights. The further proliferation of individual acts of dissent and the establishment of Helsinki monitoring groups in the years that followed the signing of the Helsinki Final Act will be a feature of each of my subsequent chapters.

4

Follow-up at Belgrade

The United States Transforms the Helsinki Process

Jimmy Carter's election in 1976 transformed United States involvement in the Helsinki process and the government's attitude toward human rights. Carter's focus on human rights, and specifically on Helsinki implementation, integrated both issues into United States foreign policy toward Eastern Europe. At the 1977–8 Belgrade Follow-up Meeting, which would become a turning point for the United States in the Helsinki process, the Carter administration made clear the importance of human rights to its foreign policy while significantly raising its profile within the CSCE negotiations. In part due to this change in United States policy, the CSCE became an ongoing process that held all participants accountable for compliance with the agreement. The new United States approach to the CSCE was essential to the long-term influence of the Helsinki process given that dissidents in Eastern Europe needed high-level allies who could utilize their reports of human rights abuses in an international framework and exert pressure on repressive governments to changes their practices. Furthermore, its emphasis on thorough Helsinki compliance was critical to later change in Eastern Europe, even if it temporarily complicated CSCE discussions.

The Belgrade Follow-up Meeting also proved significant to the development and influence of the transnational Helsinki network. First, the promise to evaluate Helsinki compliance at Belgrade provided a rationale for individual, collective, and governmental efforts to monitor adherence to the Helsinki Final Act; as the previous two chapters have shown, the result was the emergence of a variety of monitoring organizations. Second, those committed to the implementation of the Helsinki Final Act lobbied CSCE governments throughout the Belgrade Meeting, which provided a crucial forum for activists and established a pattern of relations between CSCE diplomats and private individuals going forward. Helsinki activism resonated particularly with the Carter administration and shaped the aggressive review of implementation undertaken by American diplomats there. Third, the forceful accounting conducted at the Follow-up Meeting by the United States and, to a lesser degree its allies, inspired additional groups to form and monitor Helsinki compliance in the meeting's aftermath, which will be discussed in a subsequent chapter. The Belgrade Meeting thus marked the beginning of a productive collaboration between the Helsinki network and CSCE delegations. Most importantly for the long-term influence of the CSCE and the Helsinki network, the first Follow-up Meeting led to a second and others followed; the series of subsequent review meetings fostered links among Helsinki advocates and cemented the CSCE and human rights on the international diplomatic agenda.

The United States, and over time its NATO allies, was determined to highlight Helsinki violations at Belgrade. As Carter was responsible for this new American approach to the negotiations, exploring his dedication to human rights and interest in the CSCE is essential. Carter's strong commitment to the Helsinki process once in office surprised many observers given his complicated position on the agreement during the 1976 election. Carter was sharply critical of the Helsinki Final Act early in the campaign, saying in March 1976: "At Helsinki, we signed an agreement approving the takeover of Eastern Europe. I would be very much tougher in the following years (in negotiations) with the Soviet Union."[1] At other times, he called Helsinki a "mistake" and declared that there was "no reason for us to participate in the Helsinki conference."[2] Carter similarly criticized Ford's signature of the agreement and said it had given the Soviets a "tremendous diplomatic victory."[3] He was even more explicit in an infamous *Playboy* interview, in which he condemned the entire CSCE negotiations,

---

[1] Carter Quotes on Eastern Europe, Carter on Foreign Policy (1), Box 25, Michael Raoul-Duval Papers, GRFL. For a further example, see Robert D. Schulzinger, "The Decline of Détente," in Bernard J. Firestone and Alexej Ugrinsky, eds., *Gerald R. Ford and the Politics of Post-Watergate America* (New York: Greenwood Press, 1992), 416.

[2] Reuters, "Carter on Helsinki Documents," October 10, 1976, European Question, 1976–1980, Box 251, Old Code Subject Files, Soviet Red Archives, Records of Radio Free Europe/Radio Liberty Research Institute, Open Society Archives.

[3] Carter made his comments in a speech to Lithuanian-Americans on October 2. Korey, *The Promises We Keep*, 35.

saying: "I never saw any reason we should be involved in the Helsinki meetings at all."[4] ✳

Deeper into the campaign, Carter shifted to emphasizing problems with Helsinki compliance during Ford's presidency rather than with the content of the agreement itself, alleging the Ford administration had "looked the other way" on Soviet failures to implement the Helsinki Final Act fully.[5] Scholars have often attributed this shift to pressure from Congress, and specifically the Commission.[6] More likely, it was due to the influence of Carter's closest foreign policy aide on the campaign and later national security adviser, Zbigniew Brzezinski, who had a long record of support for the CSCE and grasped the agreement's potential to foster change in Eastern Europe. (Evidence indicates that Brzezinski recognized the value of the agreement and convinced Carter to focus on the Ford administration's reluctance to pressure the Soviets to adhere to it.) For example, he wrote a memorandum for Carter explaining how

---

[4] He went on to say: "We added the stature of our presence and signature on an agreement, that, in effect, ratified the take-over of Eastern Europe by the Soviet Union. We got very little, if anything in return. The Russians promised they would honor democratic principles and permit the free movement of their citizens, including those who want to emigrate. The Soviet Union has not lived up to those promises and Mr. Brezhnev was able to celebrate the major achievement of his diplomatic life." Carter's admission in the same interview that he had "committed adultery in my heart many times" and his criticisms of former United States President Lyndon Johnson proved a significant distraction to the campaign. Transcript Excerpt, Folder 7, Box 8, Cyrus R. and Grace Sloane Vance Papers, Yale University, New Haven, Connecticut (hereafter Vance Papers). Carter's censure was effective politically because as Carter administration Press Secretary Jody Powell said, "It gave us a club that he could use against Ford for not enforcing it and against the Russians for not living up to it." William C. Green, "Human Rights and Detente," *Ukrainian Quarterly* 36:2 (1980): 142.

[5] Carter to Wurtman, September 16, 1976, Human Rights, Box 10, Myron Kuropas Files, GRFL. Carter also said on September 8, 1976, "We also regret our government's continuing failure to oppose the denial of human freedom in Eastern Europe and the Soviet Union." Carter Quotes on Eastern Europe, Carter on Foreign Policy (1), Box 25, Michael Raoul-Duval Papers, GRFL.

[6] Albright and Friendly, "Helsinki and Human Rights," in Edmund S. Muskie, Kenneth Rush, and Kenneth W. Thompson, eds., *The President, The Congress and Foreign Policy*, 304; Thomas, *The Helsinki Effect*, 134–6; and Korey, *The Promises We Keep*, 35.

[7] Patrick Vaughan, "Zbigniew Brzezinski and the Helsinki Final Act," in Leopoldo Nuti, ed., *The Crisis of Détente in Europe: From Helsinki to Gorbachev, 1975–1985* (New York: Routledge, 2009), 11–16. In 1970, he wrote: "We should think of it as a process, the purpose of which is to explore and only eventually resolve the various outstanding legacies of World War II but we will not be able to do so if the West and particularly the United States – keeps shrinking away from the challenges on the jejune argument that we can't enter a conference unless we know in advance what its outcome will be." Zbigniew Brzezinski, "Observations on East–West Relations: Détente in the '70s," *Foreign Policy* (January 3, 1970): 18.

he could put Ford "on the defensive" in the discussion of the Helsinki Final Act:

Do not attack the Agreement as a whole. The so-called "Basket III" gives us the right – for the first time – to insist on respect for human rights without this constituting interference in the internal affairs of communist states. Accordingly, this is a considerable asset for us, and you should hammer away at the proposition that the Republicans have been indifferent to this opportunity. [8]

Criticizing the Ford administration on the Helsinki Final Act proved to be politically expedient, and Carter pledged that if elected president, he would move human rights and Helsinki implementation to the top of his agenda with the Soviet Union.[9] The Democratic platform reflected Carter's position: "We should continually remind the Soviet Union, by word and conduct, of its commitments in Helsinki to the free flow of peoples and ideas and of how offensive we and other free peoples find its violations of the Universal Declaration of Human Rights."[10] The transformation of the CSCE and the Helsinki Final Act from a political liability to a heralded force in East–West relations was essential to the later influence of the Helsinki process on the end of the Cold War, and the issue remained at the forefront of United States diplomacy for many years.

Carter's increasing emphasis on human rights over the course of the campaign continued during his presidency. In office, Carter offered considerable support to the Commission, advocated an aggressive approach at the first CSCE follow-up meeting in Belgrade, and made the protection of human rights the centerpiece of his foreign policy. Despite disapproving of the Helsinki Final Act for most of his campaign, President Carter became a champion of Helsinki principles and the activists who monitored the agreement's implementation. In formulating his human rights policy, Carter was influenced by a number of external factors as well as his own sense of morality. First, from a political expediency perspective, Carter emphasized human rights because to do so at the

---

[8] Polish dissident Adam Michnik has said, "Brzezinski understood what hardly anybody could understand that that time in America – that an ideological confrontation with the Soviet bloc had to be undertaken, and the American slogan should be 'human rights.'" Vaughan, "Zbigniew Brzezinski and the Helsinki Final Act," in Nuti, ed., *The Crisis of Détente in Europe*, 16; and Brzezinski to Vance, October 6, 1976, Folder 7, Box 8, Vance Papers.

[9] "USSR/Foreign Policy," October 21, 1976, Carter Quotes – USSR, Box H34, President Ford Committee, GRFL.

[10] Human Rights and the Jackson Amendment, Carter on Foreign Policy (1), Box 25, Michael Raoul-Duval Papers, GRFL.

time was politically popular.[11] In the run-up to the convention, Carter's team had recognized that focusing on human rights was a way to build consensus within the Democratic Party.[12] In an undated memo, his aides wrote: "To groups like the Poles, Ukrainians ... and others human rights is the single most important political issue in the field of foreign policy ... The issue is of major importance to groups like the Coalition For a Democratic Majority in the Jackson-Moynihan wing of the party."[13] Carter wanted to use human rights to gain political support and recreate the domestic foreign policy consensus that had allegedly existed after World War II, but that had collapsed in the late 1960s and early 1970s.[14]

Second, in the aftermath of Vietnam, Carter's support for human rights also could enhance American international prestige. Brzezinski saw Carter's focus on human rights as important for the United States place in the world:

I felt strongly that a major emphasis on human rights ... would advance America's global interests by demonstrating to the emergent nations of the Third World the reality of our democratic system ... The best way to answer the Soviets ideological challenge would be to commit the United States to a concept which most reflected America's very essence.[15]

Furthermore, NSC staffer William Odom described Carter's human rights policy as "a very pragmatic tactic, to really beat up morally on the

---

[11] Joshua Muravchik, *Uncertain Crusade: Jimmy Carter and the Dilemmas of Human Rights Policy* (Lanham: Hamilton Press, 1986), 7; and Scott Kaufman, *Plans Unraveled: The Foreign Policy of the Carter Administration* (Dekalb: Northern Illinois University Press, 2008), 13.

[12] During the course of the campaign, Carter saw that human rights was an issue that appealed to conservatives and liberals and strengthened his appeal to ethnic communities. John Dumbrell, *The Carter Presidency: A Re-evaluation* (New York: St. Martin's Press, 1993), 117; Robert A. Strong, *Working in the World: Jimmy Carter and the Making of American Foreign Policy* (Baton Rouge: Louisiana State University Press, 2000), 73; and David Skidmore, *Reversing Course: Carter's Foreign Policy, Domestic Politics, and the Failure of Reform* (Nashville: Vanderbilt University Press, 1996), 90–2.

[13] Dumbrell, *The Carter Presidency*, 117–8; and Burton Ira Kaufman, *The Presidency of James Earl Carter, Jr.* (Lawrence: University Press of Kansas, 1993), 38.

[14] Seeking to broaden his initiative beyond Eastern European and Jewish Americans, Carter noted that it was not only Jews who wanted to leave the Soviet Union, but five million Baptists as well. Elizabeth Drew, "A Reporter at Large: Human Rights," *The New Yorker* July 18, 1977, 38; and Skidmore, *Reversing Course*, 84, 135.

[15] Dumbrell, *The Carter Presidency*, 115. See also Gaddis Smith, *Morality, Reason and Power: American Diplomacy in the Carter Years* (New York: Hill and Wang, 1986), 50.

Soviets" in the Cold War.[16] Carter was also able to use the human rights issue to distinguish his agenda from Ford and Kissinger's foreign policy, which was increasingly subject to international and domestic critics.[17]

Third, external actors such as members of Congress, his own advisors, and other concerned individuals influenced Carter's policy. Dante Fascell played an important role in Carter's commitment to human rights, suggesting talking points for his inaugural address and urging Carter to shape his discussion of morality in foreign policy by explicitly addressing human rights issues.[18] Other congressional pressure, especially from Representative Donald Fraser's House Foreign Affairs Subcommittee on International Organizations and Movements, helped develop the role of human rights in foreign policy.[19] Among his close advisers, Brzezinski's hostile outlook toward communist governments in Eastern Europe significantly influenced Carter's attitude toward the Soviet Union with regard to human rights and the CSCE, and Vice President Walter Mondale had a long record of supporting human rights during his career in the Senate.[20] Furthermore, although they had less clout than policymakers, Soviet Jews, dissidents, and other affected parties collectively shaped the president's foreign policy agenda.[21]

Beyond political motivations, Carter's emphasis on human rights was fundamentally grounded in his personal worldview, which included an inner moral dedication to human rights that then-Supreme Allied Commander in Europe Alexander Haig termed "evangelical."[22] Secretary

[16] Interview with Zbigniew Brzezinski, Madeline Albright, Leslie Dened, and William Odom, Miller Center Interview, Carter Presidency Project, Vol. XV, February 18, 1982, 49, Jimmy Carter Library, Atlanta, Georgia (hereafter JCL).

[17] Strong, *Working in the World*, 73.

[18] Fascell to Vance, January 11, 1977, document is in the author's possession.

[19] Dumbrell, *The Carter Presidency*, 117; and A. Glenn Mower, *Human Rights and American Foreign Policy: The Carter and Reagan Experiences* (New York: Greenwood Press, 1987), 81.

[20] Smith, *Morality, Reason and Power*, 38; and Forsythe, "Human Rights in U.S. Foreign Policy," 448. When discussing United States involvement in the CSCE and support for human rights in his memoirs, Brzezinski focuses most on the possibilities for change in Eastern Europe rather than scoring propaganda points against the Soviets. Zbigniew Brzezinski, *Power and Principle: Memoirs of the National Security Adviser, 1977–1981* (New York: Farrar, Straus and Giroux, 1983), 296–7; Vaughan, "Zbigniew Brzezinski and the Helsinki Final Act," in Nuti, ed., *The Crisis of Détente in Europe*, 16–7; and David Aaron Interview, 12/15/80, White House Staff Exit Interviews, 6, JCL.

[21] Paul J. Bailey and Ilka Bailey-Wiebecke, "All-European Co-operation: The CSCE's Basket Two and the ECE," *International Journal* 32:2 (1977): 394.

[22] Muravchik, *Uncertain Crusade*, 7; Strong, *Working in the World*, 73; and Alexander M. Haig, Jr. with Charles McCarry, *Inner Circles: How American Changed the World: A Memoir* (New York: Warner Books, 1992), 531.

of State Cyrus Vance would later argue that Carter's commitment to human rights was motivated by deeply held beliefs, not tactics.[23] In addition, Carter firmly believed in the civil rights movement in the United States, and some observers have suggested this commitment influenced his support for human rights internationally.[24]

Carter took office in January 1977 and immediately acted upon his campaign promise to emphasize human rights in his foreign policy. Carter writes, "The fate of human rights activists and political prisoners in the Soviet Union and Eastern Europe was one of my earliest concerns and remained important to me throughout my term."[25] The issues and the tenuous balance between human rights support and diplomacy with the Soviets became clear shortly after the inauguration when Sakharov wrote to Carter, saying, it is "our duty and yours" to "defend those who suffer because of their non-violent struggle for an open society, for justice, for other people whose rights are violated." Sakharov specifically asked the president to address the plight of Helsinki monitors in the Soviet Union.[26] Carter wrote in response, "Human rights is a central concern of my administration ... We shall use our good offices to seek the release of prisoners of conscience."[27] Soviet leaders viewed Carter's message to Sakharov as emboldening the scientist. In the KGB's view, "Sakharov regards Carter's telegram as support for the illegal activities pursued by him and his accomplices. As well as a guarantee of his personal

[23] Cyrus Vance, "'SALT II and the Growth of Mistrust': Conference #2 of the Carter-Brezhnev Project," National Security Archive; and Kaufman, *Plans Unraveled*, 13.

[24] Elizabeth Drew, "A Reporter at Large: Human Rights," *The New Yorker* July 18, 1977," 41; Marshall Shulman, "'The Collapse of Détente': From the March 1977 Moscow Meetings to the December 1979 Invasion of Afghanistan: The 'Launch' of the Carter-Brezhnev Project" (A Conference of United States and Russian Policymakers and Scholars Held at the "Playhouse" on the Rockefeller Estate, Pocantico Hills, New York, October 22–24, 1992), on file at the National Security Archive. Carter biographer Betty Glad, however, does not see Carter's support for human rights as connected with the civil rights movement; she argues he largely maintained a neutral attitude toward the civil rights movement until his gubernatorial inaugural address when he spoke out against racial discrimination. Although even in this statement, Glad asserts Carter was politically motivated as it gained him national press attention. Betty Glad, *An Outsider in the White House: Jimmy Carter, His Advisors, and the Making of American Foreign Policy* (Ithaca: Cornell University Press, 2009), 72–3.

[25] Jimmy Carter, "The American Road to a Human Rights Policy," in Samantha Power and Graham Allison, eds., *Realizing Human Rights: Moving from Inspiration to Impact* (New York: St. Martin's Press, 2000), 55.

[26] Telegram, State 02608, S.II.2.10.25, Box 55, Sakharov Papers; Andropov to the Central Committee, February 9, 1977, S. II.2.4.116, Box 46, ibid; and Lourie, *Sakharov*, 286–7.

[27] Telegram, State 02608, S.II.2.10.25, Box 55, Sakharov Papers; and Lourie, *Sakharov*, 287.

immunity."[28] Although the exchange between Carter and Sakharov ultimately proved controversial and potentially damaging to the American–Soviet relationship, Brzezinski argues that Carter could not have declined to respond to Sakharov's letter because it would be "an act of cowardice, perhaps matching Ford's unwillingness to meet with exiled Soviet author Alexander Solzhenitsyn."[29] Writing to Carter in the aftermath of the exchange, Brezhnev described the letters between Carter and Sakharov as "correspondence with a renegade who proclaimed himself an enemy of the Soviet state."[30] In retrospect, Carter acknowledges that writing to Sakharov strained Soviet–American relations but believes that it was right nonetheless, highlighting a recurring tension between championing human rights and accomplishing other American foreign policy goals during Carter's presidency.[31]

Although Sakharov was one of the most prominent human rights activists supported by the administration, Carter's policy of publicly pointing out human rights violations combined with an upsurge in

---

[28] In response, a decision was made to undertake steps to "forestall and cut short Sakharov's hostile activities." Central Committee of the CPSU Report, February 9, 1977, www.yale. edu/annals/sakharov/sakharov_english_txt/e122.txt (accessed March 27, 2006). Soviet authorities tracked reaction to the correspondence between Sakharov and Carter in the United States and French media, surveying the *Washington Post, New York Daily News, Le Figaro,* and *L'Aurore.* Carter to Sakharov, February 5, 1977, S.II.2.4.115, Box 46, Sakharov Papers.

[29] Brzezinski and Vance worked on drafting Carter's response, which was delivered in person to Sakharov at the United States Embassy in Moscow and was a forceful statement of Carter's commitment to human rights. Strong, *Working in the World,* 81; Interview Transcript, January 8, 1981, Brzezinski Interview 11/80–1/81, Box 2, S/F (P) F, #13, Brzezinski Material, NSA, JCL; and Brzezinski, *Power and Principle,* 156. The American Federation of Labor-Congress of Industrial Organizations (AFL-CIO) President George Meany had invited Ford to attend a June 30, 1975, banquet to honor Solzhenitsyn. The State Department and National Security Council, however, advised against Ford's attendance. Poor White House management of Ford's decision to decline the invitation engendered political controversy and raised questions about Ford instead receiving Solzhenitsyn at the White House, but no invitation was extended. The controversy only dissipated when Solzhenitsyn issued a statement that condemned Ford's stance on Helsinki, describing it as a "betrayal of Eastern Europe." Editorial, *Chicago Tribune,* July 23, 1975, in Buncher, *Human Rights and American Diplomacy: 1975–77,* 52; Editorial, "Europe's Act of Trust," *Chicago Sun-Times,* July 23, 1975, Press Clipping Helsinki, 1975, OSCE Archives; and Snyder, "'Jerry, Don't Go,'" 74–6.

[30] Brezhnev also wrote that he would not "allow interference in our internal affairs, whatever pseudo-humanitarian slogans are used to present it." Brzezinski, *Power and Principle,* 155; and Strong, *Working in the World,* 82.

[31] Jimmy Carter, *Keeping Faith: Memoirs of a President* (New York: Bantam Books, 1982), 146. Carter's critics charged that his open diplomacy on human rights harmed the United States relationship with the Soviet Union.

repression meant the White House and State Department responded to many reports of abuses. Indeed, Carter's first months in office produced a range of public administration comments on Eastern European human rights cases. For example, the Carter administration criticized the repression of Charter 77, publicly charging the Czechoslovak government with failing to implement the Helsinki agreement. It also admonished the Soviet government over its treatment of Helsinki monitor Alexander Ginzburg, saying that his case was "a matter of profound concern for all Americans."[32] The United States responded similarly after Orlov's arrest; to accusations that Shcharansky had worked for the Central Intelligence Agency; and to the arrests and trials of Jewish refuseniks Ida Nudel and Vladimir Slepak.[33]

Initially, Carter made direct appeals to Brezhnev on human rights but also publicly emphasized that he wanted to avoid affecting other important areas of their relationship, such as arms control.[34] Carter writes in his memoirs that although he wanted to develop better relations with the Soviets, he could not ignore their human rights abuses.[35] At first, Carter

[32] Soviet officials responded sharply to Carter's entreaties; American embassy officials in Moscow reported the Soviets had characterized United States actions as "categorically unacceptable to us" and suggested they "amount to support and direct incitement of individuals who oppose Soviet society." Telegram, AmEmbassy Moscow to SecState, February 18, 1977, S.II.2.10.30, Box 55, Sakharov Papers; Press Release, February 10, 1977, NL 101: Foreign Policy (Helsinki Violations) 2/9–10/77, Box 39, Case Papers; Kaufman, *The Presidency of James Earl Carter, Jr.*, 40; Jerel A. Rosati, *The Carter Administration's Quest for Global Community: Beliefs and Their Impact on Behavior* (Columbia: University of South Carolina Press, 1987), 119–20; Muravchik, *Uncertain Crusade*, 23–5; Betty Glad, "Carter Biographers: Discussant," in Herbert D. Rosenbaum and Alexej Ugrinsky, eds., *Jimmy Carter: Foreign Policy and the Post-Presidential Years* (Westport: Greenwood Press, 1994), 388; Strong, *Working in the World*, 79–80; Sakharov, *Memoirs*, 465; "Human Rights: Washington Keeps Speaking Up," February 8, 1977, Human Rights, 1977–1977, Box 689, Old Code Subject Files, Soviet Red Archives, Records of Radio Free Europe/Radio Liberty Research Institute, Open Society Archives; Fraser et al. to Carter, February 10, 1977, HU 3/1/77–3/31/77, HU – 1 Subject File, White House Central Files (WHCF), JCL; David Aaron Interview, 12/15/80, White House Staff Exit Interviews, 6, JCL; and Dumbrell, *The Carter Presidency*, 123.

[33] Memorandum and Attachments, Bloomfield to Brzezinski, Human Rights, 4/79–4/80, Box 29, Brzezinski Material, Subject File, NSA, JCL; Dumbrell, *The Carter Presidency*, 123; Starr to Fenwick, June 23, 1978, Helsinki/USSR, Box 271, Fenwick Papers; and Erwin C. Hargrove, *Jimmy Carter as President: Leadership and the Politics of the Public Good* (Baton Rouge: Louisiana State University Press, 1988), 152–3.

[34] The President's News Conference, February 8, 1977, http://www.presidency.ucsb.edu/ws/index.php?pid=7666&st=&st1= (accessed May 10, 2006); Press Release, Clifford Case, February 10, 1977, Folder 17, Box 274, Fenwick Papers; and Strong, *Working in the World*, 103.

[35] Carter, *Keeping Faith*, 146.

did not foresee that his emphasis on human rights was an impediment to Soviet–American détente, as he did not appreciate that his vocal support of human rights would negatively affect American–Soviet relations. Carter wrote in his first letter to Brezhnev,

We respect cooperation in the realization of further steps toward the fulfillment of the agreements reached in Helsinki regarding human rights. As I said to Ambassador Dobrynin, we hope that all aspects of these agreements can be realized. It is not our intention to interfere in the internal affairs of other countries. We do not wish to create problems with the Soviet Union, but it will be necessary for our Administration from time to time to publicly express the sincere and deep feelings which our people and I feel. Our obligation to help promote human rights will not be expressed in an extreme form or by means not proportional to achieving reasonable results. We would also welcome, of course, personal, confidential exchanges of views on these delicate questions.[36]

Carter believed he could keep his two priorities, human rights and arms control, separate, and his advisers, such as Press Secretary Jody Powell, often agreed: "Surely the Soviets are sophisticated enough to understand that the domestic flexibility we need to make progress in other areas is enhanced by your position on human rights."[37] In addition, Carter thought his criticism of non-Eastern European governments would convince the Soviets that his policy was not targeted specifically at them and thus lessen their negative reaction.[38] Yet according to former NSC staffer Robert Gates, this belief was naïve: "I believe we all underestimated just how sensitive – paranoid – the Soviets were about the dissidents. They were more aware than we by that time of the consequences of the Helsinki Accords and the spread of human rights monitoring groups in Eastern Europe and in the Soviet Union itself."[39] Indeed, Soviet Central Committee records from 1977 express its members' frustration

---

[36] Memorandum of Conversation, February 14, 1977, US-Soviet Relations, Cold War International History Project Virtual Archive.

[37] Powell to Carter, February 21, 1977, in Munteanu and Terzieva, eds., *From Global Politics to Human Rights: The CSCE Follow up Meeting, Belgrade, 1977*; and Kaufman, *The Presidency of James Earl Carter, Jr.*, 40.

[38] Kaufman, *The Presidency of James Earl Carter, Jr.*, 39. Carter said, "I think we come out better in dealing with the Soviet Union if I am consistently and completely dedicated to the enhancement of human rights, not only as it deals with the Soviet Union, but all other countries." Press Release, Clifford Case, February 10, 1977, Folder 17, Box 274, Fenwick Papers.

[39] Robert M. Gates, *From the Shadows: The Ultimate Insider's Story of Five Presidents and How They Won the Cold War* (New York: Simon and Schuster, 1996), 90.

with Carter's entreaties on human rights, regarding them as interference in their internal affairs and potentially damaging to their relationship.[40] As Carter's term progressed, the complications presented by his stance became increasingly apparent.

Soon after the election, the Carter administration commissioned a review of the role of human rights in United States foreign policy, which would determine how the government responded to human rights abuses internationally. By July 1977, a Presidential Review Memorandum was drafted, delineating the administration's view of three types of human rights: freedom from government intervention such as wrongful arrest, torture, and false imprisonment; the right to food, shelter, medical care, and education; as well as civil and political rights. It also outlined the United States human rights strategy abroad: emphasize American morals and virtue, spread the rule of law, and support and expand democratization efforts in the Soviet Union and Eastern Europe. Within the context of the memorandum, United States policymakers identified the challenges to gaining increased Eastern European compliance:

> Soviet public and private responses to our emphasis on human rights have been uniformly negative and increasingly sharp, explicitly suggesting that détente is threatened by our policy. To what extent the Soviet leadership feels their system and their hold in Eastern Europe endangered is unclear; but their objective appears to be to bring about a significant decrease in our public advocacy of the human rights cause, thus reducing its most embarrassing aspects for them, on the pretext that a "one-sided" U.S. advocacy of human rights and respect to state sovereignty cannot co-exist.[42]

According to the memorandum's drafters, the Carter administration needed to be careful not to single out particular countries and instead to emphasize the global nature of its focus. This strategy, which Carter adopted to a great extent, contrasted with his actions in his first six months in office, when he vocally denounced human rights violations in Eastern Europe, informally received Soviet dissident Vladimir Bukovsky

---

[40] Central Committee Memorandum, February 18, 1977, Perechen 25, Dokument 44, Fond 89. According to Betty Glad, Dobrynin warned Carter against publicly supporting Soviet dissidents thought public statements or invitations to the White House, saying, "let us not test Moscow." Glad, *An Outsider in the White House*, 69.

[41] Presidential Review Memorandum/NSC-28: Human Rights, July 7, 1977, Box 19, Robert J. Lipshutz Files, JCL; and Hauke Hartmann, "US Human Rights Policy Under Carter and Reagan, 1977–1981," *Human Rights Quarterly*, 23 (2001): 410.

[42] Presidential Review Memorandum/NSC-28: Human Rights, July 7, 1977, Box 19, Robert J. Lipshutz Files, JCL.

at the White House, and exchanged letters with Sakharov.[43] The administration's shift in tactics illustrates its recognition that vocally supporting human rights was imperiling other significant priorities such as détente and arms control negotiations.

Despite policy advice that Carter adopt a balanced, global approach to human rights, many contemporary and subsequent observers have criticized inconsistencies in his approach. In particular, critics have charged that for geopolitical reasons that Carter administration did not subject the human rights records of, for example, Romania, Cambodia, Iran, and China to sufficient scrutiny.[44] Others suggested he overlooked the strategic importance of South Africa or Latin American countries such as Brazil and Uruguay and focused only on their poor human rights records. His complicated relations with the Shah in Iran and Anastasio Somoza in Nicaragua also raised questions about the consistency and consequences of Carter's policies.[45]

Faced with mounting repression in Eastern Europe but concerned with the state of East–West relations, administration insiders and outside observers debated whether the United States should escalate its public and private efforts in support of human rights and what measures might lead to improvements. Brzezinski, in his memoirs, analyzed how best to influence the Soviets: "My own view is that pressure on the Soviets is justified; but it has to be measured in order to be effective. A sheer publicity campaign by itself will not achieve the desired results."[46] One opportunity arose in the close timing between the Vance–Gromyko meetings in Geneva in July 1978 and the trials of Shcharansky, Ginzburg, and two other dissidents, as well as the appeal of Vladimir Slepak's case. NSC staffer Jessica Tuchman Mathews argued the United States should either cancel the meetings or issue a presidential statement: "I also believe that

[43] In his meeting with Vice President Walter Mondale, Soviet dissident Vladimir Bukovsky reported human rights conditions in the Soviet Union had deteriorated considerably since the signing of the Helsinki Final Act. Memorandum of Conversation, March 1, 1977, in Munteanu and Terzieva, eds., *From Global Politics to Human Rights: The CSCE Follow up Meeting, Belgrade, 1977.*

[44] Glad, *An Outsider in the White House,* 237–9.

[45] For further discussion of Carter's human rights policy, see Mower, *Human Rights and American Foreign Policy;* Kaufman, *Plans Unraveled;* David F. Schmitz and Vanessa Walker, "Jimmy Carter and the Foreign Policy of Human Rights: The Development of a Post-Cold War Foreign Policy," *Diplomatic History* 28 (January 2004): 113–43; Muravchik, *Uncertain Crusade;* Dumbrell, *The Carter Presidency;* and Strong, *Working in the World.*

[46] Brzezinski, *Power and Principle,* 126.

any response less than this would lead to the widespread conclusion that the US has substantially diminished the importance it attaches to human rights."[47] The administration ultimately did neither, and Vance met with Gromyko.[48] The subsequent convictions and harsh sentences of Shcharansky, Ginzburg, and Viktoras Petkus, however, prompted the United States to take a number of other punitive measures.[49] Frustration at their trials even precipitated calls to end United States participation in the Helsinki process.[50] Yet, Soviet dissidents such as Shcharansky had

[47] Mathews to Brzezinski, July 7, 1978, HU 7/1/78–8/31/78, HU – 2, WHCF, JCL. United States Ambassador to the Belgrade Meeting Arthur J. Goldberg wanted Carter to speak out specifically on Ginzburg, Shcharansky, and Orlov and insist that Congress would not ratify a SALT agreement in the face of continuing human rights abuses. Goldberg argued that such a declaration was important for the administration's credibility on human rights. Memorandum, Eizenstat to Carter, May 17, 1978, 5/17/78, Box 86, Office of the Staff Secretary, JCL. Goldberg also condemned Orlov's trial and the arrests and legal proceedings against Shcharansky and Ginzburg, saying Soviet actions violated their commitments in the Helsinki Final Act. Statement, May 19, 1978, Folder 3, Box 148, Part I, Goldberg Papers. Members of Congress and other groups concerned about Eastern human rights abuses urged Carter to consider steps to signal American displeasure, such as postponing the SALT talks, restricting Soviet–American trade, or curbing other bilateral relations. Davis and Riseman to Carter, July 12, 1978, Correspondence, 7/12/78–8/23/78, Box 1, Ed Sanders Files, JCL; and Fascell to Carter, July 12, 1978, Name File: Fascell, [1/78–12/78], ibid. Mathews wanted to preempt congressional efforts by having Carter announce the suspension of all Soviet–American trade, government-sponsored exchanges, and technology transfers for ninety days. Mathews to Brzezinski, July 12, 1978, Human Rights, 5/77–11/78, Box 28, Subject File, Brzezinski Material, NSA, JCL.

[48] The administration only canceled the visit of science adviser Frank Press. Glad, *An Outsider in the White House*, 73–4.

[49] Measures included prohibiting the purchase of a large United States-built computer by TASS, the Soviet news agency; requiring export licenses for the sale of oil and gas equipment and technology; reviewing bilateral cultural and scientific exchanges; canceling some visits by American officials; and continuing communication of American distress at Soviet human rights abuses. Kite to Schulman, July 28, 1978, CO 165 7/1/78–9/30/78, CO – 63, WHCF, JCL; Watson to Bradley, September 21, 1978, CO 165 9/1/78–12/31/78 Executive, CO – 59, WHCF, JCL; Vernon J. Vavrina, "The Carter Human Rights Policy: Political Idealism and Realpolitik," in Rosenbaum and Ugrinsky, eds., *Jimmy Carter*, 107; Statement, July 8, 1978, Shcharansky, Anatoly, 7/14/78–3/1/78, Box 13, Al Moses Files, JCL; Memorandum and Attachments, Bloomfield to Brzezinski, Human Rights, 4/79–4/80, Box 29, Brzezinski Material, Subject File, NSA, JCL; Glad, "Carter Biographers: Discussant," 388; and Glad, *An Outsider in the White House*, 74.

[50] Commission on Security and Cooperation in Europe Hearing, "Repercussions of the Trials of the Helsinki Monitors in the USSR," July 11, 1978, Second Session, 95th Congress; and Dumbrell, *The Carter Presidency*, 125. For example, Senator Bob Dole (R-KS) characterized the trials of Soviet dissidents such as Shcharansky so close to the Belgrade Meeting as "deliberately provocative behavior" intended to "test America's commitment to human rights." Commission on Security and Cooperation in Europe Hearing, "Soviet Helsinki Watch, Reports on Repression," June 3, 1977, First Session, 95th Congress.

long implored Western officials to maintain pressure on Eastern states to comply with the Helsinki Final Act, which meant continued participation in the CSCE.[51]

Carter's approach toward the Soviet Union and Eastern Europe inspired considerable debate during his presidency and in the years that followed. One of the principal criticisms was that his administration's outspokenness on human rights provoked the Soviets to undertake further repression. Most Eastern European dissidents, however, disagreed, arguing that presidential interest in their cases gave them some level of protection and bolstered their morale. Valery Chalidze, one of many Soviet human rights activists who supported the president, wrote in the *Washington Post* that Carter was fulfilling the long-held hopes of Soviet dissidents.[52] Sakharov, whose correspondence with Carter had sparked such controversy, publicly supported the administration's policy on human rights; when asked in an ABC television interview if Carter's policy was fueling increased Soviet repression, Sakharov said, "Categorically-No!"[53] Bukovsky also challenged those who criticized Carter's human rights strategy as harmful to the dissidents' cause, noting: "The dissidents are not of this opinion. People who hold this view usually live in the West. In the Soviet Union, in Moscow, it is on the contrary argued that the more consistent Carter is in pursuing his policy, the more this would strengthen their cause."[54] In an indication of his support for Carter's policy, Petro Grigorenko, the Ukrainian Helsinki monitor, inscribed a volume of his memoirs to Carter: "The first American president to meet personally and salute former Soviet political prisoners (human rights defenders). With respect and gratitude for introducing

[51] Commission on Security and Cooperation in Europe Hearing, "Repercussions of the Trials of the Helsinki Monitors in the USSR," July 11, 1978, Second Session, 95th Congress.

[52] Valery Chalidze, "Dealing with Human Rights on a Global Scale," *Washington Post*, February 23, 1977. For a similar example, see Memorandum and attachments, Tarnoff to Brzezinski, September 28, 1977, Human Rights: Soviet Jewry 8/77–12/77, Box 54, Office of the Public Liaison, JCL; and Malcolm W. Browne, "Silent Fall," *New York Times Magazine*, October 23, 1977.

[53] Dumbrell, *The Carter Presidency*, 123; and Sakharov, *Memoirs*, 466.

[54] Norwegian Television Interview, October 2, 1977, Volume 84, File 20-4-CSCE, Volume 9097, RG 25, National Archives, Canada. In response to questions about the influence of international advocacy on his case, Bukovsky said, "Of course, as you can see. Because of that I am here now. They had to release me, exactly because of the campaign in my favour." TV Interview with Vladimir Bukovsky in Oslo on October 12, 1977, Volume 85, File 20-4-CSCE, Volume 9098, RG 25, National Archives, Canada.

and implementing the principle of human rights as a keystone of foreign policy."[55]

Not surprisingly, Carter's human rights policy was not well received in Warsaw Pact capitals.[56] Brezhnev outlined his disagreement with Carter in a harshly worded speech in March 1977, saying, "interference in the internal affairs of the Soviet Union" was in "direct opposition to further improvement of Soviet–American relations."[57] Dobrynin argues that the Soviet Union saw Carter and his stance on human rights as hostile and committed to "overthrowing [the Soviet] system."[58] As predicted by Carter's Presidential Review Memorandum, the Soviets were stung particularly by the public nature of Carter's criticisms. According to Dobrynin, the Soviets were willing to consider some progress on human rights for the sake of arms control negotiations, but "President Carter continued to attack us in public, in public, in public. Always in public!"[59] Dobrynin said Gromyko complained to him about Carter's emphasis on human rights saying, "What kind of man is he with this 'human rights?' Why won't he discuss things we can agree on. He is always bringing up human rights, human rights, human rights – what for?"[60] CIA analysts reported Soviet leaders viewed United States support for Soviet human rights activists as more damaging to Soviet–American relations than the war in Vietnam had been because "then you were bombing Hanoi, but now you are bombing Moscow." The CIA report noted, "The importance the leadership as a whole attaches to dissent can be seen by the fact that decisions about individual dissidents are sometimes made at the Politburo

---

[55] Munteanu and Terzieva, eds., *From Global Politics to Human Rights: The CSCE Follow up Meeting, Belgrade, 1977.*

[56] Carter's approach was not universally embraced in NATO capitals either. Carter's emphasis on human rights also frustrated allies such as West German Chancellor Helmut Schmidt. Helmut Schmidt, *Men and Powers: A Political Retrospective* trans. Ruth Hein (New York: Random House, 1989), 182.

[57] Furthermore, in his memoirs, Gromyko rejects Carter's concern for Soviet human rights, regarding it as an intrusion on an "internal" matter. Kaufman, *The Presidency of James Earl Carter, Jr.*, 41; Hargrove, *Jimmy Carter as President*, 134–6; and Andrei Gromyko, *Memoirs* (New York: Doubleday, 1989), 293.

[58] In Dobrynin's view, Carter's stance was driven by domestic problems and often inhibited opportunities for progress with the Soviets. Dobrynin, *In Confidence*, 389; and Dumbrell, *The Carter Presidency*, 124.

[59] Anatoly Dobrynin, "'The Collapse of Détente': From the March 1977 Moscow Meetings to the December 1979 Invasion of Afghanistan: The 'Launch' of the Carter-Brezhnev Project," National Security Archive.

[60] Anatoly Dobrynin, "'SALT II and the Growth of Mistrust': Conference #2 of the Carter-Brezhnev Project," National Security Archive.

level."[61] For example, KGB head Yuri Andropov reported to the Central Committee on Yelena Bonner's request to travel to Italy for medical treatment in 1977, demonstrating clear cognizance of the negative impact of denying her application: "One must also take into account the fact that rejection of a trip for medical treatment will entail large costs in terms of propaganda."[62]

The conflict between Carter's human rights advocacy and the Soviet insistence on controlling internal affairs would come to a head at Belgrade. The administration's early emphasis on human rights signaled the United States would play a more active role at the CSCE Belgrade Meeting than it had during the Geneva negotiations, and increased human rights activism in Eastern Europe in the intervening years assured the meeting would be focused on implementation of the agreement's human rights and human contacts provisions. These factors both ensured that Belgrade would hold great significance for the CSCE and East–West relations.

The Belgrade Meeting offered the first opportunity to evaluate Helsinki adherence publicly, and thus it spurred considerable output from Helsinki monitoring groups. For example, Charter 77 published 150 books and many periodicals as well as distributed 1,000 *samizdat* materials, all to spread information about human rights violations to politicians, delegates, and the public.[63] Many critics of Eastern compliance also utilized Moscow Helsinki Group documents to support their condemnations, marking the beginning of productive collaboration between NGOs and CSCE delegations. The Moscow Helsinki Group produced twenty-six documents and drafted 195 reports, statements, and letters to inform those at the Belgrade Meeting about the human rights situation in the

---

[61] Central Intelligence Agency, "The Soviet View of the Dissident Problem Since Helsinki," May 1977, in Munteanu and Terzieva, eds., *From Global Politics to Human Rights: The CSCE Follow up Meeting, Belgrade, 1977*. Members of the Central Committee suggested provocative American support for Soviet dissidents could undermine détente and the political, economic, and cultural cooperation that was developing. Central Committee Directive, May 19, 1977, Perechen 25, Dokument 50, Fond 89.

[62] The Soviets chose to approve her application. Andropov to the Central Committee, July 20, 1977, www.yale.edu/annals/sakharov/sakharov_english_txt/e127.txt (accessed March 27, 2006).

[63] News Release, October 24, 1979, Press Releases, Box 2442, Fascell Papers; and Falk, *The Dilemmas of Dissidence in East-Central Europe*, 251. Dissidents' focus on the upcoming Belgrade Meeting to make "anti-Soviet declamations against the Soviet system" was a source of considerable frustration to Soviet leaders. Proposal to the Central Committee of the Communist Party of the Soviet Union, January 20, 1977, *The Moscow Helsinki Group 30th Anniversary: From the Secret Files* (Washington: The National Security Archive, 2006).

Soviet Union.[64] In one instance, members of the Moscow Helsinki Group wrote to the diplomats at Belgrade to report the detention and arrests of activists in Moscow in connection with Human Rights Day.[65] In addition, Sakharov made an appeal to the parliaments of CSCE states to champion human rights at Belgrade and sought support in particular from the United States Congress and Carter.[66] During the review of implementation stage of the meeting, many delegates to the Belgrade Meeting relied upon research and reports produced by Eastern European dissidents. Through these efforts, activists began to exert influence on the delegations, especially the United States. Markku Reimaa, a Finnish delegate to the Belgrade Meeting, has called dissidents and human rights groups the "36th player" in the CSCE process.[67] This proliferation of activity, however, sparked a corresponding wave of repression; even the specter of the Belgrade Meeting did not inhibit a Soviet crackdown on domestic dissidents.[68]

Like Eastern European human rights activists, interested Western NGOs such as ethnic, religious, and human rights groups, referred to at times as the "Helsinki lobby," also closely monitored compliance with the Helsinki Final Act and significantly influenced the Follow-up Meeting.[69] The United States in particular enjoyed an open, constructive relationship

[64] Eichhorn, *The Helsinki Accords and Their Effect on the Cold War*, 193, 213; Commission on Security and Cooperation in Europe, "A Thematic Survey of the Documents of the Moscow Helsinki Groups," May 12, 1981; "Belgrade – Getting Down to Squaring the Circle," December 1, 1977, Western Cooperation: General, 1975–79, Box 60, Subject Files Relating to the Bloc, East European Research and Analysis Department, Records of Radio Free Europe/Radio Liberty Research Institute, Open Society Archives; and Dante B. Fascell, "The Helsinki Accord: A Case Study," *Annals of the American Academy of Political and Social Science* 442 (1979): 76. Sakharov also reached out directly to many Helsinki Final Act signatories; for example, he passed a document detailing Orlov's situation to the West German embassy in Moscow. Stoltenberg to Sakharov, June 22, 1978, S.III.1.2.82.3.1, Box 61, Sakharov Papers.

[65] *Arkhiv Samizdata* No. 3186, December 12, 1977, Human Rights, 1977–1977, Box 689, Old Code Subject Files, 1953–1994, Soviet Red Archives, Records of Radio Free Europe/Radio Liberty Research Institute, Open Society Archives.

[66] Telegram, AmEmbassy Moscow to SecState, September 30, 1977, S.II.2.10.36, Box 55, Sakharov Papers; and Sakharov to Parliaments, October 3, 1977, S.II.2.1.17, Box 24, ibid.

[67] Comments made at "30 Years Since the First CSCE Follow-Up Meeting in Belgrade," Belgrade, Serbia, March 2008.

[68] "USSR Weekly Review," January 26, 1978, CREST database; and William E. Griffith, "East–West Détente in Europe," in Frans A. M. Alting von Geseau, ed., *Uncertain Détente* (Alphen aan den Rijn: Sijthoff and Noordhoff, 1979), 12.

[69] Significant Western groups working on CSCE issues, many based in the United States, were the Polish American Congress, Joint Baltic American National Committee

with Western NGOs at Belgrade.[70] State Department Counselor Matthew Nimetz regularly wrote to interested groups to keep them informed of the arrangements for Belgrade and organized meetings with State Department officials.[71] This interplay represents an excellent example of "leverage politics" at work, in that groups that by themselves exerted little influence were able to press their agenda through connections to CSCE diplomats.

Members of the Commission and its staff also played a critical role in shaping United States CSCE policy for the Follow-up Meeting and the negotiations in Belgrade. As evidence of the increasing cooperation between the Commission and the State Department, the two bodies shared responsibilities as they prepared for the talks, assembling research for the delegation, compiling reports and briefing books, and transmitting NGO contributions. At the Belgrade Meeting, Commission members and staff were involved in a variety of integral tasks, including delivering speeches and facilitating contact with the press. In addition, the Commission drafted and disseminated a number of reports related to the meeting. A range of NGOs sent the Commission information on human rights abuses in Eastern Europe, and it distributed relevant documents to Amnesty International, Keston College Centre for the Study of Religion

(JBANC), the National Conference on Soviet Jewry, American Federation of American Scientists, Amnesty International, the American East European Ethnic Conference, the Committee in Support of Solidarity, World Congress of Churches, Freedom House, Assembly of European Captive Nations, the Committee of Concerned Scientists, Inc., and the American Psychiatric Association's Committee on the Abuse of Psychiatry and Psychiatrists. Mastny, *Helsinki, Human Rights, and European Security*, 197; Janie Leatherman, *From Cold War to Democratic Peace: Third Parties, Peaceful Change, and the OSCE* (Syracuse: Syracuse University Press, 2003), 16; Donald E. Pienkos, *PNA: A Centennial History of the Polish National Alliance of the United States of North America* (New York: Columbia University Press, 1984); John B. Genys, "The Joint Baltic American Committee and the European Security Conference," *Journal of Baltic Studies* 9:3 (Fall 1978): 246; and Lynne A. Davidson, "The Tools of Human Rights Diplomacy with Eastern Europe," in Newsom, ed., *The Diplomacy of Human Rights*, 27.

[70] The Carter administration also gained politically by connecting with such groups. In this context, supporting a thorough review of Helsinki implementation also was astute politically as ethnic and religious groups that traditionally supported the Democratic Party expressed significant interest in CSCE activism.

[71] Nimetz to Bolsteins, December 5, 1977, Belgrade Conference '77–'78, Box 3 Unprocessed, Joint Baltic American National Committee Records, Immigration History Research Center, University of Minnesota, Minneapolis, Minnesota; Memcon, "JBANC Meeting at White House," April 4, 1978, JBANC to White House, Box 4 Unprocessed, ibid.; "CSCE: Meeting with NGOs, September 9, 1977," September 8, 1977, Human Rights-CSCE/Helsinki Commission Articles, Printed Material 2/77–12/77, Box 53, Office of Public Liaison, JCL; and Korey, *The Promises We Keep*, 73 (hereafter JBANC).

and Communism, and others engaged in monitoring efforts.[72] During the course of the Belgrade Meeting, the Commission also shared information from closed sessions with interested NGOs.[73] The close links between the State Department, the Commission, and monitoring groups strengthened the United States commitment to the process.

At the Preparatory Meeting to set the agenda and procedures for the Follow-up Meeting, United States Ambassador Albert Sherer, Jr., argued there did not need to be "verbal fireworks" and maintained the United States desired "serious, very straightforward, very frank" talks.[74] Indeed, the State Department was hesitant about pursuing a "confrontation strategy" at Belgrade, in particular given negative ramifications for American relations with the USSR, Eastern Europe, NATO, and the neutral and nonaligned states.[75] Furthermore, the Soviets, angry about American and Western attention to their human rights record, threatened that the West's "frivolous and cavalier attitude" could create "unpleasant consequences" and lead to the "failure of our mission."[76] The two sides traded barbs for six weeks until reaching an agreement allowing for review of implementation and discussion of new proposals on "deepening of their mutual relations."[77]

---

[72] Millicent Fenwick, "The Commission on Security and Cooperation in Europe – A Unique Organization for a Unique Document," January 29, 1980, Sixteenth Meeting Between Members of the U.S. Congress and the European Parliament, Helsinki Report, Box 112, Fenwick Papers; R. Spencer Oliver Interview, February 26, 2008; and Commission on Security and Cooperation in Europe, Activities Report: 95th Congress, October 11, 1978, Commission on Security and Cooperation in Europe, 1978–79, Box 18, 4:2, Jacob Javits Collection, State University of New York at Stony Brook, Stony Brook, New York (hereafter Javits Collection).

[73] Commission on Security and Cooperation in Europe, Activities Report: 95th Congress, October 11, 1978, Commission on Security and Cooperation in Europe, 1978–79, Box 18, 4:2, Javits Collection.

[74] Proposal, CSCE/BM-P/3, June 15, 1977, Belgrade Meeting – Preparatory, Book 25, OSCE Archives; CBS Interview with Sherer, June 15, 1977, USA [United States] 1977 [3 of 4], Box 456, Yugoslav Subject Files I, Balkan Section: Albanian and Yugoslav Files, Records of Radio Free Europe/Radio Liberty Research Institute, Open Society Archives.

[75] Ambassador John Kornblum has maintained that State Department officials supported "naming of names" at Belgrade but were worried about the Commission's stridency and how it might affect opportunities for East–West diplomacy at Belgrade. Breck Walker, "'Neither Shy nor Demagogic,' – The Carter Administration Goes to Belgrade," paper presented at the conference "30 Years Since the First CSCE Follow-Up Meeting in Belgrade," Belgrade, Serbia, March 2008.

[76] "The USSR: Regional and Political Analysis," June 30, 1977, CREST.

[77] "Belgrade – Delegates Finally Reach Agreement," August 4, 1977, EUROSECURITY, 1977 [7 of 7], Box 148, Yugoslav Subject Files I, Balkan Section: Albanian and Yugoslav Files, Records of Radio Free Europe/Radio Liberty Research Institute,

Following the Preparatory Meeting, a disagreement arose between Brzezinski and Deputy Secretary of State Warren Christopher over the composition of the American delegation, which at its root was driven by conflicting visions of how aggressive the United States should be during the negotiations in Belgrade. Whereas State Department officials favored retaining Sherer as ambassador to diminish potential Soviet–American conflict at the meeting, Brzezinski pushed to appoint a more aggressive person to lead the United States delegation. Brzezinski prevailed, replacing Sherer, whom he described as "a relatively unknown State Department nominee," with Arthur Goldberg, a former Supreme Court justice, secretary of labor, and ambassador to the United Nations. In Goldberg, Carter appointed a public figure who would be willing to criticize the Soviets and whose appointment would enhance the stature of the talks.[78] This selection would prove crucial to the legacy of the Belgrade Meeting, as Goldberg's outspokenness would establish a standard for United States leadership in future CSCE meetings.

Goldberg had a long career as a labor lawyer, working primarily for the Congress of Industrial Organizations and United Steelworkers of America before President John F. Kennedy appointed him secretary of labor. He remained at the Department of Labor until Kennedy named him to the Supreme Court in 1962. Astounding most observers, Goldberg left the Court after only three years to represent the United States at the United Nations; Lyndon Johnson had appealed to Goldberg's sense of duty, arguing he needed Goldberg's negotiating skills to help avert a collapse of the United Nations and to aid Johnson in seeking a peaceful end to the war in Vietnam. Goldberg accepted based on the promise that he would lead United States negotiations on Vietnam and with the expectation that he would be reappointed to the Court afterward. Goldberg and Johnson's relationship, however, foundered on Goldberg's private criticism of Johnson's policy in Vietnam and ultimately weakened to the point

---

Open Society Archives; List of Decisions Taken, CSCE/BM-P/DEC.1, June 17, 1977, Belgrade Meeting – Preparatory, Book 25, OSCE Archives; and Memorandum, Martin Sletzinger et al. to CSCE Commissioners, August 11, 1977, Folder 16, Box 274, Fenwick Papers.

[78] Smith, *Morality, Reason and Power*, 54–5; and Carter to Mondale, September 19, 1977, 9/19/77 [1], Box 50, Office of the Staff Secretary (Presidential Handwriting File), JCL. The White House intended to highlight the symbolism of Goldberg's appointment by stating at his swearing-in that his selection signaled the "American commitment to Helsinki ideals" and describing him as "one of our greatest civil libertarians." Memorandum and attachment, Dodson to Clift, September 22, 1977, FO 2/CO/A 1/20/77–1/20/81, FO – 5, WHCF, JCL.

that Johnson did not reappoint Goldberg to the Supreme Court when the opportunity arose.[79]

Under Goldberg's leadership, the United States delegation to Belgrade intended to strike an equilibrium between "confrontation" and "platitudes" and work to "preserve the President's credibility on the subject of human rights," coordinate with interested NGOs, and communicate with the press.[80] Over the course of the meeting, however, Goldberg pursued a strategy designed to embarrass the USSR and its allies that many regarded as overly aggressive. Goldberg balanced service to a number of constituencies in his role as ambassador – the president, his delegation, and the allies – and his approach regularly raised questions of how far the United States could go in demonstrating its commitment to human rights without harming its ongoing relationship with the Soviets.[81]

The United States delegation repeatedly highlighted instances of Helsinki violations, hoping that shame might motivate Eastern European governments to observe human rights. At the Belgrade Meeting's opening session on October 4, 1977, the United States raised some criticisms, but initially avoided inflammatory statements. Goldberg emphasized the steps the United States had taken to comply with the Helsinki Final Act and alluded to problems of adherence in Eastern Europe broadly: ("In the spirit of candidness I must say to you in some nations in the East, advances have been only modest, and are still far below the Final Act's standards." Goldberg said some progress had been made on emigration, but that additional steps were needed, particularly for divided spouses. Goldberg specifically stated that he did not want a "confrontation" with the Soviets and that he planned on a "non-polemical dialogue."[82] For the moment, he avoided naming particular states that were at fault, but nonetheless did outline a number of human rights violations taking place

[79] David L. Stebenne, *Arthur J. Goldberg: New Deal Liberal* (New York: Oxford University Press, 1996), 346–79.

[80] "Proposals by Justice Goldberg to the Meeting of the PRC," September 21, 1977, Log Belgrade II, Box 6, Sherer Papers.

[81] Goldberg also indicated that he was under pressure from public opinion, and that the American people had "high expectations." Korey, "The Unanticipated Consequences of Helsinki," 8–14; Richard Davy, "The United States," in *Belgrade and Beyond: The CSCE Process in Perspective* Nils Andren and Karl E. Birnbaum, eds., East–West Perspectives No. 5 (Sijthoff & Noordhoff, December 1980), 8; and "Goldberg," Log Belgrade II (Second Part), Box 6, Sherer Papers.

[82] Statement, Arthur Goldberg (United States), October 6, 1977, CSCE/BM/PV.6, Belgrade Meeting, Book 28, OSCE Archives.

in CSCE countries.[83] Goldberg was not alone among Western representatives in both expressing disappointment at the record of Helsinki implementation but refraining from accusations as Norway, the Netherlands, and the Vatican expressed similar themes in their opening statements.[84] Acknowledging that full Helsinki implementation would take some time, the British ambassador offered strong language in his opening statement: "But after more than two years, the peoples of Europe have every right to look for substantial progress in every field covered by the Final Act."[85] In contrast with Western opening statements, the East tried to move the debate away from compliance with past agreements and instead emphasize new proposals.[86]

After the opening session, as the negotiations moved behind closed doors, Goldberg pursued a more aggressive policy than initially outlined by State Department officials for Belgrade, the shift Brzezinski had desired. The United States calculated that the Soviets, despite their protestations, would remain a part of the conference. Strong Soviet attachment to the CSCE, based in part on Brezhnev's personal prestige as well as earlier claims that the Helsinki Final Act had been a great diplomatic victory for the Soviets, enabled the United States to press human rights more vigorously.[87] Such an approach was intended to capture public and media attention and prod embarrassed states into improving their records.[88]

[83] "'Détente with a Human Face': In Belgrade, human rights are played forte, not fortissimo," *Time*, October 17, 1977, 36.

[84] Statement, M. J. van der Valk (Netherlands), October 4, 1977, CSCE/BM/VR.2, Belgrade Meeting, Book 29, OSCE Archives; Statement Th. Stoltenberg (Norway), October 4, 1977, CSCE/BM/VR.2, ibid.; Statement, Achile Silvestrini (Holy See), October 7, 1977, CSCE/BM/VR.7, ibid.

[85] Statement, Owen Goronwy-Roberts (United Kingdom), October 6, 1977, CSCE/BM/PV.6, Belgrade Meeting, Book 28, OSCE Archives.

[86] Lehne, *The Vienna Meeting of the Conference on Security and Cooperation in Europe*, 16; and Robert Rand, "New Soviet Proposals at the Belgrade conference," November 3, 1977, EUROSECURITY 1977 [4 of 7], Box 147, Yugoslav Subject Files I, Balkan Section: Albanian and Yugoslav Files, Records of Radio Free Europe/Radio Liberty Research Institute, Open Society Archives.

[87] Commission staff member Martin Sletzinger assessed the progress the United States delegation had made in the initial phase of the Belgrade Meeting, asserting, "through CSCE human rights are slowly becoming a legitimate part of international discourse. We may not yet be able to provoke a real dialogue but we have reached the stage where such issues can be mentioned without causing unalterable damage to bilateral relations." Sletzinger to Goldberg, November 10, 1977, Folder 4, Box 96, Part II, Goldberg Papers. For further discussion of Soviet motivations, see Kashlev, "SBSE v 1975–1990," in Kashlev, ed., *Khel'sinskii Protsess v Sovetskoi/Rossiiskoi Vneshnei Politike*, 19.

[88] At Brzezinski's instigation, the State Department considered a "confrontation strategy" for the Belgrade Meeting that prioritized criticizing Eastern noncompliance above all

Goldberg challenged international diplomatic norms by "naming names" and citing individual cases in his speeches in Belgrade.[89] His statements conveyed problems of implementation in a forthright manner, often with specific details. In Alfred Friendly, Jr.'s view, Goldberg's concerns about Soviet treatment of Jews shaped his tactics at Belgrade: "Arthur was a highly political Jew and truly sensitive" to Soviet behavior toward its Jewish citizens.[90] Goldberg, frustrated by the closed nature of the Belgrade sessions and the lack of press interest in the negotiations, also held regular press conferences at which he divulged details of what he had said in the presumably confidential plenary meetings in order to embarrass recalcitrant states.[91] His strategy throughout the Belgrade Meeting was to emphasize the implementation review as opposed to the negotiation of new proposals.[92] Goldberg's relatively aggressive stance in Belgrade caused distress in Soviet, neutral, and Western delegations and raised concerns about his efforts to humiliate Eastern European human rights abusers.

other objectives within the CSCE. Ultimately, the State Department recognized such an approach could threaten the opportunity to influence Eastern Europe on human rights and American relations with its allies. Brzezinski had hoped, however, that considering a more extreme strategy would "stiffen [the delegation's] backs" for Belgrade. In the end, the United States pursued the most aggressive strategy it could within the bounds of what it thought would maintain allied unity and keep the Eastern European delegations at Belgrade. "Consequences of a Confrontation Strategy in CSCE," n.d., Belgrade Instructions Letters, Box 5, Sherer Papers; and Brzezinski, *Power and Principle*, 297.

[89] Importantly for human rights activists, Goldberg consulted with Helsinki groups and relied upon their research in his speeches to the other CSCE delegates, illustrating their increased influence on the Helsinki process. Korey, *The Promises We Keep*, xxv; and Richard Schifter, "The UN Charter and the Entry of Human Rights into the Field of International Relations," in Anatoly Adamishin and Richard Schifter, *Human Rights, Perestroika, and the End of the Cold War* (Washington: United States Institute of Peace Press, 2009), 76.

[90] Alfred Friendly, Jr., Interview, May 6, 2008.

[91] At Belgrade, all plenary sessions were officially closed meetings. Telegram, WSHDC to EXTOTT GEA, November 28, 1977, Volume 90, File 20–4-CSCE, Volume 9098, RG 25, National Archives, Canada; and Korey, *The Promises We Keep*, 78. According to Goldberg, Carter instructed him to "aggressively pursue the subject of human rights, which in our government's opinion is a keystone of the Helsinki Act." "The Madrid Conference on the Helsinki Accords-Part I," February 6, 1981, Communiqué, Helsinki/ Madrid, Box 112, Fenwick Papers; and Press Briefing Transcript, November 18, 1977, Human Rights-CSCE/Helsinki Commission-Articles and Printed Matter 2/77–12/77, Box 53, Office of the Public Liaison, JCL. According to Brzezinski, he ordered the more confrontational approach at the Belgrade Meeting. In his words, "I pushed hard that the United States take the lead and be perceived as ... pushing CSCE toward higher standards." Brzezinski, *Power and Principle*, 297.

[92] Memorandum, Greenwald to Goldberg, November 2, 1977, Miscellaneous Papers, Box 6, Sherer Papers; and R. Spencer Oliver Interview, February 26, 2008.

The United States strategy was one component of the larger NATO approach for Belgrade that emphasized reviewing implementation and ensuring the Helsinki process continued. Yet, the allies questioned American overemphasis on human rights as well as Goldberg's personal, confrontational style; some European diplomats described Goldberg as an "unguided missile."[93] In evident frustration with Goldberg's tactics, one European diplomat said, "We seem to spend more time negotiating with Goldberg than negotiating with the Russians."[94] Most Western European states were more concerned than the United States about a potential Soviet withdrawal from the meeting, which led some delegates to express anxiety about the specificity of American charges at Belgrade.[95] According to one member of the United States delegation, the NATO states acted as if the United States was trying to start World War III with its policies at Belgrade.[96] Vance notes, however, that when the meeting progressed into the closed working group stage, the NATO allies were more willing to support Goldberg's strategy of naming individual cases.[97] As the Soviet Union and Eastern states ultimately did not withdraw from the CSCE process, the United States considered its aggressive approach vindicated.[98]

In order to deflect criticism at Belgrade, the Soviet Union and its Eastern European allies pursued a damage limitation strategy consisting of both defensive and offensive tactics. From a defensive perspective, the

[93] Albert W. Sherer, Jr., "Helsinki's Child: Goldberg's Variation," *Foreign Policy* 39 (1980): 154–9; R. J. Vincent, "The Response of the Europe and the Third World to United States Human Rights Diplomacy," in Newsom, ed., *The Diplomacy of Human Rights*, 33; and Michael Clarke, "Britain and European Political Cooperation in the CSCE," in Kenneth Dyson, ed., *European Détente: Case Studies of the Politics of East–West Relations* (London: Francis Pinter, 1986), 244. According to Carter, the British and Germans "were quite concerned that we might upset the sensitivities of the Soviet Union," whereas the Canadians and French were more supportive of his human rights policy. Jimmy Carter, *White House Diary* (New York: Farrar, Straus and Giroux, 2010), 49.

[94] Thomas, "Boomerangs and Superpowers," 39.

[95] In anticipation of the Belgrade Meeting, some observers suggested a failed conference could lead to the collapse of the CSCE process. Commission on Security and Cooperation in Europe, "The Belgrade Follow-up Meeting to the Conference on Security and Cooperation in Europe," Folder 19, Box 274, Fenwick Papers; and Log Belgrade II, Box 6, Sherer Papers.

[96] R. Spencer Oliver Interview, February 26, 2008.

[97] Memorandum, Friendly to CSCE Commissioners, October 31, 1977, Folder 16, Box 274, Fenwick Collection; and Commission on Security and Cooperation in Europe Hearing, June 7, 1977, First Session, 95th Congress.

[98] Memorandum, Oliver to CSCE Commissioners, January 9, 1978, Folder 16, Box 274, Fenwick Papers.

Soviets warned prior to the meeting that it was not in the CSCE states' interests for Belgrade to turn into a "complaints office," and Soviet officials criticized the West for the "hysterical campaign" they were organizing to discredit the Soviet human rights record.[99] Perhaps remembering earlier encounters with Goldberg at the UN, the Soviet Foreign Ministry characterized him as a "dangerous, powerful opponent, a polemicist inclined to aggravating situations, to sharp fights."[100] Soviet delegate Yuli Vorontsov's blustering protests to United States Senator Bob Dole (R-KS) during the meeting illustrate Soviet frustration at what they considered to be American interference in internal matters, in this case the annexation of Baltic republics: "The US does not recognize the existence of Lithuania, Latvia and Estonia as Soviet Socialist Republics. This does not bother us, we could not care less!"[101] According to one Swiss delegate, a Soviet diplomat accused the United States of "slanderous" and "propagandistic attacks."[102] Soviet officials repeatedly addressed what they saw as an anti-Soviet campaign on human rights, engineered by the agencies of the United States.[103]

The Soviet Union and its allies took some minor steps toward improved compliance, but these were primarily cosmetic changes related to provisions of the act not connected to human rights. This limited response did not prevent these countries from claiming far more progress, and they used their speeches at Belgrade to assert compliance with the Helsinki Final Act. For example, Yuli Vorontsov cited the integration of Helsinki principles into the Soviet Constitution and argued these principles were inherent in the Soviet system, saying, "In our country human rights and fundamental

---

[99] Andrei Gromyko, "The Leninist Strategy of Peace-A Unity of Theory and Practice," *Kommunist* 14 (1976) and D. A. Kunayev, "Fighting for the Consolidation of Peace and Friendship Among Nations," *Kommunist* 10 (1977) in Adamishin et al., *From Helsinki to Belgrade*, 75–6, 90.

[100] Svetlana Savranskaya, "Human Rights Movement in the USSR after the Signing of the Helsinki Final Act, and the Reaction of Soviet Authorities," in Leopoldo Nuti, ed., *The Crisis of Détente in Europe*, 37.

[101] CSCE Notes Belgrade 1977/78, Private Archive Hans-Jörg Renk, Riehen/Basel, Switzerland. I thank Thomas Fischer for bringing this transcript to my attention.

[102] Ibid.

[103] See for example, Central Committee Document, March 24, 1977, Perechen 25, Dokument 45, Fond 89. In this instance, the Central Committee agreed to combat the campaign internally and externally using press organs. See also Central Committee Document, December 9, 1976, READD-RADD Collection, National Security Archive; Andropov to the Central Committee, March 21, 1977, ibid.; and Central Committee Resolution, October 25, 1976 in Munteanu and Terzieva, eds., *From Global Politics to Human Rights: The CSCE Follow up Meeting, Belgrade, 1977*.

freedoms are more than just proclaimed and laid down in laws, they are guaranteed by our socio-economic system itself."[104] The reality, of course, was far different. The actual steps taken, which the Soviets also touted, included notifying CSCE signatories about their military maneuvers as well as moderately increasing the availability of Western culture, such as books and movies.[105] Bulgaria and Czechoslovakia resolved a number of divided family cases, and the Soviet Union granted some exit visas to long-time activists. Soviet Jewish emigration also increased during the period of the Belgrade Meeting, reaching its highest rate in four years when more than 2,000 Soviet Jews left in March 1978, but strict restrictions remained.[106] KGB archivist Vasily Mitrokhin explains that these minor steps were largely token efforts to counter the criticism of the Soviet human rights record.[107] Nevertheless, many Western delegates and NGOs viewed any progress as an important first step, one that could gain momentum over time. Commission staff member Martin Sletzinger assessed the value of holding a follow-up meeting: "It was the pressure and anticipation of a review conference which caused many East European countries, if not the Soviet Union, to improve their records, even if at the last minute ... Thus far, Belgrade has been a useful propaganda forum for calling attention to continued Soviet practices which in our view are contrary to the spirit of the Final Act."[108] According to American analysis, although the Soviets were frustrated with the review of implementation and suggested it could "rupture" the meeting, they "sat and took it all" as Western delegations criticized their record.[109]

104   Statement, Yuli Vorontsov (USSR), October 6, 1977, CSCE/BM/PV.6, Belgrade Meeting, Book 28, OSCE Archives.
105   Kashlev, "The CSCE in the Soviet Union's Politics," 68; Leonid I. Brezhnev, "From the Speech at the Berlin Conference of the Communist and Workers' Parties of Europe," June 29, 1976 and N. S. Patolichev, "Course Towards Constructive Cooperation," *Pravda* May 19, 1977, in Adamishin et al., *From Helsinki to Belgrade*, 45–50, 210.
106   National Conference on Soviet Jewry, *Wrap-up ... Leadership Report* May 1978, 95th/1st, Newspaper Clippings; News Release, May 1, 1978, Fascell-Hearings and Reports, Box 2442, Fascell Papers. In the second quarter of 1976, Soviet emigration to the United States had doubled over the previous year's rate. Memorandum for the President, Conference on Security and Cooperation in Europe, 1976 (5) NSC, Box 45, National Security Council Europe, Canada and Ocean Affairs Staff Files, GRFL.
107   Vasily Mitrokhin, "On Human Rights," Folder 51, The Chekist Anthology, The Mitrokhin Archive, Cold War International History Project Virtual Archive.
108   Sletzinger to Goldberg, November 10, 1977, Folder 4, Box 96, Part II, Goldberg Papers.
109   AmEmbassy Belgrade to SecState, November 12, 1977, Commission on Security and Cooperation in Europe (CSCE): Belgrade Review Conference, 1977 [1 of 4], Briefing Books, Legislative Relations, Dole Senate Papers.

The Belgrade Meeting did not produce new commitments, but it did facilitate an international debate about human rights in Eastern Europe and draw international attention to those states that had not fulfilled the terms of the Helsinki Final Act.[110] Goldberg's tactics represented a shift in international diplomacy and for average citizens in the East, ultimately strengthened the Helsinki process by imbuing the follow-up meetings with real repercussions. Furthermore, progress at Belgrade ensured such a discussion would recur in Madrid in 1980. Goldberg, Fascell, Brzezinski, and Carter expressed satisfaction with the results of the meeting, maintaining that the significance of Belgrade was its extension of the CSCE process.[111] Furthermore, in a February 1978 speech, Deputy Secretary of State Warren Christopher argued the United States emphasis on human rights at Belgrade had restrained violations and prevented future abuses through its strict appraisal of Helsinki compliance.[112] Consistent with this goal, in the aftermath of Belgrade, the Carter administration updated its policy on human rights with NSC 30: "It shall be a major objective of U.S. foreign policy to promote the observance of human rights throughout the world." To support such a strategy, the

[110] Summary of Statement before CSCE Commission, March 21, 1978, Ambassador Goldberg's Briefing Book, Testimony Before the CSCE Commission, Folder 5, Box 143, Part I, Goldberg Papers. Members of the Moscow Helsinki Group expressed their frustration at the Belgrade Concluding Document, complaining it did not address human rights or the fulfillment of the Helsinki Final Act. Nonetheless, the results of the Belgrade Meeting confirmed for the Group members the continuing importance of their work. *Arkhiv Samzdata* 3259, February 1978, Helsinki: Belgrade, 1977–1978, Box 114, Old Code Subject Files, Soviet Red Archives, Records of Radio Free Europe/Radio Liberty Research Institute, Open Society Archives; *Arkhiv Samzdata* 3439, March 14, 1978, Box 112, Published Samizdat, Samizdat Archive, ibid.; Moscow Helsinki Group Document, Folder 54, Box 9, Human Rights Collection, Andrei Sakharov Archives, Houghton Library, Harvard University, Cambridge, Massachusetts; and Belgrade Concluding Document, March 8, 1978, http://www.osce.org/documents/mcs/1977/10/4222_en.pdf (accessed August 19, 2009) (hereafter Human Rights Collection).

[111] H. Gordon Skilling, "The Belgrade Follow-up," in Robert Spencer, ed., *Canada and the Conference on Security and Co-operation in Europe* (Toronto: Centre for International Studies, University of Toronto, 1984), 290. Defending Carter's human rights policy, Fascell wrote, "There is nothing wrong – and a great deal right – about a policy which reminds Americans of the values our history reflects." Fascell, "Human Rights: The United States at Belgrade," 40. Goldberg wrote to Sakharov, defending his approach to the Belgrade Meeting, citing Sakharov's own interviews, which Goldberg argued supported his own strategy. He also complained that "some Western democracies sought ... to condemn in general rather than specific terms the oppression of Helsinki Watch groups in the East." Goldberg to Sakharov, December 28, 1978, S.III.1.2.82.4.0, Box 61, Sakharov Papers.

[112] "Deputy Secretary Christopher on 'Diplomacy of Human Rights,'" February 13, 1978, U.S. Policy on Human Rights, Part I, Box 7, Sherer Papers.

United States intended to use "the full range of its diplomatic tools," although the emphasis would be on positive encouragement rather than sanctions or negative reactions.[113]

Western delegations had succeeded in raising the international profile of Helsinki monitors at Belgrade; NSC staffer Robert P. Hunter argued that "virtually nobody had heard of the Orlov Group before Belgrade began," whereas afterward the plight of Helsinki monitors was well known.[114] Goldberg was convinced that his strategy at Belgrade benefited human rights monitors and others in Eastern Europe, telling a reporter,

> What we do know from various sources is that the review we conducted and the strong stand taken by the United States have given encouragement to Soviet dissenters and those in Czechoslovakia and elsewhere. We recently received a report from the Soviet monitoring group – those who are not in jail and could transmit their views through Western newspaper people – strongly commending the United States for its support of the right of the individual to engage in peaceful monitoring of the Final Act.[115]

In Shcharansky's view, the repeated CSCE review meetings ensured international community's focus would remain on imprisoned dissidents, as politicians and diplomats responded to low-level activism.[116]

Those who expressed disappointment with the Belgrade Meeting often blamed Goldberg for what they perceived as its missed opportunities. Indeed, Goldberg's leadership of the American delegation was criticized from all sides—by Eastern states unhappy over his attacks on their records, by NATO allies who worried his style was damaging détente and the sustainability of the Helsinki process, and even by members of his own delegation who worried about the impact of his actions on dissidents in Eastern Europe and United States national interests.[117] Even Yuli Vorontsov, for example, believed the Soviets benefited from the growing "unpopularity" of Goldberg.[118] Many critics questioned if

[113] Presidential Directive/NSC 30, February 17, 1978, Munteanu and Terzieva, eds., *From Global Politics to Human Rights: The CSCE Follow up Meeting, Belgrade, 1977*.

[114] Press Briefing Transcript, February 2, 1978, IT 5 1/1/78–12/31/78, IT – 1, WHCF, JCL.

[115] Transcript, February 27, 1978, Folder 3, Box 148, Part I, Goldberg Papers.

[116] Natan Sharansky Interview, November 19, 2008.

[117] Davy, "The United States," in Andren and Birnbaum, eds., *Belgrade and Beyond*; and Alexis Heraclides, *Security and Co-operation in Europe: The Human Dimension, 1972–1992* (Portland: Frank Cass, 1993), 52.

[118] Carroll Sherer, "Breakdown at Belgrade," *The Washington Quarterly* 1:4 (1978): 81.

quiet diplomacy would have been more effective.[119] According to Carroll Sherer, United States delegate to the Belgrade Meeting and wife of Albert Sherer, Goldberg was not properly suited for diplomatic negotiations, especially ones as precarious as the CSCE, although she concedes that Goldberg may have been responding to Carter's instructions.[120] She also echoed NATO criticisms that the Carter administration underestimated the fragility of the CSCE and blamed the United States for the disappointment at Belgrade, writing:

Those who try to explain the Belgrade breakdown by blaming it on Soviet intransigence are off the mark. The fact is that Belgrade should have been approached more like a china shop than a bull pen; but it was not. The White House failed to understand the fragility of the new European dialogue.[121]

Despite these criticisms, Carter said Goldberg enjoyed his strong support and praised his "tremendous success" at Belgrade, noting that Goldberg had been "particularly effective in keeping a strong posture on the human rights issue."[122] Sherer's point of view likely derived from a State Department mentality in which allied unity was of paramount concern and from displeasure at Carter and Brzezinski's replacement of her husband. Goldberg later wrote that Carter's strategy proved wise at the Belgrade Meeting, dismissing Sherer's assertion that he endangered diplomatic relations:

[It] demonstrated that naming persecuted human-rights activists and the countries responsible for their repression did not necessarily prejudice basic negotiations between the United States and the Soviet Union with respect to disarmament ...

---

[119] There was significant tension between the State Department personnel in Belgrade and other members of the delegation, including Goldberg and the public members. Telegram, WSHDC to EXTOTT GEA, January 27, 1978, Volume 94, File 20-4-CSCE, Volume 9099, RG 25, National Archives, Canada; "Human Rights," June 8, 1978, U.S. Policy on Human Rights Part II, Box 7, Sherer Papers. Sherer, "Helsinki's Child," 154–9; Jose A. Cabranes, "The Belgrade Conference: Reflections of a Public Member," April 18, 1978, Belgrade-CSCE, Box 6, Sherer Papers; and Thomas Delworth Interview, December 7, 2005. For further evidence of tension between the Commission and the State Department, see Remarks of Senator Bob Dole, Commission on Security and Cooperation in Europe (CSCE): Helsinki Commission Hearings, 1977, Briefing Books, Legislative Relations, Dole Senate Papers.

[120] Albert Sherer's daily log reveals considerable friction with Goldberg that may have colored Carroll Sherer's account.

[121] Sherer, "Breakdown at Belgrade," 84.

[122] In Brzezinski's view, Goldberg "performed admirably" in Belgrade. Candis Agnone, "Carter Praises Goldberg's Efforts at CSCE Review," in Miscellaneous Papers, Box 6, Sherer Papers; and Brzezinski, *Power and Principle*, 96.

Further, it demonstrated that by undertaking a leadership role at the first review conference, the United States did not undermine but instead strengthened its alliances and relationships.[123]

It seems unlikely that Eastern European governments would have consented to a substantive agreement at Belgrade even if Carter had appointed a different American ambassador. As Fascell wrote, "a strong Belgrade concluding document was never in the cards."[124] Facing dissent at home and international pressure, the Soviets did not intend to make new human rights or human contacts commitments.

What Goldberg accomplished was to highlight in stark terms the plight of those deprived of their human rights in Eastern Europe and invigorate the process of follow-up meetings for the future.[125] By publicly criticizing human rights abuses at Belgrade, Goldberg initiated an important component of the United States CSCE strategy until the end of the Cold War: using public embarrassment to pressure Eastern states to live up to the Helsinki Final Act more faithfully. At Belgrade, pointed criticism was part of a new assertive role for the United States, and it signaled to Eastern European states that, unless they withdrew from the CSCE, they must change their human rights practices or face international humiliation in Madrid. Fascell later wrote, "The Belgrade review period did something no other international meeting has done: it broke the silence barrier on human rights."[126] The tactics of the West, and in particular those of Goldberg, established that Helsinki follow-up meetings would actively emphasize the review of Helsinki implementation in an attempt to overcome the unenforceable nature of the agreement. As later chapters will show, Goldberg's approach of exerting pressure through the Helsinki process necessitated greater allied support to be

---

[123] Arthur J. Goldberg, "The Helsinki Final Act Revisited," *American Foreign Policy Newsletter* (April 1982): 2.

[124] Fascell, "Human Rights: The United States at Belgrade," 41. Although Sergei Kondrashev suggested if the United States had been willing to make more progress on arms control, Soviet officials might have made more concessions on human rights and humanitarian contacts at the Belgrade Meeting. Sergei Kondrashev, "'SALT II and the Growth of Mistrust': Conference #2 of the Carter-Brezhnev Project," National Security Archive.

[125] In one Reagan-era human rights official's view, Goldberg had made "the Helsinki Final Act come truly alive." Schifter, "The UN Charter and the Entry of Human Rights into the Field of International Relations," in Adamishin and Schifter, *Human Rights, Perestroika, and the End of the Cold War*, 70.

[126] Fascell, "Breaking the Silence Barrier," in Rubin and Spiro, eds., *Human Rights and U.S. Foreign Policy*, 181.

effective. For progress to result from such efforts, however, it would require leadership in Moscow with a different conception of the Soviet Union's place in the world.

Importantly, during Carter's presidency public opinion of interested constituencies shifted from worrying that the Helsinki Final Act legitimized Soviet domination of Eastern Europe to embracing its opportunities for human rights improvements. The *Wall Street Journal*, which previously had pleaded "Jerry Don't Go," was one of many to concede that "we were wrong" to tell Ford not to go to Helsinki.[127] Furthermore, Carter's administration created an effective foundation for Reagan's efforts to use the Helsinki Final Act as a tool in his struggle with the Soviet Union, and Reagan's presidency ultimately benefited from the strategy Carter initiated.[128]

The positive results were apparent in retrospect, but at the time tangible benefits were less clear. In the immediate aftermath of the Belgrade Meeting, the Soviet Union and its allies continued their repression of human rights activists. For example, Václav Havel was arrested and given a four-year sentence for his role in the founding of VONS, or the Committee to Protect the Unjustly Prosecuted, and, as mentioned earlier, the Soviets handed down a harsh sentence to Anatoly Shcharansky.[129] A further, significant development was Sakharov's arrest on January 22, 1980, for opposing the Soviet invasion of Afghanistan and his sentencing to internal exile to Gorky, a city inaccessible to foreigners.[130] Soviet officials had been increasingly threatened by what they viewed as "hostile activities" by Sakharov. In their view, he was responsible for what they regarded as repeated interferences in their internal affairs as well as anti-Soviet elements within the country. Thus, they formulated measures to restrict his activities.[131] At a January 3, 1980, Politburo meeting to discuss

---

[127] A notation on the piece in Millicent Fenwick's files read: "W. St. Journal eats crow!" "The Belgrade Watch," *Wall Street Journal* June 16, 1977, in Folder 19, Box 274, Fenwick Papers.

[128] Robert Gates writes in his memoirs, "I believe historians and political observers alike have failed to appreciate the importance of Jimmy Carter's contribution to the collapse of the Soviet Union and the end of the Cold War." Gates, *From the Shadows*, 177.

[129] William M. Brinton, "Gorbachev and the Revolution of 1989–90," in William M. Brinton and Alan Rinzler, eds., *Without Force or Lies: Voices from the Revolution of Central Europe in 1989–90: Essays, Speeches, and Eyewitness Accounts* (San Francisco: Mercury House, 1990), 377.

[130] Sakharov, *Memoirs*, 507–14.

[131] Andropov and Rydenko to the Central Committee, December 26, 1979, REEADD-RADD Collection, National Security Archive. At Orlov's trial, Sakharov scuffled with

Sakharov's fate, Gromyko said, "The question of Sakharov has ceased to be a purely domestic question. He finds an enormous number of responses abroad. All the anti-Soviet scum, all this rabble revolves around Sakharov. It is impossible to ignore this situation any longer."[132] Several months later, Andropov assessed the decision to exile Sakharov to Gorky favorably, "The termination of Sakharov's contacts with foreigners has also brought a positive change in this situation surrounding him. This has not only limited his opportunities to send hostile libelous attacks, 'statements,' 'appeals,' 'protests,' etc. to the West, but has also significantly decreased the agitation around his name conducted earlier by foreign propaganda centers."[133]

Nonetheless, Belgrade motivated existing monitoring groups to continue their work and to strengthen the Helsinki network's transnational links. In the years that followed, Sakharov and others relentlessly sent missives to the West seeking to publicize the fate of human rights activists.[134] At the same time, human rights activists in the Soviet Union, Czechoslovakia, and Poland all increased their contacts with one another. For example, Polish Helsinki activist Zbigniew Romaszewski was in communication with Charter 77 activists, and KSS-KOR and Charter 77 sent representatives to a meeting at the Polish-Czechoslovakian border in August 1978.[135] Romaszewski later visited Sakharov and other dissidents in Moscow in January 1979 and issued a statement announcing cooperation among them.[136] Subsequently, Sakharov wrote to KSS-KOR in November 1979 to request "more regular contact and for the unification

a police officer. Although the official Soviet stance had been, in the Politburo's view, extreme patience, this affront was seen as impossible to ignore. Summary of Politburo Meeting, June 8, 1978, Perechen 42, Dokument 71, Fond 89. Constantine Pleshakov argues Andropov was quite lenient toward Sakharov. Pleshakov, *There is No Freedom Without Bread!*, 89.

[132] Politburo Transcript, January 3, 1980, in Rubenstein and Gribanov, eds., *The KGB File of Andrei Sakharov*, 247.

[133] Andropov to Central Committee, April 2, 1980, in Rubenstein and Gribanov, eds., *The KGB File of Andrei Sakharov*, 253.

[134] See for example Sakharov's letter to the International Labor Organization, the Federation of American Scientists, and Federation Director Jeremy Stone describing the repression of Georgian and Ukrainian Helsinki monitors. Sakharov to International Labor Organization et al., March 8, 1978, S.II.2.2.69.1, Box 29, Sakharov Papers. Sakharov also wrote to Fascell to share with him a Moscow Helsinki Group document and update him on the plight of Orlov and other dissidents. Sakharov to Fascell, July 19, 1978, S.III.1.1.27, Box 58, Sakharov Papers.

[135] Lipski, *KOR*, 280–1.

[136] Ibid., 279–80; and Zuzowski, "The Origins of Open Organised Dissent in Today's Poland," 83.

of our [dissidents] struggle for human rights in Poland, Czechoslovakia and the Soviet Union."[137]

The implementation review also inspired new NGOs to form. In addition to the formation of Helsinki Watch and the IHF, which will be discussed in the subsequent chapter, other groups devoted to the plight of human rights activists developed. One such group, Scientists for Orlov and Shcharansky (SOS), disseminated two petitions, one of which garnered 1,750 signatures pledging scientists to "withhold all personal cooperation with the Soviet Union" until Shcharansky and Orlov were released.[138] The second was signed by 660 American scientists and pledged a more far-reaching commitment to boycott international conferences in the USSR, to withhold support for expanding Soviet–American exchanges, and to oppose most-favored-nation trading status or technology transfers for the Soviet Union.[139] American professional associations such as the Association for Computing Machinery also acted in response to the dissidents' arrest; the computer machinists voted against cooperating with or sponsoring any meeting in the Soviet Union.[140]

Although the Carter administration's approach contributed to strengthening the follow-up mechanism of the Helsinki Final Act in the long-run, in the short-term its strategy was one of the factors precipitating the decline of Soviet–American détente. The Soviet invasion of Afghanistan in 1979 effectively ended efforts at productive relations and led the United States to institute widespread sanctions. American outrage produced a range of actions including delays on the establishment of new consuls, suspension of most economic and cultural exchanges, a grain embargo, military and economic aid to Pakistan, withdrawal of the SALT II treaty from Senate consideration, and a boycott of the 1980

---

[137] Zuzowski, "The Origins of Open Organised Dissent in Today's Poland," 83.

[138] Sakharov's arrest prompted Scientists for Orlov and Shcharansky to change its name to Scientists for Sakharov, Orlov and Shcharansky. For further discussion of Western scientists' activism, see Paul Rubinson, "'For Our Soviet Colleagues': Scientific Internationalism, Human Rights, and the Cold War," in Petra Goedde, William Hitchcock, and Akira Iriye, eds., *Human Rights in the Twentieth Century: An International History* (New York: Oxford University Press, 2011), 245–64.

[139] Robert G. Kaiser, "U.S. Scientists Protest Jailings," March 2, 1979, *Washington Post*, A1. At the beginning of April 1979, the Central Committee formulated a plan of action to address activism by Scientists for Orlov and Shcharansky. Central Committee Decree, April 3, 1979, Perechen 33, Dokument 21, Fond 89.

[140] Anatoly Shcharansky, Commission on Security and Cooperation in Europe (CSCE): Belgrade Conference, 1977 [1 of 4], Briefing Books, Legislative Relations, Dole Senate Papers.

Moscow Olympics. Carter wanted to indicate that regular relations could not go forward given the Soviet intervention. In the view of some, the turn in Soviet–American relations signaled the advent of a new Cold War.[141] The Soviet invasion loomed over the CSCE meeting in Madrid, hardening Western and neutral approaches to the negotiations and fostering a more rigorous examination of the Soviet record.

[141] Raymond L. Garthoff, *Détente and Confrontation: American-Soviet Relations from Nixon to Reagan* rev. ed. (Washington: Brookings Institution, 1994), 977–1124; and *CSCE Digest*, January 11, 1980, Folder 3, Box 141, Part I, Goldberg Papers. In Dobrynin's view, Carter was obsessed with Afghanistan because he saw it as a direct threat, part of a larger "arc of crisis" spurred by Soviet expansion, and that his reaction prevented progress on any other issues. Dobrynin, *In Confidence*, 444.

5

Helsinki Watch, the IHF, and the Transnational Campaign for Human Rights in Eastern Europe

In the aftermath of Belgrade, the long-term future of the CSCE at the official level appeared temporarily secure, with the Madrid Review Meeting scheduled to open in 1980 and the United States exerting increased influence in the Helsinki process. The outlook for monitoring groups, however, was far bleaker as repression of Helsinki activists in Eastern Europe escalated.[1] To fill the void and build upon their work, NGOs outside of Eastern Europe were needed to aid the monitoring efforts. Two critical groups emerged: Helsinki Watch, a United States-based group made up of private citizens that became the most influential Western NGO devoted to Helsinki monitoring, and later the International Helsinki Federation for Human Rights, an international umbrella organization for Helsinki groups across CSCE states. Importantly, Helsinki Watch was part of a broader network of human rights organizations developing internationally in the 1970s, and it played a central role in the rising profile of human rights activism. Helsinki Watch and its allies in the IHF used their influence to press Western and neutral CSCE delegations to focus attention on the plight of Eastern Helsinki monitors and abuses of human rights more broadly. The IHF also widened nongovernmental support for Helsinki monitoring by incorporating a broader range of Western voices. It strengthened

---

[1] By May 1978 the Carter administration assessed the Soviets as having "been generally successful in hindering, if not completely suppressing, dissident activity." An update on the state of the human rights movement in the Soviet Union asserted: "The morale of the small core of activists is very low, and their hopes for the future are bleak." Memorandum, May 25, 1978, in Munteanu and Terzieva, eds., *From Global Politics to Human Rights: The CSCE Follow up Meeting, Belgrade, 1977.*

and formalized diffuse Helsinki monitoring activities, thereby heightening their effectiveness.

The establishment of Helsinki Watch was rooted not only in the increasing repression of Eastern human rights activists but also the recognition that existing Western groups were not always focused exclusively on Helsinki.[2] The respective groups that comprised the "Helsinki lobby" had varying mandates and other areas of focus. In hearings before the Commission, Goldberg noted this dynamic and identified a role for a non-governmental United States Helsinki Committee similar to the Moscow Helsinki Group and facilitated its creation by securing funding from the Ford Foundation.[3] According to Oliver, Goldberg's idea to start Helsinki Watch came from his experience working with NGOs in his years at the United Nations.[4] It is possible Goldberg was also inspired by a September 1975 proposal by Freedom House, an American NGO devoted to political rights and civil liberties, to form a "Helsinki Watch" that would "observe whether and how these accords were implemented."[5]

The mandate of Helsinki Watch, as the committee became known, was to produce reports on human rights abuses in the Soviet Union, Eastern Europe, and the United States, all of which would be released when the next CSCE meeting opened in Madrid in 1980.[6] When the

[2] There was a tradition of American concern for Soviet dissidents that pre-dated Helsinki Watch. For example, the Committee in Defense of Andrei Amal'rik pleaded for his release in 1973. The Committee was made up of prominent American writers and publishers, including Robert Bernstein. Press Release, July 19, 1973, Box 260, Accession 3560–005, Jackson Papers.

[3] The Ford Foundation granted Helsinki Watch $400,000 for two years, which it was assumed would cover the organization's costs through the end of the Madrid Meeting. Laber, *The Courage of Strangers*, 98. Funding from the Ford Foundation and other philanthropic foundations spurred considerable human rights activity in the 1970s. Cmiel, "The Emergence of Human Rights Politics in the United States," 1235, 1244. For further discussion of growing foundation support for international human rights work between 1977 and 1987, see Kathryn Sikkink, "Human Rights, Principled Issue-Networks, and Sovereignty in Latin America," *International Organization* 47 (1993): 420.

[4] R. Spencer Oliver Interview, February 26, 2008.

[5] "Mount the Helsinki Watch!" September 9, 1975, Folder 6, Box 2, Freedom House Records, Public Policy Papers, Department of Rare Books and Special Collections, Princeton University, Princeton, New Jersey. Other initiatives developed to draw attention to the plight of Helsinki monitors, including a series of events known as the International Sakharov Hearings. The hearings examined the human rights abuses in the Soviet Union and Eastern Europe, but they did not lead to sustained Helsinki monitoring.

[6] Scrutinizing United States compliance was seen as essential to maintaining international credibility. Laber, *The Courage of Strangers*, 97–99, 103, 117; Commission on Security and Cooperation in Europe, "The Belgrade Followup Meeting to the Conference on Security and Cooperation in Europe: A Report and Appraisal," May 17, 1978, Hearings and Reports 1977, Box 2442, Fascell Papers; R. Spencer Oliver Interview, February 26, 2008; and Jeri Laber Interview, April 29, 2008.

Madrid Meeting dragged on for years, Helsinki Watch became a permanent fixture of the Helsinki process, lasting far beyond its original mandate.

Those most active in the organization, including Robert Bernstein, Orville Schell, Aryeh Neier, and Jeri Laber, were drawn to human rights work through their professional and academic experiences. Robert Bernstein, president of the publisher Random House, became interested in Soviet human rights abuses due to firsthand contact with Soviet censorship in the early 1970s, his relationship with Soviet human rights advocate Andrei Sakharov, and a commitment to publishing texts banned in the Soviet Union.[7] Bernstein took the initiative in forming a nongovernmental Helsinki committee and invited both Schell and Neier to take leadership roles. Schell had been president of the New York Bar Association and had become interested in human rights after visiting the Soviet Union on a trip sponsored by the Union Councils for Soviet Jews.[8] Neier had worked as executive director of the American Civil Liberties Union (ACLU) and had come to know Bernstein through a joint Random House-ACLU lawsuit against the Central Intelligence Agency.[9] Laber, who became Helsinki Watch's executive director, had written a master's thesis on Soviet writers pressing for greater freedoms.[10] She became more involved in human rights issues, including joining an Amnesty International chapter, after reading an article by Rose Styron on torture in the *New Republic*.[11] While participating in an Amnesty International rally on behalf of Soviet dissident Vladimir Bukovsky, Laber met Bernstein, who later hired her for a position at the Association of American Publishers' International Freedom to Publish Committee. It was through this association that Laber came to work for Bernstein when he formed the Fund for Free Expression and later Helsinki Watch.[12]

Helsinki Watch was intended to complement, not replace, the Commission. According to Commission staff member Spencer Oliver, Goldberg was careful to meet with him and Fascell to assure them that this proposed committee would not be a rival to the Commission; instead it would help the Commission and broaden public support for Helsinki monitoring. As intended, the Commission and Helsinki Watch worked

---

[7] Laber, *The Courage of Strangers*, 79–80.
[8] Ibid., 98.
[9] Aryeh Neier, *Taking Liberties: Four Decades in the Struggle for Rights* (New York: Public Affairs, 2003), 149–50, 152.
[10] Laber, *The Courage of Strangers*, 54–5.
[11] Ibid., 69–71.
[12] Ibid., 74–8, 83.

together closely in the subsequent years.[13] According to Oliver, the two bodies communicated almost weekly, coordinated hearings, and were usually in agreement about questions such as the United States approach to the Madrid Meeting.[14]

Helsinki Watch was conceived as an organization devoted to advocacy and focused primarily on Eastern European human rights monitors who suffered harassment, arrest, or imprisonment for their efforts. It worked to keep their repression under an international spotlight and pursued an array of tactics to do so. Helsinki Watch's influence was built in part upon the comprehensive research reports it produced. In addition, Helsinki Watch staff members traveled regularly to Eastern Europe to offer material and moral support to human rights activists there, and in the United States and Western Europe, they worked to keep international attention focused on imprisoned monitors and those suffering state repression.

Helsinki Watch aspired to influence a range of audiences. First, it wanted to shape United States policy for the Madrid Meeting and the CSCE meetings that later followed. In speaking about the organization's relationship with United States policymakers, Helsinki Watch Vice Chair Aryeh Neier said, "[Helsinki Watch] tried to keep them honest and focused on the human rights issues."[15] Second, Helsinki Watch hoped it could win support for Helsinki monitoring among other Western and neutral CSCE diplomats. Third, and far more ambitious, Helsinki Watch aspired to reach Eastern European diplomats and officials to influence their attitudes toward the Helsinki Final Act and its monitors in the Soviet Union and Eastern Europe. Finally, Helsinki Watch recognized an important audience in the United States public, whose support of official and nongovernmental efforts in the defense of human rights was important to the long-term success of Helsinki advocacy. Spencer Oliver argues Helsinki Watch importantly fostered broad-based support for its mission, giving "definition to the Helsinki process in American public opinion."[16]

To accomplish these far-reaching goals, Helsinki Watch pursued a range of methods. Over time, it became well-known for the quality and comprehensiveness of its research reports, which were relied upon by policymakers, diplomats, and others interested in Helsinki compliance. Helsinki

[13] R. Spencer Oliver Interview, February 26, 2008.
[14] Ibid.
[15] Aryeh Neier Interview, April 24, 2008.
[16] R. Spencer Oliver Interview, February 26, 2008.

Watch, and in particular its executive director, Jeri Laber, also used more mainstream venues to highlight repressed or imprisoned individuals by issuing press releases, writing op-eds, and speaking out publicly. Finally, Helsinki Watch sought to influence CSCE diplomats through direct contact, making themselves a permanent, visible presence at CSCE meetings.

Helsinki Watch worked to maintain concerted, public pressure on the United States government to pay attention to Helsinki issues, and its press releases and research reports were essential to its efforts to employ "information politics."[17] The organization's reports were based on testimony of recent emigrants, firsthand research conducted through fact-finding missions, and documents transmitted from Eastern Europe, often from domestic monitoring groups such as the Moscow Helsinki Group. In addition, Helsinki Watch often worked with Ludmilla Alekseeva, the Moscow Helsinki Group representative in the West, to compile research reports on particular types of human rights abuses or assessments of the human rights record of a specific country. According to Aryeh Neier, the dependability and detailed nature of Helsinki Watch's research heightened its influence: "We were able to get, I think, the most reliable information that was available on the individual victims of abuse."[18]

Helsinki Watch was sophisticated in its tactics, mixing well-researched reports with poignant stories that enabled individual connections to the issue. The American public was exposed not only to the names of these Eastern activists but also to their faces, as the group accompanied as many of its reports and press releases as possible with photographs. Helsinki Watch's emphasis on visually representing dissidents had begun with Laber's first visit to Moscow in 1979, when she photographed activists gathered to meet with her in Sakharov's apartment to dramatic effect; the photos were later published in *Life* magazine.[19]

Laber's efforts were part of a concerted campaign by Helsinki Watch of "symbolic politics" to make repressed human rights activists familiar to the broader public. As Neier later said, "In order for people to rally to the human rights cause it is very often necessary for them to have an identification with individuals ... And when people started to get to know the names of someone like Yuri Orlov or Havel or Michnik, that was important."[20] In several instances, Helsinki Watch was even

[17] Keck and Sikkink, *Activists Beyond Borders*, 16.
[18] Aryeh Neier Interview, April 24, 2008; and Neier, *Taking Liberties*, 157.
[19] Laber, *The Courage of Strangers*, 118.
[20] Aryeh Neier Interview, April 24, 2008. Adam Michnik was imprisoned for his activism in Solidarity.

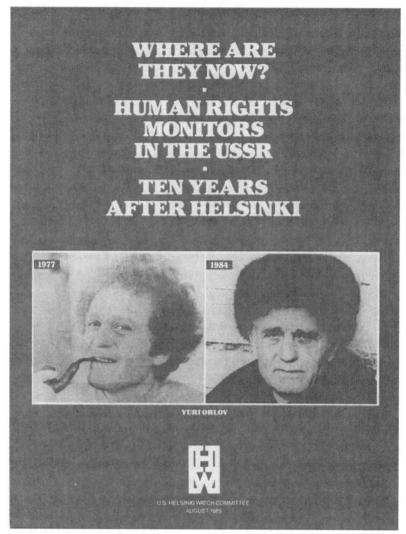

WHERE ARE
THEY NOW?
.
HUMAN RIGHTS
MONITORS
IN THE USSR
.
TEN YEARS
AFTER HELSINKI

1977   1984

YURI ORLOV

U.S. HELSINKI WATCH COMMITTEE
AUGUST 1985

FIGURE 3. Helsinki Watch produced a report entitled, "Where Are They Now?: Monitors in the USSR: Ten Years After Helsinki." The report's cover juxtaposed photos of a smiling Yuri Orlov in 1977 before his arrest and a weary Orlov in exile seven years later. Courtesy of Human Rights Watch.

able to document the toll of imprisonment on particular activists. For example, Helsinki Watch produced a report entitled, "Where Are They Now?: Monitors in the USSR: Ten Years After Helsinki." The report's cover juxtaposed photos of a smiling Orlov in 1977 before his arrest and a weary Orlov in exile seven years later.[21] According to Laber, Helsinki Watch worked to reach its primary audience, the United States public: "Our purpose was to try to dramatize the situations of these people."[22] Similarly, in 1982, Helsinki Watch began a "Forgotten Man of the Year" campaign to highlight someone "who would have been in the news if he or she had not been silenced by imprisonment." Orlov was Helsinki Watch's first "Forgotten Man of the Year"; his plight was dramatized through a poster, a press release, and repeated efforts by Helsinki Watch staff to have journalists write about his story.[23]

In a similar vein, Laber and others also published letters to the editor, articles, and op-eds in prominent national publications such as the *New York Times, Washington Post, Wall Street Journal,* and the *New York Review of Books.* Helsinki Watch's goal was to foster support for Helsinki monitors' plight and to "shame and embarrass" repressive governments. For example, in an op-ed in the *New York Times* on the occasion of the tenth anniversary of the Moscow Helsinki Group's founding, Laber wrote that Orlov had "endured in a manmade hell of physical cruelty and broken dreams."[24] In Neier's view, Laber made the stories of Eastern European dissidents immediate to a wide audience:

[She] proved an effective advocate by writing frequently for newspapers and magazines about the Russians, Poles, Czechs, and others she encountered on her

[21] U.S. Helsinki Watch Committee, "Where Are They Now?: Monitors in the USSR: Ten Years After Helsinki," August 1985, USSR: Helsinki Accords 10th Anniversary, 1985, Box 16, Country Files, Cathy Fitzpatrick Files, Record Group 7, HRWR; and Anna Husarska, "'Conscience Trigger': The Press and Human Rights," in Power and Allison, eds., *Realizing Human Rights*, 342. Recent scholarship on activism spurred by the 1973 coup in Chile suggests that Helsinki Watch's approach was reminiscent of the tactics of Amnesty International and Chilean solidarity groups. In one example, a booklet, entitled "To Save the Lives of People Kidnapped by DINA," distributed by the International Commission of Enquiry into the Crimes of the Military Junta, is similar to the Helsinki Watch publication, "Where Are They Now?" in content and layout. Patrick William Kelly, "When the People Awake: The Transnational Solidarity Movement, the Pinochet Junta, and the Human Rights Moment of the 1970s," paper presented at "A New Global Morality?: The Politics of Human Rights and Humanitarianism in the 1970s," Freiburg Institute for Advanced Studies, Freiburg, Germany, June 2010. I thank Patrick Kelly for sharing the booklet with me. See also Jan Eckel, "'Under a Magnifying Glass': The International Human Rights Campaign against Chile in the Seventies," in Hoffmann, ed., *Human Rights in the Twentieth Century*, 332.

[22] Laber reports she and her staff were very focused on the individual dissidents they were championing, because they had met many or were well acquainted with their personal stories and therefore very invested in supporting them. Jeri Laber Interview, April 29, 2008.

[23] Press Release, December 2, 1982, USSR: Orlov, Yuri: Poster [Campaign], 1982–1983, Box 59, Country Files, Files of Jeri Laber, Record Group 7, HRWR.

[24] Jeri Laber, "10 Years Later, the Legacy of the Moscow Helsinki Group," *New York Times* May 11, 1986. According to Orlov's memoirs, he suffered force-feeding in response to his

frequent travels to the region who stood up to persecution. Her impressionistic articles humanized men and women with unfamiliar-sounding names struggling against apparently all-powerful regimes with what seemed then little or no prospect of making headway. Thereby, Jeri helped many in the West care about what happened to individuals who otherwise had only a blurred collective identity as dissidents.[25]

Closely connected with Helsinki Watch's advocacy of repressed dissidents was the support it gave monitoring groups and individuals in Eastern Europe. Attention by Helsinki Watch could include offering financial support, providing some degree of protection, or simply improving morale. Helsinki Watch records demonstrate efforts over the years to secure teaching and research appointments at American universities for those facing state repression, to publish Eastern European monitoring groups' reports, and to deliver medicine and office supplies to activists in the East.

Helsinki Watch's first and strongest connections to human rights monitors in Eastern Europe were made in Moscow. Sakharov had issued an appeal for "the creation of a unified international committee to defend all Helsinki Watch members" in May 1978, and Helsinki Watch viewed its organization in that mold.[26] Laber subsequently initiated efforts to open up direct lines of communication with the Soviet and Eastern European monitoring groups; those efforts produced a joint statement by Helsinki Watch and the Moscow Helsinki Group in July 1979 that called for Helsinki monitoring groups to be established in all CSCE signatory countries.[27] To draw attention to their proposal, Helsinki Watch organized a public ceremony during which it phoned the Moscow Helsinki Group and spoke briefly with Yelena Bonner before the call was involuntarily

---

hunger strikes and was repeatedly sentenced to solitary confinement. Orlov, *Dangerous Thoughts*, 246–59.

[25] Neier, *Taking Liberties*, 156.

[26] Andrei Sakharov, "Human Rights ... A Common Goal," Support for US Helsinki Committee, 1978, Box 29, General Files, New York Office Files, Record Group 7, HRWR.

[27] The first indication that the Moscow Helsinki Group was aware of the existence of Helsinki Watch came in a March 1979 letter from Sakharov and Naum Meiman, but the letter was intended for Scientists for Orlov and Shcharansky, a scientists' advocacy group, not Helsinki Watch, demonstrating Helsinki Watch needed to enhance its ties with the Group. Meiman and Sakharov to Colleagues, March 10, 1979, S.III.1.1.33, Box 58, Sakharov Papers; Laber to Bernstein, April 26, 1979, Helsinki Watch Steering Committee, 1979, Box 3, General Files, New York Office Files, Record Group 7, HRWR; and Laber to Fishlow, December 31, 1978, Helsinki Watch – Hearings [1978–1979], Box 1, ibid.

disconnected, heightening the drama of the event.[28] Speaking to those assembled, Helsinki Watch Chair Robert Bernstein noted the irony that "nothing has done more to focus the attention of the world on human rights abuses in the USSR and Czechoslovakia than the persecution of members of the Soviet Helsinki monitoring groups and of Charter 77."[29] Further heightening the public display of solidarity between the two groups, former Soviet dissidents Alexander Ginzburg, George Vins, Petro Grigorenko, and Alekseeva also spoke at the ceremony in New York.

Helsinki Watch wanted to forge further, direct connections with the Moscow Helsinki Group by sending a representative to the Soviet Union. In September 1979, Laber traveled to Moscow, ostensibly for the Moscow Book Fair, and met with members of the Moscow Helsinki Group at Sakharov's apartment.[30] The Group discussed how best to influence Soviet leaders, garner Western press coverage for the cause, and communicate despite government efforts to block mail.[31] Laber recounted the meeting:

I told the group who I was and that we had recently formed the U.S. Helsinki Watch in response to what was happening to them. I assured them that they were not alone, that we and others abroad were aware of the arrests and imprisonment of their members and were issuing protests. I suggested that we plan some joint actions, like issuing reports together and holding press conferences simultaneously at prearranged times.[32]

Laber's trip was an important step in connecting often geographically dispersed monitoring groups into a transnational network. The relationships forged by Laber and other Helsinki Watch staff members were important to Helsinki monitors in Eastern Europe. In former Soviet dissident Anatoly

[28] For further discussion of how such transnational connections were facilitated by advances in telecommunications, see Falk, *The Dilemmas of Dissidence in East-Central Europe*, 308.

[29] Joint Statement of the Moscow Group to Promote Observance of the Helsinki Accords in the USSR and of the American Helsinki Watch, July 31, 1979, USSR: [HW] Joint Statement of the Moscow and American Watch Group, 1979, Box 53, Country Files, Jeri Laber Files, Record Group 7, HRWR; Press Release, July 31, 1979, ibid.; and Statement to the Press by Bob Bernstein, July 31, 1979, ibid.

[30] For further discussion about how conferences, book fairs, and other avenues of exchange enabled the transnationalization of civil society, see Falk, *The Dilemmas of Dissidence in East-Central Europe*, 308.

[31] Memo to the Record, n.d., USSR: Alexeyeva, Ludmilla: Correspondence, 1976, 1978–1983, Box 2, Country Files, Cathy Fitzpatrick Files, Record Group 7, HRWR.

[32] Having met and spoken openly with dissidents in an apartment undoubtedly under surveillance, Laber had attracted the authorities' attention and was refused a Soviet visa in the years that followed. Laber, *The Courage of Strangers*, 117.

Shcharansky's view, Helsinki Watch was a "powerful light directed into the Soviet Union that [showed] what [was] really happening."[33]

Helsinki Watch also worked to establish links with activists and monitoring groups in Poland and Czechoslovakia, and Laber's memoirs recount her repeated trips to Eastern Europe to communicate with dissidents there.[34] Laber first traveled to Warsaw in September 1979, where she met with members of the Committee for Social Self-Defense (KSS-KOR) and facilitated efforts to form a group devoted to Helsinki monitoring within the KOR framework.[35] According to Laber, Polish activists began organizing a Helsinki commission immediately in response to her suggestion.[36] Polish activists also shared with her their efforts to reach out to Czech dissidents and the Moscow Helsinki Group, indicating connections were being formed amongst Helsinki activists in many directions.[37] When Laber visited again in 1981, the Polish Helsinki Committee was vigorously reporting on repression of union leaders and Solidarity members, who would later play a key role in transforming Poland.[38] Helsinki Watch supported these activists throughout the years that followed.[39]

Helsinki Watch worked to maintain connections with human rights activists across Eastern Europe, with Laber visiting Czechoslovakia again in September 1979 and late 1981. During her second trip, Laber met with Ivan Havel, the brother of imprisoned Charter 77 spokesman Václav Havel who was facing trial. Ivan Havel emphasized the importance of publicizing the plight of dissidents but noted that economic pressure could be more important than public rhetoric in influencing the Czechoslovak government, highlighting the importance of governmental pressure on behalf of repressed activists.[40]

---

[33] Natan Sharansky Interview, November 19, 2009.

[34] Jeri Laber Interview, April 29, 2008.

[35] KOR had changed its name to the Committee for Social Self-Defense (KSS-KOR) in late 1977.

[36] Laber, *The Courage of Strangers*, 148.

[37] Memo for the Record, n.d., USSR: [HW] J. Laber's Memos [on Eastern Bloc Meetings], 1979, Box 53, Country Files, Jeri Laber Files, Record Group 7, HRWR.

[38] Laber, *The Courage of Strangers*, 151–2. The Polish Helsinki Committee and the Polish Helsinki Commission were distinct organizations.

[39] In one instance, Neier and his wife traveled to Poland in March 1984 to meet activists, including Zofia Romaszewska, whose husband Zbigniew was the founder of the Polish Helsinki Commission and imprisoned for his role in Solidarity. Neier, *Taking Liberties*, 246. Solidarity, the Polish trade union that became a larger social and political movement, was forced underground when Poland declared martial law on December 13, 1981.

[40] Memorandum for the Record, n.d., Czechoslovakia: Conditions – General, 1977–1983, n.d., Box 3, Country Files, Janet Fleischman Files, Record Group 7, HRWR.

Helsinki Watch worked to develop relations with dissidents broadly, including in countries where the human rights situation was less severe and activists were not as well-known. During a trip to Hungary, Laber found two groups of dissidents had emerged: Democratic Opposition and Nationalist Opposition, both focused on monitoring human rights outside of the country, in particular the situation of Hungarian minorities.[41] In 1983, members of Helsinki Watch traveled to Hungary again to meet with dissidents; while there, they met with people who had documented Helsinki violations and were interested in forming a Hungarian Helsinki group. Laber, however, discouraged formal establishment of a Hungarian group out of concern for the safety of the activists.[42]

Laber's trip reports and memoirs illuminate the challenges to making transnational human rights connections in this period. First, Laber reports she tried to remain as inconspicuous as possible during her travels, listing tourism as the reason for her visit and "housewife" as her occupation. Similarly, she rolled up her notes from conversations with dissidents and kept them at her fingertips in her coat pockets rather than risk losing them in a search of her suitcase.[43] Second, maintaining contact was a recurring problem. Despite Helsinki Watch's efforts to communicate its formation to Czech dissidents by postal mail, only some of the letters reached their recipients; news of Helsinki Watch's formation was spread more effectively by Voice of America reporting.[44] When Laber met with Czech dissidents in late 1981, one reported that he thought Helsinki Watch had become dormant given the lack of successful communication in the two years previous, a typical illustration of the difficulties in maintaining connections among Helsinki monitoring groups.[45] Third, and perhaps most significant, in many Eastern European countries discussing human rights abuses with an American was grounds for harassment, arrest, or imprisonment, making the potential costs of informal or formal connections quite high.

Despite the frustrations Laber and Helsinki Watch encountered in their efforts to keep lines of communication to Eastern Europe open, there

[41] The external focus may have been a measure of self-preservation. Laber, *The Courage of Strangers*, 154–60.

[42] Memorandum, March 8, 1982, Hungary: Independent Organizations, 1981–1987, Box 29, Country Files, Janet Fleischman Files, Record Group 7, HRWR.

[43] Laber, *The Courage of Strangers*, 134, 146.

[44] Memo for the Record, n.d., USSR: [HW] J. Laber's Memos [on Eastern Bloc Meetings]; 1979, Box 53, Country Files, Jeri Laber Files, Record Group 7, HRWR.

[45] Memorandum for the Record, n.d., Czechoslovakia: Conditions – General, 1977–1983, n.d., Box 3, Country Files, Janet Fleischman Files, Record Group 7, HRWR.

were signs that their endeavors were deeply valued by dissidents. For example, after the head of the Helsinki Committee in Poland, Zbigniew Romaszewski, was arrested, a note was smuggled out of Poland requesting someone to "please find the person from the US Helsinki Watch Committee who came to Warsaw in 1981" and ask her to act to "save the Romaszewskis."[46] Eastern European activists would later often attribute their survival, release from prison, or permission to emigrate to advocacy by Helsinki Watch. For example, in June 1985, Yugoslav dissident Mihajlo Markovic wrote to Neier asking for his help with a Yugoslav facing trial and cited Neier's work on behalf of other Yugoslav dissidents, "You have literally saved them from very long prison sentences."[47]

As its reputation developed over the course of the Madrid Meeting, Helsinki Watch was able to wield increasing influence, at times greater than states could exert. Helsinki Watch's status as a nongovernmental organization to some degree freed it from broader problems in East–West relations that prevented progress at the governmental and at the state level. Assistant Secretary of State for Human Rights and Humanitarian Affairs Paula Dobriansky has argued human rights organizations such as Helsinki Watch and Amnesty International can "sometimes accomplish more than the U.S. government. This usually occurs in dealing with individual human rights cases because a nationalistic government sometimes finds it easier to give into the demands of world public opinion than to grant the official request of the U.S. government."[48] The United States ambassador in Prague similarly emphasized the dependent nature of state-level human rights advocacy, writing to Helsinki Watch: "Our relations [with the Czechoslovak government] are so bad here that we can't help ... much!"[49]

---

[46] Bulletin #5, December 6, 1982, USSR: International Helsinki Federation for Human Rights, 1982–1987, Box 19, Country Files, Cathy Fitzpatrick Files, Record Group 7, HRWR; and Laber to the Editor, *New York Times*, December 8, 1982. According to Romaszewski, neither he nor his wife, Zofia, wrote the note asking for Helsinki Watch's intervention nor were they aware such a plea had been written. Zbigniew Romaszewski, written communication to the author, January 26, 2010. Romaszewski reported that several NGOs, including an Amnesty International chapter in the Faroe Islands, the American Society of Physicians, and a French railway trade union carefully monitored his case while he was imprisoned.

[47] Markovic to Neier, June 7, 1985, Yugoslavia: Defense [of Yugoslav dissidents] Europe, 1984–1985, Box 9, Country Files, Cathy Fitzpatrick Files, Record Group 7, HRWR.

[48] Paula J. Dobriansky, "Human Rights and U.S. Foreign Policy," *The Washington Quarterly* (Spring 1989): 167.

[49] Luers to Fitzpatrick, July 20, 1984, Czechoslovakia: General, 1984–1986, Box 16, Country Files, Files of Jeri Laber, Record Group 7, HRWR.

Surrounded by an abundance of groups trying to advance their objectives at Madrid, Helsinki Watch recognized that forming connections among like-minded groups across CSCE states could facilitate more effective human rights advocacy. Helsinki Watch's initiative built upon earlier, international efforts at coordination, including several meetings of European and American NGOs focused on human rights. One effort was organized by Eugen Voss, a leader of Faith in the Second World or G2W in German, as well as two Swiss journalists, Ulrich Kaegi and Jürg Steinacher; they invited Western European groups focused on Eastern Europe to a meeting of the Preparatory Committee for the European Helsinki Group, which was attended by representatives from twenty-three different groups.[50] The groups who attended these sessions coordinated activities for the Madrid Meeting, including meetings of nongovernmental representatives in Madrid and publications detailing violations of the Helsinki Final Act.[51] Records from these meetings make clear the international scope of Helsinki monitoring activity in advance of the Madrid Meeting.[52]

Subsequently, Helsinki Watch initiated the formation of the International Helsinki Federation for Human Rights, or IHF as it was called, which established a formal umbrella organization for Western, neutral, and Eastern national Helsinki committees. The IHF was formed at the urging of Aryeh Neier, who decided in early 1982 that Helsinki Watch should forge an alliance with NGOs in Western Europe. Identifying or establishing Helsinki groups in Western Europe to join what became the IHF, however, initially presented considerable challenges.[53] With the

---

[50] Swiss Helsinki Committee, July 28, 1988, Folder 4, Box 7, International Helsinki Federation for Human Rights Files, Record Group 7, HRWR; and Thomas Fischer, "'G2W – Faith in the Second World': Using the Helsinki Network to Overcome the East–West Divide," paper presented at the conference "Cold War Interactions Reconsidered," Helsinki, Finland, October 2009.

[51] Representatives from groups in the United States, France, the Netherlands, Switzerland, the FRG, and the United Kingdom attended. Tigrid to Sir/Madame, March 31, 1980, KSZE – Belgrad, Madrid, Stockholm (KVAE), G2W, Archiv für Zeitgeschichte, ETH Zürich (Archive for Contemporary History, Swiss Federal Institute of Technology Zurich), Zurich, Switzerland; and What Is Planned for the CSCE Conference in Madrid, May 20, 1980, ibid (hereafter ETH Zurich). A second session in June included representatives from Belgium and Sweden. I thank Thomas Fischer for sharing these documents with me.

[52] Help and Action proposal, June 25, 1980, KSZE – Belgrad, Madrid, Stockholm (KVAE), G2W, Archiv für Zeitgeschichte, ETH Zürich. One group even planned what they alternatively called a "motorcade" or a "Human Rights Relay" to draw attention to the opening of the Madrid Meeting. Essentially, they planned a caravan of vehicles from different Western European countries all traveling to Madrid; the spectacle of the "relay" was intended to draw attention to continuing human rights violations in Eastern Europe.

[53] Helsinki Watch's efforts to form the IHF were funded by the Ford Foundation and Rockefeller Foundation.

exception of monitoring groups in Eastern Europe and the Soviet Union, Helsinki Watch did not have many natural allies as other human rights organizations such as Amnesty International and the International League for Human Rights were not particularly active in that area of the world due in part to concerns about repercussions for local activists and a reluctance to undertake clandestine missions.[54] When Helsinki Watch began working on forming the umbrella group, only three countries in addition to the United States had existing groups devoted explicitly to Helsinki monitoring – the Netherlands, France, and Norway – and the groups were quite diverse.[55] For example, the Norwegian Helsinki Committee had more than 2,000 members and was funded in large part by the government. The Dutch committee, on the other hand, was comprised primarily of lawyers focused on legal aspects of the Helsinki process.

By July 1982, Laber had found representatives from eighteen countries to attend a September 1982 conference on this initiative in Lake Como, Italy.[56] By the second day of the conference, those assembled had agreed to form the IHF and to locate its headquarters in Vienna. The IHF announced its formation at a press conference in Madrid on November 9, 1982, with the founding members being Helsinki committees from Austria, Belgium, Canada, France, Norway, the Netherlands, Sweden, and the United States. Of the newly formed groups, a Swedish Helsinki Committee had been established in October 1982; its members were politicians, academics, expatriates from Eastern Europe, judges, and other professionals.[57] The Austrian Helsinki Group, which was formed officially in January 1983, included politicians, journalists, and academics, some of whom had previous involvement in Amnesty International.[58] The IHF's efforts focused on creating Helsinki committees in countries such as the FRG, Finland, Spain, and Great Britain as well as seeking money to fund the umbrella group.[59] In these early stages, however, the IHF was

---

[54] Jeri Laber Interview, April 29, 2008.
[55] The Swiss group G2W highlighted violations of human rights in Eastern Europe, with a particular focus on religious freedom. In addition, it offered direct support to Eastern Europeans by sending Bibles, clothing, food, and other supplies.
[56] Laber, *The Courage of Strangers*, 177–8.
[57] Swedish Helsinki Committee, n.d., Folder 19, Box 29, Jeri Laber: Country Files, Record Group 7, HRWR.
[58] First Official Meeting of Austrian Helsinki Committee, January 17, 1983, Folder 15, Box 4, International Helsinki Federation for Human Rights Files, Record Group 7, HRWR.
[59] Meeting Minutes, June 18–20, 1983, IHF: Coordinating Committee Meeting – Oslo, 1983, Box 2, International Helsinki Federation for Human Rights Files, Record Group 7, HRWR.

FIGURE 4. Representatives from eighteen countries attended a conference in Bellagio, Italy, in September 1982 that led to the formation of the International Helsinki Federation for Human Rights. Courtesy of Human Rights Watch.

often an organization in name only, as some committees were comprised of no more than a single concerned individual.[60] Initially it was deemed too dangerous for groups in Eastern Europe or Turkey to join officially; later the IHF came to include groups from Czechoslovakia, Denmark, the FRG, Italy, Poland, Switzerland, the United Kingdom, the Soviet Union, and Yugoslavia, among others. For the myriad of interest groups spread across CSCE countries, the IHF's founding created a means to connect with one another more easily while establishing a central organization to better guide the overarching network.

Helsinki Watch initiated the IHF to further a number of its goals against the backdrop of deteriorating American–Soviet relations. Helsinki Watch wanted to maintain its reputation as an independent organization, and the benefits that went along with it, despite the increasingly close

[60] Laber, *The Courage of Strangers*, 198–9. The national Helsinki committees that made up the IHF came to have dozens of prominent members but often limited financial resources. The exceptions were the Swedish and Norwegian Helsinki Committees, which had meaningful budgets and high membership numbers. Minnema to Bernstein, November 20, 1986, Folder 14, Box 4, International Helsinki Federation for Human Rights Files, Record Group 7, HRWR.

correlation between its objectives and the Reagan administration's policy toward the Soviet bloc. Neier believed establishing formal links to human rights groups in Western Europe would prevent Helsinki Watch from being "seen as a creature of the Reagan administration or solely as a group articulating publicly their concerns."[61] Neier writes about the IHF's creation:

The disastrous human rights situation in the Soviet Union was not the only factor in making me propose that we form an international organization. I was also concerned about our effectiveness in the US Helsinki Watch in opposing Soviet abuses. At that point, it had been a little more than a year since Ronald Reagan had become the fortieth president of the United States, and relations between Washington and Moscow had hit an all-time low.[62]

To this end, the European-based IHF offered a better opportunity to influence Soviet and Eastern European leaders as the USSR was increasingly focused on relations with Western European governments given the downturn in Soviet–American relations. According to Neier, "It seemed to me at that moment that if there were also Western European voices speaking out on violations in Soviet bloc countries, that would be more effective. If [Helsinki Watch] did it alone, we would be dismissed because of the general antagonisms at the time."[63] Neier was worried that Helsinki Watch's criticisms of the Soviet human rights record would get lost in the hostile, anti-Soviet language originating from the White House: "Prior to the establishment of the IHF, we didn't have any links with groups in Western countries that were concerned with human rights in the Soviet countries. We were only a US group concerned with the Soviet bloc countries."[64] As such, the mission of the IHF was to "generate Western European pressure against Soviet human rights abuses," and over time this goal would be realized.[65]

Importantly, the IHF was not comprised only of committees from NATO states, and in fact, Helsinki Watch explicitly sought to draw neutral and nonaligned countries into the organization at the outset. In

[61] Aryeh Neier Interview, April 24, 2008.
[62] Neier, *Taking Liberties*, 157.
[63] Aryeh Neier Interview, April 24, 2008.
[64] Ibid.
[65] Neier, *Taking Liberties*, 159. For example, in November 1982, representatives of the eight IHF national committees met with their countries' ambassadors to Madrid over dinner. Bulletin #5, December 6, 1982, USSR: International Helsinki Federation for Human Rights, 1982–1987, Box 19, Country Files, Cathy Fitzpatrick Files, Record Group 7, HRWR.

Laber's view, the IHF was established in large part as a means to reach out and influence the neutral and nonaligned delegations because they "held the balance" at the CSCE meetings.[66] The idea was that having member groups from these states would be a way to influence their respective delegations and governments to support Helsinki Watch's policy objectives.[67]

Regrettably, at the same time that Western activists were succeeding in greater organization and coordination efforts, Eastern monitoring groups declined in influence, as NGOs such as the Moscow Helsinki Group had been severely depleted in strength and numbers by arrest, exile, and imprisonment. Citing the "cruel persecution" of Moscow Helsinki Group members and in particular concerns about pending charges against 75-year-old member Sofia Kalistratova, the Group succumbed to government pressure and disbanded on September 6, 1982, announcing: "The Moscow Helsinki Group has been put into condition where further work is impossible ... Under these conditions the group ... has to cease its work."[68]

By March 1985, the IHF had committees in Austria, Canada, Denmark, the FRG, France, the Netherlands, Norway, Sweden, Switzerland, and the United States. The IHF was involved in the organization of a number of

[66] Diplomats from the neutral and nonaligned countries were often highly effective in bridging East–West differences during CSCE negotiations.

[67] Jeri Laber Interview, April 29, 2008. After the organization's formation, IHF member committees worked to exert pressure on CSCE delegates. In one example, Frantisek Janouch of the Swedish Helsinki Committee wrote to Danish, Swedish, and Dutch officials about Sakharov's case. Bodström to Janouch, February 6, 1984, USSR: Sakharov, Andrei May 1984, Box 49, Country Files, Cathy Fitzpatrick Files, Record Group 7, HRWR; Buwalda to Janouch, January 24, 1984, ibid.; Rosenthal to Janouch, January 26, 1984; ibid.

[68] Moscow Helsinki Group Document Number 195, September 6, 1982, USSR: Kalistratova, Sofia, 1982, Box 20, Country Files, Cathy Fitzpatrick Files, Record Group 7, HRWR; Statement on Closure of Moscow Helsinki Monitoring Group, September 9, 1982, USSR: Monitors, 1971–1979–1983, Box 26, ibid.; Goldberg, *The Final Act*, 278; and Laber, *The Courage of Strangers*, 182–3. Soviet officials regarded Bonner and Kalistratova's claims that they were subject to "unceasing persecution" to be a slanderous allegation. Central Committee Memorandum, September 12, 1982, REEADD-RADD Collection, National Security Archive. As one indication of the level of state repression in 1982, 229 religious leaders were imprisoned in the Soviet Union. In addition, eighteen were living in exile. The KGB had a section devoted to following activities of religious leaders. In 1982, it collected 2,500 reports of hostile activities. "Father Yakunin Says 20 Percent of USSR Clergy Worked for KGB," March 5, 1992, Folder 1, Box 70, George Lister Papers, Benson Latin American Collection, University of Texas Libraries, the University of Texas at Austin, Austin, Texas (hereafter Lister Papers). The report was based on an *Argumenty I Fakty* article published in January 1992.

conferences intended to increase interest in the CSCE.[69] IHF Executive Director Gerald Nagler traveled around Europe to maintain connections to existing IHF committees and attempting to organize new ones.[70] Activists often served as conduits of information from Eastern Europe; in one case a Dutch Amnesty International member reported to Laber a message that some Soviet political prisoners hoped could be transmitted to CSCE delegates.[71] The IHF developed a schedule of regular consultations in which representatives of many of the national committees would attend, report on their actions, and coordinate future activities. For example, Helsinki Committees worked together to celebrate Sakharov's sixty-fifth birthday as a means of highlighting his continued exile in Gorky. The committees also sought to coordinate observers at trials of dissidents and fact-finding visits to Eastern Europe.[72]

The establishment of the IHF marked a transition to a Helsinki "coalition," to use Sanjeev Khagram, James Riker, and Kathryn Sikkink's term, which could pursue a common strategy.[73] Given their shared values and common opponents, the national committees of the IHF had the potential for collective action and effective transnational advocacy.[74] Coordination among the Helsinki groups made the IHF's activism more effective as they organized fact-finding missions, publications of research reports, and fundraising. In the terminology of social movement scholars Kathryn Sikkink and Martha Finnemore, the IHF served as an "organizational platform" for those committed to human rights in the Soviet Union and Eastern Europe.[75] Greater cohesion among the disparate NGOs interested in the Helsinki process enabled them to advance their agenda more effectively, as would be seen in later CSCE meetings and in the Helsinki process as whole. First, greater consultation prevented

---

[69] Final Narrative Report, 1985, Folder 17, Box 7, International Helsinki Federation for Human Rights Files, Record Group 7, HRWR.

[70] Narrative Report 1983/4, Folder 17, Box 7, International Helsinki Federation for Human Rights Files, Record Group 7, HRWR.

[71] Boerlage to Laber, June 3, 1985, Folder 6, Box 6, International Helsinki Federation for Human Rights Files, Record Group 7, HRWR.

[72] Report, May 28, 1986, Folder 3, Box 5, International Helsinki Federation for Human Rights Files, Record Group 7, HRWR.

[73] Khagram, Riker and Sikkink, "From Santiago to Seattle," in Kagram et al., eds., *Restructuring World Politics*, 7.

[74] Sikkink, "Human Rights, Principled Issue-Networks, and Sovereignty in Latin America," 416; and Tarrow, *The New Transnational Activism*, 6.

[75] Martha Finnemore and Kathryn Sikkink, "International Norm Dynamics and Political Change," *International Organization* 52 (1998): 899.

duplicative efforts. Second, the ability to compose an international delegation or to speak with a united, international voice heightened the IHF's stature with political leaders. Third, locating the IHF's headquarters in Vienna created greater physical proximity between human rights activists and the countries they monitored.

Connections between the policymakers and activists who made up the Helsinki coalition were vital to the efficacy of the Helsinki process by providing direct access to the CSCE negotiations. Yet, at the same time Helsinki Watch was succeeding in gaining influence with Western and neutral policymakers, it faced continued frustration in shaping Eastern human rights practices. According to Neier,

The great challenge was, were you knocking your head against the wall? Did anybody really see the possibility of significant change in the Soviet bloc countries ... In general, there was a feeling of pessimism about ever having any significant impact on what was going on in the Soviet bloc countries. It was difficult to sustain a human rights effort in the face of that general pessimism.[76]

Working for years with little tangible success wore on the emotions of Helsinki Watch staff members, but they remained resolute: "We are sometimes asked how we can continue to work when so many of the individuals we seek to help remain in prison cells under harassment, when policies that we seek to change become more repressive rather than less. The answer, simply stated, is 'How can we *stop*?'"[77]

Establishment of the IHF connected Helsinki Watch and other national committees not only to one another, which was crucial in the efforts to improve the situation in Eastern Europe and the USSR, but also to a burgeoning, international human rights movement. Human rights advocates secured international legitimacy for the idea that governments' treatment of their own people is subject to international criticism and comment in part by changing ideas of national interest.[78] The Helsinki network was a key element of this broader, international movement, working to advance

---

[76] Aryeh Neier Interview, April 24, 2008.

[77] Helsinki Watch, A Report from Helsinki Watch: Annual Report, 1983, Helsinki Watch – Annual Report, 1983, Box 1, Subject Files, Cathy Fitzpatrick Files, Record Group 7, HRWR.

[78] Richard Falk, "The Infancy of Global Civil Society," in Geir Lundestad and Odd Arne Westad, eds., *Beyond the Cold War: New Dimensions in International Relations* (New York: Scandinavian University Press, 1993), 227; and Kathryn Sikkink, *Mixed Signals: U.S. Human Rights Policy and Latin America* (Ithaca: Cornell University Press, 2004), 20.

human rights at the same time as those fighting against apartheid in South Africa and those campaigning for human rights in Latin America and China.[79] Although outside the scope of this work, preliminary evidence suggests human rights movements learned from one another and improved protections of human rights overall in the years that followed.

[79] Audie Klotz, *Norms in International Relations: The Struggle Against Apartheid* (Ithaca: Cornell University Press, 1995); Keck and Sikkink, *Activists Beyond Borders;* Foot, *Rights Beyond Borders;* and Simon Stevens, "The Politics of Anti-Apartheid Activism in Britain in the Long 1970s," paper presented at "A New Global Morality?: The Politics of Human Rights and Humanitarianism in the 1970s," Freiburg Institute for Advanced Studies, Freiburg, Germany, June 2010.

6

Human Rights in East–West Diplomacy

The inability to reach a substantive concluding document at the Belgrade Meeting and increased Soviet and Eastern European repression of human rights activists in the meeting's wake raised questions about the potential promise of the Helsinki process. What followed was a complicated but important period in which political support for the Helsinki process solidified in the United States, Western allies united around CSCE objectives, and nongovernmental organizations developed a cohesive approach to promoting their agenda, but little progress was made in securing human rights observance in Eastern Europe. The significance of this period lies in the strengthening of the Western commitment to human rights such that Eastern European violations became an important component of East–West diplomacy. As this chapter illustrates, transnational connections forged in advance of and during the Madrid CSCE Review Meeting (1980–3) were a fundamental reason human rights took on such international importance. Western pressure throughout these years did not result in meaningful success but did convince Soviet leaders that progress on other questions such as trade and arms control was connected with their record on human rights. Although the sides remained at a virtual stalemate until 1985, the increasing attention to human rights in the preceding years was an integral part of the human rights reforms that arose once Mikhail Gorbachev came to power.

In stark contrast to Carter's amplified praise for the Helsinki process, Ronald Reagan openly questioned United States participation in the CSCE. In his 1976 election fight against Ford, and again during the 1980 campaign against Carter, Reagan criticized United States participation in the CSCE and Ford's signature of the Helsinki Final Act. Reagan saw a contradiction between overall American foreign policy toward the Soviet Union and United States participation in the CSCE. As an example, he noted the United States was boycotting the 1980 Moscow Olympics while maintaining plans to attend the CSCE Madrid Review Meeting: "Frankly, I have an uneasy feeling that going to Madrid is negating what we thought we could accomplish by boycotting the Olympics. If the athletes can't go, why should the diplomats go?"[1]

To those committed to the CSCE process, Reagan's election in November 1980 raised widespread apprehension and a range of questions: Would the United States pull out of the CSCE, as some conservatives and Reagan supporters were advocating? Would Reagan abandon Carter's commitment to human rights? Joshua Rubenstein, an official at Amnesty International, spoke for many human rights activists when he said, "We are concerned that the Reagan administration will not have a positive emphasis on human rights and in some parts of the world his election has been taken as a green light, an encouragement for repressive forces."[2]

The Madrid Meeting, having opened shortly before Reagan assumed office, presented him with an immediate need to formulate a policy on

---

[1] *CSCE Digest*, June 27, 1980, Folder 8, Box 138, Mazewski Papers. Senator Bob Dole supported postponing the Madrid Meeting. Czechoslovak National Council head Anna Faltus refuted such an idea, arguing, "[The] Olympics and [a] Conference on human rights are two different things." In pressing United States participation in the meeting, she wrote, "The people in the Soviet bloc countries are pinning their hopes on the Madrid Conference." Faltus to Dole, July 1, 1980, Foreign Policy – Packard – Madrid Conference Postponement, 1980, Legislative Assistants: Mike Packard, Legislative Relations, Dole Senate Papers. For similar opposition, see Day (B'Nai B'rith Women) to Dole, July 3, 1980, ibid. Many interested in the CSCE, such as the Moscow Helsinki Group, argued for continuing the Madrid Meeting as planned because postponing or canceling would enable the Soviets to avoid criticism of their human rights record. Fascell and Pell to Carter, January 22, 1980, Leg 96th/2nd, Box 35, Fascell Papers; Memorandum, Oliver to Commissioners, January 22, 1980, Box 18, 4:2, Javits Papers; Ester to Senator, January 22, 1980, ibid.; Commission on Security and Cooperation In Europe, ibid.; and New Release, January 24, 1980, Letters Co-Signed, 1979–80, Box 112, Fenwick Papers; *Arkhiv Samizdata* 4053, August 20, 1980, Box 125, Published Samizdat, 1968–1992, Samizdat Archives, Records of Radio Free Europe/Radio Liberty Research Institute, Open Society Archives; Reuter, "Moscow Helsinki Group Appeal on Madrid Conference," August 22, 1980, Helsinki: Madrid, 1979–80, Box 1115, Old Code Subject Files, Soviet Red Archives, Records of Radio Free Europe/Radio Liberty Research Institute, Open Society Archives; and *CSCE Digest*, April 25, 1980, Folder 8, Box 138, Mazewski Papers.

[2] AP, "Soviet Dissident Calls Reagan Human Rights Policy Dangerous," February 10, 1981, Human Rights, 1982–1983, Box 691, Old Code Subject Files, 1953–1994, Soviet Red Archives, Records of Radio Free Europe/Radio Liberty Research Institute, Open Society Archives.

the CSCE. In the weeks leading up to Reagan's inauguration, Washington lawyer Max M. Kampelman, whom Carter had appointed cochair of the American delegation to the Madrid Meeting, argued in the face of much skepticism that the United States would maintain its commitment to the Helsinki process:

No one should doubt American constancy to the powerful ideals of the CSCE process, to the preservation and enhancement of human freedom, to respect for the sovereignty and independence of all states, and to the effort to establish greater military security and cooperation among us.[3]

Nevertheless, there was a widespread assumption that Reagan would replace Carter's two appointees to Madrid, former Attorney General Griffin Bell and Kampelman, to the dismay of many human rights supporters.[4]

Surprisingly, in a move that foretold greater continuity in United States CSCE policy than expected, the new administration retained Kampelman to lead the delegation. Most likely Reagan's interest in Kampelman at this stage was based on ideological affinity. Although a Democrat, Kampelman was a neoconservative and affiliated with officials who would have prominent positions in Reagan's administration such as Jeane Kirkpatrick, the future ambassador to the United Nations.[5] In addition, both Kampelman and Reagan were members of the Committee on the Present Danger, indicating shared views on American foreign

[3] Statement, Max M. Kampelman, December 19, 1980, in Leonard R. Sussman, ed., *Three Years at the East-West Divide: The Words of U.S. Ambassador Max M. Kampelman at the Madrid Conference on Security and Human Rights* (New York: Freedom House, 1983), 13. On the other hand, former Finnish Ambassador Markku Reimaa indicated that in Madrid the CSCE delegates did not expect a significant shift in United States policy when Reagan was elected. Summary Notes Day 2, Oral History Conference in Vienna, February 22–3, 2007, "The Historical Experience of the Neutral and Non-aligned States in the CSCE," Oral History Workshop, Austrian Institute for International Affairs, Vienna Austria, available at: http://www.php.isn.ethz.ch/conferences/previous/documents/ViennaConf_Day2_000.pdf (accessed April 16, 2008).

[4] Kampelman had even been honored in Madrid with a farewell party. 97th Congress, Helsinki/Czechoslovakia, Box 20, Fenwick Papers; Cover Memorandum, Kampelman to Vest, December 2, 1980, Madrid Meeting of the Conference on Security and Cooperation in Europe (CSCE), Correspondence with the Department of State, December 1980, Box 15, Max M. Kampelman Papers, Minnesota Historical Society, St. Paul, Minnesota (hereafter Kampelman Papers); and Max M. Kampelman, *Entering New Worlds: The Memoirs of a Private Man in Public Life* (New York: HarperCollins, 1991), 252.

[5] Both Kirkpatrick and Kampelman had been officers of the Coalition for a Democratic Majority. Norman Podhoretz, "The Reagan Road to Détente," *Foreign Affairs* 63 (Winter 1984–5): 448; and Gil Troy, *Morning in America: How Ronald Reagan Invented the 1980s* (Princeton: Princeton University Press, 2005), 240.

policy.[6] Kampelman also suggests Reagan's relationship with former Vice President Hubert Humphrey, whom Kampelman had advised for many years, or their shared commitment to Hebrew University in Jerusalem might have inspired Reagan to keep him in Madrid.[7] Finally, the absence of any strong personal ties between Carter and Kampelman likely made the decision easier for Reagan.

Kampelman was a veteran of Washington politics, playing key behind-the-scenes roles both inside and outside the government. His background, however, had not foretold a political career. Kampelman's status as a conscientious objector during World War II led him to spend almost two years participating in a research project on semi-starvation at the University of Minnesota.[8] In Minnesota, Kampelman studied political science, having already earned a law degree before the war, and embarked upon an academic career. Soon, however, he was recruited to work for Humphrey, who was newly elected to the United States Senate. Kampelman stayed on Humphrey's staff for six years before moving on to head the Washington office of a New York law firm, Fried Frank.[9] Although out of government, he remained an informal advisor to Humphrey as the senator pondered a national campaign, and he facilitated Humphrey's designation as Lyndon Johnson's vice president after John F. Kennedy's assassination. In his memoirs, Kampelman points in particular to his work on legislation related to boycotts of American companies doing business with Israel as bringing him and his negotiating skills to the attention of the Carter administration.[10]

Although Kampelman had gained the support of those invested in the Helsinki process, Reagan's decision to keep him did not assuage broader concerns about the new president's commitment to human rights. Reagan and many within his administration had criticized elements of Carter's human rights policy. For example, Kirkpatrick in particular was critical of Carter for not prioritizing East–West issues above human rights.[11] The general charge was that Carter's policy had neglected United States national interests and had not meaningfully improved human rights

[6] The Committee on Present Danger was a bipartisan group devoted to increasing American military strength and warning about growing compliance in the face of the Soviet threat. Kampelman, *Entering New Worlds*, 233–4.

[7] Max Kampelman Interview, March 13, 2007.

[8] Kampelman, *Entering New Worlds*, 40–1, 50–1.

[9] Ibid., 118, 122–3.

[10] Ibid., 181–2.

[11] Tamar Jacoby, "The Reagan Turnaround on Human Rights," *Foreign Affairs* 64:5 (1986): 1068–9.

practices.[12] Condemnation of this type was interpreted by many to mean the Reagan administration would decrease the prominence of human rights in its foreign policy once in office, and at the outset of his presidency, Reagan's aides suggested he wanted to emphasize spreading democracy and defeating terrorism rather than championing human rights. In his first press conference as secretary of state, Alexander Haig said, "International terrorism will take the place of human rights in our concern because it is the ultimate of abuse of human rights. And it's time that it be addressed with better clarity and greater effectiveness by Western nations and the United States as well."[13] Haig's argument that combating terrorism was consistent with the protection of human rights, while accurate, signaled the administration intended to turn its attention away from violations of individual human rights. One month following the inauguration a NSC staffer wrote, "The impression of Administration policy created thus far has been that human rights are being jettisoned or severely downgraded in favor of countering terrorism or supporting authoritarian allies."[14] Facing criticism, administration officials backtracked somewhat and attempted to recast the new policy as a shift in tactics to quieter diplomacy rather than a change in strategy: "We will work to effect changes to help improve human rights, but we're going to do it quietly" said Vice President George Bush.[15]

Whatever efforts the administration made to convince skeptical observers of its dedication to human rights were weakened by Reagan's nomination of Ernest Lefever, a vocal critic of Carter's human rights policy, to head the State Department's Bureau of Human Rights and Humanitarian Affairs.[16] The nomination failed, not only damaging the perception of

[12] David Carleton and Michael Stohl, "The Foreign Policy of Human Rights: Rhetoric and Reality from Jimmy Carter to Ronald Reagan," *Human Rights Quarterly* 7:2 (May 1985): 208–9; and Forsythe, "Human Rights in U.S. Foreign Policy," 444–5.

[13] "Excerpts from Haig's Remarks at First News Conference as Secretary of," *New York Times*, January 29, 1981, A10.

[14] Lord to Allen, February 17, 1981, Folder 1, Box 1, HU, White House Office of Record Management Subject File (hereafter WHORM), Ronald Reagan Library, Simi Valley, California (hereafter RRL); Donald L. Ranard, "An appointment to mock human rights," *Boston Globe*, February 21, 1981, Folder 4, Box 139, Part I, Goldberg Papers; and Alexander Dallin and Gail W. Lapidus, "Reagan and the Russians: American Policy Toward the Soviet Union," in Kenneth A. Oye, Robert Lieber, and Donald Rothchild, eds., *Eagle Resurgent?: The Reagan Era in American Foreign Policy* (Boston: Little Brown, 1983), 221.

[15] The speech was delivered on May 24, 1981. *CSCE Digest* May 29, 1981, Helsinki/Madrid, Box 112, Fenwick Papers.

[16] For greater discussion of the controversy surrounding Lefever's nomination and how it shaped the Reagan administration's human rights policy, see Sarah B. Snyder, "The

Reagan's goals but also leaving the administration without a senior official focused on the issue for some time. Four months passed without
a new nominee, leading to consternation from groups such as Helsinki
Watch, which was not lost on the administration. Under Secretary of
State Richard Kennedy wrote, "Congressional belief that we have no
consistent human rights policy threatens to disrupt important foreign-
policy initiatives ... Human rights has become one of the main avenues
for domestic attack on the administration's foreign policy."[17] To address
such concerns, Secretary of State Alexander Haig gave a speech saying
that human rights was "the major focus" of Reagan's foreign policy.
The administration also leaked parts of a State Department memorandum entitled "Reinvigoration of Human Rights Policy," to the *New York
Times*; it stated, "Human rights is at the core of our foreign policy."[18]

In the leaked memorandum, State Department officials argued human
rights "gives us the best opportunity to convey what is ultimately at issue
in our contest with the Soviet bloc" and "must be central to our assault
on them." In addition to identifying support for human rights as useful in the Soviet–American struggle, the memorandum's authors also
noted the issue was essential to garner public and Congressional support: "'human rights' isn't something we add on to our foreign policy, but
is its very purpose ... We will never maintain wide public support for our
foreign policy unless we can relate it to American ideals and the defense
of freedom."[19] The memorandum examined administration thinking on
the relationship between human rights and foreign policy, outlining a
shift to linking human rights more closely with anticommunism and with
Jeanne Kirkpatrick's distinction between authoritarian and totalitarian
regimes.[20]

The administration also adopted a new approach publicly, working
to convey a concern for human rights to the American public and an
international audience. For example, the White House organized a May

Defeat of Ernest Lefever's Nomination: Keeping Human Rights on the United States Foreign
Policy Agenda," in Bevan Sewell and Scott Lucas, eds., *Challenging US Foreign Policy:
America and the World in the Long Twentieth Century* (London: Palgrave, 2011), 136–61.

[17] Jacoby, "The Reagan Turnaround on Human Rights," 1069–70.

[18] Excerpts from State Department Memo on Human Rights, *New York Times* November
5, 1981; Edwin S. Maynard, "The Bureaucracy and Implementation of US Human Rights
Policy," *Human Rights Quarterly* 11:2 (May 1989): 182–3; and Hartmann, "US Human
Rights Policy Under Carter and Reagan," 425–6.

[19] Underlining in original. Memorandum for the Secretary, October 26, 1981, released to
the author under the Freedom of Information Act.

[20] Jeane Kirkpatrick, "Dictators and Double Standards," *Commentary* (1979): 34–45.

1982 meeting between Reagan and Soviet émigrés at which the president stressed his commitment to religious freedom in Eastern Europe.[21] Reagan hosted a number of dissidents at the White House in May 1982. The invitees included some such as Alekseeva and Grigorenko who were active in the Helsinki network and others such as Solzhenitsyn who championed human rights in other ways. Similarly, National Security Adviser William P. Clark scheduled a meeting with Helsinki Watch members, and the NSC arranged a call between Reagan and a relative of internally exiled Soviet human rights activist Andrei Sakharov.[22] These largely superficial events illustrate the political importance human rights had developed for the United States public, but whether they represented a deeper commitment within the administration to supporting human rights is more difficult to ascertain, in part because Reagan's human rights efforts were closely linked to his anticommunism. And, Reagan, like Carter, had a decidedly mixed record on human rights.

The connection between his anticommunism and support for human rights is evident in a number of the individual cases with which Reagan became personally involved, the most prominent of which was the Pentecostal families living in the United States embassy in Moscow.[23] Reagan repeatedly raised his concern for the families, including during his first meeting with Foreign Service Officer Jack Matlock, who was returning from the United States Embassy in Moscow. According to

---

[21] Pipes to Clark, May 6, 1982, Dissident Lunch – White House May 11, 1982 (2/2), Box 22, Jack Matlock Files, RRL; and "Former Dissidents Reassured by Reagan on Human Rights," May 12, 1982, Human Rights, 1980–1982, Box 691, Old Code Subject Files, 1953–1994, Soviet Red Archives, Records of Radio Free Europe/Radio Liberty Research Institute, Open Society Archives. The meeting arose in response to congressional pressure that Reagan meet with Solzhenitsyn. Talking Points and attachments, May 11, 1982, Dissident Lunch – White House May 11, 1982 (2), Box 22, Jack Matlock Files, RRL.

[22] Clark was named National Security Adviser after Allen resigned in January 1982. Lord to Clark, June 22, 1982, Folder 12, Box 1, WHORM Subject File, RRL; and Dobriansky and Blair to Clark, December 23, 1982, "Vatican," Box 91186, NSC: Records, European and Soviet Affairs Directorate, ibid.

[23] The Vashchenko and Chmykhalov families forced their way into the United States embassy in June 1978 in an effort to secure emigration from the Soviet Union. Matlock regards Reagan's interest in Soviet human rights as genuine. Jack Matlock, Jr., *Reagan and Gorbachev: How the Cold War Ended* (New York: Random House, 2004), 55–6. Further evidence of Reagan's concern can be found in his personal letters to author Suzanne Massie, *Manchester Union Leader* publisher Nackey Loeb, and businessman Armand Hammer in which he discusses successful American efforts to secure the release of Orlov and his wife and Soviet dissidents David and Cecilia Goldfarb. Kiron K. Skinner, Annelise Anderson, and Martin Anderson, eds., *Reagan: A Life In Letters* (New York: Free Press, 2003), 382–3.

Matlock, Reagan's interest was driven by his concern for "identifiable human beings" and was linked to earlier work as a lifeguard and his desire to save people who needed help.[24] Reagan seemed to sympathize most with victims of communist repression, indicating that his strong anticommunism shaped his ideas on human rights. When two of the Pentecostals living in the embassy in Moscow undertook a hunger strike, the president sent a private letter to Brezhnev asking for his assistance in resolving the problem.[25] Reagan pressed Brezhnev for exit visas for the Pentecostal families, citing the Helsinki Final Act in support of their right to leave the Soviet Union.[26] Later, in a February 1983 meeting with Dobrynin, Reagan asked that the two families be allowed to emigrate as a signal of goodwill to the United States, promising that the United States would not draw negative attention to any Soviet action; he pledged no "crowing."[27] Although there was not a direct response, in Matlock's view, Reagan's personal emphasis facilitated the families' emigration several months later after bilateral negotiations by Kampelman at Madrid.[28] Reagan's personal investment makes it unlikely he was interested only in the propaganda benefits of Eastern human rights abuses, but discerning his thinking on the issue more broadly is a difficult task.

---

[24] Jack Matlock Interview, April 3, 2006. This analysis is echoed by Reagan's longtime ambassador to the Soviet Union, Arthur Hartman, who noted, "When he talks about human rights he's got to have a vision of who these people are." Hartman recalls Reagan's repeated emphasis on resolving the Pentecostals' plight. Arthur Hartman Interview, Folder 16, Box 2, Don Oberdorfer Papers, Public Policy Papers, Department of Rare Books and Special Collections, Princeton University Library, Princeton, New Jersey (hereafter Oberdorfer Papers). See also Nicholas Daniloff, *Of Spies and Spokesmen: My Life as a Cold War Correspondent* (Columbia: University of Missouri Press, 2008), 377. According to former State Department official Charles Hill, Reagan "was clear in his mind about human rights in the USSR and considered the deprivation of them to be Moscow's greatest weakness." He sees Reagan's role as essential to changes in Soviet human rights practices. Charles Hill, written communication with the author, March 29, 2010.

[25] Clark to Reagan, January 14, 1982, Head of State File: USSR: General Secretary Brezhnev (8190211–8290012), Box 38, Assistant to the President for National Security Affairs Records, RRL; and SecState to AmEmbassy Moscow, January 15, 1982, USSR: General Secretary Brezhnev, Box 38, NSC Records Head of State, Executive Secretariat, ibid.

[26] Telegram, SecState to AmEmbassy Moscow, January 15, 1982, USSR: General Secretary Brezhnev, Box 38, NSC Records Head of State, Executive Secretariat, RRL.

[27] According to Soviet official Andrei Aleksandrov-Agentov, Dobrynin cabled Moscow after his meeting with Reagan, urging resolution of the problem. Gromyko agreed and facilitated their emigration. Matlock, *Reagan and Gorbachev*, 54; George Shultz Interview, Folder 2, Box 3, Oberdorfer Papers; Andrei Aleksandrov-Agentov Interview, Folder 2, Box 1, ibid.; and Arthur Hartman Interview, Folder 16, Box 2, ibid.

[28] Matlock's account offers important insight into the level, style, and areas of Reagan's personal involvement in United States foreign policy. Matlock, *Reagan and Gorbachev*, 57–8.

Reagan's first-term support for human rights in Eastern Europe was manifested primarily within the CSCE context in Kampelman's vocal and active diplomacy at Madrid, while Reagan devoted his efforts, largely unsuccessfully, to private diplomacy.[29] Political instability in the Soviet Union, combined with repeated Soviet refusals to negotiate with the United States on human rights, prevented Reagan from successfully pursuing a highly personal role. Reagan attempted to exert influence in correspondence with Soviet leaders; however, Leonid Brezhnev, Yuri Andropov, and Konstantin Chernenko were each unwilling to engage substantively on human rights questions, regarding United States interest as undue interference.[30] According to Soviet diplomat Anatoly Adamishin, "From Stalin to Chernenko without interruption, the term human rights was preceded by the word so-called, and when written, surrounded by quotation marks. Human rights were officially presented as a sly, demagogical invention of the capitalist West in its struggle against socialist countries."[31] When Reagan wrote Brezhnev a lengthy letter on April 21, 1981, questioning the Soviet adherence to the Helsinki Final Act, Brezhnev not surprisingly reacted defensively in his response.[32] In mid-September, Reagan again wrote to Brezhnev to exert pressure on the

[29] Reagan occasionally voiced his concern, such as when he forcefully articulated the significance of the CSCE while condemning Polish martial law. In his address to the country on December 23, 1981, Reagan alleged the Polish government had "trampled" the Helsinki Final Act. Donald Pienkos, *For Your Freedom Through Ours: Polish American Efforts on Poland's Behalf, 1863–1991* (New York: Columbia University Press, 1991), 374–6. In addition, rhetoric such as his harsh criticism of the Soviet Union as an "evil empire" was hardly quiet.

[30] According to Reagan's memoirs, Chernenko thought that the United States should not raise human rights issues with the Soviet Union because he regarded it as an internal matter. Ronald Reagan, *An American Life* (New York: Simon and Schuster, 1990), 601.

[31] Anatoly Adamishin, "Soviet-U.S. Relations and Human Rights before Perestroika," in Adamishin and Schifter, *Human Rights, Perestroika, and the End of the Cold War*, 43.

[32] Reagan to Brezhnev, April 21, 1981, USSR: General Secretary Brezhnev Cables, Box 37, NSC Records, Head of State, Executive Secretariat, RRL. Reagan's handwritten version addressed the cases of Shcharansky and the Pentecostal families directly. Reagan asserted Shcharansky had not been involved with the United States government and called upon Brezhnev to release him and allow his emigration to Israel. Reagan emphasizes Brezhnev's action would be "strictly between us." Furthermore, he writes that if Brezhnev were to allow the Pentecostals to emigration, "this is between the two of us and I will not reveal that I made any such request. I'm sure however you understand that such actions on your part would lessen my problems in future negotiations between our two countries." Douglas Brinkley, eds., *The Reagan Diaries* (New York: Harper Collins, 2007), 13–5; Skinner, Anderson, and Anderson, eds., *Reagan: A Life in Letters*, 741; and Brezhnev to Reagan, May 27, 1981, "USSR: General Secretary Brezhnev Cables," Box 38, NSC Records: Head of State File: Records, Executive Secretariat, RRL.

Soviets to improve Soviet–American relations, including through actions at the Madrid Meeting. Reagan also expressed interest in the plight of individual activists such as Shcharansky, Sakharov, and Jewish refusenik Ida Nudel in letters to the Soviet leader.[33] Chernenko indicated he felt pressure from the Reagan administration on Jewish emigration, noting that Reagan had met with Avital Shcharansky. The Soviet leader viewed Reagan's meeting in the broader context of what he considered an anti-Soviet campaign in the American press and stated the Soviet Union was receiving hundreds of telegrams on Jewish prisoners, but Soviet authorities did not respond to the campaign.[34]

Despite the frustration of Reagan's efforts, Kampelman proved to be an effective negotiator who skillfully pursued American objectives at the Madrid negotiations. With strong White House support, Kampelman remained focused on highlighting human rights abuses, enlisting Western and neutral diplomats in his efforts, and working to free individual political prisoners at Madrid.[35] Kampelman suggests that the idea of American–Soviet negotiations on a performance requirement, or a demonstration of concrete improvements, originated with his frustration at the idea of agreeing to new formulations in Madrid that Eastern governments would never uphold. Instead, he proposed to Secretary of State George Shultz that, as a prerequisite to a concluding document at Madrid, the United States require the release and possible emigration of a number of human rights activists and Jewish refuseniks.[36] When Kampelman

---

[33] Haig to Reagan, September 18, 1981, USSR: General Secretary Brezhnev Cables, Box 37, USSR: General Secretary Brezhnev, National Security Council: Head of State File, Executive Secretariat, RRL. Reagan had a long-standing interest in Nudel, at least since a 1976 radio broadcast in which he raised her inability to obtain an exit visa as a violation of the Helsinki Final Act. Reagan was not the only prominent politician pressing Soviet leaders at the time. For example, Austrian Chancellor Bruno Kreisky wrote to Andropov, asking him to act generously by freeing Orlov. Kreisky to Andropov, July 5, 1983, Perechen 37, Dokument 38, Fond 89.

[34] Gromyko told other Soviet officials that freeing Shcharansky was not an option given the "highly unsuitable" conditions. Andropov suggested the Soviets needed to demonstrate to Americans that Shcharansky was convicted based on his espionage on behalf of the CIA and not his religion, revealing concern about the American public's support Shcharansky. Politburo Minutes, June 4, 1981, Perechen 42, Dokument 60, Fond 89.

[35] Sakharov wrote to Kampelman in appreciation for the delegation's strong support of human rights activists at the Madrid Meeting and to warn of increasing repression. Sakharov to Kampelman, January 29, 1981, S.III.1.1.68, Box 58, Sakharov Papers.

[36] Kampelman initiated and implemented the United States' strategy regarding human rights at Madrid. After George Shultz became Secretary of State July 16, 1982, he supported Kampelman's approach at a high level. In Shultz's view, Haig's past experience working with Kissinger may have led him to place insufficient emphasis on human rights. George Shultz Interview, Folder 2, Box 3, Oberdorfer Papers.

and Shultz discussed the proposal with the president, Reagan asked the CSCE ambassador to press for the emigration of the Pentecostals as part of a package agreement and pushed him to negotiate with the Soviets at Madrid to help Jewish refuseniks, saying, "Max, see what you can do to help these people," as he handed him a list. [37]

After considerable bilateral negotiations, in May 1983 Kampelman's Soviet counterpart outlined the Soviet position: They were willing to grant twenty-three Pentecostals exit visas, three Helsinki monitors would be released and allowed to emigrate, and there would be possible movement on Shcharansky and five other prominent cases. [38] The Soviets, however, later reneged on the agreement to release Shcharansky and several other Soviet dissidents, angering Kampelman. [39] In the negotiations that followed, Kampelman tried to encourage Soviet human rights progress by suggesting other potential areas for improvements in the American–Soviet relationship. Kampelman implied "if they permit a plane load of monitors and activists to leave their prisons, many benefits to them would flow and we could be more flexible on specific human rights words in Madrid." [40]

---

[37] *Washington Post* columnist George Will had argued for human rights gestures to be required in connection with a final agreement at Madrid and wrote explicitly: "no document should be signed with Anatoly Shcharansky in prison." Max M. Kampelman, "Rescue With a Presidential Push," *Washington Post*, June 11, 2004, A25; Max Kampelman Interview, March 13, 2007; Matlock, *Reagan and Gorbachev*, 57–8; and George F. Will, "Helsinki Charade," *Washington Post*, August 21, 1983, Black Binder, Box 2442, Fascell Papers.

[38] Kampelman pushed for Orlov and Sakharov to be included in the deal as well. Draft Telegram, Box 14, Kampelman Papers; Kampelman to Shultz, May 7, 1983, Madrid Conference on Security and Cooperation in Europe April–June 1983, Box 15, ibid.; Memorandum, Hill to McFarlane, October 19, 1983, Matlock CHRON October 1983 [o/11–10/24], Box 90888, Jack Matlock Files, RRL; Telegram, EXTOTT to MDRID/CSCE, May 9, 1983, Volume 9121, 20-4-CSCE-Madrid, Volume 35, RG 25, National Archives, Canada; Delworth and Marchand to MacGuigan, September 5, 1982, Volume 9118, 20-4-CSCE-Madrid, Volume 21, ibid.; and Sergei Kondrashev, in *SALT II and the Growth of Mistrust: Conference #2 of the Carter-Brezhnev Project.*

[39] Telegram, WHDC to EXTOTT, July 6, 1983, Volume 9121, 20-4-CSCE-Madrid, Volume 36, RG 25, National Archives, Canada. Writing about a July 1983 meeting between Shultz and Kampelman on the Madrid performance requirement, Reagan commented, "The Soviets are being devious about their promise to let Shcharansky go. We're going to hold them to it." Brinkley, ed., *The Reagan Diaries*, 166. At Madrid, the chief Soviet delegate told Kampelman that the Soviets would grant a request for "a release for reasons of health." Shcharansky would not accept this offer as, in his view, it implied he acknowledged the legitimacy of the judicial proceedings against him. Sharansky, *Fear No Evil*, 357–8.

[40] Kampelman estimates he spent 400 hours in bilateral negotiations with the Soviets at Madrid. Kampelman, *Entering New Worlds*, 239; Kampelman to Kovalev, November 23, 1982, November 1982, Box 13, Kampelman Papers; Kampelman to Haig, September 10, 1981, Madrid Conference on Security and Cooperation in Europe August–September

Ultimately, as mentioned previously, Kampelman did secure a pledge that if the Vashchenko and Chmykhalov families left the American embassy they would be allowed to emigrate from the Soviet Union, but he was not able to gain Shcharansky or Orlov's release.[41] The significance the White House attributed to the Pentecostals' plight can be seen in Shultz's hand-written letter to Reagan upon the emigration of the two families:

> Now that both Pentecostal families are out, you must feel relieved but also exhilarated. Giving freedom to a human being is a gift of great wonderment.
> Few people know how this all happened and I happen to be one of them. As someone with a ring side seat, let me express to you my admiration for the way you have handled this.[42]

Although granting the Pentecostal families exit visas and other actions undertaken during and immediately after Madrid were relatively small, they established a pattern that accelerated with later meetings in which the United States regarded agreement to new commitments on human rights and humanitarian issues as insufficient and sought tangible progress on compliance instead.

An important shift between the Belgrade and Madrid meetings was the high degree of allied unity regarding objectives and strategy for Madrid, coordinated through periodic NATO delegation and foreign minister meetings and influenced by external events. Madrid began in the aftermath of the Soviet invasion of Afghanistan, which had shocked the international community and drawn a unanimous response of dismay from the West. European estimations of the viability of détente, which had previously caused fissures between Western Europe and the United States, subsequently declined, leaving the West more closely aligned at the start of Madrid.

Kampelman undertook several steps to enhance allied unity at Madrid, recognizing the United States needed NATO support to pressure the

1981, Box 15, ibid.; and William Korey, *Human Rights and the Helsinki Accord* (New York: Foreign Policy Association, 1983), 55.

[41] Kampelman, "Rescue With a Presidential Push"; and Kampelman, *Entering New Worlds*, 271. Reagan wrote in his diary, "Today the Pentecostals left the Am. Embassy basement in Moscow where they've lived in the basement for 4 yrs. They left at our request. We think – well more than that we're sure we have a deal that they will be allowed to emigrate." Brinkley, ed., *The Reagan Diaries*, 144.

[42] As per its agreement with the Soviets, the United States did not publicize its role in aiding the Pentecostals. According to Ambassador Charles Hill, the Reagan administration's silence when the Pentecostals were finally permitted to emigrate helped foster Soviet–American trust. Shultz to Reagan, July 18, 1983, Folder 12, Box 2, HU, WHORM Subject File, RRL; and Charles Hill, written communication with the author, March 29, 2010.

FIGURE 5. Secretary of State George Shultz and United States Ambassador to the Madrid CSCE Review Meeting Max Kampelman discuss the negotiations in Madrid with President Ronald Reagan on July 13, 1983. Courtesy of the Ronald Reagan Library.

Soviets effectively. First, he made a tour of European capitals, consulting with allied leaders in advance of the Madrid Preparatory Meeting in an effort to avoid some of the problems that had plagued European–American relations during Belgrade.[43] Second, he worked to reestablish regular consultation among the NATO ambassadors to the Madrid Meeting. Before the meeting opened, CSCE diplomats such as those from Britain and West Germany doubted that a strong NATO caucus could be brought together again given the intraalliance problems at Belgrade.[44] Kampelman was determined to reconstitute the group and, in his telling, manipulated the NATO states, including France, to attend an inaugural session by promising to brief them on his talks with the Soviet ambassador. Given the near breakdown in Soviet–American relations at the time, the United States's allies were interested to hear the content of

---

[43] Max Kampelman Interview, March 13, 2007. Although German Foreign Minister Hans-Dietrich Genscher suggests it was he who "managed to convince [Kampelman] and win his support" for FRG and West European CSCE objectives." Genscher, *Rebuilding a House Divided*, 104.

[44] The NATO states had caucused regularly and effectively during earlier stages of the CSCE talks.

the ambassadors' discussion. His approach worked and led to regular caucus meetings during the Madrid negotiations.[45] Kampelman's extensive efforts throughout the meeting to ensure unity with the NATO allies offered Helsinki activists much needed support and prompted Richard Schifter, who became assistant secretary of state for human rights and humanitarian affairs later in the Reagan administration, to write subsequently to Kampelman: "You accomplished what Arthur [Goldberg] did not: you enlisted the West Europeans in the cause."[46]

In its opening statement at Madrid and those that followed, the United States resumed its Belgrade practice of citing specific cases of abuse, and unlike at Belgrade, here its allies eventually unified behind this strategy, albeit after considerable dissent.[47] As Western European governments had lost hope in détente with the Soviet Union in the aftermath of Afghanistan and then the imposition of martial law in Poland, they were more willing to champion human rights monitors by name and explicitly criticize Eastern violations.[48] In a contrast to Belgrade, fourteen countries raised the names of 123 people suffering human rights abuses over the course of the Madrid Meeting. The United States alone named 119 individuals of concern during the talks, including Orlov, Sakharov, Shcharansky, Yelena Bonner, Jiri Hajek, Václav Havel, Anatoly Marchenko, Naum Meiman, Ida Nudel, and Raoul Wallenberg.[49]

---

[45] Max Kampelman Interview, March 13, 2007.

[46] Schifter maintains Kampelman's efforts were key to allied unity at Madrid. Schifter to Kampelman, April 10, 1990, Box 35, Kampelman Papers; and Richard Schifter Interview, May 5, 2008. For further discussion, see Sarah B. Snyder, "The CSCE and the Atlantic Alliance: Forging a New Consensus in Madrid," *Journal of Transatlantic Studies* 8:1 (2010): 56–68. Parts of this article are reprinted here in revised form with permission from the *Journal of Transatlantic Studies.*

[47] Plenary statements and related subsequent press releases marked American efforts to publicize human rights abuses in Eastern Europe and employ international condemnation to effect change due to the closed nature of most of the sessions the public gained knowledge of the negotiations through leaks, interviews, and press conferences. Commission Staff to CSCE Commissioners, January 6, 1981, Helsinki/Madrid, Box 112, Fenwick Papers; Korey, "The Unanticipated Consequences of Helsinki," 8–14; and Memorandum, "Human Rights in the CSCE After Belgrade," File 20-4-CSCE-MDRID, Volume 9114, RG 25, National Archives, Canada.

[48] Poland imposed martial law in December 1981 in response to a crisis precipitated by the Polish trade union Solidarity's increasing popularity, growing economic problems, and pressure from Moscow, including Soviet troops menacing beyond Polish borders.

[49] Statement, Max M. Kampelman, July 15, 1983, Sussman, *Three Years at the East–West Divide,* 115; and Commission on Security and Cooperation in Europe, "The Madrid CSCE Review Meeting," November 1983, OSCE Archives; and Fenwick, *Speaking Up,* 165–6.

The Polish imposition of martial law in December 1981 similarly provided the West with actions to oppose uniformly. The Polish repression was condemned extensively in speeches at Madrid before the meeting recessed on December 18. When the meeting resumed on February 9, 1982, NATO foreign ministers delivered sharp rebukes of Polish actions.[50] Western pressure eventually forced a temporary end to the talks, leading to a nine-month recess until November 9, 1982.[51] According to West German Foreign Minister Hans-Dietrich Genscher, Haig wanted to terminate the meeting, but he was able to convince the secretary of state that doing so only benefited the Soviet bloc and harmed Western European security interests.[52] When negotiations at Madrid moved forward subsequently, they did so under a cloud of mistrust and disappointment.

The September 1, 1983, downing of Korean Airlines flight 007, a civilian airliner that mistakenly strayed into Soviet airspace, inspired further cohesion among the non-Warsaw Pact states.[53] The Soviet attack on the airliner, which coincided with the final days of the Madrid Meeting, produced an additional session of allied condemnation of the East.[54] The unified allied response to the Soviet invasion of Afghanistan, the Polish imposition of martial law, and the Soviet destruction of the Korean airplane signaled growing NATO strength within the CSCE and enabled important progress in the Madrid negotiations. Agreement among the NATO allies about their strategy for the meeting gave the West a firmer and more effective negotiating position,

---

[50] According to Genscher, at the Madrid Meeting, he implored the Polish leadership to change its policy: "Abolish martial law. Release the prisoners. Resume the dialogue with Solidarity. Allow the scholars and scientists to resume their work. Take seriously the wishes of the nations of the European Community and the Western Alliance to pave the way once again for a continuation and deepening of the CSCE process and to keep the door open to expansion of political and economic relations." Genscher, *Rebuilding a House Divided*, 81.

[51] Heraclides, *Security and Co-operation in Europe*, 64; and Jan Sizoo and Rudolf Th. Jurrjens, *CSCE Decision-Making: The Madrid Experience* (Boston: Martinus Nijhoff, 1984), 203–11.

[52] Genscher, *Rebuilding a House Divided*, 104.

[53] According to Shultz, the United States and others were angered further by initial Soviet deception about and later Soviet justification of the incident. Shultz points to Gromyko's speech at Madrid as particularly offensive as it seemed to imply the Soviets would act similarly in the future. George Shultz Interview, Folder 2, Box 3, Oberdorfer Papers.

[54] Andrei Gromyko (USSR), November 2, 1983, CSCE/RM/VR.2, Madrid Follow-up Meeting, Volume 41, OSCE Archives. Gromyko thought it was possible the United States might try to disrupt the Madrid CSCE Conference in retaliation for the KAL downing. Daniloff, *Of Spies and Spokesmen*, 301.

which it used to push proposals on human contacts, Helsinki monitors, the flow of information, terrorism, and religious freedom, among other issues.[55]

The Helsinki process was made up of thirty-five countries and interested nongovernmental observers. Nevertheless, the United States, the Soviet Union, and the complicated Soviet–American relationship had always remained at the core of the CSCE. This dynamic resulted from many factors. Initially, it was the result of the significance of their bilateral agenda. As the CSCE meetings progressed, the central United States role owed itself to sustained American criticism of noncompliance with the Helsinki Final Act. Certainly other states, most notably Canada and Great Britain, spoke out forcefully against human rights violations, but the United States geopolitical position amplified its already loud voice. As the most significant violator of the Helsinki Final Act and the head of the Eastern bloc, the Soviet Union often bore the brunt of American criticism. As such, this chapter closely examines Soviet–American discussions on human rights.

Going into Madrid, the Soviets knew to expect continued Western critiques of their Helsinki implementation, and based on the response to the Afghanistan invasion, little restraint could be expected.[56] Why then did the Soviets not pull out of the CSCE meetings altogether? The Soviets did threaten to withdraw from the CSCE prior to Madrid if the review process was not made more amenable to them. Similarly, at the Preparatory Meeting the Soviets attempted to convey disinterest in the upcoming negotiations in order to limit the time devoted to implementation review.[57] Although some European nations took their threats seriously, the United States, and particularly Kampelman, refused to modify its strategy of public criticism. Soviet

---

[55] CSCE/RM.11, December 10, 1980, Book 38, OSCE Archives; CSCE/RM.12, December 10, 1980, ibid,; CSCE/RM.14, December 11, 1980, ibid,; CSCE/RM.19, December 11, 1980, ibid,; and William E. Griffith, *The Superpowers and Regional Tensions* (Lexington: Lexington Books, 1982), 43.

[56] The deputy foreign ministers from the Warsaw Pact met in advance of the Madrid CSCE Meeting to coordinate their approach to what they expected to be a contentious meeting. Noting that diplomats at Madrid would criticize their countries for "the provision of international aid to Afghanistan and on the alleged failure to satisfy the Final Act especially in the area of human rights and freedoms," they hoped to exploit differences among Western and NNA states to avoid an "accounting." Document No. 88: Summary of the Deputy Foreign Ministers' Preparatory Meeting for the CSCE Madrid Conference, July 8–9, 1980, in Vojtech Mastny and Malcolm Byrne, eds., *A Cardboard Castle?: An Inside History of the Warsaw Pact, 1955–1991* (New York: Central European University Press, 2005), 438.

[57] Sizoo and Jurrjens, *CSCE Decision-Making*, 194.

officials continued to complain that the American approach to the Madrid Meeting interfered in their internal affairs, and Soviet Vice-Minister of Foreign Affairs Leonid Ilichev warned against turning the negotiations into a "verbal bullfight," but the Soviets remained at the meeting and endured four solid weeks of implementation review.[58]

The overriding Soviet goal for Madrid was to secure consensus for a Conference on Disarmament in Europe (CDE), which had the potential to produce an agreement on security measures, and thus the Soviets were willing to withstand the implementation review to achieve it. A number of factors, including the cost of the Soviet–American arms race, the upcoming deployment of Intermediate-Range Nuclear Forces (INF) missiles in Europe, and the desire to appeal to a growing peace movement in Western Europe, all built upon long-standing Soviet interest in utilizing the CSCE to achieve security objectives. Motives for continued Soviet participation in the CSCE included the protection of Brezhnev's personal prestige, which was linked closely with the CSCE. In addition, the Soviets hoped to exploit differences in the Western alliance, although given the invasion of Afghanistan and martial law in Poland, progress toward that objective seemed unlikely. Finally, Soviet sensitivity to Western human rights criticism may have lessened.[59]

The Madrid Meeting was a time of heightened activity by and coordination of human rights activism outside of Eastern Europe. Helsinki Watch's efforts to connect with Eastern European monitoring groups were aimed in part at enhancing the influence of NGOs at the Madrid Meeting. At Belgrade, these groups generally had been low in numbers, resources, and political clout. By the opening of the Madrid Meeting, however, evidence of a burgeoning transnational network was visible. Laber describes the opening of the Madrid Meeting as a "circus" because so many groups had emerged to participate; to political scientist H. Gordon Skilling, a specialist on dissent in Czechoslovakia, the activities of the press and human rights activists created an "Alice in Wonderland atmosphere" at

[58] Sandra Louise Gubin, *International Regimes, Agenda Setting and Linkage Groups in U.S.–Soviet Relations: The Helsinki Process and Divided Spouses* (PhD Dissertation, University of Michigan, 1990), 67; *Novoye Vremya*, November 21, in *CSCE Digest*, December 4, 1980, Folder 3, Box 140, Mazewski Papers; and Statement, Leonid Ilichev (USSR), November 14, 1980, CSCE/RM/VR.6, Madrid Follow-up Meeting, Book 40, OSCE Archives. The Soviet leadership thought that United States and Western European pressure on human rights issues was intended to embarrass the Soviets. Matlock, *Reagan and Gorbachev*, 55.
[59] February 22, 1982, Mastny, *Helsinki, Human Rights, and European Security*, 333–5.

Madrid.[60] This informal network of dissidents, human rights activists, and members of ethnic groups with varying degrees of connection to one another were there because the review meetings facilitated a unique exchange of information, providing the opportunity to disseminate work more widely and to influence not only CSCE delegates but also international and domestic public opinion. [61]

Although Helsinki Watch was joined by dozens of other NGOs, it remained the most high-profile voice on Helsinki compliance. In an effort to shape United States policy in advance of the meeting, Helsinki Watch weighed in on the recurring debate between "naming names" and "quiet diplomacy" with an op-ed in the *New York Times* that warned against cautious State Department diplomacy and advocated a strong American stance in support of imprisoned Soviet monitors.[62] During the meeting, Helsinki Watch made appeals for human rights activists in the Soviet Union, held press conferences to publicize their plight, and provided Madrid delegations with firsthand research on the situation in Eastern Europe.[63] Helsinki Watch members also repeatedly wrote to Soviet officials to convey their displeasure at Soviet human rights practices.[64]

Helsinki Watch maintained a presence in Madrid for the duration of the meeting after most NGOs and journalists had left, intending to serve a "dual function of providing a voice for the human rights spokespersons we have invited and acting as a clearinghouse for the receipt

[60] Laber, *The Courage of Strangers*, 120–1; H. Gordon Skilling, "The Madrid Follow-up" in Spencer, ed., *Canada and the Conference on Security and Co-operation in Europe*, 317; Korey, *The Promises We Keep*, xxvi; and Xinyuan Dai, *Compliance Without Carrots or Sticks: How International Institutions Influence National Policies* (PhD Dissertation, University of Chicago, 2000), 146, 186, 191.

[61] Commission staff also estimated that 1,500 members of the press, including ninety from the United States, reported from Madrid in the opening week of the meeting. Leatherman, *From Cold War to Democratic Peace*, 176; Commission Staff to CSCE Commissioners, January 6, 1981, Helsinki/Madrid, Box 112, Fenwick Papers; and CSCE Review Meeting Opens in Madrid, November 12, 1980, Folder 1, Box 140, Mazewski Papers.

[62] Calibrating the United States approach to CSCE negotiations always involved striking the right balance between public condemnation of human rights abuses and private entreaties to improve conditions in Eastern European countries. Jeri Laber, "Moscow vs. Rights," *New York Times*, July 31, 1980.

[63] U.S. Helsinki Watch Committee, "The First Fifteen Months: A Summary of the Activities of the U.S. Helsinki Watch Committee from its founding in February, 1979 to April, 1980," Helsinki Watch – Annual Report, 1979, Box 1, General Files, New York Office Files, Record Group 7, HRWR; and Helsinki Watch – Annual Report, 1986, Box 1, Subject Files, Cathy Fitzpatrick Files, ibid.

[64] For example, Bernstein and Schell to Ilichev, January 12, 1981, USSR: Political Prisoners: Campaign on their Behalf, 1981, Box 60, Country Files, Jeri Laber Files, Record Group 7, HRWR; and Bernstein and Schell to Ilichev, January 23, 1981, ibid.

and dissemination of written materials."⁶⁵ To that end, Helsinki Watch employed a permanent representative and local support staff in Madrid to continue exerting pressure on delegates and publicizing Helsinki Watch's research.⁶⁶ As the Madrid Meeting dragged and press interest waned, however, Helsinki Watch struggled at times to capture attention for its cause.⁶⁷ When Laber stopped in Madrid at the end of a twenty-five-day trip to Eastern Europe, United States CSCE ambassador Max Kampelman arranged a luncheon with fourteen NATO and NNA ambassadors. To Laber's surprise, as she conveyed her findings, she sensed she was giving the ambassadors new information and educating them about the situation in these countries: "I realized that many of them were focusing for the first time on the personal tragedies caused by human rights violations. Their response led me to believe that in the future they would raise human rights issues more vociferously with the Eastern bloc delegates at the conference."⁶⁸ Laber's experience in Madrid further demonstrated the potential for Helsinki Watch to influence CSCE diplomats. Finding its ongoing presence effective, Helsinki Watch pursued a similar strategy at subsequent CSCE meetings.

As Helsinki Watch and the other IHF national committees worked on building their network, the United States government also became interested in facilitating and supporting Helsinki monitoring groups in Western Europe.⁶⁹ Governmental interest may have been connected with Kampelman's observation that Western European delegates at Madrid

---

⁶⁵ Jeri Laber Interview, April 29, 2008; and The Madrid Office, March 19, 1980, Madrid pre-conference plans, 1979–1980, Box 37, General Files, New York Office Files, Record Group 7, HRWR.

⁶⁶ Laber, *The Courage of Strangers*, 123. In addition to the office Helsinki Watch established in Madrid, a number of European Helsinki groups jointly organized an information center for the meeting, and the Commission ran a public affairs office as well.

⁶⁷ Helsinki Watch's full-time representatives in Madrid, however, were bolstered by periodic visits by Laber, Helsinki Watch board member Orville Schell, and others who could draw the attention of CSCE delegates. Report from Madrid – November 2, 1982, Madrid: November 9, 1982, Box 38, General Files, New York Office Files, Record Group 7, HRWR.

⁶⁸ In 1981, Helsinki Watch decided that it needed to move beyond its strategy of collecting information and begin conducting its own research into human rights practices in the countries it was monitoring. So, in the fall, Laber embarked on a solo research trip to Czechoslovakia, Poland, Hungary, and Yugoslavia. Laber later reported on a trip to Romania and argued against holding the next CSCE conference there, as Romanian President Nicolai Ceausescu wished. Laber, *The Courage of Strangers*, 132–3, 162, 198–9.

⁶⁹ Kampelman to Laber, August 5, 1983, National Endowment for Democracy, 1983–1984, Box 49, Subject Files, New York Office Files, Record Group 7, HRWR.

were under no public pressure to push Eastern governments on human rights, leading them to pursue less activist policies in the CSCE negotiations. He hoped "energizing European NGO's" might help pressure Western European delegations.[70]

Eastern European dissidents also tried to influence the talks, although government repression made such efforts more difficult. In one example, the Helsinki group in Poland had hoped its head, Zbigniew Romaszewski, would be able to attend the meeting, but his passport was seized and he was not permitted to travel to Madrid. Instead, it authored a 182-page report detailing Helsinki violations during martial law, which it sent to Madrid. As noted in a cover memorandum to the report, "The preparation in clandestine conditions of such an exhaustive and extensive report comprising more than 600 pages with the appendices, required enormous effort and implied grave risks for the underground activists."[71] In addition, Orlov made a plea to Madrid delegates for amnesty for all political prisoners and declared a two-day hunger strike on May 15, 1980, to draw attention to the issue. He also drafted and smuggled out of prison a document about prison and camp life to be sent to CSCE diplomats. His highly personal appeal said, "I'm sewing bags on the machine. I'm not allowed to have eye glasses. I'm fighting for the right of correspondence ... Our hope rests only with Europe."[72] Soviet political prisoners

---

[70] Helman to Laber, January 10, 1984, National Endowment for Democracy, 1983–1984, Box 49, General Files, New York Office Files, Record Group 7, HRWR.

[71] It was later published by Helsinki Watch as *Prologue to Gdansk*. Zbigniew Romaszewski, written communication to the author, January 26, 2010; Bugajski and Pollack, *East European Fault Lines*, 115; Thomas, "The Helsinki Accords and Political Change in Eastern Europe," in Risse, et. al., eds., *The Power of Human Rights*, 216–17, 221; Laber, *The Courage of Strangers*, 156–7; Milewski to Delegation Heads, March 16, 1983, Folder 4, Box 151, Part I, Goldberg Papers; Wanda Jarzabek, "Home and Reality: Poland and the Conference on Security and Cooperation in Europe, 1964-1989," Cold War International History Project, Working Paper No. 56, Woodrow Wilson Center for Scholars, 55; and Lipski, *KOR*, 364.

[72] Yuri Orlov, "To the Madrid Conference," *Freedom Appeals* 6 (October 1980): 29. Orlov's wife also wrote directly to the Madrid Conference and Kampelman to discuss her husband's case. Orlova to the Conference in Madrid, January 17, 1981, USSR: Orlov, Yuri, 1981, Box 34, Country Files, Cathy Fitzpatrick Files, Record Group 7, HRWR; and Orlov, *Dangerous Thoughts*, 234, 242–4. Prisoners from Mirov, Czechoslovakia, also appealed to the Madrid delegates in January 1981 declaring, contrary to what Czechoslovak representatives were saying, they had been sentenced because they "raised the question of violations of human rights." In another instance, Sakharov and Naum Meiman called upon the diplomats at Madrid to aid Orlov, who they characterized as under a regime of "extended torture," pointing to his life of "exhausting forced labor, extremely poor diet, and humiliating treatment." Mastny, *Helsinki, Human Rights, and European Security*, 196; and Press Release, March 18, 1981, Press Releases, March

also wrote to Madrid delegates in late 1981 to urge them to draw their attention to ongoing violations of human rights in the Soviet Union and to press for amnesty of political prisoners in all CSCE states.[73] The Ukrainian Helsinki Group appealed to Madrid delegates to put forth a "Declaration on the Right of Citizens to Monitor Compliance with the Helsinki Final Act and the Inadmissibility of Criminal and Administrative Reprisals for Participation in Such Monitoring."[74] Shcharansky's mother also petitioned the Madrid Meeting to focus on his case, saying, "How can one discuss new proposals when innocent living people are still in prison? ... You bear the heavy responsibility and duty to defend these unjustly convicted people."[75] Through their communications with diplomats and activists in Madrid, Eastern European dissidents and their advocates attracted international attention to their plight, but they had limited influence on Eastern European human rights practices. According to Fenwick, those oppressed in Eastern Europe "hung like a cloud over all the proceedings of the conference."[76]

At odds with his campaign rhetoric on the issue, Reagan ultimately supported a continuation of Carter's CSCE policy. He did not boycott the Madrid Meeting or withdraw from the CSCE, as some had feared; instead, he retained Kampelman and established what would become unexpected consistency with Carter's support of the Helsinki process and use of open diplomacy in multilateral forums such as the CSCE to push human rights compliance.[77] Under Reagan's direction, Kampelman and

1981, Box 32, General Files, New York Office Files, Record Group 7, HRWR. In January 1982, Irina Orlova, Sakharov, and Meiman again appealed to Madrid delegates to press the Soviets to release Orlov from labor camp prison given the great danger to his health. "On the Camp Imprisonment of my Husband, Yuri Orlov," January 19, 1982, Folder USSR: Orlov, Yuri 1982, Box 35, Country Files, Cathy Fitzpatrick Files, Record Group 7, HRWR; and Sakharov and Meiman to the CSCE Madrid Meeting, January 10, 1982, ibid.

[73] *Arkhiv Samizdata* 4477, January 9, 1981, Human Rights, 1980–1982, Box 691, Old Code Subject Files, Soviet Red Archives, Records of Radio Free Europe/Radio Liberty Research Institute, Open Society Archives. Bonner wrote to Kampelman, raising the case of Moscow Helsinki Group member Tanya Osipova's imprisonment as well as the ongoing plight of the Kovalev family. Bonner to Kampelman, April 14, 1982, S.II.2.2.77.0, Box 29, Sakharov Papers.

[74] Grigorenko to Bernstein, September 12, 1980, USSR: Ukrainian [Helsinki] Group, 1974–1984, Box 66, Country Files, Jeri Laber Files, Record Group 7, HRWR.

[75] An Appeal to the Madrid Meeting from Anatoly Shcharansky's Mother, February 1981, USSR: Moscow Helsinki Watch Group, 1980–1981, Box 27, Country Files, Cathy Fitzpatrick Files, Record Group 7, HRWR.

[76] Fenwick, *Speaking Up*, 164.

[77] Mower, *Human Rights and American Foreign Policy*, 99.

subsequent CSCE ambassadors continued Goldberg's policy of "naming names." The Reagan administration, like Carter's, publicly admonished Eastern European states for human rights abuses if warranted, such as with Poland in 1981, and like Carter, Reagan and his aides often raised human rights cases in bilateral meetings with the Soviets. Reagan's administration was active in, and at times essential to, the CSCE meetings during his presidency; in this vein, the United States remained committed to the Madrid CSCE Meeting despite increasing East–West tension caused by Soviet actions in Afghanistan and Polish imposition of martial law in 1981.[78] Due in part to this sustained American involvement, the talks facilitated progress in the CSCE process.

In contrast to the Belgrade Meeting that had ended without a substantive document, the Madrid Concluding Document was a notable negotiating achievement for the West; its significance, however, lay primarily in the mandates for subsequent interim meetings. Western states, in particular Canada and the United States, pressed for and secured one meeting in Ottawa on human rights and fundamental freedoms as well as one in Bern on human contacts in exchange for agreeing to a conference on confidence- and security-building measures (CSBMs).[79] The document's new commitments on issues related to Baskets One and Three were not surprisingly less ambitious than those of the Helsinki Final Act. Moreover, agreement on the Madrid Concluding Document was bittersweet for many in light of the still unfulfilled Helsinki Final Act provisions. The West succeeded in its efforts to use Madrid as a forum to press for Eastern European compliance, but there seemed little hope the Eastern European states would improve their human rights records in the near term. Although the delegates had reached a concluding document at Madrid, the prospects for eventual implementation of either

---

[78] William Korey, "Helsinki, Human Rights, and the Gorbachev Style," *Ethics and International Affairs* 1 (1987): 113–133; and Hyland, *Mortal Rivals*, 232.

[79] Proposals in Ottawa would deal with gender equality, access to health care, the right to participate in religious education, and freedom from torture, whereas those at Bern would address such issues as family visits, postal communication, access to a passport, exit visa fees, and facilitating tourism. Lehne, *The Vienna Meeting of the Conference on Security and Cooperation in Europe*, 23; CSCE Staff to CSCE Commissioners, May 27, 1981, Helsinki/Madrid, Box 112, Fenwick Papers; CSCE/RM.16, December 12, 1980, Book 38, OSCE Archives; CSCE/RM.48, November 9, 1982, ibid; CSE/RM.49, November 9, 1982, ibid; and Sizoo and Jurrjens, *CSCE Decision-Making*, 260. For further discussion of the significance of the interim meetings that followed Madrid, see Sarah B. Snyder, "The Foundation for Vienna: A Reassessment of the CSCE in the mid-1980s," *Cold War History* 10:4 (2010): 493–512.

the commitments in the original agreement or the concluding document were unclear.

In the years that followed, violations of the Helsinki Final Act and repression of dissent continued unabated. For example, in 1984 Soviet authorities charged Bonner with drafting a 1977 Moscow Helsinki Group document, "An Appeal to the Belgrade Conference" and transporting it to Italy for which she was sentenced to five years in exile.[80] Jeri Laber describes the feeling at Helsinki Watch that they were "hitting our heads against a stone wall" for many years because so few governments responded to their entreaties and so few prisoners were released.[81] As Charter 77 architect Jiri Hajek has written, "The problem is, however, that there is no way of compelling a delinquent state to mend its ways."[82] Under a succession of Soviet leaders in the early 1980s, there was no sign that the USSR had any intention of changing its practices; in the words of Soviet diplomat Anatoly Adamishin: "The vast humanitarian field was practically shut for any dialogue between two superpowers whatsoever: One cannot call mutual reproaches and accusations a dialogue."[83]

Not until the emergence of Mikhail Gorbachev in 1985, and the development of a new Soviet–American relationship, did meaningful progress on East–West security and human rights negotiations restart. Gorbachev and a group of close advisers helped foster a culture of reform within the Soviet government; it began with respect to military and security measures, including a progressive agreement in Stockholm to allow on-site military inspections for the first time, and gradually evolved to include an array of human rights improvements. Outside of the CSCE framework, Gorbachev's pursuit of reform enabled Eastern European activists to advocate political and social changes that, once implemented, resulted in the collapse of communist regimes across the region. Collectively, Gorbachev's reforms would change the dynamics of the Soviet "empire" as well as East–West relations, ultimately facilitating the end of the Cold War.

Initial appraisals of Gorbachev pointed to significant differences from his immediate predecessors but did not predict how fundamentally he

[80] Elena Bonner, *Alone Together* trans. Alexander Cook (New York: Alfred A. Knopf, 1986), 83–4, 95. Bonner's exile severed Sakharov's links with the outside world as it meant she could no longer freely travel between Gorky, a city closed to foreigners, and Moscow.

[81] Jeri Laber Interview, April 29, 2008.

[82] Jiří Hájek, "What Can We Expect from Madrid?" May 1980 in Skilling, *Charter 77 and Human Rights in Czechoslovakia*, 322.

[83] Adamishin, "Soviet-U.S. Relations and Human Rights before Perestroika," in Adamishin and Schifter, *Human Rights, Perestroika, and the End of the Cold War*, 43.

would reform the Soviet state.[84] In a March 1985 speech nominating Gorbachev to be general secretary, Gromyko alluded to Gorbachev's considerably younger age and better health, citing Gorbachev's "boundless creative energy, his determination to do more, and to do it better."[85] There is substantial debate as to whether he came to office in March 1985 with a plan of reform; regardless, he was forced to formulate responses to extensive challenges, including tense international relations and a troubled economy at home.[86]

Gorbachev's rise to power was essential to the improved Soviet–American relationship that characterized most of Reagan's second term. Almost immediately, the two began addressing critical bilateral issues, including arms control, because Gorbachev realized that improved relations with the West were needed to facilitate domestic reform efforts.[87] Gorbachev's overriding focus on invigorating the Soviet economy necessitated reducing Soviet military expenditures, thus producing his strong interest in reaching arms control agreements with the United States. Anatoly Chernyaev, a personal adviser with daily access to Gorbachev, described the "one vital goal of *perestroika*," or restructuring, as "easing the military burden."[88] Gorbachev also slowly recognized that in addition to reducing military expenditures through arms control agreements, the moribund Soviet economy needed Western technology, trade, and financial support. However, in order to improve economic relations

---

[84] Born into a peasant family in Southern Russia on March 2, 1931, Gorbachev went on to study at Moscow State University. Gorbachev entered politics in 1955 and rose to be party chief of the Stavropol region by 1970; he moved to Moscow in 1978 to become secretary of the Central Committee.

[85] "Session of the Politburo of the CC CPSU," March 11, 1985, *To the Summit: Perestroika and the Transformation of U.S.-Soviet Relations* (Washington: The National Security Archive, 2005), no. 172, http://www.nsarchive.org (accessed May 22, 2006). A different Politburo member cited his "sprit of innovation." His trips abroad to the United Kingdom, Canada, Bulgaria, the FRG, and Italy were shown as evidence of his ability to conduct foreign policy. Fedor Burlatsky Interview, Folder 5, Box 1, Oberdorfer Papers; Valentin M. Falin Interview, Folder 6, ibid; and Vladimir Petrovsky Interview, Folder 18, ibid.

[86] Others have attributed Gorbachev's receptivity to change to his upbringing, curiosity, and foreign contacts. Brown, *The Gorbachev Factor*, 155; Tony Judt, *Postwar: A History of Europe Since 1945* (New York: Penguin Press, 2005), 594; and Matthew Evangelista, *Unarmed Forces: The Transnational Movement to End the Cold War* (New York: Cornell University Press, 1999), 262.

[87] Jack Matlock, *Autopsy of an Empire: The American Ambassador's Account of the Collapse of the Soviet Union* (New York: Random House, 1995), 69.

[88] Anatoly Chernyaev, *My Six Years with Gorbachev* (University Park: Pennsylvania State University Press, 2000), 80.

or garner international assistance, he would need to normalize relations with the West, which required an improved Soviet human rights record.[89]

Unlike his predecessors, Gorbachev was anxious to engage Reagan in active dialogue, although like them, the Soviet leader was reluctant to address the issue of human rights. In their first correspondence, Reagan affirmed the United States commitment to human rights, whereas Gorbachev ignored the issue in his reply, indicating only an interest in a summit meeting to ease Soviet–American tension.[90] In a subsequent letter, Reagan raised questions about Gorbachev's commitment to improving relations, citing continued Soviet human rights abuses in violation of CSCE agreements: "Let me turn to an issue of great importance to me and to all Americans. As the Vice President informed you in Moscow, we believe strongly that strict observance of the Universal Declaration of Human Rights and of the Helsinki Final Act is an important element of our bilateral relationship."[91] Reagan's repeated efforts helped convince Gorbachev of the United States commitment to human rights; Gorbachev later wrote that Americans had "an almost missionary passion for preaching about human rights and liberties" despite what he termed "a disregard for ensuring those same elementary rights in their own home."[92] Facing American and other entreaties on the issue, Gorbachev suggested he was willing to discuss human rights broadly with the West, but not individual cases.[93]

Western leaders' early meetings with Gorbachev and his new foreign minister indicated that improving relations with the Soviet Union might be possible under his leadership but made clear progress would be evolutionary, not immediate. Bush, as vice president, met Gorbachev for the first time while in Moscow for Chernenko's funeral.[94] Bush remembers that Gorbachev bristled when he tried to discuss human rights but ultimately showed a willingness to consider Bush's message, a change from

[89] Thomas, "The Helsinki Accords and Political Change in Eastern Europe," in Risse, et. al., ed., *The Power of Human Rights*, 229.

[90] Gorbachev to Reagan, March 24, 1985, USSR GSG 8590272–8590419, Box 39, National Security Council: Head of State File, Executive Secretariat, RRL.

[91] Reagan to Gorbachev, April 30, 1985, USSR GSG 8590475–8590495, Box 39, National Security Council: Head of State File, Executive Secretariat, RRL.

[92] Mikhail Gorbachev, *Perestroika: New Thinking for Our Country and the World* (New York: Harper and Row, 1987), 215.

[93] Ibid., 205.

[94] Herbert S. Parmet, *George Bush: The Life of a Lone Star Yankee* (New York: Scribner, 1997), 304.

past Soviet leaders. Nevertheless, Bush noted that Gorbachev clearly resented being lectured on the topic.[95]

Gorbachev's rise to power initiated a number of changes in the top Soviet leadership, of which one of the most significant was the replacement of longtime Soviet Foreign Minister Andrei Gromyko with Eduard Shevardnadze, who was first secretary of the party in the republic of Georgia and with whom Gorbachev had a long friendship.[96] Shevardnadze's selection surprised almost all domestic and foreign observers, as he had virtually no foreign experience, which he himself stressed to Gorbachev in their first meeting on the appointment. Gorbachev, however, replied, "No experience? Well, perhaps that's a good thing. Our foreign policy needs a fresh eye."[97]

Foreign ministers from the thirty-five CSCE states gathered in Finland in 1985 to mark the tenth anniversary of the Helsinki Final Act, offering an opportunity for the first meeting between Shevardnadze and his CSCE peers, including Shultz, who delivered a tough critique of Soviet human rights abuses.[98] The anniversary meeting in Helsinki came less than a month after Shevardnadze's appointment as foreign minister, and he described it as his "coming out party."[99] George Shultz writes that at Helsinki he told Shevardnadze, "Until the Soviet Union adopts a different policy on humanitarian issues, no aspect of our dealings will be truly satisfactory, nor will your society be able to progress as it can and should."[100] Although Shevardnadze was offended by Shultz's pressure on human rights, Shevardnadze soon recognized it would be a necessary

[95] George Bush and Brent Scowcroft, *A World Transformed* (New York: Vintage Books, 1998), 4.

[96] Soviet translator Viktor Sukhodrev writes about how Gorbachev successfully put his people in place in the Politburo, including giving Gromyko a "shove upstairs" to become head of the Presidium of the Supreme Soviet. V. M. Sukhodrev, *Iazyk Moĭ–Drug Moĭ: Ot Khrushcheva do Gorbacheva* (Moscow: AST, 1999), 425.

[97] Former Soviet official Valentin Falin argues Shevardnadze's inexperience was important for Soviet foreign policy as he had "no burden of old stereotypes on his shoulders." In the view of Soviet official Andrei Aleksandrov-Agentov, Gorbachev was drawn to Shevardnadze's "flexible" and "creative mind." Brown, *The Gorbachev Factor*, 108; Valentin M. Falin Interview, Folder 6, Box 1, Oberdorfer Papers; and Andrei Aleksandrov-Agentov, Folder 2, ibid.

[98] Don Oberdorfer, *From the Cold War to a New Era: The United States and the Soviet Union, 1983–1991* (Baltimore: Johns Hopkins University Press, 1998), 121–2.

[99] Eduard Shevardnadze, *The Future Belongs to Freedom* trans. Catherine A. Fitzpatrick (New York: Free Press, 1991), 60.

[100] George P. Shultz, "Foreword," in Adamishin and Schifter, *Human Rights, Perestroika, and the End of the Cold War*, xii.

component of the American–Soviet relationship.[101] Shevardnadze's presentation in Helsinki immediately struck Shultz, who thought Shevardnadze's approach might signal a shift in the way the Soviets would conduct their diplomacy. Throughout his memoirs, Shultz notes how different Shevardnadze was from his predecessor, Gromyko, who was often referred to as "Mr. Nyet" for his uncompromising stances. Shevardnadze, on the other hand, could engage personally – even laughing and joking with Reagan about communists – and avoided a polemical negotiating style.[102]

In the years that followed, Shultz and Shevardnadze would engage in increasingly productive negotiations on a range of issues, including human rights. When the two met for a second time in New York in September 1985, in what Shevardnadze termed his "preemptive game," he told Shultz that they should begin their meeting by discussing human rights; this tact surprised Shultz, as the Soviets had long resisted discussing those issues. Thereafter, Shevardnadze was more willing to consider humanitarian issues and the Soviet record.[103] According to Shultz, in the year after their meeting, Shevardnadze acted on a list of dissidents and refuseniks, pardoning or releasing all of them.[104] The productive beginning to Shultz's and Shevardnadze's interaction offered hope that the United States and Soviet Union would be able to improve their relationship in subsequent years.

Many Western observers, such as Matlock and Brent Scowcroft, who served as George Bush's national security adviser, suspected Shevardnadze held liberal ideas on human rights and foreign policy. These suspicions were borne out by Shevardnadze's later articulation of his opposition to Soviet exit visa policy:

By closing our borders to our own citizens, and screening those allowed to make trips abroad almost like cosmonauts going to the moon, we left people no choice … It was wrong to lock people in the church, never to let them out of the country,

---

[101] Matlock, *Reagan and Gorbachev*, 131.

[102] George P. Shultz, *Turmoil and Triumph: Diplomacy, Power, and the Victory of the American Ideal* (New York: Simon and Schuster, 1993), 574–5, 577. Shevardnadze credits Shultz with setting a positive tone for their relationship in their meeting at Helsinki. Eduard Shevardnadze Interview, Folder 21, Box 1, Oberdorfer Papers.

[103] Shevardnadze, *The Future Belongs to Freedom*, 85; and Raymond Garthoff, *The Great Transition: American–Soviet Relations and the End of the Cold War* (Washington: Brookings Institution, 1994), 321.

[104] Shultz, "Foreword," in Adamishin and Schifter, *Human Rights, Perestroika, and the End of the Cold War*, xiii.

claiming that beyond our borders reigned sin and corruption. A person should have the freedom to make and follow his own choice.[105]

Shevardnadze's willingness to discuss human rights was consistent also with slowly changing ideas within the USSR about dissidents and the international implications of Soviet repression.[106] This evolution can be seen in an August 1985 Politburo meeting in which members discussed Sakharov's request that his wife, Yelena Bonner, be allowed to travel abroad for medical treatment despite her internal exile.[107] Cognizant of the negative publicity rejecting the request would bring, members of the Politburo debated this appeal with Gorbachev asking, "What will hurt us more – to allow Bonner to go abroad or to forbid it?" Soviet leaders weighed the goodwill such a step might engender against potential negative publicity caused by Bonner's actions abroad. Ultimately, they decided to allow her to travel.[108]

---

[105] Shevardnadze, *The Future Belongs to Freedom*, 63. Scowcroft viewed Shevardnadze as almost an "apostle for fundamental change." Bush and Scowcroft, *A World Transformed*, 154.

[106] Soviet reports on the fifth annual International Sakharov Hearings offer evidence that Soviet authorities remained frustrated at the ongoing attention to their record and include complaints the attendees were fixated on implementation of the Helsinki Final Act and on influencing public opinion against the Soviet record. Kashlev to the Central Committee, May 27, 1985, S.II.2.6.1.36, Box 51, Sakharov Papers.

[107] Sakharov had begun a hunger strike in May 1984 to press the Soviets to permit his wife to receive medical treatment abroad. The United States government took a range of steps to demonstrate its concern, including raising Sakharov's situation in bilateral contacts, releasing State Department statements, utilizing American embassies in foreign countries to pressure the Soviets, discussing Sakharov's case with visiting foreign dignitaries, as well as consulting with interested parties such as the National Academy of Sciences and Sakharov's family members in the United States. In response to American efforts, the Soviet leadership accused the United States of "having conspired with the Sakharovs to create the present situation." Helsinki Watch also tried to generate pressure in support of Sakharov, communicating with the IHF about influencing Western European governments to speak out on the couple's plight. Shultz to Reagan, May 18, 1984, Matlock CHRON May 1984 (2), Box 4, Jack Matlock Files, RRL; and U.S. Helsinki Watch to International Helsinki Federation for Human Rights, May 24, 1984, USSR: Sakharov, Andrei May 1984, Box 49, Country Files, Cathy Fitzpatrick Files, Record Group 7, HRWR. Sakharov's step-son-in-law Efrem Yankelevich was in touch with the White House about Sakharov's hunger strike, deteriorating health, and force-feeding. Semyonov to Bush, n.d. S.II.2.3.302, Box 50, Sakharov Archives; and Semyonov to Matlock, n.d. S.II.2.3.303, ibid.

[108] "Meeting of Politburo of CPSU," August 29, 1985, *To the Geneva Summit: Perestroika and the Transformation of U.S.-Soviet Relations* (Washington: The National Security Archive, 2005), no. 172, http://www.nsarchive.org (accessed May 22, 2006).

To demonstrate the United States commitment to human rights, Shultz made it one of the four points on the agenda he formulated for discussions with the Soviets. The list included human rights, regional issues, arms control, and bilateral issues and was intended to ensure that the Soviet-American relationship would not be dominated solely by arms control discussions.[109] The four-point agenda was instrumental in convincing the Soviet leadership that progress on human rights was essential to improving Soviet–American relations. For former Assistant Secretary of State for Human Rights and Humanitarian Affairs Richard Schifter, the key was that Shultz never practiced direct linkage, which would have been counterproductive, but instead always mentioned human rights and arms control in the same context, leading Soviet officials to be able to tell military leaders that making progress on human rights could ease the Soviet economic burden through mutual arms reduction.[110] The United States objective was to convince Gorbachev such changes were in Soviet national interests rather than a mandate from Washington.

At Geneva in 1985, the first Soviet–American summit in six years, the Reagan administration intended to raise human rights but in a nuanced manner. Reagan's briefing paper for the summit advised him to express American concern at low Jewish emigration, Sakharov's exile, political prisoners, and divided spouses, among other concerns. It also reported that the Soviets were attempting to "eliminate all forms of internal dissent" and that they had succeeded in dismantling the Moscow Helsinki Group by late 1982.[111] Reagan wrote notes to himself in advance of the meeting; of the four and a half double-spaced pages he drafted, one full page was devoted to his thoughts on human rights: "We are somewhat publicly on the record about human rights. Front page stories that we are banging away on them on their human rights abuses will get us some cheers from the bleachers, but it won't help those who are being abused."[112] Reagan's

---

[109] Shultz, *Turmoil and Triumph*, 266n.

[110] Richard Schifter Interview, May 5, 2008. See also James Mann, *The Rebellion of Ronald Reagan: A History of the End of the Cold War* (New York: Viking, 2009), 246.

[111] "Human Rights in the Soviet Union," "Soviet Union (binder)," Box 91097, Tyrus W. Cobb Files, RRL.

[112] Pressing the Soviets on human rights would certainly earn Reagan support from the many private citizens and politicians who wrote Reagan in advance of the Geneva summit, although Reagan wanted to affect change as well as score political points. Matlock, *Reagan and Gorbachev*, 152. For a representative sample, see Hammen to Reagan, October 18, 1985, Folder 6, Box 2, FO 006-09, WHORM Subject File, RRL; Adram to McFarlane, September 9, 1985, Folder 4, ibid.; Broomfield to Oglesby,

consideration of strategy reflected the continuing debate over the most effective volume and tactics with which to approach the Soviet Union on human rights. Vocal public diplomacy made more sense during a CSCE meeting, whereas quiet pursuit of Helsinki objectives was more effective at other times during his presidency.

In their two days of meetings, Reagan told Gorbachev about American concern for divided families, and he suggested that movement on human rights would facilitate other types of cooperation, such as trade.[113] Gorbachev recounted his discussions with Reagan at Geneva:

Reagan began by saying that if the Soviet Union intended to improve its relations with the United States, it would do well to change its reputation with respect to individual freedom. He argued that the American public was very sensitive with respect to individual freedom. He argued that the American public was very sensitive about the issue and that therefore no American politician could ignore it.[114]

In an important step for human rights improvements over time and the future of their relationship, Reagan also expressed a willingness to avoid propaganda if the Soviets made some concessions on human rights. In response, Gorbachev charged that anti-Soviet groups and even the president were using the issue of human rights for political reasons. Reagan later wrote in his diary,

I explained that I wasn't telling him how to run his country – I was asking for his help; that I had a better chance of getting support at home for things we'd agreed to if he would ease some of the restrictions on emigration, etc. I told him I'd never mention what he was doing out loud but he'd find that I could better meet some of his requests for trade, etc. He argued back sort of indicating that he thought they treated their people better than we did ours.[115]

Reagan assured Gorbachev he would not claim responsibility if the Soviets moved forward on some cases, and Gorbachev eventually agreed

November 4, 1985, Folder 16 ibid; and Flis to Reagan, October 29, 1985, Folder 12, ibid.; Specter et al. to Reagan, October 24, 1985, Folder 7, ibid.; and D'Amato et al. to Reagan, November 5, 1985, Folder 1, Box 32, PR 007, WHORM Subject File, RRL. Commissioner Steny Hoyer issued an appeal for Gorbachev to release Sakharov and Bonner from internal exile to build confidence going into the summit. CSCE News Release, September 4, 1985, Leg. 99th/1st 1985 CSCE Press Releases, Box 2480, Fascell Papers.

[113] Lou Cannon, *President Reagan: The Role of a Lifetime* rev. ed. (New York: Public Affairs, 2000), 675; and Bernard Weinraub, "President Links Rights in Soviet to Summit Success," *New York Times*, October 8, 1986, Human Rights Issue, Box 1 Processed, JBANC.

[114] Gorbachev, *Memoirs*, 408.

[115] November 20, 1985, Brinkley, ed., *The Reagan Diaries*, 370.

to examine the situations.[116] The two did not make significant progress on human rights at Geneva, but they did sign a bilateral exchanges agreement that Matlock saw as important for its potential to open the Soviet Union to outside influences.[117] In addition, the personal relationship they established there was a foundation to future improvements in Soviet–American relations.[118]

After Geneva, Reagan wrote to Gorbachev to outline his concerns about Soviet human rights, emphasizing progress was critical to improving the broader U.S.–Soviet relationship. He noted with pleasure Soviet efforts to reunite divided spouses in the aftermath of the summit but also outlined a number of other areas he hoped Gorbachev would address, including dual citizens and family reunification requests.[119] The issues, according to Reagan, included:

The broad question of emigration, whether members of such groups as Jews, Armenians and others, or of some internationally known individuals. In both categories, we are talking about quite poignant cases. The young pianist I mentioned to you falls into the category of someone whose requests to emigrate have been refused. The political importance of resolving such well known cases as the Sakharovs, Scharansky [sic] and Yuri Orlov cannot be overestimated. We are not interested in exploiting these cases. Their resolution will permit greater prominence for other issues in our relationship ... the issues I have laid out in this letter are serious ones. Progress here would provide an enormous impetus to the resolution of other outstanding problems. Lack of progress will only hold us back.[120]

---

[116] Matlock, *Reagan and Gorbachev*, 161; and Memorandum of Conversation, November 20, 1985, Geneva: Memcons (Reagan–Gorbachev Memcons Geneva Meeting 11/19–21/1985) 2 of 3, Box 92137, Jack Matlock Files, RRL. Gorbachev was not persuaded by Reagan's efforts to convince him of the power of public opinion in the United States and challenged Reagan's claims that Soviet human rights problems complicated his foreign policy, saying he doubted that Reagan could be constrained by interest groups. Memorandum of Conversation, November 20, 1985, Soviet Union–Geneva Summit, 2 of 2, Box 9215, Peter Rodman Files, RRL.

[117] Jack Matlock Interview, April 3, 2006. According to Assistant Secretary of State for European and Canadian Affairs Rozanne Ridgway, the Soviets did not want human rights to be mentioned in the Geneva communiqué: "They insisted that human rights didn't translate into Russian," but the term's inclusion was very important to the United States. Rozanne Ridgway Interview, Folder 30, Box 2, Oberdorfer Papers.

[118] Gorbachev aide Andrei Grachev recalled that the general secretary saw his meeting with Reagan as an important opportunity to convince the president that he was different from previous Soviet leaders. Valentin M. Falin Interview, Folder 6, Box 1, Oberdorfer Papers; and Andrei Grachev Interview, Folder 8, ibid.

[119] Shultz to Reagan, December 4, 1985, USSR GSG 8591241–8591245, Box 40, Executive Secretariat, NSC: Head of State File, RRL; and Reagan to Gorbachev, December 7, 1985, USSR GSG 8591241–8591245, ibid.

[120] Reagan, *An American Life*, 645.

After the summit, Reagan told his cabinet that he would no longer pressure the Soviet Union on human rights publicly.[121] He hoped to convince Gorbachev that respecting human rights was in the best interests of the Soviet Union, and he recognized that Gorbachev would be much more likely to implement changes if it did not appear as if he was reacting to Western demands, particularly because Gorbachev had indicated that the Soviet Union would not change its policies under American pressure.[122] Reagan argues in his memoirs that his Geneva commitment to Gorbachev to use quiet diplomacy facilitated progress on human rights over time.[123]

Despite Gorbachev's stance at Geneva, his advisers were more interested in resolving a number of broad human rights issues that inhibited Soviet policy priorities. For example, his aide Alexander Yakovlev advocated changes as early as December 1985, writing:

There should be a law on individual rights and their guarantees, a law on personal integrity, personal property and domicile, on privacy of correspondence, telephone conversations and personal life.

[There should be] organizational forms of practicing the right to hold rallies, freedom of speech, religion, press, assembly, and the right of free travel.

We want everybody to have great civic responsibilities, but that is only possible if there are great civil rights.

Yakovlev's memorandum advocated other far-reaching reforms of the Soviet system, including an independent judiciary, a legitimate legislature chosen through multicandidate elections, and "all-around glasnost," many of which Gorbachev ultimately adopted.[124] In addition,

---

[121] Jacoby, "The Reagan Turnaround on Human Rights," 1082–3.

[122] Jack Matlock Interview, April 3, 2006; and Memorandum, Shultz to Reagan, January 14, 1986, 90024, Box 40, USSR GSG 8690024–8690124, National Security Council: Head of State File, Executive Secretariat, RRL. As part of Reagan's commitment not to "crow" when Gorbachev took positive steps on human rights, he declined to receive Bonner when she visited the United States for medical treatment. Instead, she met with National Security Adviser John Poindexter. Soviet officials, however, interpreted Reagan's decision as evidence of American displeasure at Sakharov's criticism of SDI. David Hoffman, "President Declines Visit From Bonner," *Washington Post*, March 21, 1986, A1; Chebrikov to the Central Committee, May 11, 1986, in Joshua Rubenstein and Alexander Gribanov, ed., *The KGB File of Andrei Sakharov*: http://www.yale.edu/annals/sakharov/documents_frames/Sakharov_187.htm (accessed September 12, 2009). Central Committee records from mid-July indicate Soviet leaders wanted to take steps to combat what they saw as an anti-Soviet campaign on the issue of human rights by disseminating materials disputing allegations of Soviet violations of human rights. Central Committee Directive, July 31, 1986, Perechen 18, Dokument 102, Fond 89.

[123] Reagan, *An American Life*, 686.

[124] Memorandum, Yakovlev to Gorbachev, December 25, 1985, *To the Geneva Summit: Perestroika and the Transformation of U.S.-Soviet Relations* (Washington: The

two months earlier Chernyaev had described the "Jewish question" as the "most burning among human rights problems" that must be solved, as the plight of Jewish refuseniks was a constant obstacle to improved relations with the United States and other Western and neutral states.[125] Yakovlev and Chernyaev's writings both indicated sympathy for changes advocated by dissidents and Western leaders as well as early recognition that the USSR's human rights record inhibited Soviet foreign policy.

After Geneva, Reagan continued to stress the connections between human rights and economic relations in his personal correspondence with Gorbachev and in meetings between Soviet and American officials. Gorbachev generally did not respond to repeated American entreaties on human rights and publicly refuted allegations about Soviet human rights violations.[126] In this context, Reagan sent a highly specific letter to Gorbachev enumerating seventeen divided spouses, twenty-three cases involving dual citizenship, and 129 family reunification cases the United States hoped could be resolved.[127] Gorbachev's December 1985 response did not address Reagan's message on human rights, which led Shultz to doubt Gorbachev was prepared to undertake broad human rights reforms. The Soviet leader, however, took a number of steps on human rights issues in the subsequent months, including granting exit visas for eight divided spouses and releasing several dissidents such as Shcharansky and Orlov in prisoner exchanges. His small steps, such as resolving divided family cases, raised some American hopes that the Soviets might make more

National Security Archive, 2005), no. 172, http://www.nsarchive.org (accessed May 22, 2006). His memorandum demonstrates that Matlock was warranted in regarding Yakovlev as an important force in strengthening Soviet observance of human rights. Matlock, *Autopsy of an Empire*, 76.

[125] Chernyaev, *My Six Years with Gorbachev*, 41. Throughout his diary entries in 1985, even before Gorbachev's assumption of Soviet leadership, Chernyaev was enthusiastic about the prospects of reform, including allowing the publication of Anatoli Rybakov's banned novel *The Children of Arbat*, set in the years of Soviet leader Joseph Stalin's purges. Chernyaev recognized the scope of challenges facing the new Soviet leader, arguing a "revolution from the top" was necessary. January 4, 1985, March 13, 1985, *The Diary of Anatoly Chernyaev: The First Installment* (Washington: The National Security Archive, 2006), no. 192, http://www.nsarchive.org (accessed May 28, 2006).

[126] In February 1986, Gorbachev told *L'Humanite*, "Now, about political prisoners, we don't have any. Likewise, our citizens are not prosecuted for their beliefs. We don't try people for their opinions." Gilligan, *Defending Human Rights in Russia*, 66. After this interview, Sakharov wrote to Gorbachev to dispute his assertion and call upon Gorbachev to release still imprisoned political prisoners. Sakharov to Gorbachev, February 19, 1986, S.II.4.17, Box 45, Sakharov Papers.

[127] Reagan to Gorbachev, December 7, 1985, USSR General Secretary Gorbachev 8591241–8591245, Box 40, National Security Council: Head of State File, Executive Secretariat, RRL.

significant changes. whereas others suggested his actions at the time were calculated only to maximize the public relations value of each human rights move.[128]

Shcharansky's memoirs end with a moving account of his reunification with his wife Avital in February 1986 after his expulsion from the Soviet Union and recount the beginnings of their new life together in Israel. But his story could have ended in tragedy if his plight had not garnered high-level and widespread international attention. Members of the Reagan administration regularly communicated with his wife and repeatedly pressed Soviet officials for his release.[129] Indeed, Reagan had written to Brezhnev in October 1982 urging him to resolve Shcharansky's hunger strike and allow him to emigrate to Israel; the president raised Shcharansky's case with Gorbachev as well.[130] Avital Shcharansky met with high-level officials in the Reagan administration, including Secretary of State Haig, Shultz, and Vice President Bush, and received assurances from American leaders that they were committed to resolving her husband's case.[131] American entreaties had failed to prompt Soviet action for many years, but in February 1986, the Soviet Union, still asserting that Shcharansky had worked for the CIA, included him in a spy exchange.

Yuri Orlov's release from exile and expulsion from the Soviet Union in October 1986 further lifted hopes among Westerners that the Helsinki process might finally begin to yield progress. The process through which his release was secured demonstrates the close, working relationship between Helsinki Watch and Reagan administration officials on such

[128] Senator Alfonse D'Amato (R-NY) suggested in hearings on Soviet human rights practices that the USSR was making tactical concessions to disguise continued repression, stating "there is reason to believe that recent promising developments were nothing more than another cynical attempt by Soviet leaders to manipulate the Western media and, through them, Western political leaders and public opinion." Commission on Security and Cooperation in Europe Hearing, "Human Rights and the CSCE Process in the Soviet Union," February 27, 1986, 99th Congress, 2nd Session.

[129] Brinkley, ed., *The Reagan Diaries*, 21. Reports from the United States embassy in Moscow detailed meetings with Shcharansky's family, his health, and punishments in prison. See, for example, AmEmbassy Moscow to SecState, May 18, 1981, Dissidents (2/23), Box 23, Jack Matlock Files, RRL.

[130] Reagan to Brezhnev, October 20, 1982, Dissidents (9/23), Box 23, Jack Matlock Files, RRL. Brezhnev's response indicated he would not act as Reagan had requested and noted Shcharansky was "a Soviet citizen, sentenced for espionage and other grave anti-Soviet crimes." Brezhnev to Reagan, October 30, 1982, Dissidents (9/23), Box 23, Jack Matlock Files, RRL.

[131] Allen to Bush, May 19, 1981, CO 165 USSR (025700–028799), Box 1 WHORM Subject Files, RRL; and Shultz, *Turmoil and Triumph*, 121. Central Committee records indicate Soviet leaders were sufficiently concerned with international attention

FIGURE 6. Anatoly Shcharansky and Elena Bonner celebrate the tenth anniversary of the formation of the Moscow Helsinki Group. Shcharansky had recently been sent into exile by the Soviet Union, and Bonner was in the United States for medical treatment. The two had not seen one another since Shcharansky's arrest in March 1977. Photo by Janet Fleishman. Courtesy of Human Rights Watch.

issues. Orlov's liberation was part of a negotiated deal involving a Soviet spy in the United States, Gennadiy Zakharov, and a falsely accused American journalist, Nicholas Daniloff, in the Soviet Union.[132] Reagan had refused to make an equal exchange of Zakharov for Daniloff, fearing it would encourage the Soviets to make other unfounded arrests. Assistant Secretary of State for European and Canadian Affairs Rozanne Ridgway turned to Helsinki Watch for advice on whose release the United States should seek. According to Aryeh Neier, staff members "had heard Orlov was in bad physical condition out in Siberia and needed help ... So, we

given to Shcharansky's plight to try to combat rumors that he was in grave health. Central Committee Memorandum, February 16, 1983, Perechen 11, Dokument 121, Fond 89.

[132] Iu. V. Dubinin, *Vremia Peremen: Zapiski Posla v SshA* (Moscow: Aviarus-XXI, 2003), 100, 117; Daniloff, *Of Spies and Spokesmen*, 1–5, 366–84; and George Shultz Interview, Folder 2, Box 3, Oberdorfer Papers.

said Orlov."[133] After the Soviets added Orlov to the deal, stripping him
of his citizenship and sending him into exile, Ridgway called Helsinki
Watch and said, "Tell Jeri [Laber] she's got her man."[134] Upon his arrival
in the United States, Orlov met with journalists and members of Congress
and visited the White House, where Reagan called him a "hero of our
time."[135] Although overjoyed at Orlov's release, some American observers questioned if the Soviet release was a signal of broadening respect for
human rights or simply a tactical maneuver by Gorbachev. Laber was
skeptical of Soviet motives and suggested Orlov's release and exile were
intended to curry favor at the upcoming Vienna CSCE Review Meeting.[136]
White House officials similarly regarded high-profile Soviet actions such
as Orlov's release as intended to obscure the Soviets' overall poor record
on human rights.[137]

Achieving improvements in Soviet human rights practices was a frus-
tratingly slow process. Yet, increased Soviet–American contacts facilitated progress, and American policymakers continued to press for change,
often in close contact with human rights activists. For example, when
Orlov met Reagan at the White House on October 7, 1986, he said, "We
talked about the problems of peace, security and how these problems
are related to the issue of human rights." Orlov advised Reagan to press
for Sakharov's release at his upcoming summit meeting.[138] In a different

---

[133] Aryeh Neier Interview, April 24, 2008. In April 1985, Orlov had been badly beaten to
the point of unconsciousness and suffered problems with his eyesight in subsequent
months. Orlov, *Dangerous Thoughts*, 282–3.

[134] Ridgway later said, "One of the nicest phone calls I was ever able to make was to call
Helsinki Watch in New York and tell the staff there that Yuri Orlov would be leaving
the Soviet Union." Orlov, *Dangerous Thoughts*, 296–8; Reagan, *An American Life*, 667;
and Laber, *The Courage of Strangers*, 253–5, 258.

[135] After his release, Orlov met with a number of other foreign leaders, including British
Prime Minister Margaret Thatcher, former West German Chancellor Willy Brandt, and
FRG Chancellor Helmut Kohl to press the plight of Soviet political prisoners. Orlov,
Dangerous Thoughts, 300; and John Fry, *The Helsinki Process: Negotiating Security and
Cooperation in Europe* (Washington: National Defense University Press, 1993), 108.

[136] Poland was far more successful in changing its image when it released almost all of
its political prisoners just before the Vienna Meeting opened. Laber, *The Courage of
Strangers*, 255–8; Pleshakov, *There Is No Freedom Without Bread!*, 156.

[137] Weinraub, "President Links Rights in Soviet to Summit Success." Though in a Politburo
meeting in October 1986, Gorbachev looked ahead to the Reykjavik summit and said,
"On human rights. Let us see what we can do ... All in all, we should step up our work
on these issues." From Chernyaev's notes, it is unclear on which issues in particular
Gorbachev intended to make progress. Anatoly Chernyaev's Notes from the Politburo
Meetings, October 8, 1986, READD-RADD Collection, National Security Archive.

[138] Orlov, *Dangerous Thoughts*, 300. Of Orlov, Reagan said, "The West owes him a profound debt, both for his courage and for his fortitude under unspeakable conditions, and

instance, Shultz consulted with Laber and Helsinki Watch staff member Cathy Fitzpatrick about individual cases and systemic abuses he should be raising when meeting with Soviet leaders at an upcoming summit.[139] Such high-level contacts offer evidence of the close links between human rights activists and Western politicians committed to improving Helsinki compliance.

As in Geneva, the principal issue under discussion at the October 1986 Reykjavik summit was arms control. Nevertheless, Reagan intended to press Gorbachev on human rights issues, announcing he would link them to other areas of the U.S.–Soviet relationship: "I will make it amply clear to Mr. Gorbachev that unless there is real Soviet movement on human rights, we will not have the kind of political atmosphere necessary to make lasting progress on other issues."[140] At Reykjavik, Gorbachev agreed to discuss what he called "humanitarian issues" but resented Reagan's efforts to press human rights before other, broader discussions occurred.[141] In their talks, Reagan told Gorbachev that he wished the Soviets could go further on human rights to facilitate more cooperation, and he gave him a list of 1,200 Soviet Jews who were waiting to emigrate.[142]

Some observers see Reykjavik as denoting an important shift in Soviet attitudes toward human rights, marking a reconsideration of Soviet policy toward dissidents to gain support from Western European leaders, elites, and public opinion. According to Anatoly Adamishin, Gorbachev declared in a Politburo meeting after the summit, "It is necessary to free political prisoners from jails. They are there for saying the words that I, as the Secretary General, am saying today."[143] Similarly, Gorbachev told

---

for reminding us how precious are the freedoms that we sometimes take for granted." Weinraub, "President Links Rights in Soviet to Summit Success."

[139] Jeri Laber Interview, April 29, 2008.

[140] A host of other ethnic and human rights organizations, members of Congress, and private citizens wrote to Reagan asking him to raise different human rights concerns in his meeting with Gorbachev. Weinraub, "President Links Rights in Soviet to Summit Success"; Overall Briefing Book, October 10–12, 1986, President Reagan's Trip to Reykjavik, Iceland October 10–12, 1986: Overall Briefing Book, Box 92085, Fritz Ermath Files, RRL; Letter and Attachments, Broomfield to Ball, October 7, 1986, 428917, HU, WHORM Subject File, ibid.; and Hoyer et al. to Reagan, October 6, 1986, 451246, FO 006, WHORM Subject File, ibid.

[141] Matlock, *Reagan and Gorbachev*, 218.

[142] Shultz proposed a working group to discuss human rights and regional issues. Matlock, *Reagan and Gorbachev*, 226; and Cannon, *President Reagan*, 687.

[143] Anatoly Adamishin, "The Human Rights Agenda," in Adamishin and Schifter, *Human Rights, Perestroika, and the End of the Cold War*, 116. The memoir account of the Soviet ambassador to the United States at the time, Yuri Dubinin, similarly indicates a new approach, in particular regarding activists such as a son of Vladimir Slepak who

the Politburo in November 1986 that the USSR needed to improve its stance on human rights: "We need to work out a conception of human rights, both at home and abroad, and to put an end to the routine. It only produces dissidents." His comments on the recent prisoner exchanges, however, indicate he was not motivated by sympathy for political prisoners' plight: "It is not a loss, it is a gain if all kinds of trash got out of the country [abroad]. What, essentially, did we have to give up? Orlov and Shcharansky? Let's sweep out with a broom everyone whom we can send abroad without hurting our security."[144]

Matlock argues that after Reykjavik, Gorbachev realized he could achieve normalized relations with the United States only if he was willing to deal with "the full agenda of issues," which included human rights.[145] Reykjavik was one significant event amid a broad pattern of international pressure on Gorbachev. Other leaders such as British Prime Minister Margaret Thatcher also raised human rights concerns with Gorbachev, warning him the Soviets would never develop international relations based on trust if they did not respect human rights and democracy.[146] During a March 1987 visit to Moscow, Margaret Thatcher said,

The extent to which you, the Soviet Government, meet the commitments which you have freely undertaken in the Helsinki Final Act will determine how far other countries and other peoples have confidence in the undertakings which you give on, for instance, arms control. The greater your readiness to release prisoners of

---

had been denied permission to emigrate to Israel. According to Dubinin, the two were on the same flight back to New York after the end of the Reykjavik Summit. Slepak had been warned against approaching Dubinin, but Dubinin writes that he enjoyed talking with the varied passengers, including journalists, cultural figures, and human rights activists on the flight. Dubinin, *Vremia Peremen*, 150.

[144] Anatoly Chernyaev's Notes form the Politburo Session, November 13, 1986, READD-RADD Collection, National Security Archive; Politburo Minutes, November 13, 1986, in Anatoliia Cherniaeva, ed., *B Politbiuro CK KPSS … Po Zapisiam Anatoliia Cherniaeva, Vadima Medvedeva, Georgiia Shakhnazarova (1985–1991)* (Moscow: Al'pina Biznes Buks, 2006), 112; Thomas, "Human Rights Ideas, the Demise of Communism, and the End of the Cold War," 131; and Zubok, *A Failed Empire*, 298.

[145] Matlock, *Autopsy of an Empire*, 97. Other scholars such as Robert English have maintained the nuclear accident at Chernobyl in April 1986, not Reykjavik, spurred Gorbachev to focus more on respect for human rights issues, as it demonstrated the dangers of Soviet secrecy and the need to open the Soviet system. English, *Russia and the Idea of the West*, 220.

[146] Margaret Thatcher, *The Downing Street Years, 1979–1990* (New York: Harper Perennial, 1993), 772–3; Robert English, "The Sociology of New Thinking: Elites, Identity Change, and the End of the Cold War," *Journal of Cold War Studies* 7:2 (Spring 2005): 66; and Anatoly Chernyaev's Notes from the Politburo Session, May 8, 1987, REEADD-RADD, National Security Archive.

conscience and to allow those who wish to do so freely to leave their country, and we welcome the steps which you have already taken, the greater the readiness that you will find in the west to believe that peaceful and friendly relations with the Soviet Union cannot only be maintained but extended.[147]

Gorbachev's first months in office and early contacts with Western leaders highlighted for him what they had emphasized for some time, that the United States under Reagan, Britain under Thatcher, and other like-minded governments determined their relations with the Soviet Union based on its commitment to upholding international agreements and, in the case of the Helsinki Final Act, on its internal record on human rights. Reagan and Thatcher's message seems to have penetrated Gorbachev's policymaking in late 1986, when his efforts to pursue domestic reforms accelerated during the course of the Vienna Meeting.

---

[147] Margaret Thatcher, "Speech at Soviet Official Banquet," March 30, 1987, Margaret Thatcher Foundation, www.margaretthatcher.org. During her visit to the Soviet Union, Thatcher met with refuseniks and reported their spirits were raised by the knowledge that allies outside the Soviet Union kept attention focused on their cases. Margaret Thatcher, Public Statement: Prime Minister's Visit to the Soviet Union, April 2, 1987, Margaret Thatcher Foundation, www.margaretthatcher.org.

7

"A Debate in the Fox Den About Raising Chickens"

The Moscow Conference Proposal

Over the years of the CSCE Vienna Review Meeting, the Soviet attitude toward compliance with the Helsinki Final Act transformed. The pace and scope of change demonstrated a fundamentally different approach to human rights in the Soviet Union. Western pressure, ineffective for so many years, finally began to result in meaningful improvements, as Soviet leaders recognized they were necessary to improving relations. The new Soviet outlook also shaped the dynamics throughout the region, leading Eastern European governments to adopt a range of responses to demands for greater freedom. This chapter focuses on efforts by Gorbachev and Shevardnadze to prod the Soviet Union and Eastern Europe toward greater compliance with the Helsinki Final Act. Although other observers dispute the suggestion that pressure from Helsinki activists influenced Soviet behavior, I argue the Soviet proposal at the Vienna CSCE Review Meeting to host a conference on human rights in Moscow, as well as subsequent efforts to secure consensus for the proposed meeting, demonstrate the direct and indirect influence of transnational Helsinki activism.[1] A key element of this transformation was the Soviet decision to invite its prominent critics, including the International Helsinki Federation for Human Rights and the Commission, to Moscow in order to secure Western support for its new reform agenda.

---

[1] For skepticism about the influence of Helsinki activism, see Gubin, *International Regimes, Agenda Setting and Linkage Groups in U.S.–Soviet Relations*, 168; N. Edwina Moreton, "Security, Change, and Instability in Eastern Europe," in Derek Leebaert, ed., *European Security: Prospects for the 1980s* (Lexington: Heath, 1979); and Jonathan Luxmoore, "And So to Vienna ... The CSCE Eleven Years On," *Contemporary Review* 249:1451 (1986): 307.

Before the CSCE meeting in Vienna opened, little in Soviet behavior foretold the changes that would soon follow. As of early 1986, Gorbachev had yet to embrace human rights reforms, and small steps such as the release of Shcharansky and Orlov contrasted with an overall policy of repression and a continued reluctance to negotiate on human rights issues.[2] As Matlock has noted regarding this period, "Gorbachev had not yet acknowledged that protection of human rights was a legitimate subject for negotiation; the number of Jewish refuseniks continued to grow, and most of the political prisoners arrested in the 1970s and early 1980s remained in labor camps."[3] The death of Soviet dissident Anatoly Marchenko in prison on December 8, 1986, shortly after the negotiations at Vienna began, further heightened the considerable criticism from the West and demonstrated the costs of continuing human rights abuses. Marchenko's death, after months on a hunger strike advocating the release of political prisoners and an end to physical brutality in prisons, shook the delegates in Vienna and the human rights community more broadly. He had been a founding member of the Moscow Helsinki Group, joining from prison, and recently had written to the CSCE delegates in Vienna to draw attention to human rights abuses in the Soviet Union. With Marchenko's death as the latest signal of Soviet intransigence, many engaged in the Helsinki process doubted whether the Vienna Meeting would produce any meaningful change.

Despite such pessimism, the years of the Vienna Meeting, November 1986 to January 1989, ultimately corresponded with a period of fundamental reform in the Soviet Union that produced changes inconceivable to most participants in the Helsinki process. Signs of meaningful Soviet progress began with the release of Sakharov and his wife Yelena Bonner from internal exile in Gorky on December 16, 1986, and continued throughout Gorbachev's years in office; further steps such as the end of radio jamming, the easing of restrictions on emigration, and changes in the Soviet legal code were key elements of his reforms.[4]

---

[2] Lehne, *The Vienna Meeting of the Conference on Security and Cooperation in Europe*, 36–7.

[3] Matlock, *Reagan and Gorbachev*, 174–5.

[4] Discussion of ending Sakharov's internal exile had begun as early as September 1986 due to a growing belief that "Sakharov's return to Moscow will entail fewer political costs than his continued isolation in Gorky." Ligachev, Chebrikov, and Marchuk to the Central Committee, September 12, 1986, in Joshua Rubenstein and Alexander Gribanov, eds., *The KGB File of Andrei Sakharov*: http://www.yale.edu/annals/sakharov/documents_frames/Sakharov_191.htm (accessed on September 12, 2009). A final decision on Sakharov's and Bonner's fates was taken on November 10, 1986. Politburo Minutes, November 10, 1986

The Soviets' surprising proposal, announced at the outset of the Vienna Meeting, to host a human rights conference in Moscow became a central factor in reforms in this period. Many Western leaders would consider the meeting only if the Soviet Union met a long list of requirements, making the issue a critical bargaining chip within East–West relations. Gaining Western support necessitated far-reaching implementation of the Helsinki Final Act and fulfillment of many long-held Western objectives. The Soviet proposal and the efforts taken to secure it, demonstrate the long-term influence of transnational Helsinki activism, as international pressure exerted through the Helsinki process was a significant factor in the Soviet maneuvers.

When the Vienna Meeting began on November 4, 1986, almost all of the foreign ministers' opening statements reiterated long-standing positions. Western speeches emphasized religious freedom, the right to leave one's country, freedom of movement, the rights of national minorities, and the release of imprisoned Helsinki monitors.[5] British Foreign Secretary Sir Geoffrey Howe said that at Vienna the CSCE states would "aim to improve the quality of life for all Europeans," and Shultz delivered a forceful opening statement explicitly criticizing a range of human rights problems in Eastern Europe.[6] Predictably, most Eastern states used their speeches to resist the Western emphasis on human rights.

and Meeting with Members of the Politburo and the Secretaries of the Central Committee, December 1, 1986, in Cherniaeva, ed., *B Politbiuro CK KPSS ... Po Zapisiam Anatoliia Cherniaeva, Vadima Medvedeva, Georgiia Shakhnazarova (1985–1991),* 105, 114. The memoirs of Italian Communist Party official Antonio Rubbi indicate the party pressed Soviet officials on the treatment of dissidents and specifically Sakharov's internal exile. Antonio Rubbi, *Incontri con Gorbaciov: I colloqui di Natta e Occhetto con il leader sovietico: giugno 1984-novembre 1989* (Rome: Editori Riuniti, 1990), 65, 82. Sakharov wrote to Gorbachev soon after his return to Moscow, pressing him to grant an amnesty to political prisoners to solidify his democratization process for the Soviet Union. Sakharov to Gorbachev, January 20, 1987, S.II.1.4.19, Box 45, Sakharov Papers; and Joshua Rubenstein, "Introduction: Andrei Sakharov, the KGB, and the Legacy of Soviet Dissent," in Rubenstein and Gribanov, eds., *The KGB File of Andrei Sakharov,* 53. In the aftermath of Sakharov's release, many asked if his return to Moscow signified meaningful change in Soviet human rights practices. Sakharov himself adopted a cautious approach, signaling he hoped for widespread progress but needed more time to assess the changes taking place in the Soviet Union. Transcript, "This Week with David Brinkley," December 28, 1986, Folder 2, Box 4ad, Human Rights Collection, Sakharov Archives; and Chebrikov and Medvedev, October 19, 1988, REEADD-RADD Collection, National Security Archive.

5 Lehne, *The Vienna Meeting of the Conference on Security and Cooperation in Europe,* 70.
6 Shultz mentioned by name Helsinki monitors Anatoly Marchenko and Anatoly Koryagin as well as the internal exile of Andrei Sakharov, the plight of divided spouses, and the repression of Charter 77, the Jazz Section, Solidarity, and religious believers, among others. Geoffry Howe (United Kingdom), November 4, 1986, CSCE/WT/VR.2, OSCE Archives; and George Shultz (United States), November 5, 1986, CSCE/WT/VR.3, ibid.

The Soviet opening statement thus was extremely unexpected, and Shevardnadze shocked many of the assembled delegations with his proposal that the Soviet Union host a conference on human contacts, information, culture, and education in Moscow as one of the experts meetings to follow Vienna.[7] According to Soviet diplomat Yuri Kashlev, "The heads of the delegations froze with their mouths gaping" after hearing Shevardnadze's speech.[8] The Soviet proposal was the second of the entire Vienna Meeting, formally submitted on December 10, 1986, and it remained under consideration for the entire conference. As the Soviets only briefly outlined what they envisioned, the proposal bred confusion as delegations were unsure what stance to adopt.[9] Up to this point in the CSCE process, the only meeting held in a Warsaw Pact country was the 1985 Budapest Cultural Forum, at which the Hungarian government amassed a mixed record of openness, including the prohibition of a planned IHF counterconference (The Soviet Union, however, was a far more notorious human rights offender than Hungary.)

Some delegates were adamant that they would not consider the proposal given the USSR's abysmal rate of Helsinki compliance, whereas others thought its merits should be explored.[10] The United States, Canada, and Great Britain in particular resisted agreeing to the meeting.[11] A Canadian delegate likened it to "Hitler suggesting in 1938 that Berlin should host a conference on the welfare of the Jews," and an editorial in the Austrian *Die Presse* suggested the fulfillment of

[7] CSCE/WT.2, December 10, 1986, OSCE Archives; Eduard Shevardnadze (USSR), November 5, 1986, CSCE/WT/VR.3, OSCE Archives; and Bohdan Nahaylo, "Shevardnadze Proposes International Conference on Humanitarian Issues in Moscow," November 5, 1986, Human Rights, 1986–1987, Box 692, Old Code Subject Files, Soviet Red Archives, Records of Radio Free Europe/Radio Liberty Research Institute, Open Society Archives. According to Soviet diplomat Yuri Kashlev the conference proposal was developed clandestinely. Y. B. Kashlev, "Khel'sinskii Protsess I Prava Cheloveka," and Kashlev, "SBSE v 1975–1990," in Y. B. Kashlev, ed., *Khel'sinskii Protsess v Sovetskoi/ Rossiiskoi Vneshnei Politike*, 22, 70–1.

[8] The exception was the Warsaw Pact diplomats who had been alerted to the proposal several hours in advance. Ibid., 70–1.

[9] CSCE/WT.2, December 10, 1986, OSCE Archives.

[10] Some Western delegates also asked what effect a Moscow human rights meeting would have on the psyche of Soviet prisoners and dissidents. Memorandum, IHF to National Helsinki Committees, February 10, 1987, Memos, 1987, Box 20, Correspondence and Memoranda, Records of the International Helsinki Federation for Human Rights, Open Society Archives.

[11] Leatherman, *From Cold War to Democratic Peace*, 185; and Richard Schifter, "A Goal-Oriented Human Rights Dialogue Begins," in Adamishin and Schifter, *Human Rights, Perestroika, and the End of the Cold War*, 135.

such a proposal would be like "a debate in the fox den about raising chickens."[12] As the Soviets were slow to expand fully on their proposal, Western delegations, in consultation with NGOs such as the IHF, began amassing a list of conditions that might be necessary for its acceptance.[13] The proposal became the defining issue of the Vienna negotiations; for many observers, progress on the proposed Moscow conference served as a barometer of Eastern advancement on human rights, as the acceptance of the Moscow conference proposal and thus agreement on a concluding document was conditioned on Soviet progress on human rights.

Regardless of subsequent Soviet intransigence at Vienna, the Soviet proposal indicated a changed attitude toward the CSCE and a growing recognition that demonstrating a positive record on human rights was beneficial to Soviet interests. It outlined potential topics of discussion, covering a broad range of humanitarian issues, including freedom of expression, the right to employment, and access to medical care, among others. Soviet Deputy Foreign Minister and Vienna delegate Anatoly Kovalev declared the conditions of the meeting would be "in keeping with international standards," although he did not explain what this meant. Nor did Soviet delegation head Yuri Kashlev offer effective clarification: "We do not exclude the possibility that organizations involved in the Helsinki process could participate ... But at present it is difficult to be more specific. We'll have to take into account the existing norms and standards in this particular area."[14] Some observers suggested that Soviet authorities anticipated a significant propaganda bonus from hosting a humanitarian meeting and expected to be able to minimize damage by repressing open dissent during the meeting, which if effective, would be an "ingenious,

[12] Leatherman, *From Cold War to Democratic Peace*, 184; and Laber, *The Courage of Strangers*, 260.

[13] Roland Eggleston, "West Considers Soviet Proposal for Humanitarian Meeting in Moscow," Radio Liberty Research, December 4, 1986, Helsinki: Vienna, 1986–1989, Box 1118, Old Code Subject Files, Soviet Red Archives, Records of Radio Free Europe/Radio Liberty Research Institute, Open Society Archives; and Letter, Howe to Avebury, May 7, 1987, Correspondence: National Committees: United Kingdom, 1986–1992, Box 19, Correspondence and Memoranda, Records of the International Helsinki Federation for Human Rights, ibid.; and Confidential Memorandum, October 19, 1987, Folder 8, Box 7, International Helsinki Federation for Human Rights Files, Record Group 7, HRWR.

[14] Roland Eggleston, "USSR Talks About Proposed Moscow Conference," Radio Liberty Research, December 11, 1986, Human Rights, 1986–1987, Box 692, Old Code Subject Files, Soviet Red Archives, Records of Radio Free Europe/Radio Liberty Research Institute, Open Society Archives.

political move."[15] Subsequent accounts have suggested Soviet leaders also hoped a conference would facilitate reform.

Although the Soviet proposal suggested that Vienna could evolve differently than prior meetings had, CSCE diplomats nonetheless initially maintained familiar positions at Vienna. The United States delegation continued its long-standing strategy: focus on the review of implementation and emphasize individual cases. United States Ambassador Warren Zimmermann declared his intention to follow Goldberg's and Kampelman's policy of publicly naming specific cases of concern.[16] He noted the meeting offered an opportunity for "semipublic debate" in which the United States could assess the entire Soviet record.[17] The United States pushed the Soviets to make significant progress on releasing all political prisoners, addressing family reunification cases, increasing emigration, and ceasing jamming.[18] Some in the United States, and in particular members of Congress, wanted to withhold agreement on a final document until Soviet human rights practices improved. Their slogan was said to be "no compliance, no deal."[19]

[The Vienna Meeting offers important insight into the way Helsinki activists functioned and influenced the policy process.] For Helsinki

[15] Roland Eggleston, "Warsaw Pact Proposes Meetings to Follow Vienna Conference," December 18, 1986, Human Rights, 1986–1987, Box 692, Old Code Subject Files, Soviet Red Archives, Records of Radio Free Europe/Radio Liberty Research Institute, Open Society Archives; and Chris van Esterik and Hester Minnema, "The Conference that Came in from the Cold," in A. Bloed and P. Van Dijk, eds., *The Human Dimension of the Helsinki Process: The Vienna Follow-up Meeting and its Aftermath* (Boston: Martinus Nijhoff, 1991), 5.

[16] Zimmermann, a long-time Foreign Service Officer, had served as Kampelman's deputy at Madrid.

[17] Commission on Security and Cooperation in Europe Hearing, 99th Congress, 2nd Session, September 11, 1986; "Ambassador Zimmermann Testifies on Vienna Meeting," *CSCE Digest* September 1986, CSCE Digest, Box 6 Unprocessed, JBANC; and Victor Fedoseyev, "Interview with Head of US Delegation at CSCE Meeting in Vienna," Radio Liberty Research, June 10, 1987, Helsinki: Vienna, 1986–1989, Box 1118, Old Code Subject Files, Soviet Red Archives, Records of Radio Free Europe/Radio Liberty Research Institute, Open Society Archives. Fedoseyev interviewed Zimmermann on May 14.

[18] Commission on Security and Cooperation in Europe Hearing, 99th Congress, 2nd Session, September 11, 1986; and Leatherman, *From Cold War to Democratic Peace*, 181.

[19] Lehne, *The Vienna Meeting of the Conference on Security and Cooperation in Europe*, 69; and Telegram, VCSCE to EXTOTT, January 16, 1987, 20-4-CSCE-VIENN, Vol. 2, Historical Division, Ministry of Foreign Affairs, Ottawa, Ontario, Canada (hereafter Historical Division, Canada). Eastern European states and particularly the USSR, which was the target of the bulk of criticism in the early months in Vienna, responded negatively to the United States' continuing practice of naming names.

activists, the review meetings offered the best forum to shape Eastern practices either through new agreements or the attendant publicity of a condemnatory statement by a CSCE delegate.[20] Advocacy groups were active in Vienna and pursued a range of tactics to influence Western and neutral delegations, dispensing information and maintaining pressure on delegates. The connections among delegates and NGOs were manifested in a number of ways, including written correspondence, regular meetings, research reports, and personal contacts. As at Belgrade and Madrid, NGOs not only pressured CSCE delegates to raise specific cases at Vienna but also provided supporting documentation for such a strategy and even aided in drafting of the concluding document.[21] As many of the delegations did not have enough staff to conduct their own research, they worked with NGOs to stay apprised of Eastern European human rights abuses.[22] At Jeri Laber's urging, the IHF served during the Vienna Meeting "both as a coordinator of NGO and other activities and as a source of information for delegations and for the press." Furthermore, Laber recommended publishing a newsletter addressing the closed negotiations in an effort to "establish the IHF as a necessary center for all activities in Vienna." [23]

The interconnected nature of the Helsinki network and the international cooperation among interested NGOs was illustrated prominently at Vienna. One telling example was the repeated practice of Eastern dissidents joining Western Helsinki groups upon their emigration or exile.

[20] In advance of the Vienna Meeting, United States officials and NGOs engaged in the CSCE process met for a two-day conference on United States human rights policy in the CSCE context. Agenda, September 7–8, 1986, USSR: CSCE Follow-up Meeting, Vienna, 1985–1986, Box 47, Country Files, Jeri Laber Files, Record Group 7, HRWR. More than fifty NGOs were present for the opening session. Laber, *The Courage of Strangers*, 259.

[21] IHF Proposal, June 1988, Correspondence: National Committees: Germany, 1984–1992, Box 18; and Letter, Howe to Avebury, May 7, 1987, Correspondence: National Committees: United Kingdom, 1986–1992, Box 19, Correspondence and Memoranda, Records of the International Helsinki Federation for Human Rights, Open Society Archives.

[22] More striking is that policymakers regularly contacted NGOs unsolicited, illustrating the groups' scope of influence. For example, Zimmermann was so concerned about maintaining a strong relationship with Helsinki Watch that when he thought the United States position had been misrepresented as "backsliding," he wrote directly to Laber to clarify his stance. Letter and attachments, Zimmermann to Laber, October 24, 1988, CSCE: Third Follow-Up Meeting, Vienna: Miscellaneous, 1987–1989, Box 8, OSCE/CSCE Files, Records of the International Helsinki Federation for Human Rights, Open Society Archives.

[23] Memorandum from Jeri Laber, CSCE – Vienna Conference, 1986, Box 40, General Files, New York Office Files, Record Group 7, HRWR.

For example, Ludmilla Alekseeva worked with Helsinki Watch for many years as a part-time consultant after she left the Soviet Union and represented the group at Vienna.[24] Similarly, after his exile from the Soviet Union, Orlov attended the Vienna Meeting as the new honorary chair of the IHF.[25] Furthermore, during Vienna, Eastern European activists sought to enhance their connections regionally. According to Charter 77 signatory Jan Urban, "From the end of 1987, we Czech dissidents had concluded that it wasn't enough to make links with groups in the West, welcome as that was. We had to develop a broader context, and even cooperation, with dissidents in other parts of Eastern Europe."[26]

Lobbying Western and neutral diplomats was the focus of NGOs, but activists also attempted to influence Eastern Europe officials directly. For example, Anatoly Chernyaev notes that Gorbachev received many letters asking him to act to release Soviet dissidents.[27] Similarly, Helsinki Watch tried to communicate with Yuri Kashlev about the proposed Moscow conference.[28] Although largely repressed at this point, Eastern European activists also tried to influence the diplomats and negotiations at Vienna. For example, members of Czechoslovakia's Jazz Section appealed to the CSCE delegates, claiming their arrest and trial contravened the Helsinki agreement.[29] In another instance, Bulgarian dissidents wrote to Vienna diplomats alleging violations of the Helsinki agreement by their

[24] Laber, *The Courage of Strangers*, 121; and Orlov, *Dangerous Thoughts*, 301.

[25] Memorandum, Nagler and Minnema to National Committees, November 20, 1986, Memos, 1986, Box 20, Correspondence and Memoranda, Records of the International Helsinki Federation for Human Rights, Open Society Archives; Orlov, *Dangerous Thoughts*, 301, 309–10; and Korey, *The Promises We Keep*, 226.

[26] Pleshakov, *There Is No Freedom Without Bread!*, 154.

[27] Anatoly Chernyaev Diary, December 15, 1986, The National Security Archive. For example, Orlov, Alekseeva, and others wrote to Gorbachev on behalf of political prisoners living in "special regime" camps, where the conditions were so harsh, the authors pointed out one sixth of the prisoners, or ten of sixty, had died in the last three years. In particular, they raised the cases of eight Helsinki monitors serving sentences in "special regime" camps. Checlav Milosh et al. to Gorbachev, February 17, 1987, USSR: [Political] Prisoners, Jan–Feb 1987, Box 39, Country Files, Cathy Fitzpatrick Files, Record Group 7, HRWR.

[28] Bernstein to Kashlev, February 2, 1987, USSR: CSCE: Vienna, 1986–Feb 1987, Box 10, Country Files, Cathy Fitzpatrick Files, Record Group 7, HRWR.

[29] Appeals such as the Jazz Section's demonstrate that Eastern European dissidents believed gaining attention for their cause during a CSCE meeting could potentially improve their treatment. Zimmermann Statement, December 5, 1986, Warren Zimmermann Papers, Special Collections Research Center, Georgetown University, Washington, District of Columbia (hereafter Zimmermann Papers). The Jazz Section was an organization of musicians devoted to jazz music, but Czechoslovakian authorities charged it was engaging in antistate activities and repressed its leadership in the mid-1980s.

government.[30] In addition, many private citizens, without professional involvement in the cause, wrote letters to political officials and prison wardens seeking medical care, family visits, and releases for political prisoners. For much of the history of the Helsinki process thus far, however, such direct appeals had proved ineffective and held significance primarily as symbolic gestures.

Human rights and human contacts issues dominated much of the negotiations at Vienna. The plight of Helsinki monitors was an ongoing concern for Western and neutral CSCE delegates as well as NGOs at the Vienna Meeting.[31] Western states proposed expanding the right to monitor implementation of the Helsinki commitments and mandating that all CSCE states republish the Helsinki Final Act, the Madrid Concluding Document, the Vienna Concluding Document, and other documents related to human rights. It is likely Western ambassadors expected publication to spur increased monitoring activity, much as publishing the Helsinki Final Act had twelve years previously.[32]

A central component of the West's focus was creating a means to react formally to abuses when no CSCE meeting was in session. To this end, Western delegations introduced an outline for a human dimension mechanism. Different options available as part of the mechanism included requesting information from a government, initiating bilateral meetings, alerting other states of a problem, and enabling an ad hoc meeting of the thirty-five states to address the issue.[33] It would be used frequently in the years that followed to draw attention to human rights abuses, in particular the deteriorating situation in Yugoslavia.

The Soviet proposal for a human rights conference in Moscow was a preemptive response to years of international criticism and was the centerpiece of a calculated strategy to respond to Western scrutiny by projecting an improved Soviet image to the West. To this end, the Soviet delegation went to extensive lengths to interact with journalists in the early stages of the Vienna Meeting, holding six press conferences in one

---

[30] See Information from D. Stoyanov and M. Balev, April 24, 1987, Bulgaria in the Cold War, Cold War International History Project Virtual Archive.

[31] At the outset of the Vienna Meeting, forty-one Helsinki monitors were imprisoned in the Soviet Union. Czechoslovakia was also a target for human rights criticism for its treatment of Charter 77, VONS, and the Jazz Section. Lehne, *The Vienna Meeting of the Conference on Security and Cooperation in Europe*, 92.

[32] CSCE/WT.38, February 13, 1987, OSCE Archives.

[33] CSCE.WT.19, February 4, 1987, OSCE Archives.

week alone.[34] In contrast with previous meetings, Soviet delegates were willing to accept lists of refuseniks and political prisoners as well as to meet with a range of NGOs and individuals.[35] In the words of one observer, the Soviets tried to draw a contrast between their new openness and "the bad old days."[36] According to Shevardnadze, the Soviet Union's policy of increased contact with the press there was due to the influence of *glasnost'*. [37]

Despite the ostensibly open attitude and progressive promises, the West was frustrated by the incongruity between Gorbachev's talk about *perestroika* and *glasnost'* and the Soviet negotiating positions at Vienna. As in past conferences, the Soviet Union and its allies employed varied strategies to deflect Western human rights criticisms, including introducing new proposals and accusing the West of violations. The strategy of the Warsaw Pact diplomats at Vienna was to insist on compliance with economic, social, and cultural rights to counteract the Western emphasis on civil and political rights, causing the first year of debate in Vienna to be unproductive as the two sides pursued their own agendas, talking past each other rather than working together to reach mutual compromises.[38]

[34] In Helsinki Watch's analysis, "The Gorbachev government, in an unexpected series of acts and declarations, has apparently put human rights concerns at the top of its public agenda and is taking the initiative in related matters. Whatever the motivation behind the gestures that have been made, certain implications are clear. International concern about human rights abuses in the Soviet Union has not gone unnoticed by Soviet leaders." Annual Report, Helsinki Watch, A Report from Helsinki Watch: Annual Report, 1986, Box 1, General Files, New York Office Files, Record Group 7, HRWR.

[35] American embassy officials in Moscow spent considerable time formulating the list of cases on which the United States would formally ask the Soviets to act. Larry Napper Interview, October 1, 2009.

[36] Korey, "Helsinki, Human Rights, and the Gorbachev Style," 113–133; Roland Eggleston, "The New Soviet 'Openness in Vienna: Many Words, Little Substance," Radio Liberty Background Report, November 10, 1986, Helsinki: Vienna, 1986–1989, Box 1118, Old Code Subject Files, Soviet Red Archives, Records of Radio Free Europe/Radio Liberty Research Institute, Open Society Archives; Memorandum, Nagler and Minnema to National Committees, November 20, 1986, Memos, 1986, Box 20, Correspondence and Memoranda, Records of the International Helsinki Federation for Human Rights, ibid.; Korey, *The Promises We Keep*, 227, 271; and Orest Deychakiwsky, "Helsinki Review Process: Making Progress Slowly, but Surely," *Ukrainian Weekly*, January 18, 1987, 7. Deychakiwsky was a staff member of the Commission.

[37] Shevardnadze, *The Future Belongs to Freedom*, 44.

[38] Lehne, *The Vienna Meeting of the Conference on Security and Cooperation in Europe*, 74.

An additional tactic the Soviets pursued to deflect attention from their record was creating governmental bodies that supposedly addressed domestic human rights. First, they established a bureau on humanitarian affairs in the foreign ministry whose leader, Yuri Kashlev, also headed the Soviet delegation in Vienna.[39] American policymakers initially were unsure how to regard the new humanitarian and cultural affairs administration. Zimmermann and others ultimately discerned there was little substance behind it, but that it nonetheless signaled progress. In their view:

The primary function of the office, rather, seems to be propaganda, i.e., to defend Soviet human rights practices and to criticize Western countries for alleged abuses of human rights. The fact that the Soviets felt obliged to create such an office, however, does indicate increased Soviet sensitivity to Western human rights criticism.[40]

Soviet efforts indicated the leadership saw value in projecting a changed attitude to the international community.[41]

The Soviet Union also formed the Public Commission for International Cooperation in Humanitarian Problems and Human Rights in late 1987. Headed by Fedor Burlatsky, a Gorbachev adviser, it was charged with monitoring Soviet and other CSCE states' Helsinki compliance as well as reforming Soviet legislation.[42] According to an official statement, the Public Commission was designed "to achieve conformity of Soviet legislation with the obligations assumed by the Soviet Union in the Helsinki Final Act and in UN human rights documents."[43] In Burlatsky's view, the

[39] Korey, *The Promises We Keep*, 220.

[40] Commission on Security and Cooperation in Europe Hearing, September 11, 1986, 99th Congress/2nd Session.

[41] The Ministry of Foreign Affairs later changed the name of the Department of Humanitarian Cooperation to the Department of Humanitarian Cooperation and Human Rights, which in Schifter's view indicated "a fundamental change in the Soviet leadership's outlook on the subject of human rights." Richard Schifter, "Putting the Vienna CSCE Meeting on Our Bilateral Agenda," in Adamishin and Schifter, *Human Rights, Perestroika, and the End of the Cold War*, 168.

[42] Julia Wishnevsky, "Burlatsky on Goals of Soviet Human-Rights Commission," Radio Liberty Research, February 17, 1988, Human Rights, 1988–1988, Box 692, Old Code Subject Files, Soviet Red Archives, Records of Radio Free Europe/Radio Liberty Research Institute, Open Society Archives; Alexander Rahr, "USSR-Fedor Burlatsky to Head New Human Rights Commission," December 1, 1987, Politics: Human Rights: General, 1987–1988, Box 20, New Code Subject Files, ibid.; and Korey, *The Promises We Keep*, 220.

[43] Viktor Yasmann, "An Official Human Rights Organization in the USSR: 'New Thinking' or Propaganda?" Radio Liberty Research, January 12, 1988, Human Rights, 1988–1988, Box 692, Old Code Subject Files, Soviet Red Archives, Records of Radio Free Europe/Radio Liberty Research Institute, Open Society Archives; and Gilligan, *Defending Human Rights in Russia*, 74–5.

Public Commission served as a "legal opposition," focusing on political and civil rights and recognizing the rights of informal political groups.[44] At least initially, however, the Public Commission was designed more for propaganda purposes than to advocate or implement change.[45] A Helsinki Commission member described the Burlatsky Commission as "part of [the] overall effort of [the Soviet Union] to get out in front of [the human rights] issue."[46] Bonner denigrated it as "a creature of the KGB and the Politburo." [47]

Despite assessments that the Public Commission was intended as window dressing, Helsinki Watch and other human rights activists reached out to Burlatsky in the hope that a relationship might prove productive over time. Helsinki Watch began writing to Burlatsky's Commission to raise cases of Soviet human rights abuses, and representatives from the two organizations met in Paris in May 1988.[48] In Helsinki Watch's view, it was focused on the resolution of outstanding human rights cases whereas Burlatsky seemed interested in forging a broad relationship and garnering favorable press coverage.[49] Representatives of Amnesty International also met with members of the Public Commission in May 1988; the two groups reportedly talked about changes to Soviet criminal law, the reform of psychiatric practices, religious freedom, and the rights of conscientious objectors.[50] Helsinki Watch later organized a meeting for Burlatsky with human rights leaders in the United States based on his stated interest in learning from their "experience in shaping public opinion in order to influence the government." At the session, Burlatsky

---

[44] Stephen F. Cohen and Katrina Vanden Heuvel, *Voices of Glasnost: Interviews with Gorbachev's Reformers* (New York: W. W. Norton Company, 1989), 174.

[45] The Commission's creation may have been prompted by concerns about potential criticism of the Soviet human rights record in Washington during Gorbachev's visit there, as the announcement of its establishment came only a few days before Gorbachev traveled to the United States.

[46] Steno Notebook, November 1988, Folder 18, Box 175, Dennis DeConcini Papers, University of Arizona, Tucson, Arizona (hereafter DeConcini Papers).

[47] Gilligan, *Defending Human Rights in Russia*, 75.

[48] See for example, U.S. Helsinki Watch Committee to Burlatsky, July 22, 1988, Burlatsky, Fyodor: Correspondence, 1988–1989, Box 44, Country Files, Jeri Laber Files, Record Group 7, HRWR.

[49] Memorandum, USSR: Burlatsky, Fyodor: Meetings, 1988, Box 44, Country Files, Jeri Laber Files, Record Group 7, HRWR.

[50] Amnesty International Press Release, May 13, 1988, USSR – Reports and Information, 1985–1988, Box 364, Series 2: Country Files, Record Group IX: Communications Department/Media Relations Files, Amnesty International USA Archives, Center for Human Rights Documentation and Research, Rare Book and Manuscript Library, Columbia University Library, New York, New York.

equated his commission to "the legal opposition to the bureaucracy" but said the "hardest thing for us to do is individual cases."[51]

Soviet actions thus far suggested only cosmetic changes, and Western delegates largely perceived the Soviets to be unwilling to engage in productive negotiations. By March 1987, the Soviet Union had sponsored thirty-two proposals, of which none addressed substantive human rights and human contacts questions. Indeed, some Western diplomats saw the Soviet efforts as characteristic of earlier meetings in which *glasnost'* was not yet the official policy in Moscow. In the words of one Western diplomat: "We have heard a lot from Moscow and various Soviet officials about new thinking in regard to such problems as exit visas for those who want to go abroad to meet their families. One would expect the USSR to show it is serious by presenting some of these ideas in Vienna. But the table is bare."[52] To the great frustration of the delegates, progress had been more apparent in Moscow than at the negotiating sessions.[53]

The British delegation, led by Laurence O'Keefe, was the most vocal in its frustration that human rights policies in the East were not changing fast enough. O'Keefe noted that although some political prisoners had been released, high numbers remained in jail, labor camps, and psychiatric institutions.[54] Richard Schifter argued similarly that the Soviet steps had amounted only to a "heightened media consciousness" but did not reflect an authentic effort at human rights reform.[55] Canadian ambassador

[51] Notes on Meeting with Burlatsky, June 1988, USSR: Public [Human Rights] Commission, May 1988–1989, Box 43, Country Files, Cathy Fitzpatrick Files, Record Group 7, HRWR.

[52] Roland Eggleston, "Gorbachev's 'New Thinking' and the Vienna Conference," Radio Liberty Research, March 18, 1987, Helsinki: Vienna, 1986–1989, Box 1118, Old Code Subject Files, Soviet Red Archives, Records of Radio Free Europe/Radio Liberty Research Institute, Open Society Archives; and Lehne, *The Vienna Meeting of the Conference on Security and Cooperation in Europe,* 75. Helsinki Watch was concerned about the makeup of Burlatsky's Commission given indications that some members were not committed to human rights, including one person a Helsinki Watch staff member described as a "real bad egg in psychiatry." Memorandum, n.d., USSR: Burlatsky, Fyodor: Meetings, 1988, Box 44, Country Files, Jeri Laber Files, Record Group 7, HRWR.

[53] Memorandum, IHF to National Helsinki Committees, February 10, 1987, Memos, 1987, Box 20, Correspondence and Memoranda, Records of the International Helsinki Federation for Human Rights, Open Society Archives.

[54] Statement, O'Keefe, May 22, 1987, OSCE Archives; Statement, O'Keefe, July 31, 1987, ibid.; and Esterik and Minnema, "The Conference that Came in from the Cold," in Bloed and Van Dijk, eds., *The Human Dimension of the Helsinki Process,* 18.

[55] Eggleston, "Schifter Speech in Vienna on Developments in the USSR," January 28, 1987, Politics: Human Rights: General, 1986–7, Box 19, New Code Subject Files, Soviet Red Archives, Records of Radio Free Europe/Radio Liberty Research Institute, Open Society Archives.

William Bauer said, "The Soviet human rights record remains deplorable. The new wind which we are told blows from Moscow brings no refreshing change."[56] Given Western sentiment, the Soviets faced a difficult challenge in gaining acceptance for their proposal to hold a conference in Moscow.

Not only did the lack of meaningful Soviet proposals at Vienna frustrate diplomats there, but the USSR and its satellite states continued to violate their citizens' human rights. Speaking about several long-time Soviet refuseniks on hunger strikes in an effort to secure permission to emigrate, Zimmermann said, "Is it really necessary for people to starve themselves in order to exercise a right which all the participating states recognized in signing the Final Act?"[57] In another instance, Charter 77 activist Pavel Wonka died tragically in Czechoslovak custody. His death came less than two months after he appealed to the Vienna delegates to ensure that his "voice is not silenced – under some pretext – in prison."[58]

In this context of Western frustration, the Soviets elaborated on their conference proposal through a July 1987 addendum, notably indicating they wanted the conference to begin at the level of foreign minister and the sessions to be open to the media and the public. In a press conference that followed, Kashlev indicated only that the Soviets would adhere to the pattern of other CSCE meetings concerning access for NGOs, journalists, and other foreigners: "The procedures will be the same as here in Vienna and as have existed in Madrid, Ottawa, Berne, and other cities."[59] A few months later at a panel organized by the IHF, however, Soviet delegate Yuri Kolosov backed away from earlier Soviet commitments, saying NGOs would be permitted in Moscow during the conference, but not everyone who wanted to travel to Moscow would be allowed: "Every state has its own rules on issuing visas. We also have our rules. Every state has a list of unwanted people. The list is computerized.

---

[56] Lehne, *The Vienna Meeting of the Conference on Security and Cooperation in Europe*, 89.

[57] Zimmermann Statement, March 27, 1987, Zimmermann Papers.

[58] Zimmermann Statement, April 29, 1988, Zimmermann Papers.

[59] Statement, Zimmermann, July 28, 1987, OSCE Archives; Mala Tabory, "The Vienna CSCE Concluding Document: Some General and Jewish Perspectives," *Soviet Jewish Affairs* 19:1 (1989): 3–18; Roland Eggleston, "Disappointing Soviet Statement on Human-Rights Conference," Radio Liberty Research, July 25, 1987, Human Rights, 1987–1987, Box 692, Old Code Subject Files, Soviet Red Archives, Records of Radio Free Europe/Radio Liberty Research Institute, Open Society Archives; CSCE/WT.2/ Add.1, July 24, 1987, OSCE Archives; and Statement, Yuri Kashlev (USSR), July 24, 1987, ibid.

If any person in the computer is regarded as *persona non grata* with respect to entering our country, such a person will not be admitted."[60] Leaving aside the content of his remarks, that a Soviet official participated in an IHF panel demonstrated a shift in tactics for the Soviets, in a bid to gain support for their conference proposal, the Soviet delegation courted NGOs. Soviet efforts reflected the significance they attributed to improving their image, realizing that listening to NGO concerns was important for their international reputation and agenda, and by extension a way to influence Western delegations. Nonetheless, the mixed Soviet messages complicated a Western decision on the proposal.

The Soviet proposal produced differences of opinion among the Western states as to the prerequisites for agreeing to such a conference. Most notably, the United States and the United Kingdom were vehement that they would not agree to the conference without meaningful implementation of past agreements, whereas others identified the conference itself as an opportunity to spotlight the Soviet human rights record.[61] Canada, France, Portugal, the Netherlands, and Monaco did not support the initiative, with France offering to hold the conference in Paris instead. Italy favored setting conditions for an agreement, whereas Spain expressed concerns that such conditions could be seen by the Soviets as a refusal.[62] Others, such as the FRG, were more moderate in their stance

[60] The influence of NGOs on Soviet policy also can be seen in Soviet efforts to improve their record on psychiatric abuse before reapplying to the World Psychiatric Association from which it had withdrawn under threat of expulsion in 1983. As part of that effort, Burlatsky's commission planned a hearing on psychiatric abuse in the Soviet Union in late November 1988. Roland Eggelston, "The Vienna Debate on the Proposed Moscow Human-Rights Meeting," Radio Liberty Research, October 27, 1987, Human Rights, 1987–1987, Box 692, Old Code Subject Files, Soviet Red Archives, Records of Radio Free Europe/Radio Liberty Research Institute, Open Society Archives; and Letter, Fitzpatrick to Nagler and Minnema, October 13, 1988, Correspondence: National Committees: USA/Helsinki Watch, 1988–1992, Box 19, Correspondence and Memoranda, Records of the International Helsinki Federation for Human Rights, ibid.

[61] Annette McGill, "Thatcher on Moscow Human Rights Conference," October 28, 1988, Politics: Human Rights: General, 1988–1988, Box 22, New Code Subject Files, Soviet Red Archives, Records of Radio Free Europe/Radio Liberty Research Institute, Open Society Archives; Heraclides, *Security and Co-operation in Europe*, 98; and Brinkley, ed., *The Reagan Diaries*, 657. Internal National Security Council documents address American concerns that agreeing to a Moscow conference proposal could confer "extraordinary legitimacy" on the Soviet system and Gorbachev's leadership in particular. One NSC staffer wrote that agreeing to a human rights conference in Moscow was "mind-boggling, if not obscene" and threatened to undermine "15 years of Western human rights policy." Rodman to Carlucci, September 25, 1987, Soviet Union 1987–1988 Memos, etc. [5 of 7], Box 92158, Nelson Ledsky Files, RRL.

[62] Update, July 7, 1987, Memos, 1986, Box 20, Correspondence and Memoranda, Records of the International Helsinki Federation for Human Rights, Open Society Archives;

and argued that a conference could offer support to Soviet dissidents.[63] Genscher writes, "For my part I believed that an open human-rights conference in Moscow would positively affect human rights within the Soviet Union even before the fact."[64]

Like many other controversial proposals, Moscow's push to hold a human rights conference prompted considerable dialogue among dissidents, human rights activists, and CSCE diplomats, illustrating again their close transnational connections. Interested groups and individuals shared their views with CSCE delegates as to what conditions should be imposed on Moscow in exchange for agreeing to the conference.[65] By and large, the conditions focused on two categories: improvements in Soviet human rights practices before agreeing to the conference and commitments on the circumstances of the meeting in Moscow, such as open sessions, guaranteed entry to the Soviet Union for the duration of the meeting, as well as opportunities for parallel meetings and demonstrations. Only months after Shevardnadze made his proposal, the IHF urged the Western delegations to support it as long as the Soviet Union

---

Roland Eggleston, "Question Mark over Moscow Humanitarian Conference," June 9, 1988, Human Rights, 1988–1988, Box 692, Old Code Subject Files, Soviet Red Archives, Records of Radio Free Europe/Radio Liberty Research Institute, ibid.; and Heraclides, *Security and Co-operation in Europe*, 88.

[63] Heraclides, *Security and Co-operation in Europe*, 87.

[64] Explaining his position further, Genscher writes, "I could not understand why many of my Western colleagues hesitated or rejected the proposal. A CSCE conference on human rights in Moscow could only expand the potential of our human-rights policy; I expressed this thought openly in my support of the Soviet suggestion." Genscher, *Rebuilding a House Divided*, 109, 195–6.

[65] Memorandum, IHF to Delegations to the Vienna CSCE Meeting, February 4, 1987, Memos 1987, Box 20, Correspondence and Memoranda, Records of the International Helsinki Federation for Human Rights, Open Society Archives; Letter, Howe to Avebury, May 7, 1987, Correspondence: National Committees: United Kingdom, 1986–1992, Box 19, ibid.; "Appeal by Doctor Yuri Orlov to the Vienna CSCE Meeting," January 27, 1987, Memoranda, 1987, Box 20, ibid.; and Official Response of U.S. Helsinki Watch Committee, January 21, 1987, USSR: CSCE: Vienna, 1986–Feb 1987, Box 10, Country Files, Cathy Fitzpatrick Files, Record Group 7, HRWR. The Vladimir Bukovsky Foundation, located in Amsterdam, also undertook an assessment of what conditions would make a conference in Moscow acceptable. The foundation initially outlined the unconditional release and rehabilitation of all political prisoners; an end to the abuse of psychiatry; protection for religious freedom; open access to Moscow during the conference to NGOs, the press, and human rights activists, regardless of where they reside and their prior records in the Soviet Union; freedom of movement and assembly during the conference; and protections for the free flow of information during the meeting. Yet, it suggested such conditions were not possible in the Soviet Union and that to agree to such a meeting would be unprincipled and risky, undermining the integrity of the Helsinki process. Robert van Voren, "Is a Human Rights Conference in Moscow Acceptable?" August 1987, Folder 2, Box 37, Human Rights Collection, Sakharov Archives.

met certain requirements, including the release of all Helsinki monitors and other political prisoners from jails, labor camps, internal exile, and psychiatric institutions.[66] Separately, Orlov advocated considerable stipulations, including freeing all political prisoners and admission to the meeting for journalists, human rights groups, activists, and Soviet citizens. If such steps were taken, Orlov said that he would travel to Moscow himself for the meeting.[67] Sakharov, whom Shultz asked for his view, said that the United States should have two key conditions: the Soviet withdrawal from Afghanistan and the release of political prisoners.[68]

In the talks at Vienna, and in diplomatic contacts elsewhere, United States officials repeatedly noted they were evaluating Soviet human rights abuses with the proposed Moscow conference in mind. Zimmermann enumerated an ambitious list of changes he felt the Soviet Union needed to undertake to demonstrate compliance with the Helsinki Final Act. He kept the focus on those still imprisoned, denied the right to emigrate, and limited in their access to information.[69] In addition to significant steps such as amnestying all political prisoners, he also called for an institutionalization of such changes by abolishing the articles in the Soviet criminal code that facilitated politically motivated arrests and sentences.[70]

[66] Memorandum, IHF to Delegations to the Vienna CSCE Meeting, February 4, 1987, Memos 1987, Box 20, Correspondence and Memoranda, Records of the International Helsinki Federation for Human Rights, Open Society Archives.

[67] Orlov, *Dangerous Thoughts*, 304–5; and Eggleston, "Yuri Orlov Sets Conditions for Moscow Human Rights Conference," November 22, 1988, Human Rights, Declarations, 1988–1990, Box 693, Old Code Subject Files, Soviet Red Archives, Records of Radio Free Europe/Radio Liberty Research Institute, Open Society Archives. According to Orlov, he had differences with some human rights activists including members of Helsinki Watch about the conditions to which the Soviets should be held with regard to agreement on the Moscow meeting. Orlov was firm that all political prisoners should be released. Yuri Orlov Interview, March 27 and 28, 2008.

[68] Sakharov was less concerned with emigration as an issue and more concerned with the rights of those living in the Soviet Union. Matlock, *Reagan and Gorbachev*, 291.

[69] For example, Zimmermann Statement, May 5, 1987, Zimmermann Papers. Sakharov wrote to Zimmermann in early January 1987 expressing his gratitude for the support of the American delegation at Vienna and to the ambassador personally, suggesting their consistent defense of Sakharov and Bonner contributed to their release from internal exile. Sakharov to Zimmermann, January 25, 1987, in the possession of the author; Sakharov to Zimmermann, n.d., S.III.1.2.53, Box 61, Sakharov Papers; and Warren Zimmermann Interview, December 10, 1996, *The Foreign Affairs Oral History Collection of the Association for Diplomatic Studies and Training*, Library of Congress, http://memory.loc.gov/ammem/collections/diplomacy/ (accessed March 6, 2010).

[70] Whitehead Statement, June 23, 1987, Zimmermann Papers; and Zimmermann Statement, May 5, 1987, ibid.

The Soviet Union undertook more meaningful steps to improve its human rights record in 1987, releasing political prisoners, acting on family reunification cases, and curbing radio jamming. Of particular significance to the United States was the emigration of Jewish refusenik Ida Nudel whose case had first come to Reagan's attention in the 1970s; Shultz later said he regarded the Soviet decision to grant her an exit visa as one of his most significant accomplishments.[71] In a further sign of increased Soviet willingness to resolve human rights cases, the Soviet government responded for the first time to Helsinki Commission entreaties by resolving 137 cases of the 442 the Commission had raised several months earlier. Commission Cochair Steny Hoyer (D-MD) called the Soviet response "a positive move forward because it is the first time the Soviets have ever responded directly to a list presented by the official United States commission monitoring the Helsinki Accords. Hopefully this is an indication that the Soviets are willing to take specific steps to fulfill their Helsinki humanitarian commitments." According to the Commission, the 137 cases that the Soviets resolved involved more than 300 individuals long-seeking emigration from the Soviet Union.[72]

By 1987, aides to Gorbachev and Shevardnadze were also working on reforming Soviet emigration policy. According to Anatoly Adamishin, the view of some Soviet officials was that "Those who want to emigrate from the country should be in a position to do so. It is not only a moral imperative ... but also our international obligation." Similarly, they noted that "a positive evolution in this field of human rights will bring not only political and propaganda benefits but eventually material advantages as well; it will help remove such pleasant phenomena as trade embargoes, denial of most-favored-nation status, and restrictions on technology supplies." Adamishin remembers that in discussions of liberalizing emigration at a Politburo meeting, Gorbachev said, "Let people travel the way it is done all over the world."[73]

---

[71] Shultz describes Nudel's phone call to him from Israel upon her arrival there as "a very emotional moment" for him. Rozanne Ridgway Interview, Folder 30, Box 2, Oberdorfer Papers; George Shultz Interview, Folder 2, Box 3, ibid.; and George Shultz Interview, December 18, 2002, Reagan Presidential Oral History Project, Miller Center, University of Virginia, Charlottesville, Virginia.

[72] "Soviets Announce Resolution of Commission Cases," *CSCE Digest* April 1987, CSCE Digest, Box 6, JBANC.

[73] Anatoly Adamishin, "Enter Gorbachev," in Adamishin and Schifter, *Human Rights, Perestroika, and the End of the Cold War*, 86–7.

Zimmermann and the United States delegation believed there was a "growing basis for hope" on human rights questions but noted the Soviet Union needed to make greater progress and institutionalize changes in human rights practices.[74] The litany of conditions considered by Western governments would have seemed entirely implausible a few years earlier, but by fall 1987 Adamishin told Richard Schifter that in response to a question about political prisoners, the Soviet Union had decided to bring itself into compliance with all international agreements.[75] The Soviet Union made important strides that year, including releasing 140 political prisoners in February, ceasing to jam Voice of America in May, and allowing German and Jewish emigration to rise significantly.[76]

By the summer of 1988, the status of the Soviet conference proposal remained unclear, as the issue had not been formally raised at Vienna in some time. Some Western diplomats thought the Soviets finally might have acknowledged opposition to their proposal was insurmountable, as pressure on the Soviet Union and its allies to resolve human rights cases continued unabated.[77] For example, in August 1988, Zimmermann suggested the Soviet Union needed to make more progress: "Why can't all prisoners of conscience be released? ... Why can't all monitors be freed?"[78] This idea would later be termed a "zero option" by Hoyer; the United States wanted there to be no remaining political prisoners, divided spouses, or divided families by the end of the Vienna Meeting.[79]

Nevertheless, the USSR remained interested in the proposed conference, and Soviet officials continued to indicate they were committed to making the necessary concessions; for example, Kashlev proactively asked Zimmermann for a list of prisoners about whom the United States was concerned in an attempt to gain favor.[80] Jack Matlock similarly points to the 1988 Party Conference theses as a genuine turning point for Soviet

---

[74] Zimmermann Statement, September 22, 1987, Zimmermann Papers.

[75] Richard Schifter Interview, May 5, 2008.

[76] Lehne, *The Vienna Meeting of the Conference on Security and Cooperation in Europe*, 106.

[77] Roland Eggleston, "Question Mark Over Humanitarian Conference," Radio Liberty Research, June 9, 1988, Human Rights, 1988–1988, Box 692, Old Code Subject Files, Soviet Red Archives, Records of Radio Free Europe/Radio Liberty Research Institute, Open Society Archives; and Eggleston, "USSR Revives Proposal for Humanitarian Meeting in Moscow," July 1, 1988, Politics: General: Human Rights, 1988–1988, Box 21, New Code Subject Files, ibid.

[78] Underlining in original. Zimmermann Statement August 5, 1988, Zimmermann Papers.

[79] Hoyer Statement, November 11, 1988, Zimmermann Papers.

[80] Cable, AmEmbassy Vienna to SecState, June 20, 1988, Eastern Europe (General) 1987–1988 Memos, Cables, Reports, Articles (1 of 2), Box 92440, Nelson Ledsky Files, RRL.

commitment to human rights: "Never before had I seen in an official Communist Party document such an extensive section on protecting the rights of citizens." For Matlock, the theses signaled that Gorbachev was incorporating respect for human rights as an element of *perestroika*.[81] Gorbachev also articulated his new approach to the other leaders of Warsaw Pact states:

The development of relations with the governments of the West presumes the development of humanitarian contacts as well. On this topic, our western partners have long seen a weak spot in us. This in itself has been facilitated by our avoiding serious conversation about human rights and, at times – we must be honest here – our dogmatic position, as if Socialism had not already achieved its goals, and had limits in the area of civil rights and freedoms ... Of course, we have not allowed anyone to preach at us, nor to meddle in our internal affairs. But we approach the matter with the understanding that humanitarian problems, human rights – these are subjects of legal concern to the entire world community.[82]

As CSCE diplomats negotiated in Vienna, Shultz, Schifter, and Arthur Hartman, the United States ambassador in Moscow, pressed the Soviets in bilateral channels as well.[83] Schifter describes considerable diplomacy outside of formal negations, in which both he and Adamishin tried to work around their bureaucracies. In the first half of 1988, Soviet and American officials were meeting every six weeks to discuss human rights concerns.[84] According to Adamishin, by this point human rights had risen

---

[81] Matlock, *Autopsy of an Empire*, 122–3.

[82] Document No. 135: Speech by Gorbachev at the Political Consultative Committee Meeting in Warsaw, July 15, 1988, in Mastny and Byrne, ed., *A Cardboard Castle?*, 612–13.

[83] At one point, Shevardnadze's deputy, Anatoly Adamishin, asked Schifter if they could agree to the human rights conference without "haggling as if we were in a bazaar." Richard Schifter Interview, May 5, 2008. As high-level discussions ensued about agreement to the conference, the State Department carefully followed political prisoners' releases in the Soviet Union with members of the embassy there working to stay on top of the developments. John Finerty, written communication with the author, June 24, 2008; and Larry Napper Interview, October 1, 2009. American officials pressed other Eastern European officials on their human rights records as well. For example, John Whitehead, United States Under Secretary of State, told Bulgarian leader Todor Zhivkov that Bulgaria and the United States "do not share a common view of what human rights are." Whitehead went on to say, "I think that all major differences stem from [the issue of human rights and human freedoms]; it is in this sphere that mutual understanding is most difficult to reach." Memorandum of Conversation, Whitehead and Zhivkov, February 4, 1987, *Cold War International History Project Bulletin* 14/15 (Winter 2003/Spring 2004): 429–32.

[84] Schifter, "Putting the Vienna CSCE Meeting on Our Bilateral Agenda," and Schifter, "A Goal-Oriented Human Rights Dialogue Begins," in Adamishin and Schifter, *Human Rights, Perestroika, and the End of the Cold War*, 144, 149.

in significance as an issue in the Soviet view of its relations with the United States such that it was at times regarded on par with disarmament.[85]

Consistent with its policy, the Reagan administration continued its practice of always including human rights on its agenda for meetings with Soviet leaders. Shultz in particular was committed to pressing the issue, as Reagan noted in his diary after a meeting with Shultz: "He presented some material on his coming trip to Moscow having to do with Human Rights. He really wants to go after observance by the Soviets of the Helsinki Pact."[86] The following month, Shultz invited Jewish refuseniks to a Seder at Spaso House over Passover in April 1987, which both Kampelman and former State Department official Charles Hill suggest had an important influence of Soviet authorities as it highlighted that Jewish emigration was a priority for Shultz.[87] Shultz's emphasis on the issue slowly produced results, and he began to see genuine change in the Soviet position when Shevardnadze told him in September 1987, "Give me your lists and we will be glad to look at them."[88] By October 1987, the Soviets had granted exit visas to 6,000 people, more than six times the number in 1986, although 7,500 cases remained. After meeting with Shevardnadze in Moscow, Shultz believed the Soviet system of reviewing applications was finally effective. Not only was Shevardnadze an improvement over Gromyko in his willingness to listen to Shultz's concerns and occasionally act on cases Shultz had mentioned, but by 1987, United States Ambassador to the Soviet Union Jack Matlock argues, "Shevardnadze actually began to try to change the system."[89]

[85] Anatoly Adamishin, August 5, 1989 Interview Transcript, Folder 1, Box 1, The Hoover Institution and the Gorbachev Foundation (Moscow) Collection, Hoover Institution Archives, Stanford, California. Copyright Stanford University.

[86] March 18, 1987, Brinkley, ed., *The Reagan Diaries*, 484.

[87] Max Kampelman Interview, June 24, 2003, *The Foreign Affairs Oral History Collection of the Association for Diplomatic Studies and Training*, Library of Congress, http://memory.loc.gov/ammem/collections/diplomacy/ (accessed March 8, 2010); Charles Hill, written communication with the author, March 29, 2010; and Beckerman, *When They Come For Us, We'll Be Gone*, 511–13.

[88] Shultz, *Turmoil and Triumph*, 986. According to Ridgway, Shultz's repeated entreaties convinced Soviet leaders changing their human rights practices was in the best interests of their reform efforts. Rozanne Ridgway Interview, Folder 30, Box 2, Oberdorfer Papers. Hill emphasizes Shultz's role in convincing Gorbachev and Shevardnadze that human rights violations were a "practical problem" for the Soviet Union. Charles Hill, written communication with the author, March 29, 2010.

[89] Matlock, *Reagan and Gorbachev*, 265; and AP, "Soviets Sending Positive Signals on Human Rights, Shultz Says," October 22, 1987, Politics: Human Rights: General, 1987–1987, Box 19, New Code Subject Files, Soviet Red Archives, Records of Radio Free Europe/Radio Liberty Research Institute, Open Society Archives.

Nevertheless, the large number of exit visas outstanding indicated many problems remained, raising questions about the depth of the Soviet commitment to change.

Although most NGOs had directed their efforts at inducing Western leaders to advance their agenda for much of the CSCE process, as the Vienna Meeting progressed, some shifted their attention to lobbying Eastern states. By 1987, Laber suggests that Helsinki Watch was beginning to have real influence in Eastern Europe:

They were responding – to our prisoner lists, our recommendations. We saw an opportunity to become active players in the Soviet Union and Eastern Europe and began seeking direct contacts with formerly unapproachable officials. We, and the Helsinki committees in Western Europe that we had organized, were virtually the only Western human rights groups that had been consistently involved in the region. Now everyone was turning to us – seeking our information and asking us for direction.[90]

At the end of 1988, the IHF wrote in its annual report that changes in Eastern countries had led to less resistance to IHF inquiries. It reported a shift to "dialogue" with these countries, which enabled the IHF to be more productive on human rights issues, including the opening of a channel of communication with the Soviet Union through its trip to Moscow.[91]

As the Vienna Meeting advanced, human rights activists in Eastern European states tested the limits of reform. For example, Press Club Glasnost, a Soviet affiliate of the IHF as of October 1987, decided to organize a seminar of nongovernmental organizations to evaluate the government's attitudes toward unofficial meetings and conferences.[92] The seminar was held in December 1987 and, in a positive development, was not harassed or obstructed by Soviet security forces. Nevertheless, Soviet officials developed a plan to contain the "provocative actions" of the seminar's participants, including blocking entry by some activists from the West and Poland as well as restricting the access of some Soviet human rights advocates.[93]

---

[90] Laber, *The Courage of Strangers*, 276.

[91] Laber suggests that after the IHF's trip to Moscow, other Eastern European countries felt compelled to receive it as well. Annual Report, 1988, Box 1, Publications, Records of the International Helsinki Federation for Human Rights, Open Society Archives; and Laber, *The Courage of Strangers*, 296.

[92] Appeal, September 2, 1987, USSR: Press Club Glasnost, 1987, Box 60, Country Files, Jeri Laber Files, Record Group 7, HRWR; and Central Committee Declaration, December 4, 1987, Perechen 18, Dokument 120, Fond 89.

[93] Central Committee Declaration, December 28, 1987, Perechen 18, Dokument 121, Fond 89.

The limits on political dissidence in Eastern Europe varied at this point, as the Czechoslovakian government prevented "Czechoslovakia '88," an event examining the historical significance of the country in European history, from going forward. Instead, police detained many potential Czechoslovakian participants and warned foreigners against holding the symposium.[94] In Krakow, Poland, on the other hand, more than 1,000 people participated in a human rights meeting in August 1988.[95]

Gorbachev's visit to the United States in 1987 from December 8 to 10 highlighted the contradictions in Soviet policy as he gave conflicting signals about his willingness to make strides on human rights.[96] Matlock writes that by the time of the Washington summit in December, Soviet aides were willing to include human rights discussions on the meeting's agenda, but talks on the subject did not go smoothly; Gorbachev was particularly irritated at Reagan's attempts to press for increased Jewish emigration and human rights.[97] According to one account, when Reagan brought up human rights and Jewish emigration at the outset of the summit, Gorbachev told his translator Reagan was "blathering on again."[98]

[94] Zimmermann Statement, November 15, 1988, Zimmermann Papers. Shortly thereafter in response to a reporter's question about Czechoslovakia's "outcast" status as the result of its actions, Zimmermann said, "I think the conduct of the Prague regime is really so far in contradiction to the ideals of the Helsinki process that one has to think twice about contributions which the Prague government offers for the Helsinki process." Press Conference Transcript, November 18, 1988, Zimmermann Papers. Compelled to monitor Czechoslovakian compliance in the wake of a government crackdown, a Czechoslovak Helsinki Committee formed at the end of 1988 and affiliated with the IHF. According to a Canadian diplomat, Czechoslovak authorities allowed a small demonstration to commemorate Human Rights Day in December 1988 in conjunction with French President Françoise Mitterrand's visit to Czechoslovakia. In his view, the permission was a cynical ploy to gain favor with the French and to convey an impression of greater liberalization than existed at the time. Rob McRae, *Resistance and Revolution: Václav Havel's Czechoslovakia* (Ottawa: Carleton University Press, 1997), 13.

[95] Zimmermann Statement, October 21, 1988, Zimmermann Papers.

[96] Reagan's aides suggested he should use the overlap between Human Rights Day and Gorbachev's visit to highlight the American commitment to the issue by holding the traditional White House ceremony celebrating the event. Ermath to Powell and Griscom, November 13, 1987, Human Rights Day, Box 92251, Lisa Jameson Files, RRL.

[97] Matlock, *Reagan and Gorbachev*, 268; Letter, Fitzpatrick to Minnema, December 16, 1987, Delegation to Moscow: Briefing Materials, 1987, Box 3, Project Files, Records of the International Helsinki Federation for Human Rights, Open Society Archives; and Reagan, *An American Life*, 698. Reagan's talking points for the summit emphasized linkage: "The pace at which the cause of human rights advances to a great extent sets the political pace of our relationship." Talking Points, Background Book for Meeting between President Reagan and General Secretary Gorbachev, 12/1987 (1/4), Box 91605, Stephen I. Danzansky Files, RRL.

[98] Mann, *The Rebellion of Ronald Reagan*, 269.

"What right does [the United States] have to be teacher – who gave it the moral right?" Gorbachev asked rhetorically.[99] Although Gorbachev wanted to improve relations with the United States and recognized that protecting human rights could facilitate such progress, he nonetheless resented any semblance of American superiority, and American officials appreciated the need to be sensitive on this point.[100] Although according to one Gorbachev aide, American pressure was useful in internal debates over Soviet policy: "Gorbachev's team, which was pushing for internal reforms, in particular in the area of emigration policy, used U.S. requests in the humanitarian field as a lever in our internal debates."[101]

An additional factor complicating Gorbachev's reform efforts was internal bureaucratic resistance to his efforts. Entrenched Soviet apparatchiks were often unresponsive to Gorbachev's reform policies. Adamishin describes how difficult it was to implement changes in Soviet human rights practices:

The Americans usually presented their requests to our ministry, while we, even considering many of them fair, had difficulty obtaining positive answers from our domestic agencies. Those matters were the responsibility of domestic agencies, but the agencies would forward their answers – often unpalatable ones – to us to deliver to foreign representatives. In short, to be involved in human rights issues meant, almost automatically, to be involved in constant disputes with other Soviet government agencies, with little capability to influence them.[102]

In his efforts to improve the Soviet human rights record, Shevardnadze pointed out to Schifter that he faced resistance from the Soviet Ministry of the Interior, which after all, had arrested, convicted, and imprisoned the country's political prisoners.[103] Furthermore, Shevardnadze complained to Shultz, in an April 1988 meeting, about the intransigence of the Soviet delegation in Vienna, many of which were technically his own subordinates.[104]

Outside of bilateral contacts with the Americans, Soviet leaders pursued a range of other steps to win support for their proposed conference,

[99] Letter and attachments, Culvahouse to Dawson, January 15, 1988, Folder 7, Box 6, HU, WHORM Subject File, RRL.
[100] Jack Matlock Interview, April 3, 2006.
[101] Adamishin, "Soviet–U.S. Relations and Human Rights before Perestroika," in Adamishin and Schifter, *Human Rights, Perestroika, and the End of the Cold War*, 45.
[102] Adamishin, "Enter Gorbachev," in Adamishin and Schifter, *Human Rights, Perestroika, and the End of the Cold War*, 94.
[103] Richard Schifter Interview, May 5, 2008.
[104] Memorandum of Conversation, April 21, 1988, *The Moscow Summit: 20 Years Later*, National Security Archive Electronic Briefing Book.

including inviting some of their most ardent critics to Moscow: the IHF and the Helsinki Commission.[105] Swiss activist Eugen Voss suggests he thought of the idea to press for a fact-finding mission to Moscow as a test of the Soviet commitment to change in their effort to secure the human rights conference.[106] According to Laber, one of the unintended benefits of having established the IHF was that when the Soviets wanted to reach out to an international nongovernmental organization dedicated to Helsinki compliance, one was in place.[107] In Laber's view, the Soviets chose to invite the IHF due to its influence with the CSCE delegates at Vienna and the Soviets' overwhelming desire to host a human rights conference.[108] Describing Soviet motivations for the invitation, Kashlev said, "We are engaged in a dialogue on human rights in the Soviet Union not only with those who like us but those who criticize us as well."[109]

The IHF prepared intensely for its January 1988 trip to the Soviet Union, which was being watched closely by CSCE delegations for evidence of Soviet progress.[110] It was the first time that IHF members had

[105] "Commission Delegation Holds Human Rights Discussions in Moscow," *CSCE Digest*, January–February 1989, CSCE 1989: London Conference, Box 2 Unprocessed, JBANC.

[106] Fischer, "'G2W – Faith in the Second World': Using the Helsinki Network to Overcome the East–West Divide,

[107] In Laber's view, the Soviets would never have invited Helsinki Watch because it was solely a United States-based group. Jeri Laber Interview, April 29, 2008. Helsinki groups from Austria, Canada, Denmark, the FRG, the Netherlands, Norway, Sweden, Switzerland, and the United States sent representatives as part of the IHF mission to Moscow.

[108] Letter, Schwarzenberg to Gorbachev, November 27, 1987, Delegation to Moscow: General, 1987, Box 3, Project Files, Records of the International Helsinki Federation for Human Rights, Open Society Archives; and Laber, *The Courage of Strangers*, 283.

[109] On September 18, 1987, the Soviet embassy announced that an IHF delegation had been invited to visit Moscow to meet with a variety of government ministries. Judy Dempsey, "Moscow Go-ahead for Rights Group," in Annual Report 1988, Box 1, Publications, Records of the International Helsinki Federation for Human Rights, Open Society Archives.

[110] The IHF had a ten-point agenda of issues to raise in their meeting with Soviet officials, including: the Soviet proposal to host a human rights conference; issues related to political prisoners including those incarcerated in psychiatric institutions; six proposals to reform the Soviet legal code; emigration; travel; religious freedom; Helsinki monitoring; Soviet intervention in Afghanistan; freedom of the press; access to information; and communication. "International Helsinki Federation Delegation to the USSR: Issues to Raise," October 17, 1987, Delegation to Moscow: Correspondence, 1987–1988, Box 3, Project Files, Records of the International Helsinki Federation for Human Rights, Open Society Archives; Memorandum, To Members of the IHF Delegation to Moscow, October 30, 1987, Delegation to Moscow Correspondence, 1987–8, ibid.; "Perm Labor Camp Visit Refused," *News from Helsinki Watch* II:1 (February 22, 1988) in

held official meetings with Soviet officials in the USSR.[111] In Laber's view, the mission was "strictly window dressing" and demonstrated the USSR was run by the "same old bureaucrats" doing only a "slightly different number."[112] Laber regarded her Soviet hosts as disingenuous and argues they had no intention of examining the prisoner lists presented by the IHF.[113] Furthermore, despite the changed image Soviet officials tried to project, some old practices remained. Consistent with Laber's characterization, Soviet authorities moderated their repressive tactics somewhat during the IHF's stay, but still recorded meetings between the IHF and its Soviet member the Press Club Glasnost, which intimidated certain activists.[114]

Nevertheless, a number of the IHF meetings were valuable. In particular, the informal meetings with a range of Soviet groups strengthened connections among disparate activists and enabled the IHF delegates to learn more about current human rights practices in the USSR. The IHF met with representatives of human rights groups, members of a free trade-union, a full range of religious groups, and representatives of ethnic minorities such as the Crimean Tatars and Lithuanian nationalists.[115] In addition, Laber considered one of the most important moments of the trip to be when Soviet representatives allowed Lev Timofeyev, a Soviet dissident, former political prisoner, and head of Press Club Glasnost, to speak at a meeting between IHF and Soviet officials, marking the first public debate on Soviet human rights between Soviet authorities and

Delegation to Moscow: General, 1987, ibid.; Laber, *The Courage of Strangers*, 287; and Zimmermann Statement, January 22, 1988, Zimmermann Papers.

[111] They had undertaken unofficial visits to the Soviet Union before and held all official meetings with Soviet officials thus far in Vienna. In Moscow, the IHF delegation met with representatives from the Ministries of Foreign Affairs, Internal Affairs, Justice, and Health. International Helsinki Federation for Human Rights, *On Speaking Terms: An Unprecedented Human Rights Mission to the Soviet Union* (Vienna: International Helsinki Federation for Human Rights, 1988), iii–iv, 19–23, 27.

[112] Jeri Laber Interview, April 29, 2008.

[113] Laber, *The Courage of Strangers*, 288; "Political Prisoners," *News from Helsinki Watch* II:1 (February 22, 1988) in Delegation to Moscow: General, 1987, Box 3, Project Files, Records of the International Helsinki Federation for Human Rights, Open Society Archives; and Letter, Schwarzenberg to Adamishin, March 15, 1988, Delegation to Moscow, Correspondence 1987–1988, ibid.

[114] International Helsinki Federation for Human Rights, *On Speaking Terms*, 5, 7.

[115] "International Helsinki Federation Mission to Moscow," *News from Helsinki Watch* II:1 (February 22, 1988) in Delegation to Moscow: General, 1987, Box 3, Project Files, Records of the International Helsinki Federation for Human Rights, Open Society Archives; and Diary, Frantisek Janouch, January 24–31, 1988, ibid.

FIGURE 7. International Helsinki Federation for Human Rights Executive Director Gerald Nagler, Helsinki Watch Executive Director Jeri Laber, and Lef Timofeyev of Press Club Glasnost consult during a meeting with the Soviet Union's Public Commission on Human Rights in December 1987. Courtesy of Human Rights Watch.

Western and Eastern human rights activists. Such a step did not come easily. Before Timofeyev was given the floor to speak, there was heated debate between the IHF delegates and Fedor Burlatsky, chair of the Public Commission for International Cooperation on Humanitarian Issues and Human Rights. Burlatsky accused the IHF of provoking a "scandal," by forcing the Commission to allow members of the Press Club Glasnost to participate in the discussion.[116]

Swedish delegate Frantisek Janouch's firsthand account of his time in Moscow with the IHF delegation differs from Laber's and illustrates the extent to which the Soviets wanted to curry favor for their proposed conference and cultivate the support of human rights activists from Western and neutral countries. Janouch wrote, "Almost anything was permitted during that one week: Jewish demonstrations as well as demonstrations

[116] Laber, *The Courage of Strangers*, 292–3; and International Helsinki Federation for Human Rights, *On Speaking Terms*, 3, 8, 11–7.

of Hare Krishna devotees, and many more things, unknown or at least unusual in Moscow."[117] According to Janouch, Shevardnadze's deputy, Anatoly Adamishin, tried to persuade the IHF to support the conference proposal, even going so far as "promising everything under the sun." The IHF's report, however, characterized Adamishin's comments on the conditions for such a conference to be "evasive."[118] Although the IHF representatives encountered a wide spectrum of views on the proposed conference among those they met in Moscow, Janouch personally saw value in allowing a conference to induce the Soviets to develop a favorable human rights record:

I am convinced that the organization of a conference on humanitarian issues in Moscow could have a positive influence on future developments in the USSR. The earliest date the conference could meet in Moscow is 1990, probably one or two years later. During the period of preparation the Soviet authorities will logically make sure that fundamental human rights are respected. This means that the present relatively liberal attitude of the Soviet authorities will go on for several more years – and will clearly progress even further during the actual conference.[119]

In Janouch's view and many others', agreeing to the conference would ensure an initial period of respect for human rights, and by the time the conference closed, it would be too late for the Soviets to reverse course and return to repressive human rights practices.

Janouch's thinking was in line with the approach the IHF adopted. After returning from Moscow, the organization shared its impressions with the Vienna CSCE delegations and began a public campaign in support of a Moscow conference. Leading the effort, Laber wrote an opinion piece for the *International Herald Tribune* outlining the argument in favor of the meeting:

A Moscow human rights conference would ... give the Soviet people a forum for discussing their government's past, present and future human rights practices. It

[117] Diary, Frantisek Janouch, January 24–31, 1988, Box 3, Project Files, Records of the International Helsinki Federation for Human Rights, Open Society Archives.

[118] International Helsinki Federation for Human Rights, *On Speaking Terms*, 45–7; and Diary, Frantisek Janouch, January 24–31, 1988, Box 3, Project Files, Records of the International Helsinki Federation for Human Rights, Open Society Archives.

[119] Diary, Frantisek Janouch, January 24–31, 1988, Box 3, Project Files, Records of the International Helsinki Federation for Human Rights, Open Society Archives; and International Helsinki Federation for Human Rights, *On Speaking Terms*, 46–7.

would allow an infusion of Western ideas and values, including the concept that respect for human rights cannot merely be legislated from above but requires the active participation and vigilance of private citizens.[120]

There is some irony that its trip to Moscow led the IHF to work toward the same goal as the Soviet Union, although clearly for different reasons. There is also incongruity in the Soviet courting of the IHF, which had long fought against Soviet repression of Helsinki monitors. The reach of IHF's influence with CSCE delegations, however, was such that Soviet authorities saw value in winning over this transnational coalition and their sensitivity to their international image.

As he had during the Washington summit, Reagan pressed his human rights concerns in a number of ways in connection with the Moscow summit from May 29 to June 2, 1988.[121] First, en route to Moscow, Reagan stopped in Finland where he delivered a speech heralding the Helsinki Final Act as "a singular statement of hope." In Reagan's words,

The Final Act set new standards of conduct for our nations and provided the mechanisms by which to apply those standards ... For all the bleak winds that have swept the plains of justice since that signing day in 1975, the accords have taken root in the conscience of humanity and grown in moral, and increasingly, diplomatic authority ... It reflects an increasing realization that the agenda of East–West relations must be comprehensive – that security and human rights must be advanced together, or cannot truly be secured at all.[122]

Reagan used his visit to the Soviet Union to convey his support and that of the American people for Soviet dissidents, religious believers, and others.

While in Moscow, Reagan also met with more than a hundred Soviet dissidents and citizens at Spaso House, the American ambassador's

[120] Annual Report, 1988, Box 1, Publications, Records of the International Helsinki Federation for Human Rights, Open Society Archives. It is clear the American delegation benefited from the IHF visit to Moscow. For example, Zimmermann's February 12 statement cited its findings on the state of psychiatric abuse in the Soviet Union. Statement, Zimmermann, February 12, 1988, OSCE Archives; and Laber, *The Courage of Strangers*, 287, 305.

[121] National Security Decision Directive Number 305, April 26, 1988, Folder 6, Box 2, NSDD, RRL.

[122] Bodin, "Reagan Calls Helsinki Act Beacon of Hope for Future," May 27, 1988, Politics: Human Rights: General, 1988–1988, Box 21, New Code Subject Files, Soviet Red Archives, Records of Radio Free Europe/Radio Liberty Research Institute, Open Society Archives; Lehne, *The Vienna Meeting of the Conference on Security and Cooperation in Europe*, 119–20; and Matlock, *Reagan and Gorbachev*, 295.

residence.[123] In his remarks to the assembled guests, Reagan praised Soviet progress on human rights, but in a common theme of the trip, emphasized that more work was needed to fulfill the obligations of the Helsinki Final Act and the Universal Declaration on Human Rights.[124] In his speech, Reagan said, "I've come to Moscow with this human rights agenda because … it is our belief that this is a moment of hope."[125] According to long-time Commission staffer John Finerty, the most remarkable event was an "embassy reception with dozens of former Soviet political prisoners who had been released earlier in the year. It was as if Kronid Lubarsky's annual List of Political Prisoners had come alive."[126] Reagan's meeting was not well received by Soviet officials, demonstrating the limits of the supposedly new Soviet approach. One Soviet official interviewed on the evening news said, "What a shame that [Reagan] would come all this way for an important meeting and waste his time on something like this." Other Soviet officials disparaged those at Spaso House, as "not the flower of our society, quite the opposite."[127] Yet, after the Moscow Summit, others such as the Director of the Institute of United States and Canada Georgi Arbatov wrote to Gorbachev that "even those events that were planned by Reagan as a direct propaganda action (the meeting with the dissidents, meetings with the religious public figures), in the West was mainly perceived as a confirmation of glasnost and perestroika in the USSR."[128]

According to Reagan, Gorbachev was more receptive to his concerns about religious freedom and human rights during the Moscow summit than ever before.[129] During the summit, Reagan visited the Danilov

[123] Orlov had met with Shultz and Reagan before the Moscow summit and pushed them to offer public support to Soviet dissidents by meeting separately with them and with refuseniks during their time in Moscow. Orlov, *Dangerous Thoughts*, 308.

[124] Oberdorfer, *From the Cold War to a New Era*, 297; Eichhorn, *The Helsinki Accords and Their Effect on the Cold War*, 273; Cannon, *President Reagan*, 705–6; Press Briefing, May 30, 1988, Moscow Summit 1988 (7) OA 18291, Katherine Chumachenko Files, RRL; and Brinkley, ed., *The Reagan Diaries*, 613–4.

[125] Cannon, *President Reagan*, 705–6.

[126] John Finerty, written communication with the author, June 24, 2008. Kronid Lubarsky, a former Soviet political prisoner, maintained what was regarded as the most reliable list of those imprisoned for political reasons in the USSR.

[127] David Remnick, "Reagan, Soviet Dissidents Meet in Moment of Hope," May 31, 1988, Politics: Human Rights: General, 1988–1988, Box 21, New Code Subject Files, Soviet Red Archives, Records of Radio Free Europe/Radio Liberty Research Institute, Open Society Archives.

[128] Memorandum, Arbatov to Gorbachev, June 1988, *Reagan, Gorbachev and Bush at Governor's Island* (National Security Archive Electronic Briefing Book No. 261, December 2008).

[129] Reagan, *An American Life*, 709.

FIGURE 8. President Ronald Reagan visits Danilov Monastery to demonstrate his support for religious freedom. Courtesy of the Ronald Reagan Library.

Monastery to underline his commitment to religious freedom. There he said, "We in our country share this hope for a new age of religious freedom in the Soviet Union ... We pray that the return of this monastery signals a willingness to return to believers the thousands of other houses of worship which are now closed, boarded up, or used for secular purposes."[130] The monastery visit was one of a number of symbolic stops made by Reagan that were designed to demonstrate his commitment to human rights. Even one item removed from the summit agenda made an impression on Soviet leaders, specifically Nancy Reagan had proposed visiting a refusenik couple in Moscow before meeting with Gorbachev. Although the plan was shelved, Reagan had convinced Gorbachev of his concern for the issue, and the couple emigrated soon thereafter.[131]

In Moscow, Reagan tried to convey to Gorbachev the domestic pressure he faced on Soviet human rights abuses. He emphasized congressional opposition to Soviet human rights violations as the impediment to increased Soviet–American trade and urged Gorbachev to address the problem.[132]

---

[130] Brinkley, ed., *The Reagan Diaries*, 613; and Remarks by the President, May 30, 1988, Human Rights Day 1988 (5), Box OA 19268, Chumachenko Files, RRL.
[131] Matlock, *Reagan and Gorbachev*, 296–8.
[132] Reagan, *An American Life*, 705.

Reagan repeatedly stressed that American concern over human rights abuses was linked to ethnic and religious coreligionists who felt a connection to those repressed in the Soviet Union.[133] Reagan's repetition began to gain traction in Moscow, and in their first one-on-one meeting, Gorbachev said Soviet leaders were ready to work with the Reagan administration and the United States Congress to resolve outstanding humanitarian issues.[134] That said, Gorbachev at times bristled at being lectured by the American president. In advance of the summit, Gorbachev had expressed frustration with Reagan's "sermons": "We are not going to re-educate the United States and do not accept that it has any right to re-educate us."[135] The United States needed to be careful not to let its advocacy undermine Gorbachev's authority on human rights. When Reagan gave Gorbachev a list of fourteen cases the United States wanted addressed, the Soviet leader replied he would study the list carefully, but also said, "There are too many lists," indicating a struggle to balance the need to reform human rights practices with national pride.[136]

Although Gorbachev had to endure Reagan's "sermons" and meetings with dissidents, the Soviet leader received an important "endorsement" from Reagan during the summit.[137] When Gorbachev and Reagan visited

---

[133] For example, see two interviews given by the president before his departure. Press Release, May 26, 1988, Moscow Summit 1988 (6), Box OA 18291, Chumachenko Files, RRL; and Press Release, May 26, 1988, ibid.

[134] Memorandum of Conversation, May 31, 1988, *The Moscow Summit: 20 Years Later*, National Security Archive Electronic Briefing Book.

[135] Reuter, "Gorbachev Signals he is tired of 'Sermons' From Reagan," April 27, 1988, Politics: Human Rights: General, 1988–1988, Box 20, New Code Subject Files, Soviet Red Archives, Records of Radio Free Europe/Radio Liberty Research Institute, Open Society Archives. Reagan faced pressure on this issue from many sides; while Gorbachev warned of damage to their relationship, members of Congress wrote to Reagan to persuade him to meet with Lithuanian human rights activists during his visit to the Soviet Union. Letter, Riegle et al. to Reagan, May 1, 1988, Folder 14, Box 6, HU, WHORM Subject File, RRL. Some members of Congress were concerned that human rights would not be as forcefully pressed at the Moscow summit as issues of arms control. Winter, "U.S. Congressmen Urge Human Rights Emphasis at Moscow Summit," May 5, 1988, Politics: Human Rights: General, 1988–1988, Box 21, Old Code Subject Files, Soviet Red Archives, Records of Radio Free Europe/Radio Liberty Research Institute, Open Society Archives; and Winter, "Reagan Urged to Press Human Rights," May 17, 1988, Politics: General: Human Rights, 1988–1988, Box 21, New Code Subject Files, ibid.

[136] Memcon, May 31, 1988, 1988 IS-Soviet Summit Memcons, May 26–June 3, 1988, Box 92084, Fritz Ermath, RRL; Cannon, *President Reagan*, 703; and David Remnick, "Reagan, Soviet Dissidents Meet in Moment of Hope," May 31, 1988, Politics: Human Rights: General, 1988–1988, Box 21, New Code Subject Files, Soviet Red Archives, Records of Radio Free Europe/Radio Liberty Research Institute, Open Society Archives.

[137] Matlock, *Autopsy of an Empire*, 123.

Red Square, a reporter inquired if Reagan still viewed the Soviet Union as an "evil empire." Reagan replied that he did not.[138] When asked who deserved credit for the changes underway in the Soviet Union, Reagan said, "Mr. Gorbachev deserves most of the credit as the leader of this country .... And it seems to me that with *perestroika* things have been changed in the Soviet Union. Judging from what I read about *perestroika*, I could agree with a lot of it." In Gorbachev's estimation, Reagan's comments in Red Square were "one of the genuine achievements of his Moscow visit."[139]

During the Helsinki Commission's November 1988 mission to Moscow, the Soviets similarly worked to convey an impression of progress and openness, while also conceding more needed to be done and articulating a commitment to undertake further improvements.[140] The congressional delegation focused primarily on religious freedom, legal reform, emigration, and the working conditions of journalists in its sessions with Soviet officials. In addition, members of the Commission organized meetings with nongovernmental activists during their time in Moscow. One member of the delegation reported a changed attitude among Soviet officials in their talks about efforts to reform legislation governing exit and entry practices: "There was a willingness not only to discuss the issues, but a forthcoming that I've never seen from Soviet officials, one of [which said]: 'We have made a lot of mistakes, and we are going to change and concern ourselves more with individual liberties. And we're going to do it because it's in the best interest of our people and it's going to help our economy do better.'"[141] At the conclusion of the congressional visit,

---

[138] In Shevardnadze's view, Reagan's comments on Red Square were evidence of the transformation of his attitudes toward the Soviet Union. Eduard Shevardnadze Interview, Folder 21, Box 1, Oberdorfer Papers.

[139] Mikhail Gorbachev, *Memoirs* (New York: Doubleday, 1996), 457; and Matlock, *Reagan and Gorbachev*, 302. Reagan had described the Soviet Union as an "evil empire" in a March 1983 speech to the Annual Convention of the National Association of Evangelicals. In Soviet official Anatoly Adamishin's view, Reagan's concession was an important victory for Gorbachev and ended the Soviet Union's isolation outside the circle of righteous countries. Anatoly Adamishin, August 5, 1989 Interview Transcript, Folder 1, Box 1, The Hoover Institution and the Gorbachev Foundation (Moscow) Collection, Hoover Institution Archives, Stanford, California. Copyright Stanford University.

[140] "Commission Delegation Holds Human Rights Discussions in Moscow," *CSCE Digest*, January–February 1989, CSCE 1989: London Conference, Box 2 Unprocessed, JBANC; and Steno Notebook, November 1988, Folder 18, Box 175, DeConcini Papers.

[141] Sean Griffin, "De Concini observes new Soviet attitude," *Phoenix Gazette*, November 24, 1988, Folder 18, Box 175, DeConcini Papers. See also Mickey Edwards, "Is Moscow Due That Rights Session?" *Washington Times*, January 10, 1989, F1–4; and Memorandum,

FIGURE 9. Ronald Reagan talks with General Secretary Mikhail Gorbachev in Red Square during the May 1988 Moscow Summit. Courtesy of the Ronald Reagan Library.

the Soviets resolved 147 exit visa cases, although none of the 200 political prisoners about whom members of Congress had inquired were
released.[142] An embassy cable reported, "Several Supreme Soviet deputies,
however, signaled an awareness of the need for tangible improvements in
Soviet human rights performance. They hinted this would be forthcoming, while pleading for patience."[143] About the progress possible due to
the congressional visit, Commission Cochair Steny Hoyer said, "They
want to get this stage behind them – the stage of continual harping by
Congress on human rights issues."[144] Nevertheless, as with the IHF, Soviet
eavesdropping on the Commissioners in their hotel rooms raised questions about the degree of the Soviet conversion.[145]

The Soviets took a number of other last-minute steps to demonstrate
concrete improvement. According to Yuri Kashlev, in the final phase of
the Vienna Meeting, Gorbachev established a special subcommittee in the
Politburo to respond to the Soviet delegation's queries regarding humanitarian cases.[146] In November 1988, the Soviets agreed to resolve the cases
of 120 refuseniks before Reagan left office. The number was based on
Richard Schifter's calculation of the number of cases that could be acted
on in the working days remaining before the Vienna document would
have to be decided.[147] In addition, the Soviets agreed to an exchange of
visits by psychiatrists during which American psychiatrists would assess
if Soviet abuses had ended. The *Washington Post* described the Soviets as

Susan to Edwards, January 10, 1989, Folder 11, Box 56, Mickey Edwards Collection, Carl Albert Center Congressional Archives, University of Oklahoma, Norman, Oklahoma (hereafter Edwards Collection).

[142] Press Conference: Soviet Union Trip, November 23, 1988, Folder 18, Box 175, DeConcini Papers.

[143] AmEmbassy Moscow to SecState, November 22, 1988, Folder CSCE Codels 11/99, Box 1, Lot Files 90D481, released through the Freedom of Information Act.

[144] During the meetings, there was talk of instituting a "pink telephone" to address human rights concerns, in reference to the red telephone used to facilitate direct communication in international crisis. Felicity Barringer, "For 2 Days, Dissidents Are Toast of Moscow," *New York Times*, November 21, 1988, A5; "Suggestions for Working Groups," Folder 19, Box 175, DeConcini Papers; and Press Conference: Soviet Union Trip, November 23, 1988, Folder 18, ibid.

[145] Mickey Edwards, "Is Moscow Due That Rights Session?" *Washington Times*, January 10, 1989, F1–4; and Memorandum, Susan to Edwards, January 10, 1989, Folder 11, Box 56, Edwards Collection.

[146] Kashlev, "Khel'sinskii Protsess I Prava Cheloveka," in Kashlev, ed., *Khel'sinskii Protsess v Sovetskoi/Rossiiskoi Vneshnei Politike*, 70–1.

[147] Schifter, "Putting the Vienna CSCE Meeting on Our Bilateral Agenda," in Adamishin and Schifter, *Human Rights, Perestroika, and the End of the Cold War*, 169–71; Richard Schifter Interview, May 5, 2008; and Richard Schifter Interview, September 8, 2003, *The*

applying "the techniques of arms control verification to this politically sensitive area of medicine."[148]

As Reagan and Gorbachev's meetings progressed, the Soviet Union made greater strides in the Vienna negotiations and in improving its domestic human rights record. When the two leaders met again in New York in December 1988 and discussed human rights, among other issues, there was increasing evidence of Soviet progress.[149] Adamishin describes Soviet efforts to end the country's isolation from Europe, to cease to be a castaway, and instead to "be accepted in its embrace."[150] Most significantly, while in New York Gorbachev gave a speech that he intended to be "an anti-Fulton – Fulton in reverse," in reference to former British Prime Minister Winston Churchill's famous iron curtain speech in Fulton, Missouri.[151] Gorbachev spoke to the United Nations General Assembly and announced a unilateral withdrawal of Soviet troops from Eastern Europe. The decision enabled Eastern European states to pursue reform as they saw fit without fear of Soviet intervention. He also stated publicly, "We intend to expand the Soviet Union's participation in the human rights monitoring arrangements in the United Nations and the Conference on Security and Cooperation in Europe" and pledged to end arrests and trials for political offenses.[152] Reviewing Gorbachev's performance at the

Foreign Affairs Oral History Collection of the Association for Diplomatic Studies and Training, Library of Congress, http://memory.loc.gov/ammem/collections/diplomacy/ (accessed March 5, 2010).

[148] David Ottaway, "U.S. Psychiatrists to Visit Soviet Mental Hospitals," *Washington Post*, November 22, 1988, A22; and Editorial, "Dealing With Soviet Psychiatry," *Washington Post*, November 27, 1988, D6.

[149] Reagan advocated the release of the remaining political prisoners and action on all long-time refusenik applications. "Text of Reagan's Rights Remarks," December 9, 1988, Human Rights deklaratsia, 1988–1990, Box 693, Old Code Subject Files, Soviet Red Archives, Records of Radio Free Europe/Radio Liberty Research Institute, Open Society Archives; Letter, Hornblow to Bauzys, January 13, 1989, Folder 9, Box 7, HU, WHORM Subject File, RRL; and Memorandum of Conversation, December 7, 1988, *Reagan, Gorbachev and Bush at Governor's Island* (National Security Archive Electronic Briefing Book No. 261, December 2008).

[150] Anatoly Adamishin, August 5, 1989 Interview Transcript, Folder 1, Box 1, The Hoover Institution and the Gorbachev Foundation (Moscow) Collection, Hoover Institution Archives, Stanford, California. Copyright Stanford University.

[151] Memorandum of Conversation, October 31, 1988, *Reagan, Gorbachev and Bush at Governor's Island* (National Security Archive Electronic Briefing Book No. 261, December 2008).

[152] Gorbachev declared the Soviet Union would respond to requests for exit visas "in a humane spirit" and end the problem of refuseniks. AP, "The Gorbachev Visit; Excerpts from Speech to U.N. on Major Soviet Military Cuts," *New York Times*, December 8, 1988; and Tabory, "The Vienna CSCE Concluding Document," 15.

United Nations, Chernyaev wrote, "[A]fter an hour of holding its breath the audience erupted in an endless ovation. The U.N. has never seen anything like it."[153]

Comments by Gorbachev and his advisers suggest the extent to which they too realized that human rights, whether as an element of Gorbachev's UN address or in other contexts, could be used as a tool in the Cold War. Gorbachev and Shevardnadze's approach through the years of the Vienna Meeting suggest they were determined to approach such issues offensively rather than only reacting to Western pressure. Gorbachev thought his speech had changed the international image of the Soviet Union, telling a session of the Politburo:

We can state that our initiatives pulled the rug from under the feet of those who have been prattling, and not without success, that new political thinking is just about words. The Soviet Union, they said, still needs to provide evidence. There was plenty of talk, many nice words, but not a single tank is withdrawn, not a single cannon. Therefore the unilateral reduction left a huge impression and, one should admit, created an entirely different background for perceptions of our policies and the Soviet Union as a whole.[154]

The impact of Gorbachev's United Nations speech was so pronounced that Shultz said, "If anybody declared the end of the Cold War, he did it in that speech. It was over."[155]

Gorbachev continued to accelerate the pace and expand the scope of his reforms in the final months of 1988. By December 1988, Schifter saw the Moscow human rights conference as an important means for liberalization in the Soviet Union and believed "U.S. engagement in a human rights dialogue encouraged the leadership to effect the changes that they themselves thought were needed" through "informal linkage."[156] According to Adamishin and Schifter, "The Soviet–U.S. human rights dialogue of the late 1980s achieved significant results because each of us knew the

---

[153] Chernyaev, *My Six Years with Gorbachev*, 201; Anatoly Chernyaev Diary, December 17, 1988, The National Security Archive.

[154] Memorandum of Conversation, December 27–28, 1988, *Reagan, Gorbachev and Bush at Governor's Island* (National Security Archive Electronic Briefing Book No. 261, December 2008).

[155] Pavel Palazchenko, *My Years with Gorbachev and Shevardnadze: The Memoir of a Soviet Interpreter* (University Park: The Pennsylvania State University Press, 1997), 370.

[156] Schifter, "Putting the Vienna CSCE Meeting on Our Bilateral Agenda," in Adamishin and Schifter, *Human Rights, Perestroika, and the End of the Cold War*, 177, 180. See also Jacqueline Hayden, *The Collapse of Communist Power in Poland: Strategic Misperceptions and Unanticipated Outcomes* (New York: Routledge, 2006), 5–6.

thinking of our respective bosses, who wanted to remove the obstacle to good relations that disagreement on human rights issues presented."[157] In Shultz's view, the dialogue between Schifter and Adamishin "produced concrete results: an end to abuse of psychiatry, the release of political prisoners, the repeal of laws restricting freedom of expression, an end to the repression of religion, and a fundamental shift in the laws and regulations that governed emigration."[158]

By the end of 1988, 600 political prisoners had been released, emigration had swelled to 80,000, and jamming had ended. In addition, Gorbachev announced he was ending Soviet involvement in Afghanistan, withdrawing all troops by February 15, 1989, and reducing Soviet force levels in Eastern Europe by 500,000 soldiers and 10,000 tanks.[159] In a sign of the scope of Soviet changes, Eastern emigration had risen to such numbers that the United States government had to consider increasing the refugee limits for Eastern Europe and the Soviet Union.[160]

As the end of Reagan's term approached, the United States and its allies faced a difficult choice on the Moscow conference. The Soviet Union had made considerable progress, but the Reagan administration risked domestic criticism if it relented on the proposal before all of its conditions had been met.[161] As of November 1988, the United Kingdom, Canada, France, and other NATO states had not been persuaded they should agree to the Moscow conference.[162] Nevertheless, the American

[157] Anatoly Adamishin and Richard Schifter, "Introduction," in Adamishin and Schifter, *Human Rights, Perestroika, and the End of the Cold War*, 3.

[158] Shultz, "Foreword," in Adamishin and Schifter, *Human Rights, Perestroika, and the End of the Cold War*, xiv.

[159] Laber, *The Courage of Strangers*, 304; and Milan Hauner, "A Softening of the Soviet Stance on Human Rights?" Radio Liberty Research, December 7, 1988, Human Rights, 1988–1989, Box 693, Old Code Subject Files, Soviet Red Archives, Records of Radio Free Europe/Radio Liberty Research Institute, Open Society Archives.

[160] The 1988 budget included funding for 15,000 refugees from Eastern Europe and the Soviet Union. The United States Coordinator for Refugee Affairs Jonathan Moore suggested that the president consider raising the ceiling by 15,000. Arguing for the declaration of an "unforeseen refugee emergency," Moore noted that "it would be an embarrassment to the United States if we were to turn away or create a significant backlog of Soviet refugees both when our diplomatic efforts are bearing fruit and on the eve of a U.S.–Soviet summit." Memorandum, Moore to Reagan, March 21, 1988, Soviet Union–1987–1988 (USSR), Memos–Letters–Cable–Reports–Articles (1 of 7), Box 92158, Nelson C. Ledsky Files, RRL.

[161] Lehne, *The Vienna Meeting of the Conference on Security and Cooperation in Europe*, 129–30.

[162] Telegram, VCSCE to EXTOTT, November 7, 1988, 20-4-CSCE-VIENN, Volume 11, Historical Division, Canada; and Frédéric Bozo, *Mitterrand, The End of the Cold War and German Unification* trans. Susan Emmanuel (New York: Berghahn Books, 2009), 33.

presidential election put pressure on the delegations to reach an agreement before likely delays caused by a new administration in January.[163]

The United States chose to approve the Moscow conference conditionally, in part because Shultz wanted the Vienna document signed before the end of Reagan's term.[164] In Shultz's view, the Vienna Concluding Document was the culmination of Reagan's record of dedication to the CSCE, and thus he wanted the president to garner the deserved credit for its commitments.[165] The United States decision, as outlined in a White

---

[163] Lehne, *The Vienna Meeting of the Conference on Security and Cooperation in Europe*, 124; Oberdorfer, *From the Cold War to a New Era*, 324–5; Roland Eggleston, "NATO Allies Drawing up Conditions for Moscow Conference," November 10, 1988, Human Rights Declaration, 1988–1990, Box 693, Old Code Subject Files, Soviet Red Archives, Records of Radio Free Europe/Radio Liberty Research Institute, Open Society Archives; and Eichhorn, *The Helsinki Accords and Their Effect on the Cold War*, 273.

[164] American and Soviet negotiators outlined a timetable for Soviet changes. Lehne, *The Vienna Meeting of the Conference on Security and Cooperation in Europe*, 130; and Gubin, *International Regimes, Agenda Setting and Linkage Groups in U.S–Soviet Relations*, 89. Schifter reports concerns within the incoming Bush administration that Reagan and his advisors had gone too far in negotiating with the Soviets. According to Schifter, the sense was that Shultz was "too weak in dealing with the Soviets" and that Reagan "had gone soft on communism" "in his old age." Differences of opinion such as these shaped the decision to end the Vienna Meeting before Reagan left office. Richard Schifter Interview, May 5, 2008. According to Zimmermann, Bush did not support the decision to agree to the Moscow human rights conference, suggesting that if the meeting had lasted several more days, the outcome might have been quite different. Warren Zimmermann Interview, December 10, 1996, *The Foreign Affairs Oral History Collection of the Association for Diplomatic Studies and Training*, Library of Congress, http://memory.loc.gov/ammem/collections/diplomacy/ (accessed March 6, 2010). It was not only members of the incoming administration that saw Schifter and Shultz as too quick to believe Soviet promises of fundamental change and too invested in supporting Gorbachev's agenda. Critics within the administration included one staffer who described the proposed conference as "this conference in hell" and suggested the United States was working to "thwart [it] directly." Dorminey Memorandum, December 1, 1988, Moscow Human Rights Conference [11/07/1988–12/02/1988] Box 92254, Lisa Jameson Files, RRL.

[165] This reasoning prompted some consternation. Helsinki Watch Chairman Robert Bernstein suggested the United States had undercut its ability to gain compromises by concluding the Vienna Meeting before Bush's inauguration: "Our major regret is that the conference was brought to an abrupt end because of a desire on the part of the United States State Department to conclude the conference before the new Administration took office in the U.S. The ending came at a time when further concessions by the Soviet Union seemed likely and when the momentum for the release of the remaining political prisoners in the Soviet Union was building." Zimmermann disagreed, indicating that he believed the Western position was strongest in December and January and that he did not think there would necessarily have been more Soviet concessions if the meeting had continued. Press Release, January 17, 1989, CSCE: Third Follow-Up Meeting, Vienna: Miscellaneous,

House press release, was based on the idea that the conference would serve as a "means of encouraging continuation of the significant progress in human rights that has taken place in the Soviet Union over the past three years. That progress has included the release of hundreds of political prisoners and exit permission for many people long refused the right to emigrate."[166] Influenced by American thinking and Soviet concessions, the United States allies also agreed to the Vienna Concluding Document and its mandate for a conference in Moscow.

In his speech marking the end of the Vienna Meeting, Shultz outlined achievements over the course of the talks, including an end to jamming, the release of Soviet political prisoners, increased freedoms to demonstrate and organize in Eastern Europe, and expanding freedom of movement. He pointed out that the three upcoming Conferences on the Human Dimension, of which the Moscow meeting was one, as well as the human dimension mechanism provided the CSCE an ongoing process to monitor human rights.[167] Yet, Shultz also noted that repression that contravened Helsinki principles continued in Eastern Europe, Czechoslovakia, the GDR, and Romania. He challenged those who signed the Vienna document to implement the "comprehensive human rights agenda" therein.[168] Other Western speakers such as the foreign ministers from Ireland and Portugal hailed the concluding document for its substance and the dramatic strides that had been made since Madrid.[169] Many of the concluding speeches at Vienna, including Poland's, referenced Gorbachev's image of a common European home

1987–9, Box 8, OSCE/CSCE Files, Records of the International Helsinki Federation for Human Rights, Open Society Archives; and Commission on Security and Cooperation Hearing, "Conclusion of the Vienna Meeting and Implications for U.S. Policy," February 23, 1989, 100th Congress/1st Session.

[166] The White House statement announcing the decision clearly echoed IHF's analysis. Announcement by the White House Press Office, January 4, 1989 in Vojtech Mastny, ed., *The Helsinki Process and the Reintegration of Europe, 1986–1991* (New York: Institute for East–West Security Studies, 1992), 131; and USIS, "White House Statement on Moscow Rights Conference," January 5, 1989, MD: Helsinki: Moscow, Box 129, Subject Files, Samizdat Archives, Records of Radio Free Europe/Radio Liberty Research Institute, Open Society Archives.

[167] In addition to the meeting scheduled for Moscow in 1991, conferences on the human dimension also were mandated to be held in Paris in 1989 and Copenhagen in 1990.

[168] George Shultz, Secretary's Address, January 17, 1989, *Department of State Bulletin* (March 1989): 50–1.

[169] Brian Lenihan (Ireland), January 18, 1989, CSCE/WT/VR.12, OSCE Archives; and José Manuel Durao Barroso (Portugal), ibid.

and likened the Vienna agreement and the Helsinki process to elements in his vision.[170]

The close of the Vienna Meeting on January 19, 1989, represented the end to the traditional East–West divide that characterized the CSCE and Europe and marked the end of the Cold War.[171] The Soviet proposal to host a human rights conference, Western conditions for their agreement, and Soviet efforts to meet those terms denoted one of the most remarkable stories of the CSCE and a significant moment of change in the Cold War.[172] As Laber notes in her memoirs, "Reforms we had demanded as conditions for the Moscow human rights conference – the release of political prisoners, free emigration, and an end to jamming of foreign radio stations – had actually come to pass."[173] Zimmermann characterized the concluding document as "the most comprehensive statement of human rights commitments that has ever existed in the East–West framework."[174] Shevardnadze later described the Vienna Meeting as a "watershed." According to him, "Europe had never known such a dialog – intense, at times dramatic, but purposeful and democratic in a way that was without precedent."[175] Yuri Kashlev has written that "without the achievements reached in Vienna communist regimes in Eastern European countries would have fallen much later."[176]

That the Soviet Union would propose hosting a conference on human rights, meet numerous conditions to gain its acceptance, and agree to the far-reaching Vienna Concluding Document represented the culmination of years of governmental and nongovernmental human rights advocacy on both sides of the Iron Curtain.[177] The agenda of transnational

---

[170] Tadeusz Olechowski (Poland), January 18, 1989, CSCE/WT/VR.11, OSCE Archives. The FRG also used this image in their closing speech. Hans-Dietrich Genscher (FRG), January 18, 1989, CSCE/WT/VR.12, OSCE Archives.

[171] Schifter and Adamishin also see the Cold War as ending with the adoption of the Vienna Concluding Document. Richard Schifter, "Concluding Thoughts," in Adamishin and Schifter, *Human Rights, Perestroika, and the End of the Cold War*, 243.

[172] Activists such as Orlov also saw Vienna as a significant breakthrough in Soviet thinking about political prisoners and human rights. Yuri Orlov interview, March 27 and 28, 2008.

[173] Laber, *The Courage of Strangers*, 304.

[174] Heraclides, *Security and Co-operation in Europe*, 102.

[175] Shevardnadze, *The Future Belongs to Freedom*, 128–9.

[176] Kashlev, "The CSCE in the Soviet Union's Politics," 71.

[177] The Vienna Concluding Document included a mandate to begin Conventional Forces in Europe talks, leading many to point to the close of the Vienna Meeting as marking the beginning of a new era for Europe.

advocates – that Eastern observance of Helsinki human rights provisions was necessary for Eastern states to have productive relations with the West – shaped Gorbachev's course of reform and contributed to the political, social, and economic changes that followed. Years of activism ensured human rights a permanent place on the East–West agenda, inducing Gorbachev to address human rights issues to achieve his international diplomatic goals. As Zimmermann wrote, "The West made the Soviets pay dear[ly] for Western agreement to the conference, but this did not change the fact that the Soviet Union had embraced the Western human rights agenda."[178]

In the case of the Moscow conference proposal, Gorbachev and Shevardnadze were pressuring others in the Soviet government to make faster, more far-reaching progress. Shevardnadze explained the rationale for the conference proposal, focusing on its demonstrative value: "I was convinced that the conference was essential in order to show the country and world how far we intended to go and, beyond that, to provide an impetus for democratization and the perestroika of legislation in everything relating to human affairs."[179] Shevardnadze's thinking about the conference may have been shaped by repeated Western complaints that Gorbachev's policies were fundamentally shifts in rhetoric rather than policy. It is unclear if the conference's proponents realized the degree of concessions that would be necessary for its achievement.[180] Nonetheless, they remained committed to the proposal and to demonstrating a changed stance on human rights.

Over time, Gorbachev would pursue reforms beyond the minimum necessary to win approval of his proposal and facilitate improved relations with the West. The scope of changes undertaken under his leadership reveal a greater commitment to human rights than was required by external pressure. The writings of Shevardnadze, Chernyaev, Adamishin, Yakovlev, and Gorbachev indicate a degree of commitment to human

---

[178] Warren Zimmermann, "CSCE: Past and Future," paper presented at the conference "Conference on Germany, Europe, and the Future Security System for the 1990s," Berlin, Germany, November 1990, Zimmermann Papers.

[179] Shevardnadze, *The Future Belongs to Freedom*, 86.

[180] Yakovlev suggests Gorbachev may not have realized the consequences of the fundamental reforms he was implementing. Similarly, Burlatsky argues that Gorbachev did not want to liberate Eastern Europe but to inspire "mini-Gorbachev reformers" and did not anticipate the course of events there. Alexander Yakovlev, *Sumerki* (Moscow: Materik, 2003), 492; and Fedor Burlatsky Interview, Folder 9, Box 1, The Hoover Institution and the Gorbachev Foundation (Moscow) Collection, Hoover Institution Archives, Stanford, California. Copyright Stanford University.

rights ideals. According to Anatoly Adamishin, "Some people believed that moving forward in the field of human rights was not a concession to the West but an indispensable prerequisite for the country's development, which needed long-overdue democratic reforms."[181] Such views undoubtedly influenced their responses to the challenges facing the Soviet Union and their decision not to support embattled regimes in Eastern Europe, thus enabling the collapse of the Soviet bloc.

---

[181] Anatoly Adamishin, "Vienna," in Adamishin and Schifter, *Human Rights, Perestroika, and the End of the Cold War,* 153.

8

"Perhaps Without You, Our Revolution Would Not Be"

The pace of progress accelerated in the months following the Vienna Meeting, ushering in significant developments in the Helsinki process. Within the CSCE framework, almost all contentious issues were resolved, enabling agreements on such topics as adherence to the principles of pluralistic democracy, market capitalism, and the rule of law. More broadly, stunning changes transformed Eastern and Central Europe between 1989 and 1991, and Helsinki monitors were active in the movements that toppled communist leadership in Czechoslovakia and Poland. The broader Helsinki network was one element in a kaleidoscope that shaped the changes across Eastern Europe and the Soviet Union throughout this period. This chapter, which draws its title from a speech given by Charter 77 activist and Czechoslovak President Václav Havel to Helsinki Watch in February 1990, demonstrates how Helsinki activism influenced the transformation of Europe both directly and indirectly. The steps taken by Gorbachev to ensure the acceptance of the Moscow conference had signaled a momentous shift in Soviet attitudes toward human rights and the CSCE. Concessions such as the release of political prisoners, granting exit visas to long-time refuseniks, and allowing travel to the West were crucial to the broader end of the Cold War. My work suggests the Helsinki process was one factor that shaped Gorbachev's thinking about human rights, self-determination, and nonviolence, all of which contributed to the demise of communism in Eastern Europe and the collapse of the Soviet Union.

Scholars have debated at length what factors led Gorbachev to undertake such fundamental reform.[1] Unanticipated by most contemporary observers, a range of internal and external factors inspired Gorbachev's pursuit of reform.[2] Gorbachev, younger than his predecessor by nineteen years, had fresh ideas to address Soviet problems. As the youngest member of the Politburo and the first representative of his age group to reach the pinnacle of Soviet leadership, Gorbachev brought a new generation's approach to the problems facing the Soviet system. These difficulties included a stagnating economy; an accelerating arms race; lagging technological progress; overextension abroad, including most devastatingly in Afghanistan; tension with China, the United States, and Western Europe; and fading international prestige. The Soviet Union had suffered under years of geriatric leadership, with the previous seven years being particularly ineffective. In contrast to his predecessors, Gorbachev brought vigor to the general secretaryship. He regarded himself as a member of the 1960s generation, a group that was influenced by Soviet leader Nikita Khrushchev's 1956 "Secret Speech" denouncing Stalin, ideas about reforming communism, and the Prague Spring.[4] Gorbachev's "new thinking" was not just a new tactic or policy to confront a problem but rather represented the widespread adoption of a different system of values and beliefs.[5]

Above all, Gorbachev undertook reforms such as *perestroika* to address the USSR's economic problems. Increased contacts with the West, among other factors, had highlighted the disparity between Soviet and Western standards of living. In order to ease the strain on the Soviet economy, Gorbachev sought to curb the arms race with the United States, withdraw troops from Afghanistan, limit aid to socialist allies, and improve relations with Western Europe. As time went on, he recognized the need for some liberalization of the Soviet political system to facilitate his economic reforms.

---

[1] See in particular, English, *Russia and the Idea of the West*, 192, 197; and Brown, *The Gorbachev Factor*, 13.

[2] Social movements scholars' models, developed largely in response to disturbances of the 1960s, were not sufficient to predict the revolutions in Eastern Europe. Sidney Tarrow, "'Aiming at a Moving Target': Social Science and the Recent Rebellions in Eastern Europe," *PS: Political Science and Politics* 24:1 (March 1991): 12.

[3] Gorbachev also had personal experience with state repression; during the 1930s his paternal grandfather had been sent into internal exile and his maternal grandfather was arrested and tortured. Brown, *The Gorbachev Factor*, 25–6.

[4] Ibid., 40.

[5] English, "The Sociology of New Thinking," 43; and Checkel, *Ideas and International Political Change*, 25.

As Soviet abuses were complicating relations with the West, Gorbachev worked to improve the Soviet human rights record to encourage international cooperation with his economic agenda. The review meetings, and in particular the Madrid Meeting, had put the Soviets "in [the] dock before public opinion."[6] In Richard Schifter's view, Gorbachev and Shevardnadze had been uncomfortable with the public criticism of the Soviet human rights record at Madrid; they were "conscious" of the "shortcomings of the Soviet Union" in human rights and "responded accordingly."[7] Although earlier Soviet leaders had addressed this problem in a piecemeal fashion, they had not undertaken fundamental reforms. Matlock suggests that Gorbachev eventually transformed himself into a "champion of universal human values" who recognized that the Soviet Union needed to join the international community.[8] That Gorbachev saw improving the Soviet human rights record as a step to developing deeper relations with the West points to the reach of Helsinki activism.

A number of external actors, including Western leaders, prominent foreign communists, his advisers, and even Soviet dissidents, influenced Gorbachev's policies.[9] Repeated conversations with Western leaders such as Margaret Thatcher, Reagan, and Shultz, led Gorbachev and his close advisers to see human rights as an element of their new foreign policy, an interlocking component of the larger agenda.[10] Through his exposure to the West and in particular his meetings with Western European political leaders in 1987 and 1988, Gorbachev came to believe that Western European democratic socialism had more effectively implemented socialist ideals than the Soviet Union had.[11] In addition, he was influenced personally by reformers such as his law school classmate and close friend Zdeněk Mlynář, who was involved with the Prague Spring and later with Charter

---

[6] Warren Zimmermann, Handwritten Notes, Zimmermann Papers; and Brown, *The Rise and Fall of Communism*, 464.

[7] Richard Schifter Interview, May 5, 2008.

[8] Matlock, *Autopsy of an Empire*, 658; and David Lane, *The Rise and Fall of State Socialism: Industrial Society and the Socialist State* (Cambridge: Polity Press, 1996), 180, 184.

[9] For further discussion of the influence of dissidence on *perestroika*, see Robert Horvath, *The Legacy of Soviet Dissent: Dissidents, Democratisation and Radical Nationalism in Russia* (New York: Routledge Curzon, 2005), 1, 3, 237.

[10] Fedor Burlatsky Interview, Folder 9, Box 1, The Hoover Institution and the Gorbachev Foundation (Moscow) Collection, Hoover Institution Archives, Stanford, California. Copyright Stanford University.

[11] Thomas, "Human Rights Ideas, the Demise of Communism, and the End of the Cold War," in Risse, ed., *The Power of Human Rights*, 112, 125, 138; English, *Russia and the Idea of the West*, 10; and Evangelista, *Unarmed Forces*, 262.

77; Italian Communist leader Enrico Berlinguer; and Spanish Prime Minister Felipe González, who urged Gorbachev to implement democracy and a free market in order to reinvigorate socialism in the Soviet Union. Gorbachev was particularly impressed by González's leadership of Spain as the country shifted away from its recent history of dictatorship.[12]

Using what historian Archie Brown has called his "power of appointment," Gorbachev selected advisers who were similarly disposed to consider reform, including Alexander Yakovlev and Shevardnadze.[13] One of Gorbachev's most important advisers, Alexander Yakovlev, had studied at Columbia University in the 1950s and spent over a decade serving as Soviet ambassador to Canada.[14] Gorbachev helped facilitate Yakovlev's return to Moscow to head the Institute of World Economy and International Relations, and when Gorbachev came to power, he made Yakovlev one of his chief aides. Valery Boldin, Gorbachev's Chief of Staff for Party Affairs from 1987 to 1991, emphasizes the considerable significance Yakovlev had on Gorbachev's reforms, arguing, "The notion of perestroika, together with all its basic components, was mainly the work of Yakovlev. Practically all of Gorbachev's speeches were also based on Yakovlev's thinking."[15]

Political scientist Robert English has identified a long-term process of Westernization of Soviet elites that led to new thinking in foreign and domestic policy under Gorbachev.[16] In that vein, human rights had gained

---

[12] English, "The Sociology of New Thinking," 60; and Andrei S. Grachev, *Final Days: The Inside Story of the Collapse of the Soviet Union* trans. Margo Milne (Boulder: Westview Press, 1995), 74.

[13] Brown, *The Gorbachev Factor*, 89, 107; and Bennett, "The Guns That Didn't Smoke," 103.

[14] Yakovlev describes his time as a graduate student at Columbia in the 1950s as more influential on him than his later years in Canada. Richmond, *Cultural Exchange and The Cold War*, 29, 90–1; and Alexander Yakovlev Interview, Folder 25, Box 1, Oberdorfer Papers. In Ottawa, Yakovlev faced questions from Canadian politicians about the plight of Solzhenitsyn, Sakharov, and other dissidents in the Soviet Union and encountered picketers at the Soviet embassy who pressed for family reunification. One observer has suggested Soviet repression frustrated Yakovlev and that he shared his feelings during Gorbachev's visit to Canada in 1983. Christopher Shulgan, *The Soviet Ambassador: The Making of the Radial Behind Perestroika* (Toronto: McClelland and Stewart, 2008), 146, 165, 191, 266.

[15] Valery Boldin, *Ten Years That Shook the World: The Gorbachev Era as Witnessed by His Chief of Staff* trans. Evelyn Rossiter (New York: Basic Books, 1994), 113.

[16] English, *Russia and the Idea of the West*, 5–8. Cultural contacts and exchanges shaped this process of Westernization. KGB official Oleg Kalugin who studied at Columbia University in the late 1950s, and has said, "Exchanges were a Trojan Horse in the Soviet Union. They played a tremendous role in the erosion of the Soviet system. They opened

salience in Eastern Europe since the Helsinki Final Act was signed in
1975, influencing Soviet leaders who wanted to move away from heavy-
handed repression. Increased access to information from abroad through
travel and the spread of modern communications facilitated the dissemination of Western ideas. Soviet and Eastern European leaders also experienced increased exposure to dissident thinking and some may have begun
to internalize it. Thomas argues that certain advisers who were close to
Gorbachev had considerable exposure to human rights literature, such as
Yakovlev when he was ambassador to Canada, and Shevardnadze, who
had known a number of Georgian dissidents.[17] Burlatsky, however, suggests Western pressure and concerns about the Soviet Union's technological progress were the key factors inspiring Soviet reform; he attributes
less significance to dissidents, saying that the party intelligentsia did not
read their writings at that time.[18] Nonetheless, some members of Eastern
governments began to understand dissidents' critiques slowly, started
to identify themselves more broadly as European, and, to use Daniel
Thomas's term, were "persuaded" of human rights as a formal norm.[19]
A common complaint in Gorbachev's early years was that dissidents had
been imprisoned for advocating *glasnost'* and *perestroika* ahead of their
time.[20] Describing his reform efforts, Gorbachev wrote,

up a closed society. They greatly influenced younger people who saw the world with more
open eyes, and they kept infecting more and more people over the years." Richmond,
Cultural Exchange and The Cold War, 32.

[17] Thomas, "Human Rights Ideas, the Demise of Communism, and the End of the Cold
War," 11–21; Andrew and Mitrokhin, *The Sword and the Shield*, 333; and Thomas,
"The Helsinki Accords and Political Change in Eastern Europe," 229. Mlynář eventu-
ally emigrated to the West. Mikhail Gorbachev and Zdeněk Mlynář, *Conversations with
Gorbachev: On Perestroika, the Prague Spring, and the Crossroads of Socialism* (New
York: Columbia University Press, 2002); Thomas, "Human Rights Ideas, the Demise
of Communism, and the End of the Cold War," 119–21; and Dai, *Compliance Without
Carrots or Sticks*, 196.

[18] Fedor Burlatsky Interview, Folder 9, Box 1, The Hoover Institution and the Gorbachev
Foundation (Moscow) Collection, Hoover Institution Archives, Stanford, California.
Copyright Stanford University.

[19] Thomas defines persuasion as happening when actors learn about new ideas and accept
their "explanatory power" or "moral or social legitimacy." Thomas, "Human Rights
Ideas, the Demise of Communism, and the End of the Cold War," 112. I use "norm" to
define the expected behavior of an actor given its identity. Peter J. Katzenstein, ed., *The
Culture of National Security: Norms and Identity in World Politics* (New York: Columbia
University Press, 1996), 5; and Thomas, *The Helsinki Effect*, 7.

[20] One Soviet diplomat made the link between the Helsinki Final Act and new political
thinking explicit, saying the agreement gave "legitimacy and prominence to some of the
concepts that later became New Thinking." Vladimir Petrovsky Interview, Folder 18,
Box 1, Oberdorfer Papers.

For many long years the Soviet Union considered human rights as some sort of false issue that had been manufactured artificially (even the phrase human rights was published in our country only in quotation marks preceded by the word so-called). For a totalitarian system, the very posing of the question of human rights is a challenge, a vicious assault on the very essence of its policies. And only perestroika brought this to an end.[21]

The evolution of Soviet leaders' attitudes toward human rights since the signing of the Helsinki Final Act was striking. In the agreement's immediate aftermath, Soviet officials criticized reporting on human rights abuses as interference in internal affairs. Their intransigence continued for so many years that when the Soviet Union began to criticize Western countries' records, it was a welcome shift as it acknowledged human rights were a matter of international concern. Later, Soviet willingness to discuss human rights violations as part of the Reagan administration's four-part agenda was regarded as important progress. Gorbachev has written about the slow process by which human rights policy emerged:

The concept of human rights – especially the possibility of outside intervention to ensure that these rights are observed – is a relatively new phenomenon. It is the result of a gradual development in political culture that included the awareness of these rights, which arose primarily in Europe and North America. In Europe, for example, the universality of human rights is recognized by all governments. This implies acceptance of international intervention in the name of preserving human rights.[22]

The eventual transformation of Soviet attitudes toward dissent, religion, and emigration represented a fundamental shift, which enabled Gorbachev's talk of the Soviet Union sharing a common home with Europe to be imbued with real meaning.[23]

The manifestations of changing attitudes began to emerge at the Paris Conference on the Human Dimension, which opened five months after Vienna closed and amid accelerating reform in Central and Eastern Europe. There, the Soviet Union was a more cooperative participant in

---

[21] Mikhail Gorbachev, *Gorbachev: On My Country and the World* trans. George Shriver (New York: Columbia University Press, 2000), 267. See also A. G. Kovalev Interview, Folder 6, Box 2, The Hoover Institution and the Gorbachev Foundation (Moscow) Collection, Hoover Institution Archives, Stanford, California. Copyright Stanford University.

[22] Gorbachev, *Gorbachev*, 266.

[23] For further discussion of Gorbachev's use of the term "common European home," see Marie-Pierre Rey, "'Europe is our Common Home': A Study of Gorbachev's Diplomatic Concept," *Cold War History* 4:2 (January 2004): 33–65.

CSCE meetings, distancing itself from many other Eastern European states that maintained a hard line. Changes in Soviet policy led to less intransigence on Helsinki issues and enabled the CSCE to become a more productive forum.[24] Sensing the improved dynamic, new United States President George Bush saw the Paris Conference as an opportunity for the CSCE to facilitate further change in Eastern Europe:

I propose we strengthen and broaden the Helsinki process to promote free elections and political pluralism in Eastern Europe ... The foundation for lasting security comes not from tanks, troops, or barbed wire. It is built on shared values and agreements that link free people.[25]

Western diplomats submitted a range of proposals seeking not only to advance respect for human rights but also to promote broad democratic values. For example, Western proposals sought to ensure religious freedom, minority rights, freedom of movement, the rule of law, trade union rights, and freedoms of assembly, association, and expression.[26] Reflecting the wider possibilities, Commission Chair Steny Hoyer even introduced a proposal on free, multiparty elections.[27] The decision to introduce such an aggressive outline for political reform may have reflected Bush's desire to push for more far-reaching political change, but Hoyer's proposal was at the least overly optimistic. Nonetheless, the nature of reforms envisioned in the proposals at Paris foretold important changes to come within the CSCE and in Europe more broadly.

The progress in Eastern Europe fostered improvements in East–West relations and facilitated some positive steps at Paris. According to a Commission report, the Paris meeting was the first instance in which Eastern delegates did not try to prevent delegations from reviewing specific countries' records of Helsinki implementation.[28] Hungary, for

---

[24] In another signal of progress under Gorbachev, Soviet dissidents including Sakharov, Bonner, and Timofeyev appealed to leaders of the CSCE states to address Czechoslovak, not Soviet, repression at the upcoming Paris CHD. Bonner et al. to CSCE heads of state, January 29, 1989, *Jan Palach Week, 1989: The Beginning of the End for Czechoslovak Communism* (National Security Archive Electronic Briefing Book No. 271, January 2009).

[25] Korey, *The Promises We Keep*, 279–80.

[26] CSCE/CDHP.1, June 14, 1989, OSCE Archives; CSCE/CDHP.2, June 14, 1989, ibid.; CSCE/CDHP.6, June 16, 1989, ibid.; CSCE/CDHP.8, June 16, 1989, ibid.; CSCE/CDHP.29, June 19, 1989, ibid.

[27] CSCE/CDHP.33, June 20, 1989, OSCE Archives.

[28] The Paris CHD was held from May 30 to June 23, 1989. Commission on Security and Cooperation in Europe Hearing, "Paris Human Dimension Meeting: Human Rights in the Helsinki Process," July 18, 1989, 100th Congress/First Session; and Commission on

example, which had shifted away from the traditional Warsaw Pact position on exit visas when it opened its borders, submitted a proposal with the United States and Austria pressing for greater freedom of movement.[29] Other states, however, remained in their traditional CSCE roles: Romania, Bulgaria, Czechoslovakia, and the GDR were the most targeted for their human rights abuses, and their persistent obstinacy prompted explicit criticism from CSCE delegates, including British representative Sir Anthony Williams:

> But where – we shall ask – is the GDR in all of this? It still has its walls and its moats. Its soldiers still go on shooting people who try to cross that wall and those moats. Those people appear to be exercising that fundamental right to leave which is, we understood, recognized by the government of the GDR. Why is this right denied them? Why does this wall still exist? Why are people still being shot?[30]

Despite the continuing progress, some observers remained skeptical; Lithuanian-American activist Dr. C. K. Bobelis remarked, "The big surprise of the Paris conference was the new face put on by the Soviet Union. The Soviet delegation held several press conferences, filled the press tables with countless experts and was able to cut and weave through tough questions by hiding behind the façade of future progressive legislation."[31] Concerns, however, about the superficiality of Soviet actions were assuaged during the course of the meeting. While the Paris Conference was in session, the Soviet Union resolved twenty human contacts cases

---

Security and Cooperation in Europe, "From Vienna to Helsinki: Report on the Inter-Sessional Meetings of the CSCE Process," 102nd Congress/2nd Session.

[29] Commission on Security and Cooperation in Europe Hearing, "Paris Human Dimension Meeting: Human Rights in the Helsinki Process," July 18, 1989, 100th Congress/First Session.

[30] Korey, *The Promises We Keep*, 282; and Opening Statement, Sir Anthony Williams (United Kingdom), May 31, 1989, Conference on the Human Dimension, Paris: Statements, 1989, Box 8, OSCE/CSCE Files, Records of the International Helsinki Federation for Human Rights, Open Society Archives. A Memorandum for Alexander Yakovlev noted the differences that had developed among Eastern European countries on the issue of human rights: "In a similar fashion, the humanization of international relations [and their] confirmation of human rights is perceived by the leadership of some governments as a threat to socialism; for others it serves as an additional impulse to enter the road to 'openness' in their own countries." Memorandum, International Department of the Central Committee of the CPSU to Yakovlev, February 1989, *Cold War International History Project Bulletin* 12/13 (Fall/Winter 2001): 66.

[31] Commission on Security and Cooperation in Europe Hearing, "Paris Human Dimension Meeting: Human Rights in the Helsinki Process," July 18, 1989, 100th Congress/First Session.

and released fifteen political prisoners, and it made continued progress after the meeting ended.[32]

More broadly, the Helsinki process was fueling change across Europe. Governing in a new atmosphere without a security guarantee from the Soviet Union, Eastern European leaders were acceding to their population's demands, many of which were tied explicitly to Helsinki principles. The events there, often driven by activists influenced by Helsinki ideals, transformed the European landscape, largely from below. Helsinki monitors were "being catapulted up on to political platforms, speaking in front of mass rallies, organizing demonstrations, and forming political organizations."[33]

The Helsinki process was by no means the only factor driving political change in Eastern Europe; economic concerns, nationalism, and political aspirations were all important as well. Nevertheless, observers at the time recognized the influence of the CSCE, and their analysis remains valid today. Steny Hoyer described the Helsinki process as a force for change: "Although the leadership of Mikhail Gorbachev has been an undisputed element in the reform movement taking place in the Soviet Union, and indeed Hungary and Poland, it is the Helsinki Final Act, and the process it established, which have been the constant driving forces behind this process."[34] He alluded to the roundtable negotiations that facilitated political change, most notably in Poland, and the role of the CSCE as a productive forum when he described the CSCE as "a round table writ large."[35] Furthermore, leaders of movements in Eastern Europe highlighted the role of activist organizations in enabling such changes. Speaking to Helsinki Watch in February 1990 during his first visit to the United States as president of Czechoslovakia, Havel said, "I feel that I'm here as a friend among friends. I know very well what you did for us, and perhaps without you, our revolution would not be."[36]

---

[32] Kovalev, *Azbuka Diplomatim*, 193.

[33] Letter, Fitzpatrick to Nagler and Minnema, October 13, 1988, Correspondence: National Committees: USA/Helsinki Watch, 1988–1992, Box 19, Correspondence and Memoranda, Records of the International Helsinki Federation for Human Rights, Open Society Archives; and Laber to Helsinki Watch Staff, Helsinki Watch Program, 1989, Box 30, General Files, New York Office Files, Record Group 7, HRWR.

[34] Plenary Statement, Steny Hoyer – United States, June 19, 1989, *CSCE Digest* June–July 1989, CSCE 1989, Box 2 Unprocessed, JBANC.

[35] Hoyer, Speech to the Woodrow Wilson International Center for Scholars, April 23, 1990 in Samuel J. Wells, Jr., ed., *The Helsinki Process and the Future of Europe* (Washington: The Wilson Center Press, 1990), 175.

[36] Laber, *The Courage of Strangers*, 349; and William I. Hitchcock, *The Struggle for Europe: The Turbulent History of a Divided Continent, 1945 to the Present* (New York: Anchor Books, 2004), 347. According to Warren Zimmermann, Havel also

FIGURE 10. Czechoslovak President Václav Havel with Helsinki Watch Executive Director Jeri Laber in February 1990. During his visit to Helsinki Watch's New York office, Havel declared, "I feel that I'm here as a friend among friends. I know very well what you did for us, and perhaps without you, our revolution would not be." Photo by Star Black.

Further evidence of the significance of these transnational connections can be seen in the Czechoslovak/Czech Helsinki Committee's unanimous election of Laber to be an honorary member: "We all highly appreciate your friendly and understanding approach to our situation in the difficult situation of the years 1987–1989, when you courageously supported our first steps to found, on the basis of Charter 77, our Helsinki Committee."[37]

Essential to Eastern European reform was the Soviet decision to let the satellite states pursue individual paths. Earlier reform movements, such

thanked him for his efforts. Warren Zimmermann Interview, December 10, 1996, *The Foreign Affairs Oral History Collection of the Association for Diplomatic Studies and Training*, Library of Congress, http://memory.loc.gov/ammem/collections/diplomacy/ (accessed March 6, 2010).

[37] Kadlecova et al. to Laber, December 23, 1992, Member Committees – Czechoslovakia, 1988–1996, Box 5, Files on the International Helsinki Federation for Human Rights, Group 7, HRWR.

as in Hungary in 1956 and Czechoslovakia in 1968, had been suppressed violently on Soviet orders. The Soviet Union's conception of security, however, changed over the course of the CSCE meetings and negotiations with the West, resulting in a different approach to Eastern Europe.[38] In a July 1989 speech to the Council of Europe, Gorbachev said that reform in Eastern Europe was "entirely a matter for the people themselves."[39] Later that summer, on August 16, 1989, in response to struggles between Solidarity and the Communist Party in Poland, the Soviet Foreign Ministry stated, "We do not interfere in the internal affairs of Poland. The Poles must solve their problems themselves."[40] Emphasizing the point again, in October 1989, Gorbachev visited Finland and disavowed Soviet intervention in Eastern Europe, proclaiming what has since been called "the Sinatra doctrine." Gorbachev said, "Hungary and Poland are doing it their way." He went on to assert the "Brezhnev doctrine is dead."[41] The relationship between the Soviet Union and Eastern Europe had become burdensome to the Soviet Union in the late 1980s, and Gorbachev worked to change it.[42]

---

[38] Mastny, *The Helsinki Process and the Reintegration of Europe*, 3.

[39] Judt, *Postwar*, 632; and Csaba Békés, "Back to Europe: The International Background of the Political Transition in Hungary, 1988–90," in András Bozóki, ed., *The Roundtable Talks of 1989: The Genesis of Hungarian Democracy: Analysis and Documents* (Budapest: Central European University Press, 2002), 241.

[40] Norman Davies, *God's Playground: A History of Poland*, Volume II, rev. ed. (New York: Columbia University Press, 2005), 504. Soviet official Yevgeny Primakov asserts that Soviet interference was never discussed: "It was quite clear that we should not intervene." Yevgeny Primakov Interview, Folder 19, Box 1, Oberdorfer Papers.

[41] Timur Kuran, "Now Out of Never: The Element of Surprise in the East European Revolution of 1989," *World Politics* 44:1 (October 1991): 38. In addition, Gorbachev had indicated Soviet forces would not participate in such actions. Timothy Garton Ash, *The Magic Lantern: The Revolution of '89 Witnessed in Warsaw, Budapest, Berlin and Prague* (New York: Vintage Books, 1993), 140–2; and Stephen Kull, *Burying Lenin: The Revolution in Soviet Ideology and Foreign Policy* (Boulder: Westview Press, 1992), 139–40. Vladislav Zubok suggests Gorbachev and his advisers were influenced by residual guilt leftover from the crackdown in Hungary in 1956 and invasion of Czechoslovakia in 1968. Vladislav M. Zubok, "New Evidence on the 'Soviet Factor' in the Peaceful Revolutions of 1989," *Cold War International History Project Bulletin* 12/13 (Fall/Winter 2001): 10. See also Svetlana Savranskaya, "In the Name of Europe: Soviet Withdrawal from Eastern Europe," in Frédéric Bozo et al., eds., *Europe and the End of the Cold War: A Reappraisal* (New York: Routledge, 2008), 38, 41. Gorbachev's position was shaped in part by economic factors: "Today some people criticize us: they say, what is the Soviet Union doing – allowing Poland and Hungary to 'sail' to the West [?] But we cannot take Poland on our balance." Memorandum of Conversation, November 1, 1989, End of the Cold War, Cold War International History Project Virtual Archive.

[42] Savranskaya, "In the Name of Europe," 37.

Changes in the Soviet Union directly and indirectly influenced developments in its satellite states. Historian Mark Kramer has examined what he calls the "indirect spillover" of Gorbachev's reforms on Eastern Europe: "Gorbachev's boldness in implementing reforms in the Soviet Union made it increasingly difficult for the hard-line Communist regimes in Eastern Europe to hold out against the 'winds of change.'"[43] Gorbachev's restraint removed the threat of Soviet intervention and deprived other communist leaders of their authority, undermining the states' stability.[44] Given their economic problems, Eastern European regimes needed the Soviet military support, which Gorbachev was unwilling to provide.[45] Furthermore, the Helsinki process and the growing salience of respect for human rights had raised the international stakes for domestic repression such that Eastern European states did not use violence to suppress the revolutions.[46] Once initiated, the fall of communism in Eastern Europe occurred relatively quickly as each communist party that collapsed undermined the legitimacy of those remaining.[47] In stunning speed, nearly half a century of Soviet domination came to an end.

One of the most important ways the Helsinki process enabled the revolutions in Eastern Europe was through the development of a "second society" in the Soviet Union, Hungary, Poland, Czechoslovakia, and elsewhere.[48] This "second society," which was often inspired by the Helsinki Final Act and formally linked with Helsinki monitoring groups,

[43] Mark Kramer, "The Collapse of East European Communism and the Repercussions within the Soviet Union (Part 2)," *Journal of Cold War Studies* 6:4 (Fall 2004): 4; Archie Brown, *Seven Years that Changed the World: Perestroika in Perspective* (New York: Oxford University Press, 2007), 157, 229; and Pleshakov, *There Is No Freedom Without Bread!*, 6.

[44] Judt, *Postwar*, 632–3.

[45] Steven Saxonberg, *The Fall: A Comparative Study of the End of Communism in Czechoslovakia, East Germany, Hungary and Poland* (Amsterdam: Harwood Academic Publishers, 2001), 366. Speaking with the leader of the Yugoslav Presidium, Gorbachev explained that even though the Soviet Union had the ability to impose its will on other states, it would not do so. Excerpt, March 14, 1988, REEADD-RADD Collection, National Security Archive.

[46] For greater discussion of the process by which norms such as human rights are accepted, see Finnemore and Sikkink, "International Norm Dynamics and Political Change," 895, 902.

[47] A record of economic failure also undermined the regimes, spurred social opposition, and led to a loss of confidence in Eastern European leaders. J. F. Brown, *Surge to Freedom: The End of Communist Rule in Eastern Europe* (Durham: Duke University Press, 1991), 2–4.

[48] Some scholars such as Stephen Kotkin disagree with the assertion that a civil society or "second society" existed in Eastern Europe at this time. See Stephen Kotkin, *Uncivil Society: 1989 and the Implosion of the Communist Establishment* with a contribution by

laid a foundation for political change.[49] This "second society" was comprised of people committed to a wide range of political and social causes, which uniquely prepared them to participate in the transformation of their states and partake in postcommunist governance in meaningful ways. Once a movement for change began, organizations, activists, and structures already existed to replace the Communist Party. These second societies existed to varying degree across Eastern Europe. Many elements were fostered by the Helsinki process, and Western states, organizations, and individuals supported these movements until Gorbachev's process of liberalization offered the opportunity for reform in Eastern Europe.[50]

Helsinki activism was always one factor in a host of forces that precipitated change in Eastern Europe. Its influence was stronger in countries such as Czechoslovakia and Poland where Helsinki monitors had been active since the late 1970s.[51] Poland was the first country in which significant change began in 1988 when strikes and protests, prompted by rising consumer prices, compelled the government to initiate roundtable talks with Solidarity, the banned trade union.[52] These negotiations led to the union's relegalization in 1989 and were followed by a number of reforms,

---

Jan T. Gross (New York: Modern Library, 2009), xiv. Padraic Kenney, however, argues, "Protest became a ubiquitous part of everyday life in major cities." Padraic Kenney, *A Carnival of Revolution: Central Europe 1989* (Princeton: Princeton University Press, 2002), 12.

[49] Other movements such as those devoted to labor rights, peace, the environment, and national identity were also important. Leatherman, *From Cold War to Democratic Peace*, 222; Sabrina P. Ramet, *Social Currents in Eastern Europe: The Sources and Consequences of the Great Transformation* (Durham: Duke University Press, 1995), 317; Ash, *The Magic Lantern*, 14; Brown, *Surge to Freedom*, 168; Grzegorz Ekiert and Jan Kubik, *Rebellious Civil Society: Popular Protest and Democratic Consolidation in Poland, 1989–1993* (Ann Arbor: The University of Michigan Press, 1999), 44; Mark R. Beissinger, "Nationalism and the Collapse of Soviet Communism," *Contemporary European History* 18:3 (2009): 331–47; and Kenney, *A Carnival of Revolution.*

[50] Observers who have highlighted the small number of dissidents in countries such as the USSR, GDR, and Romania in the late 1980s are correct. I agree that there was meaningful regional variation in the quantity and significance of activists across Eastern Europe. Arguments for their influence, however, cannot be undermined solely on the basis of the total bodies. Using parameters such as the resonance of their ideas, the existence of support for their agenda, as well as their effectiveness in securing attention and support for their causes seems far more meaningful. See for example, Brown, *The Rise and Fall of Communism*, 576; and Kotkin, *Uncivil Society*, 7.

[51] In other countries, the influence of the Helsinki process was weaker, although broader human rights concerns were often apparent.

[52] Bush pointed to the role of the Helsinki Final Act as a catalyst for change in remarks marking the Polish government's April 17, 1989, relegalization of Solidarity, which one observer described as the "engine" of change in Eastern Europe. Pienkos, *For Your Freedom Through Ours*, 403; and Ramet, *Social Currents in Eastern Europe*, 345.

including elections for a new assembly.[53] Solidarity's overwhelming success in the June 1989 elections, in which it won 99 out of 100 seats in the Senate and all 161 seats for which it could field candidates in the Sejm, signaled the end of Communist Party domination in Poland. Solidarity leader and Polish President Lech Wałesa has said the Helsinki Final Act and resulting human rights movement was instrumental in the formation of Solidarity as it was a "turning point on the road to Gdańsk," where Solidarity was born.[54]

The next Soviet satellite to fall was Hungary: Protests began in Budapest in June 1989 in honor of 1950s Hungarian leader Imre Nagy, who had been executed in the aftermath of the 1956 Soviet invasion. At Nagy's long-overdue funeral, Hungarians paid tribute to his efforts at liberalization and condemned the subsequent Soviet invasion.[55] Likely owing to Hungary's status as the most liberal Eastern European state, change there came primarily through formal negotiations on reforming the political process as opposed to large-scale public demonstrations. There was no violence or even any threats to use violence.[56] Instead, agreement on multi-party democracy signaled the end of communist domination in Hungary. As discussed earlier, the Hungarian government had not been as repressive as its neighbors, and this was reflected in the relatively smooth transition there. In a similar vein, the Helsinki process influenced developments in Hungary less because the party's relatively liberal policies meant the conditions that prompted Helsinki monitoring groups in other states had not existed to the same degree. Nonetheless, a small democratic opposition had been active, if secretly, in Hungary for much of the 1980s, and Hungarian opposition figures pressed for

---

[53] Poland had a longer tradition of mass protests inspired by political and economic issues than other Eastern European countries. The support Western human rights groups, trade unions, and political parties offered to Solidarity after the imposition of martial law and in the years that followed had helped sustain it underground. Grzegorz Ekiert, *The State against Society: Political Crises and Their Aftermath in East Central Europe* (Princeton: Princeton University Press, 1996), 21, 290; Ash, *The Polish Revolution*, 371; and Judt, *Postwar*, 606–7.

[54] Thomas, "The Helsinki Accords and Political Change in Eastern Europe," in Thomas Risse et al., ed., *The Power of Human Rights*, 220–1.

[55] András Bozóki emphasizes a long-term process facilitated change in Hungary with the reburial of Nagy as just one point along a longer continuum. András Bozóki, "Hungary's Road to Systemic Change: the Opposition Roundtable," *East European Politics and Societies* 7:2 (Spring 1993): 277.

[56] Bruszt László, "1989: The Negotiated Revolution in Hungary," *Social Research* 57:2 (Summer 1990): 366–7; and Pleshakov, *There Is No Freedom Without Bread!*, 139, 169.

reforms similar to those advanced at the Paris Conference on the Human Dimension (CHD).[57]

In comparison to some of its neighbors, human rights activism in the GDR had a relatively short history. This was due in part to divisions between those who wished to emigrate and those who sought reform of the system. In the 1980s, East Germans dissidents were largely focused on peace and environmental issues.[58] The emphasis on these two issues was connected in part to the Lutheran Church's attention to peace activism and its role as a "free space" for dissident activity in the GDR.[59] Later, East German human rights activism led to the formal establishment of the Initiative for Peace and Human Rights in January 1986. The IFM, as it was known, followed the model of similar dissident groups and drew up documents that enumerated human rights violations by the government. It also began to publish a newsletter *Grenzfall* in mid-1986; before *Grenzfall* there had been little *samizdat* literature in the GDR. The IFM, however, was small in size and had little contact with other dissident groups.[60] In the late 1980s a new strand of activists developed – largely younger activists who embraced Western style capitalism for East Germany, further complicating the emergence of a unified movement.[61]

The fall of the Berlin Wall produced perhaps the most enduring symbol of the collapse of communism in Eastern Europe, and the CSCE had a distinct role. The Hungarian decision to open its border with Austria to East German vacationers at the end of the summer prompted the crisis that ultimately forced the GDR to follow suit. In changing its policy, Hungary cited its commitment in the Vienna Concluding Document to the right to leave one's country and the costs associated with maintaining the fence.[62] Recent accounts have suggested Hungarian claims regarding maintenance costs were a cover for reform-minded leaders such as Hungarian Prime Minister Miklos Nemeth to dismantle the border in part to gain favor

---

[57] Saxonberg, *The Fall*, 18.
[58] Torpey, *Intellectuals, Socialism, and Dissent*, 89; and Maier, *Dissolution*, 172.
[59] Torpey, *Intellectuals, Socialism, and Dissent*, 80, 89, 94; and Kotkin, *Uncivil Society*, 60–1.
[60] As mentioned earlier, there were no Helsinki monitoring groups in the GDR before the IFM's establishment. Torpey, *Intellectuals, Socialism, and Dissent*, 95–97, 99; and Kenney, *A Carnival of Revolution*, 109–13.
[61] Mary Elise Sarotte, *1989: The Struggle to Create Post–Cold War Europe* (Princeton: Princeton University Press, 2009), 91.
[62] Leatherman, *From Cold War to Democratic Peace*, 189; Lehne, *The Vienna Meeting of the Conference on Security and Cooperation in Europe*, 188–9; Korey, *The Promises We Keep*, 305; Pleshakov, *There Is No Freedom Without Bread!*, 181; and Kotkin, *Uncivil Society*, 56.

with Western leaders.[63] Thereafter East German citizens could reach the FRG by using Hungary as an escape point, precipitating waves of departures from the GDR. The Pan-European Picnic held in Sopron, Hungary in August 1989 in particular served as a means for East German citizens to exit Warsaw Pact territory.[64] In confronting this problem, East German leaders ultimately decided to allow freedom of movement between the GDR and the FRG, leading to the opening and dismantling of the Berlin Wall.[65] The fall of the Berlin Wall in 1989 exemplified the dramatic change in Europe as a divided Berlin had long been a flashpoint for Cold War tension and symbolic of the broader division of Europe. Former Polish Foreign Minister Adam D. Rotfeld later singled out the CSCE as the first step toward these events: "All in all, the road to the dismantling of the Berlin Wall and unification of Europe began in Helsinki."[66]

In Bulgaria, the events leading to the downfall of that regime were stimulated in part by a crackdown against members of Ecoglasnost, the Bulgarian NGO that organized protests during a CSCE meeting on the environment in Sofia in October and November 1989.[67] One observer

[63] Such developments have led observers to characterize the political changes in Hungary as a "revolution from above." Michael Meyer, *The Year That Changed the World: The Untold Story behind the Fall of the Berlin Wall* (New York: Scribner, 2009), 28, 36, 67; and Pleshakov, *There Is No Freedom Without Bread!*, 169.

[64] George Paul Csicsery, "The Siege of Nógrádi Street, Budapest, 1989," in Brinton and Rinzler, eds., *Without Force or Lies*, 300–1. Journalist Michael Meyer has characterized the Pan-European Picnic as an explicit attempt to encourage East Germans to cross the Hungarian border to Austria. Furthermore, according to Meyer, Nemeth said, "Yes, I foresaw that opening the border could lead to the collapse of the German Democratic Republic, and of the Czech regime as well." Meyer, *The Year That Changed the World*, 98, 114.

[65] The spillover or "Gorbachev effect" was particularly strong in the GDR due to the degree of its dependence on the USSR. Peter Grieder, "'To Learn from the Soviet Union is to Learn How to Win': The East German Revolution, 1989–90," in McDermott and Stibbe, eds., *Revolution and Resistance in Eastern Europe*, 171. East Germans protesting on the anniversary of the founding of the GDR made such connections explicit by chanting, "Help us, Gorbachev." Demonstrators in Leipzig in October 1989 also chanted Gorbachev's name. Telegram, October 9, 1989, End of the Cold War, Cold War International History Project Virtual Archive; and Konrad H. Jarausch, *The Rush to German Unity* (New York: Oxford University Press, 1994), 46.

[66] Adam D. Rotfeld, "The Helsinki Process: Status Quo v. Fundamental Change," Address at "Thirty Years Since the Helsinki Final Act," Rüschlikon (Switzerland) September 8–10, 2005, 1–2, in the author's possession.

[67] Bulgaria did not have a long history of opposition groups; those that did develop in the late 1980s focused on environmental problems, human rights, and general reform. It did, however, have an abysmal record in its treatment of Bulgarians of Turkish descent. Jordan Baev, "1989: Bulgarian Transition to Pluralist Democracy," *Cold War International History Project Bulletin* 12/13 (Fall/Winter 2001): 165; Robert L. Hutchings, *American Diplomacy and the End of the Cold War: An Insider's Account of*

suggests Bulgarian leader Todor Zhivkov wanted to use the CSCE meeting as a way to shore up his prestige, which seemed imperiled in the wake of GDR General Secretary Erich Honecker's fall.[68] At the same time, Ecoglasnost protester Krassen Stanchev later said, "We saw [the CSCE meeting] as a great opportunity to get more widely known. There would be foreign politicians, civil servants and journalists here and the police and security services couldn't keep us away from these delegates. We were still campaigning on environmental issues, like the hydroelectric dam project and Rila Monastery. But these were a pretext, our activities were really anti-regime in general and everyone knew it."[69] The repression incited sharp condemnation by the CSCE delegates there, with Bulgaria ultimately apologizing and promising its actions would not be repeated. This bolstered independent activism in Bulgaria. Zhivkov's removal several weeks later was likely influenced by the physical presence of CSCE negotiations, protests prompted by the CSCE, and condemnation by CSCE delegates, although ultimately he lost power in a political struggle.[70] Zhivkov's resignation was characterized by Bulgarian officials as a "victory for the 'Gorbachev's supporters [*gorbachiovistilor*]" rather than a democratic revolution.[71]

As in Poland, Czechoslovak protests were influenced by the terms of CSCE agreements and led by activists inspired by the Helsinki Final Act. In Prague, the spark for revolution was a demonstration held on November 17, 1989, to mark the fiftieth anniversary of the Nazi murder of Czechoslovakian student Jan Opletal, although earlier protests such as those in January and August 1989 had also undermined the regime.[72] The Czechoslovak police harshly repressed the demonstration, leading to

US Diplomacy in Europe, 1989–1992 (Baltimore: The Johns Hopkins University Press, 1997), 80–1; and Pleshakov, *There Is No Freedom Without Bread!*, 196.

[68] Brown, *Surge to Freedom*, 195–6. In the face of increasing protests, Honecker was forced to resign in October 1989.

[69] Sebestyen, *Revolution 1989*, 361.

[70] Laber, *The Courage of Strangers*, 330–4; Telegram, AmEmbassy Sofia to SecState, November 2, 1989, www.foia.state.gov/documents/foiadocs/677b.PDF (accessed May 22, 2006); Lehne, *The Vienna Meeting of the Conference on Security and Cooperation in Europe*, 187–8; and Brown, *Surge to Freedom*, 197.

[71] Telegram, November 10, 1989, End of the Cold War, Cold War International History Project Virtual Archive. See also Hutchings, *American Diplomacy and the End of the Cold War*, 81.

[72] Kincl to Adamec, January 25, 1989, *Jan Palach Week, 1989: The Beginning of the End for Czechoslovak Communism* (National Security Archive Electronic Briefing Book No. 271, January 2009). Czechoslovak Secret Police document conveys the frustration the regime felt toward the Czechoslovak Helsinki Committee, which it viewed as "incit[ing] a

student strikes and protests against the government and the 1968 Warsaw Pact invasion. Protests for political freedoms led by opposition forces such as Charter 77 and the Czechoslovak Helsinki Committee quickly gained wider adherents. Charter 77 did not topple the regime in Prague, rather it as well as like-minded groups and individuals capitalized on disillusionment with the government and mobilized masses of protesters to press for fundamental change.[73] The Civic Forum, an effort to unify opposition elements in Czechoslovakia, outlined collective complaints in late November: "the disregard of several human rights, especially the right of free assembly and association, the right of free expression of opinion, and the right to partake in the decision of public affairs."[74] In the face of growing demonstrations and without support from Moscow, the communist government, which was no longer willing to repress the demonstrators by force and lacking political legitimacy, resigned.[75] This action brought to power playwright and long-imprisoned human rights activist Václav Havel, who had risen to political prominence through his involvement with Charter 77.[76] Continuing a trend, success of opposition demonstrations in one Eastern European country, this time Czechoslovakia, reverberated elsewhere in the region.[77]

confrontation with citizens demanding democratic renewal." Czechoslovak Secret Police Memorandum, August 1989, *Cold War International History Project Bulletin* 12/13 (Fall/Winter 2001): 194–5. The Czechoslovak Secret Police saw evidence of Hungarian, Polish, and Western support for opposition activism. Polish Solidarity, the Hungarian Democratic Forum, and Czechoslovak émigrés were all specifically cited as supporting the "internal enemy." Czechoslovak Secret Police Memorandum, August 20, 1989, *Cold War International History Project Bulletin* 12/13 (Fall/Winter 2001): 198.

[73] Falk, *The Dilemmas of Dissidence in East-Central Europe,* 255. See Tarrow for a discussion of how people in Eastern Europe reacted in response to smaller and obscure opportunities for protest. Tarrow sees the protests as collective responses to opening of political opportunities, which raised the possibility or reward and lowered the costs. Tarrow, "'Aiming at a Moving Target,'" 14–15.

[74] Draft Thesis of the Program of the Civic Forum, November 24, 1989, *Cold War International History Project Bulletin* 12/13 (Fall/Winter 2001): 212. The Civic Forum's counterpart in Bratislava was Public Against Violence.

[75] George Lawson argues "that revolutions take place when the legitimacy of a ruling regime fatally collapses and an opposition group exists that espouses an alternative ideology, offers a viable plan for radical change, holds sufficient resources to proffer a credible challenge, and carries the support of significant social groups and members of the public. All these conditions bar one existed in Czechoslovakia in 1989." George Lawson, *Negotiated Revolutions: The Czech Republic, South Africa and Chile* (Burlington: Ashgate, 2005), 87.

[76] IHF Chairman Karl von Schwarzenberg, a Czechoslovakian exile, was actively involved in Czech events and served as chancellor to new Czechoslovakian President Václav Havel after the revolution. Ash, *The Magic Lantern,* 80–2.

[77] Timur Kuran, "Now Out of Never: The Element of Surprise in the East European Revolution of 1989," in Nancy Bermeo, ed., *Liberalization and Democratization: Change*

The Romanian dictator Nicolae Ceauşescu was overthrown and executed in December 1989 in a revolution that was rooted more in opposition to his dictatorship than in a broad-based social or political movement. Yet in Romania, as in other Eastern European states at the time, protests against the regime were instigated in part by attempts to repress human rights activism. In the Romanian case, the precipitating incident was an effort to arrest a priest active in defending the rights of ethnic Hungarians living in Romania.[78] The resulting protests and Ceauşescu's orders for the military to suppress them provoked a backlash, triggering his eventual capture and execution.

Despite the progressive dismantling of the informal Soviet empire, Gorbachev remained firm in his disavowal of the Brezhnev Doctrine. Gorbachev opposed the use of force in Eastern Europe, seeing past Soviet interventions in Afghanistan and Angola as ineffective militarily and certainly politically. Moreover, recently he had witnessed the international condemnation of the crackdown in Tiananmen Square as well as the shock of Soviet citizens at the repression of protesters in Tbilisi in 1989.[79] Gorbachev also was cognizant that international opposition to Soviet intervention could cripple his efforts at domestic reform, which remained his foremost priority.

As communist regimes continued to fall, the CSCE responded to new circumstances on the ground. The dramatic changes in Eastern Europe in the year between the CHD meetings in Paris and Copenhagen meant that many traditional Helsinki points of controversy between East and West were no longer contentious. Instead, the 1990 CHD meeting in Copenhagen charted the way for Eastern Europe to adopt democratic pluralism.[80] One of the most far-reaching and widely supported proposals at Copenhagen advocated the significance of the rule of law

---

in the Soviet Union and Eastern Europe (Baltimore: The Johns Hopkins University Press, 1992), 39.

[78] Mircea Munteanu, "New Evidence on the 1989 Crisis in Romania," Cold War International History Project e-Dossier No. 5 (December 2001); Pleshakov, There Is No Freedom Without Bread!, 216–7; and Kotkin, Uncivil Society, 94–5.

[79] Bennett, "The Guns That Didn't Smoke," 93–4; Savranskaya, "In the Name of Europe," in Bozo et al., ed., Europe and the End of the Cold War, 36–7; Nigel Swain, "Negotiated Revolution in Poland and Hungary, 1989," in McDermott and Stibbe, eds., Revolution and Resistance in Eastern Europe, 152; Sebestyen, Revolution 1989, xix; and Chen Jian, "Tiananmen and the Fall of the Berlin Wall: China's Path Toward 1989 and Beyond," in Jeffrey A. Engel, ed., The Fall of the Berlin Wall: The Revolutionary Legacy of 1989 (New York: Oxford University Press, 2009), 114.

[80] The Copenhagen Conference was held in the context of the international showdown with Saddam Hussein over Kuwait and a recent show of force by Soviet troops in Lithuania.

and such rights as freedom of expression; freedom to assemble and demonstrate; freedom of association, including membership in a trade union; freedom of thought; freedom of movement; and freedom to own private property.[81] That such a proposal could gain support from both Eastern and Western states was evidence of the dramatic shifts that had taken place in Europe. Indeed, United States Secretary of State James Baker said, "My friends, we are present at the creation of a new age of Europe."[82] Systemic changes in CSCE states were reflected at Copenhagen in the proposals submitted and the partnerships delegations formed. For example, the GDR announced it was cosponsoring eight Western proposals on freedom of expression, freedom of association, and the role of NGOs.[83] United States Ambassador to the Copenhagen Meeting Max Kampelman described the new dynamic: "The Soviets have been extremely cooperative with me and ready to accept most anything within reason. The newly initiated democracies began to feel their oats."[84]

Traditional CSCE issues such as divided families and political prisoners were largely resolved by the end of the Copenhagen Conference, but the fall of communism produced new challenges for the CSCE to confront.[85] The CSCE states turned their attention to dilemmas such as ethnic tension, the future role of European military alliances, and CSCE institutionalization. The rising tension and violence in Yugoslavia, in particular, presented a considerable crisis for the CSCE, which did not

Commission on Security and Cooperation in Europe, "From Vienna to Helsinki: Report on the Inter-Sessional Meetings of the CSCE Process," 102nd Congress, 2nd Session. Albania was granted observer status at Copenhagen, whereas Estonia, Latvia, and Lithuania were not. The Baltic states wanted to join the CSCE, at least as observers and in their request they had considerable support, but as the CSCE was governed by consensus, the Soviet veto prevented it. Korey, *The Promises We Keep*, 359; John J. Maresca, "Ensuring CSCE Promises Are Kept," *ODIHR Bulletin* 3:3 (Fall 1995): 33; "CSCE Summit," n.d., Box 36, Kampelman Papers; Heraclides, *Security and Co-operation in Europe*, 118; and Lehne, *The Vienna Meeting of the Conference on Security and Cooperation in Europe*, 190.

[81] CSCE/CHDC.16, June 8, 1990, OSCE Archives.

[82] Press Release, June 11, 1990, C.S.C.E. Ministerial 10/1/90, Chronological File, 1989–93, Speech File Backup Files, White House Office of Speechwriting, George Bush Library, College Station, Texas (hereafter GBL).

[83] CSCE/CHDC.Inf.4, June 14, 1990, OSCE Archives. See also CSCE/CHDC/Inf.2, June 11, 1990, OSCE Archives; CSCE.CHDC/Inf.5, June 18, 1990, ibid.

[84] Telegram, AmEmbassy Copenhagen to SECSTATE, June 27, 1990, Box 35, Kampelman Papers.

[85] Helsinki Commission Staff to EUR/RPM, March 28, 1990, Box 35, Kampelman Papers.

have an effective deterrent mechanism, raising questions about possible modifications to the CSCE framework.[86]

With a concluding document declaring an explicit connection between Europe, the CSCE, and pluralistic democracy, the Copenhagen CHD moved the Helsinki process beyond emphasizing human contacts and human rights. At Copenhagen, the CSCE states committed themselves to free elections, representative government, the rule of law, and a range of fundamental freedoms not previously adhered to under communist regimes.[87] The Copenhagen agreement also included protections against torture and promoted democratic values. "The promise of the 1975 Helsinki Accords now has become a program of democratic action," a White House statement declared.[88] The dramatic scope of the terms agreed to at Copenhagen was significant but the likelihood that these provisions would actually be implemented throughout the CSCE, still a new phenomenon in the Helsinki process, was even more important.

CSCE delegates to Copenhagen repeatedly remarked on the fundamental changes in Eastern Europe. Cypriot Foreign Minister George Iacovou reflected the sentiments of many when he said:

When in January 1989 we adopted the Vienna Concluding Document, few if any, would have predicted the changes in Europe that were to come. When we met in Paris over a year ago, to discuss the Human Dimension of the CSCE, the confrontations atmosphere of yesteryear prevailed with only a hint of dawn in Eastern Europe.[89]

The Finnish Minister of Foreign Affairs echoed similar sentiments, calling the changes in Eastern Europe "nothing less than a transformation of our Continent." He went on to attribute considerable responsibility to the CSCE for these changes, saying, "The CSCE is at the core of these developments ... it was also a blueprint for action ... when Europe now speaks

---

[86] In Yugoslavia, loss of political support for the Communist Party had coincided with rising nationalist aspirations by different republics and provinces within the federation leading to the collapse of Yugoslavia and the outbreak of bitter fighting. Ramet, *Social Currents in Eastern Europe*, 341–5.

[87] According to Baker, the United States and the United Kingdom sought to expand the definition of human rights to include the right to free elections. Press Briefing, June 4, 1990, Folder 16, Box 163, James A. Baker III Papers, Public Policy Papers, Department of Rare Books and Special Collections, Princeton University Library, Princeton, New Jersey (hereafter Baker Papers).

[88] Statement by the President, June 29, 1990, Box 35, Kampelman Papers.

[89] Statement, George Iacovou (Cyprus), June 5, 1990, CSCE, Conference on the Human Dimension, Copenhagen, Statements, 1990 [1 of 3], Box 8, OSCE/CSCE Files, Records of the International Helsinki Federation for Human Rights, Open Society Archives.

of human rights, it increasingly does so in one language."[90] Responding to such changes, many CSCE members states questioned how the CSCE should evolve.[91]

At the November 1990 Paris summit, which many CSCE observers regarded as marking the end of the Cold War, the sweeping shifts in the East–West relationship were formalized and, as Gorbachev noted, "[It] heralded a new, post-confrontational era in European history."[92] At the summit opening, French President François Mitterrand noted the unique nature of the changes in Eastern Europe: "It is the first time in history that we witness a change in depth of the European landscape which is not the outcome of a war or a bloody revolution." He went on to say, "For forty years we have had stability without freedom in Europe. Henceforth we want freedom with stability."[93] Representatives from all CSCE states signed two documents there: the Charter of Paris for a New Europe and the Vienna Document on Confidence and Security Building Measures, which expanded and strengthened the CSBM terms agreed to at the Stockholm Conference in 1986.[94] The Charter of Paris for a New Europe declared, "The era of confrontation and division of Europe has ended," and further emphasized the CSCE commitments to human rights, democracy, rule

---

[90] Statement, Pertti Paasio (Finland), June 5, 1990, CSCE, Conference on the Human Dimension, Copenhagen, Statements, 1990 [1 of 3], Box 8, OSCE/CSCE Files, Records of the International Helsinki Federation for Human Rights, Open Society Archives. Minister of Foreign Affairs of Portugal, João de Deus Pinheiro also eloquently outlined similar ideas. Statement, João de Deus Pinheiro (Portugal), June 6, 1990, CSCE, Conference on the Human Dimension, Copenhagen, Statements, 1990 [3 of 3], Box 9, OSCE/CSCE Files, Records of the International Helsinki Federation for Human Rights, Open Society Archives.

[91] The Bush administration repeatedly talked about developing a "new architecture" for Europe, and it intended the CSCE to play an important role as the one institution that bridged Western, Central, and Eastern Europe as well as including Canada and the United States. Yet, although the United States was willing to consider the establishment of a small secretariat, it was not interested in a significant expansion of the CSCE. Press Release, May 2, 1990, Folder 1, Box 163, Baker Papers; and Press Briefing, June 4, 1990, Folder 16, ibid. I will not address the considerable debates regarding institutionalization of the CSCE, possible NATO expansion, or new frameworks for Europe. For a full discussion, see Sarotte, *1989.*

[92] Gorbachev, *Memoirs*, 548.

[93] Mitterrand had wanted the CSCE Paris Summit represent an end to the Cold War. Statement, Francois Mitterrand, November 19, 1990, Conference on Security and Cooperation in Europe, Box 1, Subject Files, Press Office, GBL; Melvin Croan "Germany and Eastern Europe," in Joseph Held, ed., *The Columbia History of Eastern Europe in the 20th Century* (New York: Columbia University Press, 1992), 388; and Bozo, *Mitterrand, The End of the Cold War and German Unification*, 279.

[94] The negotiations that produced the Vienna Document on CSBMs had been in session since March 9, 1989, and were the second phase of the Stockholm conference held from 1984 to 1986.

of law, and market economics.[95] It also established structures and institutions to develop the Helsinki process further.[96] Institutionalization of the CSCE, which broadened its activities, was one of a number of steps taken to heal the former East–West divide in Europe.[97] The NATO and Warsaw Pact states also signed the Treaty on Conventional Armed Forces in Europe and the Joint Declaration of Twenty-Two States, which declared an end to East–West conflict between the two alliances.[98] After the important agreements on democracy and market economics signed at Copenhagen and Bonn, declaring an end to East–West military animosity suggested further confirmation of the end of the Cold War.[99]

Although the Paris summit was hailed as an achievement for Gorbachev and evidence of the transformation of the communist bloc, the period after the summit was at times difficult for the Soviet leadership. Gorbachev, Shevardnadze, and their aides had many domestic opponents to their program of reform. For example, Adamishin, head of the humanitarian department in the Ministry of Foreign Affairs, suggests that his proposals for reform were watered down as they worked their way through the ministry.[100] Shevardnadze wrote similarly about his struggle to change human rights in the Soviet Union:

---

[95] Charter of Paris for A New Europe, November 1990, www.osce.org/documents/ mcs/1990/11/4045_en.pdf (accessed May 22, 2006); and Rob Zaagman, "The Second Basket of the CSCE: History, Helsinki-II and Afterwards," in Arie Bloed, ed., *The Challenges of Change: The Helsinki Summit of the CSCE and its Aftermath* (Boston: Martinus Nijhoff, 1994), 181.

[96] Charter of Paris for A New Europe, November 1990, www.osce.org/documents/ mcs/1990/11/4045_en.pdf (accessed May 22, 2006); Press Briefing, July 1, 1992, National Security Council, Walter Kanskiner Trip Files 6/92–7/92 President's Trip to … [8] Pre-Summit Prep., Box 2 of 5, 2000–1333-F, GBL; and Commission on Security and Cooperation in Europe, "The Conference on Security and Cooperation in Europe: An Overview of the CSCE Process, Recent Meetings and Institutional Development," February 1992; Heraclides, *Security and Co-operation in Europe*, 137; and Korey, *The Promises We Keep*, 357.

[97] Andrew J. Pierre, "The United States and the New Europe," *Current History* 89:550 (November 1990): 354.

[98] Joint Declaration of Twenty-Two States, Conference on Security and Cooperation in Europe, Box 1, Subject Files, Press Office, GBL; and Heraclides, *Security and Co-operation in Europe*, 144–5.

[99] The Negotiation on Conventional Armed Forces in Europe (CFE) produced an agreement that limited conventional forces in Europe and was described by a Bush administration official as "probably the most ambitious arms control treaty ever concluded." Press Briefing, November 15, 1990, Conference on Security and Cooperation in Europe, Box 1, Subject Files, Press Office, GBL.

[100] Anatoly Adamishin, August 5, 1989 Interview Transcript, Folder 1, Box 1, The Hoover Institution and the Gorbachev Foundation (Moscow) Collection, Hoover Institution Archives, Stanford, California. Copyright Stanford University.

It cost immense effort to bring back from exile and banishment several outstanding scientists, writers, and theater directors – honest, conscientious people whose only offense had been refusing to accept the canon of violence and falsehood. But it was even harder to restore the good name of the country where the best people had been treated that way.

It was difficult to persuade even my colleagues on the simplest point: Since we had signed the Helsinki Final Act and had assumed obligations under international conventions and agreements, we had thereby acknowledged the right of other participants in these agreements to inquire into all issues and to insist that we observe the obligations we had undertaken. By that time it had become perfectly obvious to me that the human dimension in international security was crucial. But many of our partners had yet to believe in the sincerity of my statements on that score.[101]

The long-awaited Moscow Conference on the Human Dimension opened in September 1991, three weeks after the failed coup that would overshadow much of the meeting. In his opening speech, Gorbachev characterized the defeat of the coup against him as a triumph for human rights.[102] Baker echoed Gorbachev in his opening statement: "[The] CSCE has no divisions of tanks. It has instead the moral authority that flows from [the Paris Charter] principles. But as we saw on the streets of this city three weeks ago, at critical moments people armed with principles have overwhelmed tanks."[103] Baker also lamented that change came to the Soviet Union too late "for the eleven Helsinki monitors who perished in Soviet prison camps, or in foreign exile, and who, before their deaths, were made to suffer long years of persecution for defending human rights."[104] Most of the issues originally slated for discussion at Moscow, such as

---

[101] His memoirs offer important evidence of the adoption of Helsinki ideals by Gorbachev's aides and other Soviets leaders at the time. In December 1990, Shevardnadze resigned, warning of a conservative backlash against Gorbachev's policies. Shevardnadze, *The Future Belongs to Freedom*, 86, 204.

[102] Max Kampelman again headed the United States delegation with advisers from the Commission, the State Department, and members of the public. The Soviets questioned going forward with the Moscow CHD given the turmoil in the Soviet Union but polled CSCE ambassadors in Moscow who argued that it would offer support to the reforms undertaken by the Gorbachev government. Chernyaev, *My Six Years with Gorbachev*, 390.

[103] Korey, *The Promises We Keep*, 393. In the aftermath of the failed coup, the three Baltic states gained international recognition; therefore, at Moscow for the first time, Estonia, Latvia, and Lithuania joined the CSCE. James A. Baker, *The Politics of Diplomacy: Revolution, War, and Peace, 1989–1992* (New York: G. P. Putman's Sons, 1995), 527; and Statement, Algirdas Saudargas (Lithuania), September 10, 1991, OSCE Archives.

[104] James A. Baker III, "Democracy's Season," September 11, 1991, Folder 27, Box 167, Baker Papers.

release of political prisoners and freedom to leave one's country, had been addressed in the earlier CHD meetings in Paris and Copenhagen and implemented in the intervening months. Instead, given the situation in Yugoslavia, the Moscow conference closely examined the outbreak of nationalist tensions, among other issues.[105] One of the most significant concerns about a human rights meeting in Moscow had been access for NGOs to the conference and delegations, which had become increasingly part of the fabric of the CSCE; given subsequent developments, openness was not a problem once the meeting began, and abundant Soviet NGOs were active in connection with the meeting.[106] In conjunction with the meeting, Helsinki Watch organized independent, unofficial activities in Moscow during the meeting and other parallel events in Lithuania, where the reconstituted Moscow Helsinki Group also held hearings.[107] Helsinki Watch's activities in Moscow included seminars on prison conditions in the Soviet Union, the plight of deported peoples, and the recent incidents of use of force against civilians by the Soviet military. As evidence of the transformation of the Soviet involvement in the CSCE, long-time human rights activist Sergei Kovalev, speaking in his capacity as the chair of the Russian Federation Parliament Committee on Human Rights, addressed one of the meeting's plenary sessions.[108]

The Moscow Concluding Document, like the text agreed to at Copenhagen, demonstrated how far acceptance of human rights had progressed in the previous years. The CSCE states noted continuing progress on Helsinki compliance and the challenges of rising ethnic, national, and religious discrimination and violence. They expressed concern about human rights, democracy, and the rule of law as well as capital punishment,

[105] CSCE/CHDM.33, September 25, 1991, OSCE Archives; CSCE/CHDM.36, September 25, 1991, ibid.; CSCE/CHDM.37, September 26, 1991, ibid.; CSCE/CDHM.46, September 26, ibid.; CSCE/CHDM.47, September 26, 1991, ibid.; and Laber, *The Courage of Strangers*, 365.

[106] DeConcini and Hoyer to Petrovskiy, June 14, 1991, Box 36, Kampelman Papers; and Laber, *The Courage of Strangers*, 366–9.

[107] Soviet activists had reestablished the Moscow Helsinki Group in July 1989. Laber to Zeltman and Nagler, March 21, 1991, IHF General, 1991, Box 1, International Helsinki Federation for Human Rights Files, Record Group 7, HRWR; Nowicki to Helsinki Watch, April 26, 1991, USSR: CSCE: Conference on the Human Dimension, Moscow, 1991, Box 47, Country Files, Jeri Laber Files, ibid.; Laber to Nowicki, May 15, 1991, USSR: CSCE – Conference – Moscow – Correspondence, 1991 [3 of 3], Box 6, Country Files, Chris Pancio Files, ibid.; Minutes, July 10, 1991, Helsinki Watch (HW) Meeting – HW Committee (July 10, 1991), Box 9, General Files, New York Office Files, ibid.

[108] "Russian Human Rights Chairman Briefs CSCE," September 18, 1991 *FBIS*, Folder 1, Box 70, Lister Papers.

migrant workers, the protection of journalists and artistic freedom.[109] The Moscow Concluding Document expanded the human dimension mechanism, outlined a commitment to an independent judiciary, addressed situations of public emergency such as a coup, and contained commitments on freedom of domestic travel, protections for journalists, preservation of cultural heritage and safeguards for migrant workers. Soviet political liberalization and other reforms enhanced the stature of other political leaders who eventually challenged Gorbachev's leadership, and only two months after the Moscow Conference, the Soviet Union collapsed into fifteen individual states. Internal forces, many of which were fostered and facilitated by Gorbachev's reforms, had brought down the Soviet Union.

Many observers and policymakers on both sides of the East–West divide have argued the Helsinki process, and the activism it inspired, influenced the end of the Cold War. Former British Foreign Secretary Douglas Hurd described the Helsinki process as a slow but steady force for change: "Constant drops of water began to wear away the stone."[110] Former Soviet officials offer similar interpretations of the influence of the Helsinki process; in Soviet diplomat Yuri Kashlev's words, "It is difficult to imagine what our society would have become without all of those democratic changes that were to a very large extent related to our participation in the Helsinki process."[111] Former Czechoslovakian leader Alexander Dubcek saw the signing of the Helsinki Final Act as an important turning point: "The treaty brought about a qualitative change in the whole situation. After Helsinki, what the Soviets and their lackeys in Eastern Europe continued to do was illegal under international law."[112] In former Jewish refusenik and Soviet human rights activist Anatoly Shcharansky's view, reform in the Soviet Union was possible because Soviet dissidents were "ready to risk their freedom to speak the truth" and "leaders of the free world who [were] ready to support [them] directly and consistently."[113]

Nevertheless, in retrospect some of the CSCE's most ardent cheerleaders as well as others involved in East–West diplomacy have simplified the trajectory of the Helsinki process to suggest the collapse of communism

---

[109] CSCE/CHDM.49/Rev.1, October 3, 1991, OSCE Archives.

[110] Douglas Hurd, *The Search for Peace* (New York: Little, Brown and Company, 1997), 105–6. See also Hyland, *Mortal Rivals*, 128; Gates, *From the Shadows*, 89; Yuri Fokine et al., "Helsinki 30 Years Later," *International Affairs* (May 2005): 199; and R. Spencer Oliver Interview, February 26, 2008.

[111] Fokine, "Helsinki 30 Years Later," 188.

[112] Jiri Hochman, ed., and trans. *Hope Dies Last: The Autobiography of Alexander Dubcek* (New York: Kodansha International, 1993), 263.

[113] Natan Sharansky Interview, November 19, 2008.

in Eastern Europe and the end of the Cold War were inevitable. As this book has shown, the Helsinki process helped shape the end of the Cold War, but such a development was not a foregone conclusion when the Helsinki Final Act was signed. Accounts that draw a straight line from 1975 to 1989 neglect the significance of human agency and individual actions to the influence of the CSCE and the movement it inspired. Helsinki monitoring groups were an unanticipated consequence of the Helsinki Final Act, launching a movement for change "from below" that worked together with those engaged in the Helsinki process at an official level to affect change "from above."[114] The power of ideas and ideals, as set out in the Helsinki Final Act, was important to the spread of reform in Eastern Europe, yet the individuals who made up the Helsinki network were the critical actors to this transformation.

[114] Patricia Chilton, "Mechanics of Change: Social Movements, Transnational Coalitions, and the Transformation Processes in Eastern Europe," in Thomas Risse-Kappen, ed., *Bringing Transnational Relations Back In* (Cambridge: Cambridge University Press, 1995), 200–1; Sebestyen, *Revolution 1989*, xviii; and Falk, *The Dilemmas of Dissidence in East-Central Europe*, xxi–xxii. George Lister, a State Department official long active on human rights, emphasized the role of activists in a 1990 speech: "Of course I do not wish to imply that these dramatic changes in Eastern Europe are solely the result of our human rights policy. Obviously not. The main credit for this progress goes to such heroic giants as Andrei Sakharov and Lech Walesa, and to those countless others who struggled courageously and died in oblivion." George Lister, "The Human Rights Cause: How We Can Help," February 20, 1990, Folder 4, Box 18, Lister Papers.

Conclusion

The largely peaceful collapse of communism in Eastern Europe in 1989, the reunification of Germany in 1990, and the disintegration of the Soviet Union in 1991 traditionally signify the end of the Cold War, which had dominated international relations for more than forty-five years. The end of the Cold War has been attributed to a multitude of factors including economic decline, imperial overstretch, military competition, nationalism, the transmission of Western culture, scientific and educational contacts, and the personalities of key political leaders, among others. I have argued that the Helsinki process and the transnational network of human rights advocates also contributed to the transformation of Europe, and that the development of this network established human rights as an integral component of international relations. My research shows that the Helsinki process directly and indirectly influenced both Western and Eastern governments to pursue policies that facilitated the rise of organized dissent in Eastern Europe, freedom of movement for East Germans, and improved human rights practices in the Soviet Union – all factors in the end of the Cold War. Finally, I have suggested that January 19, 1989, may be the appropriate date to consider as the end of the Cold War; on that day CSCE representatives agreed to the Vienna Concluding Document, which included legitimate commitments to enhance religious freedom, facilitate the spread of information, and address human rights and human contacts in three subsequent conferences. The reforms implemented during the course of the meeting and its culminating agreement signaled a fundamentally new approach to East–West relations.

The most important scholarly work on the Helsinki Final Act thus far has been Daniel Thomas's *The Helsinki Effect: International Norms,*

Human Rights, and the Demise of Communism, which analyzes the influence and acceptance of human rights norms, using reaction to the Helsinki Final Act in the Soviet Union, Czechoslovakia, and Poland as his case studies.[1] Although my work has similarly highlighted the importance of human rights in the end of the Cold War, my research on the Helsinki process has led me to emphasize human rights advocacy as opposed to the power of human rights norms. Helsinki activism grew increasingly effective as the movement gained supporters who would incorporate Helsinki compliance into high-level diplomacy. The ability to point to international norms certainly aided Helsinki activists, but it was their work cataloguing repeated violations of the Helsinki Final Act and humanizing those who suffered from abuses that gained devoted champions such as Arthur J. Goldberg, Jimmy Carter, and George Shultz. Monitoring by Helsinki activists and their utilization of the follow-up meetings, not simply the 1975 commitments of Soviet diplomats, fundamentally altered Eastern politics.

The development and influence of a transnational Helsinki network was due to several key individuals without whom the principles and baskets of the Helsinki Final Act would have had little lasting significance. The network's creation can be traced to 1975, when Representative Millicent Fenwick returned from a congressional delegation to the Soviet Union. Her trip took place shortly after the signing of the Helsinki Final Act, when most American politicians, reporters, and ethnic groups were highly critical of the agreement. Her meetings with dissidents and their families in Moscow convinced her that the United States needed to press Eastern European states more aggressively to comply with the Helsinki Final Act. Recognizing that the Ford White House would not support her campaign, Fenwick turned to Congress. Her efforts led to the creation of the Commission on Security and Cooperation in Europe, one of the two early pillars of the transnational Helsinki network. Fenwick and the Commission generated the initial momentum for the Helsinki process to gain support in the United States, which Jimmy Carter built upon when he became president.[2] The Commission championed the

---

[1] Thomas argues that the establishment of human rights as a "formal norm" in the Helsinki Final Act transformed Soviet bloc states and East–West relations. Thomas, *The Helsinki Effect,* 258.

[2] Fenwick remembered the Commission as her most significant legislative achievement in a 1985 interview. Millicent Fenwick Interview, December 17, 1985, *The Foreign Affairs Oral History Collection of the Association for Diplomatic Studies and Training,* Library of Congress, http://memory.loc.gov/ammem/collections/diplomacy/ (accessed March 8, 2010).

efforts and sacrifices of Eastern Helsinki monitors but more importantly offered a channel for their *samizdat* to reach a wider, sympathetic audience. The events that led to the establishment of a transnational Helsinki network are among the most important in the development of the Helsinki process as a powerful force in the latter years of the Cold War, and thus Fenwick's role should not be overlooked.

Yuri Orlov's establishment of the Moscow Helsinki Group also was critical to the development of a transnational Helsinki network. Although the Commission publicized Helsinki violations and attempted to exert government-level pressure to curb them, its awareness of instances of noncompliance and evidence to support allegations of Helsinki violations often depended on reporting by Eastern NGOs. Furthermore, groups such as the Moscow Helsinki Group dramatized the plight of dissidents and Helsinki monitors in Eastern Europe, inspiring many others to join in pressing for Helsinki implementation, and through "symbolic politics" the difficulties of Helsinki monitors like Orlov and Shcharansky came to epitomize the cruel repression of the communist regimes. Orlov's leadership of the Moscow Helsinki Group, his efforts to connect with a broader network in the Soviet Union and abroad, his courage and resilience in the face of government repression, and his continued activism in the United States after his exile stimulated the expansive nature of the Helsinki network.

Jimmy Carter's determination to press human rights in foreign policy and reevaluate the United States role in the CSCE offered nongovernmental activists their most powerful supporter. Carter's administration adopted an aggressive strategy regarding compliance with the Helsinki Final Act and implementation review at the Belgrade Meeting. Under Carter, the United States strategy at Belgrade transformed the American role within the CSCE and established thorough accounting of Helsinki implementation as an integral component of American policy at follow-up meetings. The advocacy pursued by Carter and Goldberg at Belgrade forged tight bonds among different actors committed to the same cause and strengthened the network going forward. Reagan, Shultz, and Kampelman continued the Carter administration's policy toward the Helsinki process, incorporating human rights into the United States agenda for relations with Eastern Europe. The advocacy of these and other Western actors, including Helsinki Watch and IHF activists, maintained an international spotlight on Eastern repression and laid the foundation for later progress.

Gorbachev's role in the end of the Cold War is unparalleled, and his significance to the Helsinki process is similarly essential.[3] When Gorbachev became general secretary, the Soviet Union's international image was poor and its record of human rights abuses was one of a number of issues that prevented constructive East–West relations. Influenced in part by the Helsinki process, Gorbachev pursued a new foreign policy that reduced tension with the West and contributed to improving Soviet standing in Europe. Recognizing that the Soviet failure to implement the Helsinki Final Act was an obstacle to his policy priorities, Gorbachev adopted a new approach to the CSCE at Vienna and began to comply more fully with existing Helsinki agreements. Without Gorbachev's commitment to implementing elements of the Helsinki Final Act, the CSCE could have been mired in ineffective debates on human contacts and the peaceful settlement of disputes for years. Instead, Gorbachev put into motion a series of reforms for which improved relations with the West were crucial; unlike his predecessors, Gorbachev engaged the United States and the West in substantive negotiations and, due to both external pressure from Western governments and evolving internal attitudes toward human rights, the Soviet Union began actively complying with its CSCE commitments. Gorbachev's concerted efforts to change the international image of the Soviet Union suggest international shaming can be effective on those who wish to be seen as a full member of the international community.

In 1975, at the signing of the Helsinki Final Act, few participants and observers expected the Helsinki process to have such far-reaching and significant influence. Yet, the Helsinki Final Act, a voluntary agreement quickly dismissed by many international commentators, was successful in affecting the end of the Cold War as a result of the interventions of key actors in the years that followed. Such developments were unanticipated, but they utilized several structural aspects of the document that led to the network's surprising strength. First, the CSCE was governed by consensus – all decisions needed the agreement of each CSCE state. This dynamic heightened the level of compromise and manifested itself in the constant balancing of Soviet-favored security issues with Western-desired humanitarian provisions, an exchange that was embedded in the

[3] Adamishin notes the Nobel Peace Prize Committee recognized the key role of Gorbachev and his reform policies in ending the Cold War. Anatoly Adamishin, August 5 1989 Interview Transcript, Folder 1, Box 1, The Hoover Institution and the Gorbachev Foundation (Moscow) Collection, Hoover Institution Archives, Stanford, California.

Helsinki Final Act. The pattern of give and take began even before the first CSCE negotiating session—the Soviets wanted to hold a European Security Conference and were forced also to discuss human contacts to achieve their goal. Throughout the fifteen years that followed, this balance ensured Eastern states had to accede on humanitarian and human rights issues in order to achieve their objectives. Such compromises were commonplace in CSCE sessions, the most prominent being agreement on a conference on human rights in Moscow in return for significant progress on emigration and the release of political prisoners. It is a credit to the transnational Helsinki network's far-reaching political influence that throughout these years, the West's focus in the negotiations was to secure greater respect for human rights in foreign countries rather than to concentrate on the agreement's trade or security aspects. Furthermore, the follow-up mechanism outlined in the fourth basket and shaped by Goldberg's tactics offered repeated opportunities to assess implementation of the Helsinki Final Act. Basket Four inspired a range of Western and Eastern groups to undertake monitoring efforts because the follow-up meetings provided a crucial and unique means to disseminate information, without which the Helsinki monitors would have been less effective. Essential to the CSCE's success, particularly in the United States, was that the diverse transnational actors championing the Helsinki Final Act effectively utilized the follow-up meetings to pressure policymakers to make progress on implementation of the agreement.

Regardless of the efforts of the activists, the success of the Helsinki process depended on the eventual efforts of Eastern European leaders to improve their countries' human rights practices. Although some limited progress had been made prior to Vienna, the meeting was a turning point for both the USSR role in the CSCE and Eastern compliance with Helsinki commitments. Domestic and international considerations drove Gorbachev's and Shevardnadze's formulation of the proposal to hold a conference on human rights in Moscow; they hoped proposing and holding the conference would improve relations with Western states and thus facilitate domestic objectives as well. The proposal reflected a genuine realization among Soviet leaders that concerns about human rights had become entrenched in Western foreign policy; nevertheless, it also demonstrated a limited understanding of the repercussions of fulfilling the West's requirements. Soviet positions at Vienna influenced other Eastern European governments to permit more liberalization and likewise Eastern dissidents to press for more concessions. The result was that the Helsinki process rapidly accelerated the momentum of reform in Eastern Europe.

In the years that followed, the degree and pace of reform varied across Central and Eastern Europe, but the changes were dramatic and far-reaching in nearly all respects. Nevertheless, many concerned with human rights in Eastern Europe declared victory too soon. Human rights violations persist to varying degrees in the successor states to the Soviet Union. In Russia alone, abuses at the most extreme end of the spectrum include disappearances and extrajudicial killings.[4] In a prominent example of continuity with the past, Ludmilla Alekseeva was featured on the front page of the *New York Times* in January 2010; the accompanying photo showed her detained by the police in Moscow several days earlier.[5] In that instance, Alekseeva was one of many activists targeted for demonstrating on behalf of the freedom to assemble as she and other members of the reconstituted Moscow Helsinki Group continue to press for protection of human rights. As in Soviet times, Russian activists currently endanger themselves through their human rights advocacy. Prison conditions are notoriously poor, and several prominent prisoners have died due to limitations on their access to medical care in recent years; human rights activists have also been kidnapped and murdered. Thus, the story of the transnational Helsinki network is not a triumphal one, even if it does demonstrate that nongovernmental activism can affect positive political change.

[4] In most successor states to the Soviet Union, widespread violations of human rights persist.
[5] Barry, "Russian Dissident's Passion Endures Despite Tests," *New York Times* January 12, 2010, A1.

Bibliography

Manuscript Collections

Carl Albert Collection, Carl Albert Center Congressional Archives, University of Oklahoma, Norman, Oklahoma.

American Latvian Association of the United States Records, Immigration History Research Center, University of Minnesota, Minneapolis, Minnesota.

Amnesty International USA Archives, Center for Human Rights Documentation and Research, Rare Book and Manuscript Library, Columbia University Library, New York, New York.

Archiv für Zeitgeschichte, ETH Zürich (Archive for Contemporary History, Swiss Federal Institute of Technology Zurich), Zurich, Switzerland.

Assembly of Captive European Nations Records, Immigration History Research Center, University of Minnesota, Minneapolis, Minnesota.

James A. Baker III Papers, Public Policy Papers, Department of Rare Books and Special Collections, Princeton University Library, Princeton, New Jersey.

Clifford Case Papers, Rutgers University, New Brunswick, New Jersey.

Frank Church Collection, Boise State University, Boise, Idaho.

Richard Clark Papers, University of Iowa, Iowa City, Iowa.

Cold War International History Project, Washington, District of Columbia.

Council on Foreign Relations Records, Public Policy Papers, Department of Rare Books and Special Collections, Princeton University Library, Princeton, New Jersey.

Dennis DeConcini Papers, University of Arizona, Tucson, Arizona.

Robert J. Dole Senate Papers, Robert J. Dole Institute of Politics, The University of Kansas, Lawrence, Kansas.

Robert F. Drinan Papers, Boston College, Chestnut Hill, Massachusetts.

Mickey Edwards Collection, Carl Albert Center Congressional Archives, University of Oklahoma, Norman, Oklahoma.

Dante Fascell Papers, University of Miami, Coral Gables, Florida.

Millicent Fenwick Papers, Rutgers University, New Brunswick, New Jersey.

Freedom House Records, Public Policy Papers, Department of Rare Books and Special Collections, Princeton University Library, Princeton, New Jersey.

Arthur J. Goldberg Papers, Radford University, Radford, Virginia.

Arthur J. Goldberg Papers, Manuscript Division, Library of Congress, Washington, District of Columbia.

The Hoover Institution and the Gorbachev Foundation (Moscow) Collection, Hoover Institution Archives, Stanford, California.

Human Rights Collection, Andrei Sakharov Archives, Houghton Library, Harvard University, Cambridge, Massachusetts.

Human Rights Watch Records, Center for Human Rights Documentation and Research, Rare Book and Manuscript Library, Columbia University Library, New York, New York.

Hubert Humphrey Papers, Minnesota Historical Society, St. Paul, Minnesota.

International Helsinki Federation for Human Rights Records, Open Society Archives, Budapest, Hungary.

International League for Human Rights Records, Manuscripts and Archives Division, Humanities and Social Sciences Library, The New York Public Library, New York, New York.

Henry M. Jackson Papers, University of Washington, Seattle, Washington.

Jacob Javits Collection, State University of New York at Stony Brook, Stony Brook, New York.

Joint Baltic American National Committee Records, Immigration History Research Center, University of Minnesota, Minneapolis, Minnesota.

Max M. Kampelman Papers, Minnesota Historical Society, St. Paul, Minnesota.

Keston Archive and Library, Oxford, England.

George Lister Papers, Benson Latin American Collection, University of Texas Libraries, the University of Texas at Austin, Austin, Texas.

Aloysius A. Mazewski Papers, Immigration History Research Center, University of Minnesota, Minneapolis, Minnesota.

Daniel P. Moynihan Papers, Manuscript Division, Library of Congress, Washington, District of Columbia.

National Security Archive, Washington, District of Columbia.

Don Oberdorfer Papers, Public Policy Papers, Department of Rare Books and Special Collections, Princeton University Library, Princeton, New Jersey.

Organization for Security and Cooperation in Europe Archives, Prague, Czech Republic.

Claiborne Pell Papers, University of Rhode Island, Kingston, Rhode Island.

William Proxmire Papers, Wisconsin Historical Society, Madison, Wisconsin.

Radio Free Europe/Radio Liberty Collection, Hoover Institution Archives, Stanford, California.

Radio Free Europe/Radio Liberty Research Institute Records, Open Society Archives, Budapest, Hungary.

John J. Rhodes Minority Leader Papers, Arizona State University, Tempe, Arizona.

Papers of Andrei Sakharov, Andrei Sakharov Archives, Houghton Library, Harvard University, Cambridge, Massachusetts.

Scientists for Sakharov, Orlov and Shcharansky Records, Hoover Institution Archives, Stanford, California.

Albert William Sherer, Jr., Papers, Yale University, New Haven, Connecticut.
Ukrainian National Association Records, Immigration History Research Center, University of Minnesota, Minneapolis, Minnesota.
Cyrus R. and Grace Sloane Vance Papers, Yale University, New Haven, Connecticut.
Thomas J. Watson, Jr., Papers, Brown University, Providence, Rhode Island.
Clement J. Zablocki Papers, Marquette University, Milwaukee, Wisconsin.
Warren Zimmermann Papers, Special Collections Research Center, Georgetown University, Washington, District of Columbia.

Government Documents

Unpublished

Historical Division, Ministry of Foreign Affairs, Ottawa, Ontario, Canada.
CIA Records Search Tool, National Archives, College Park, Maryland.
George Bush Library, College Station, Texas.
Jimmy Carter Library, Atlanta, Georgia.
General Records of the Department of State, Record Group 59, National Archives, College Park, Maryland.
Gerald R. Ford Library, Ann Arbor, Michigan.
Lyndon B. Johnson Library, Austin, Texas.
National Archives, Ottawa, Ontario, Canada.
Nixon Presidential Materials Project, National Archives, College Park, Maryland.
Ronald Reagan Library, Simi Valley, California.
Margaret Thatcher Foundation, www. margaretthatcher. org.
Records of the United States Information Agency (USIA), Record Group 306, National Archives, College Park, Maryland.

Published

Bennett, G. and K. A. Hamilton, eds. *Documents on British Policy Overseas: Britain and the Soviet Union, 1968–72 Series III: Volume I.* London: The Stationery Office, 1997.
Documents on British Policy Overseas: The Conference on Security and Cooperation in Europe, 1972–1975 Series III: Volume II. London: The Stationery Office, 1997.
Documents on British Policy Overseas: Détente in Europe, 1972–1976 Series III: Volume III. London: The Stationery Office, 2001.
Carter, Jimmy. *Public Papers of the President, 1978, Volume I.* Washington: Government Printing Office, 1979.
Public Papers of the President, 1980–81: Volume I. Washington: Government Printing Office, 1981.
Cherniaeva, Anatoliia, ed. *B Politbiuro CK KPSS ... Po Zapisiam Anatoliia Cherniaeva,Vadima Medvedeva, Georgiia Shakhnazarova (1985–1991).* Moscow : Al'pina Biznes Buks, 2006.

Fond 89: Communist Party of the Soviet Union on Trial, Archives of the Soviet Party and Soviet State Microfilm Collection, Yale University, New Haven, Connecticut.

Ford, Gerald R. *Public Papers of the President 1975: II.* Washington: Government Printing Office, 1975.

Iakovlev, A. A. *Aleksandr Iakovlev Perestroika: 1985– 1991: Neizdannoe, Maloizvestnoe, Zabytoe.* Moscow: Mezhdunarodnyi Fond "Demokratiia," 2008.

Kavass, Igor I. and Jacqueline P. Granier, eds. *Human Rights, the Helsinki Accord and the United States.* 3 Vol. New York: W. S. Hein, 1982.

Kavass, Igor I., Jacqueline Paquin Granier and Mary Frances Dominick, eds. *Human Rights, European Politics, and the Helsinki Accord: The Documentary Evolution of the Conference on Security and Co-operation in Europe.* 7 Vol. New York: W. S. Hein, 1981–1995.

United States Department of State. *The Conference on Security and Cooperation in Europe: Public Statements and Documents, 1954–1986.* Washington: U. S. Department of State, Bureau of Public Affairs, Office of the Historian, 1986.

Foreign Relations of the United States, 1964–8: XVII: Eastern Europe. Washington: Government Printing Office, 1996.

Foreign Relations of the United States, 1969–1976: XXXIX: European Security, 1969–1976. Washington: Government Printing Office, 2007.

Interviews

Catherine Cosman, April 8, 2008.

Thomas Delworth, December 7, 2005.

Patt Derian, John C. Stennis Oral History Project, Mississippi State University, Mississippi State, Mississippi.

Ethnic Groups and American Foreign Policy Project, Oral History Research Office, Butler Library, Columbia University, New York, New York.

The Foreign Affairs Oral History Collection of the Association for Diplomatic Studies and Training, Library of Congress, Washington, District of Columbia.

Millicent Fenwick Oral History, Oral History Research Office, Butler Library, Columbia University, New York, New York.

Alfred Friendly Jr., May 6, 2008.

James Goodby, April 1, 2005.

Max Kampelman, March 13, 2007; July 12, 2010.

Jeri Laber, April 29, 2008.

Jack Matlock, April 3, 2006.

Larry Napper, October 1, 2009.

Aryeh Neier, April 24, 2008.

R. Spencer Oliver, February 26, 2008.

Yuri Orlov, March 27 and 28, 2008.

Richard Schifter, May 5, 2008.

Natan Sharansky, November 19, 2008.

George Shultz Interview, December 18, 2002, Reagan Presidential Oral History Project, Miller Center, University of Virginia, Charlottesville, Virginia.
Ted Wilkinson, October 12, 2004.

Unpublished Manuscripts

Dai, Xinyuan. *Compliance Without Carrots or Sticks: How International Institutions Influence National Policies.* PhD Dissertation, University of Chicago, 2000.

Domber, Gregory F. *Supporting the Revolution: America, Democracy, and the End of the Cold War in Poland, 1981–1989.* PhD Dissertation, George Washington University, 2008.

"Power Politics, Human Rights, and Trans-Atlantic Relations." Paper presented at the conference "European and Transatlantic Strategies in the Late Cold War Period to Overcome the East–West Division of Europe," Copenhagen, Denmark, November–December 2007.

Eichhorn, Robert Kennedy. *The Helsinki Accords and Their Effect on the Cold War.* M. A. Thesis, California State University, Fullerton, 1995.

Fischer, Thomas. "'G2W – Faith in the Second World': Using the Helsinki Network to Overcome the East–West Divide." Paper presented at the conference "Cold War Interactions Reconsidered," Helsinki, Finland, October 2009.

Goodby, James E. "The Origins of the Human Rights Provisions in the Helsinki Final Act." Unpublished manuscript, in the possession of the author.

Gubin, Sandra Louise. *International Regimes, Agenda Setting and Linkage Groups in U.S.–Soviet Relations: The Helsinki Process and Divided Spouses.* PhD Dissertation, University of Michigan, 1990.

Hodgman, Edward Bailey. *Détente and the Dissidents: Human Rights in U. S. – Soviet Relations, 1968–1980.* PhD Dissertation, University of Rochester, 2003.

Hong, Ki-joon. *The CSCE Security Regime Formation: From Helsinki to Budapest.* PhD Dissertation, Katholieke Universiteit Leuven, January 1996.

Kelly, Patrick William. "When the People Awake: The Transnational Solidarity Movement, the Pinochet Junta, and the Human Rights Moment of the 1970s." Paper presented at "A New Global Morality?: The Politics of Human Rights and Humanitarianism in the 1970s," Freiburg Institute for Advanced Studies, Freiburg, Germany, June 2010.

Leatherman, Janie Lee. *Engaging East and West: Beyond the Bloc Divisions: Active Neutrality and the Dual Role Strategy of Finland and Sweden in the CSCE.* PhD Dissertation, University of Denver, 1991.

Lomellini, Valentine. "1975–1981, Return Journey: Italian Left and Eastern Dissent. Two Worlds Compared." Paper presented at the conference "European and Transatlantic Strategies in the Late Cold War Period to Overcome the East–West Division of Europe," Copenhagen, Denmark, November–December 2007.

Nathans, Benjamin. "Soviet Dissidents and Human Rights," paper presented at "A New Global Morality?: The Politics of Human Rights and Humanitarianism in the 1970s," Freiburg Institute for Advanced Studies, Freiburg, Germany, June 2010.

Nuenlist, Christian. "Switzerland, the Neutrals, and the Early CSCE Process, 1969–1975." Paper presented at Society for Historians of American Foreign Relations Annual Meeting, Lawrence, Kansas, June 2006.

Paczkowski, Andrzej. "From Amnesty to Amnesty: the Authorities and the Opposition in Poland, 1976–1986." Paper presented at the conference "From Helsinki to Gorbachev, 1975–1985: The Globalization of the Bipolar Confrontation," Artimino, Italy, April 2006.

Richardson-Little, Ned. "'No Human Rights without Socialism – No Socialism without Human Rights!': Socialist Human Rights and the Helsinki Accords in East Germany." Paper presented at "A New Global Morality?: The Politics of Human Rights and Humanitarianism in the 1970s," Freiburg Institute for Advanced Studies, Freiburg, Germany, June 2010.

Robson, John Sinclair Petifer. *Henry Jackson, The Jackson-Vanik Amendment and Détente: Ideology, Ideas, and United States Foreign Policy in the Nixon Era.* PhD Dissertation, The University of Texas at Austin, 1989.

Romano, Angela. "The Main Task of the European Political Cooperation: Fostering Détente in Europe." Paper presented at the conference "European and Transatlantic Strategies in the Late Cold War Period to Overcome the East–West Division of Europe," Copenhagen, Denmark, November–December 2007.

Rose, Curt Lewis. *Political Suicide: The Controversial Decisions of the Ford Administration.* M. A. Thesis, Virginia Commonwealth University, 1996.

Sargent, Daniel Jonathan. *From Internationalism to Globalism: The United States and the Transformation of International Politics in the 1970s.* PhD Dissertation, Harvard University, 2008.

Savranskaya, Svetlana. "The Battles for the Final Act: the Soviet Government and Dissidents' Efforts to Define the Substance and the Implementation of the Helsinki Final Act." Paper presented at the conference "European and Transatlantic Strategies in the Late Cold War Period to Overcome the East–West Division of Europe," Copenhagen, Denmark, November 30–December 1, 2007.

Selvage, Douglas. "The Struggle Against Transnational Resistance: The East German Ministry for State Security, Charta 77, and Opposition in East Germany, 1977–1980." Paper presented at Society of Historians of American Foreign Relations Annual Meeting, Falls Church, Virginia, June 2009.

Shulman, Colette. "A Symposium on US–USSR: Confrontation or Cooperation," Seven Springs Center, November 1978.

Stevens, Simon. "The Politics of Anti-Apartheid Activism in Britain in the Long 1970s." Paper presented at "A New Global Morality?: The Politics of Human Rights and Humanitarianism in the 1970s," Freiburg Institute for Advanced Studies, Freiburg, Germany, June 2010.

Vaughan, Patrick. "Zbigniew Brzezinski and the Helsinki Final Act." Paper presented at the conference "From Helsinki to Gorbachev, 1975–1985: The Globalization of the Bipolar Confrontation," Artimino, Italy, April 27–9, 2006.

Walker, Breck. "'Neither Shy nor Demagogic,' – The Carter Administration Goes to Belgrade." Paper presented at the conference "30 Years Since the First CSCE Follow-Up Meeting in Belgrade," Belgrade, Serbia, March 2008.
'Yesterday's Answers' or 'Tomorrow's Solutions'?: The Cold War Diplomacy of Cyrus Vance. PhD Dissertation, Vanderbilt University, 2007.

Periodicals

Department of State Bulletin
International Herald Tribune
The Nation
New York Review of Books
New York Times
New York Times Magazine
New Yorker
Time
Ukrainian Weekly
Wall Street Journal
Washington Post

Articles

Acimovic, Ljubivoje. "CSCE and the Non-Aligned States," *Survival* 18:3 (May–June 1976): 112–5.

Adams, Tenley. "Charter 77 and the Workers' Defense Committee (KOR): The Struggle for Human Rights in Czechoslovakia and Poland," *East European Quarterly* 26:2 (Summer 1992): 219–38.

Adomeit, Hannes. "Soviet Policy in Europe: Trends and Issues in the Post-Helsinki Period," *Soviet Studies* 31:4 (October 1979): 585–595.

Alexeyeva, Ludmilla. "The Human Rights Movement in the USSR," *Survey* 23 (Autumn 1977–8): 72–85.

Andelman, David A. "The Road to Madrid," *Foreign Policy* 39 (1980): 159–72.

American Association of the International Commission of Jurists. "Toward an Integrated Human Rights Policy," New York: The American Association of International Commission of Jurists, 1979.

Arangio-Ruiz, Gaetano. "Autodeterminazione Dei Popoli e Diritto Internazionale. Dalla Carta delle Nazioni Unie All'atto di Helsinki," *Rivista di Studi Politici Internazionali* 50:4 (1983): 523–52.

Arato, Andrew. "Civil Society Against the State: Poland 1980–81," *Telos* 47: 24–47.

Bailey, Paul J. and Bailey-Wiebecke, Ilka. "All-European Co-operation: The CSCE's Basket Two and the ECE," *International Journal* 32:2 (1977): 386–407.

Bange, Oliver and Stephan Kieninger. "Negotiating One's Own Demise?: The GDR's Foreign Ministry and the CSCE Negotiations: Plans Preparations, Tactics and Presumptions," Cold War International History Project, e-Dossier No. 17, Woodrow Wilson International Center for Scholars.

Beissinger, Mark R. "Nationalism and the Collapse of Soviet Communism," *Contemporary European History* 18:3 (2009): 331–47.

Bennett, Andrew. "The Guns That Didn't Smoke: Ideas and the Soviet Non-Use of Force in 1989," *Journal of Cold War Studies* 7:2 (Spring 2005): 81–109.

Bertsch, Herbert. "The CSCE Process: Politico-institutional Aspects," *Peace and Sciences* 2–3 (1989): 50–62.

Beyer, Gregg A. "The Evolving United States Response to Soviet Jewish Emigration," *Journal of Palestinian Studies* 21:1 (Autumn 1991): 139–156.

Birnbaum, Karl E. "The Member States of the Warsaw Treaty Organization and the Conference on the Security and Cooperation in Europe," *Cooperation and Conflict* 9:1 (1974): 29–34.

"Human Rights and East–West Relations," *Foreign Affairs* 55 (July 1977): 783–99.

Birnbaum, Karl E. and Ingo Peters. "The CSCE: A Reassessment of its Role in the 1980s," *Review of International Studies* 16:4 (1990): 305–319.

Bloed, Arie. "Helsinki II: The Challenges of Change," *Helsinki Monitor* (April 1993): 37–50.

Bloodworth, Jeff. "Senator Henry Jackson, the Solzhenitsyn Affair, and American Liberalism," *Pacific Northern Quarterly* (Spring 2006): 69–77.

Bowker, Mike and Phil Williams. "Helsinki and West European Security," *International Affairs* 61:4 (Autumn 1985): 607–18.

Bozóki, András. "Hungary's Road to Systemic Change: the Opposition Roundtable," *East European Politics and Societies* 7:2 (Spring 1993): 276–308.

Brinkley, Douglas. "The Rising Stock of Jimmy Carter: The 'Hands on' Legacy of Our Thirty-Ninth President," *Diplomatic History* 20 (Fall 1996): 505–29.

Bromke, Adam. "The CSCE and Eastern Europe," *The World Today* (May 1973): 196–207.

Brooks, Stephen G. and William C. Wohlforth. "Clarifying the End of Cold War Debate," *Cold War History* 7:3 (August 2007): 447–54.

Brown, Archie. "The Change to Engagement in Britain's Cold War Policy: The Origins of the Thatcher-Gorbachev Relationship," *Journal of Cold War Studies* 10:3 (Summer 2008): 3–47.

"Perestroika and the End of the Cold War," *Cold War History* 7:1 (February 2007): 1–17.

Brown, J. F. "Détente and Soviet Policy in Eastern Europe," *Survey* (Spring/ Summer 1974): 46–58.

Brzezinski, Zbigniew. "Observations on East–West Relations: Détente in the '70s," *Foreign Policy* (January 3, 1970): 17–18.

Buergenthal, Thomas. "The Copenhagen CSCE Meeting: A New Public Order for Europe," *Human Rights Law Journal* 11 (1990): 217–31.

Bugajski, Janusz and Maxine Pollack. "East European Dissent: Impasses and Opportunities," *Problems of Communism* XXXVII: 2 (March–April 1988): 59–67.

Byrnes, Robert F. "United States Policy Towards Eastern Europe: Before and After Helsinki," *Review of Politics* 37 (October 1975): 435–63.

Campbell, John C. "European Security After Helsinki: Some American Views," *Government and Opposition* 11:3 (Summer 1976): 322–36.

Carleton, David and Michael Stohl. "The Foreign Policy of Human Rights: Rhetoric and Reality from Jimmy Carter to Ronald Reagan," *Human Rights Quarterly* 7:2 (May 1985): 205–29.

Chernoff, Fred. "Negotiating Security and Disarmament in Europe," *International Affairs* 60:3 (1984): 429–37.

Clark, Ann Marie. "Non-Governmental Organizations and their Influence on International Society," *Journal of International Affairs* 48:2 (Winter 1995): 507–25.

Clavin, Patricia. "Defining Transnationalism," *Contemporary European History* 14:4 (2005): 421–39.

Cmiel, Kenneth. "The Emergence of Human Rights Politics in the United States," *The Journal of American History* 86:3 (December 1999): 1231–50.

Cortell, Andrew P. and James W. Davis, Jr. "How Do International Institutions Matter? The Domestic Impact of International Rules and Norms," *International Studies Quarterly* 40:4 (December 1996): 451–78.

Cosman, Catherine. "Soviet Dissent and the Helsinki Process," *Scandinavian Journal of Development Alternatives* 3:3 (September 1984): 84–94.

Cox, Michael and Steven Hurst. "'His Finest Hour?' George Bush and the Diplomacy of German Unification," *Diplomacy and Statecraft* 13:4 (December 2002): 123–50.

Critchley, Julian. "East–West Diplomacy and the European Interest: CSCE, MFR and SALT II," *Round Table* 255 (1974): 299–306.

Cronin, Thomas. "A Resurgent Congress and the Imperial Presidency," *Political Science Quarterly* 95:2 (Summer 1980): 209–37.

Dallman, Wilfred. "The Future of the CSCE Process," *Peace and the Sciences* 2 (1987): 19–23.

Davy, Richard. "The ESCE Summit," *The World Today* 31:9 (September 1975): 349–53.

"Helsinki Myths: Setting the Record Straight on the Final Act of the CSCE, 1975," *Cold War History* 9:1 (March 2009): 1–22.

Deletant, Dennis and Mihail Ionsecu. "Romania and the Warsaw Pact, 1955–1989," Cold War International History Project Working Paper Number 43, Woodrow Wilson International Center for Scholars.

Dijk, P. van. "The Final Act of Helsinki – A Basis for Pan-European System?" *Netherlands Yearbook of International Law* 11 (1980): 97–124.

Dobriansky, Lev E. "CSCE and the Captive Nations," *Ukrainian Quarterly* 31 (Autumn 1975): 247–57.

"Helsinki, Human Rights, and U. S. Foreign Policy," *Ukrainian Quarterly* (Summer 1977): 122–33.

"The Unforgettable Gaffe," *Ukrainian Quarterly* 33:4 (1977): 366–77.

Dobriansky, Paula J. "Human Rights and U. S. Foreign Policy," *The Washington Quarterly* (Spring 1989): 151–67.

Dubinin, Iuri Vladimirovich. "Khel'sinki 1975: Detali Istorii," *Voprosy Istorii* 11–12 (1995): 101–19.

Deudney, Daniel and G. John Ikenberry. "Who Won the Cold War?" *Foreign Policy* (Summer 1992): 123–38.

Edwards, Geoffrey. "Belgrade and Human Rights," *Government and Opposition* 13:3 (1978): 307–22.

"Human Rights and Basket III Issues: Areas of Change and Continuity," *International Affairs* 61:4 (Autumn 1985): 631–42.

"The Conference on Security and Co-operation in Europe After Ten Years," *International Relations* 8:4 (1985): 397–406.

English, Robert D. "Sources, Methods, and Competing Perspectives on the End of the Cold War," *Diplomatic History* 21:2 (Spring 1997): 283–94.

"Power, Ideas, and New Evidence on the Cold War's End," *International Security* 26:4 (Spring 2002):70–92.

"The Sociology of New Thinking: Elites, Identity Change, and the End of the Cold War," *Journal of Cold War Studies* 7:2 (Spring 2005): 43–80.

Fall, Brian. "The Helsinki Conference, Belgrade, and European Security," *International Security* 2:1 (Summer 1977): 100–105.

Fascell, Dante B. "Did Human Rights Survive Belgrade?" *Foreign Policy* 31 (Summer 1978): 104–118.

"The Helsinki Accord: A Case Study," *Annals of the American Academy of Political and Social Science* 442 (1979): 69–76.

"The Madrid CSCE Meeting," *The Washington Quarterly* (Autumn 1982): 202–8.

"Helsinki, Gdansk, Madrid," *The Washington Quarterly* 7:4 (Fall 1984): 170–80.

Fink, Carole. "Minority Rights as an International Question" *Contemporary European History* 9:3 (November 2000): 385–400.

Finnemore, Martha and Kathryn Sikkink. "International Norm Dynamics and Political Change," *International Organization* 52 (1998): 887–917.

Fischer, Thomas. "A Mustard Seed Grew into a Bushy Tree': The Finnish CSCE Initiative of 5 May 1969," *Cold War History* 9:2 (May 2009): 177–201.

Flynn, Gregory A. "The Content of European Detente," *Orbis* 20 (Summer 1976): 401–16.

Fokine, Yuri, et al. "Helsinki 30 Years Later," *International Affairs* (May 2005): 184–200.

Forsberg, Tuomas. "Economic Incentives, Ideas, and the End of the Cold War: Gorbachev and German Unification," *Journal of Cold War Studies* 7:2 (Spring 2005): 142–64.

Forsythe, David P. "Human Rights in U. S. Foreign Policy: Retrospect and Prospect," *Political Science Quarterly* 105:3 (Autumn 1990): 435–54.

Fraser, Donald. "Freedom and Foreign Policy," *Foreign Policy* 26 (Spring 1977): 140–56.

Gaddis, John Lewis. "Hanging Tough Paid Off," *Bulletin of American Scientists* (January/February 1989): 11–4.

Galey, Margaret E. "Congress, Foreign Policy, and Human Rights Ten Years after Helsinki," *Human Rights Quarterly* 7:3 (August 1985): 334–72.

Galtung, Johan. "European Security and Cooperation: A Skeptical Contribution," *Journal of Peace Research* 21:3 (1975): 165–78.

Gati, Charles. "The 'Europeanization' of Communism," *Foreign Affairs* 55:3 (1977): 539–53.

Genys, John B. "The Joint Baltic American Committee and the European Security Conference," *Journal of Baltic Studies* 9:3 (Fall 1978): 245–58.

Goldberg, Arthur J. "The Helsinki Final Act Revisited," *American Foreign Policy Newsletter* (April 1982): 1–6.

"The Madrid CSCE Conference-'Twas a Hollow Victory," *American Foreign Policy Newsletter* 7:1 (February 1984): 1–5.

"A Reply," *American Foreign Policy Newsletter* 8:2 (April 1985): 1, 10–1.

Gorbachev, Mikhail, et al. "The Soviet View of the State of Human Rights in the United States and Western Europe," *Survey* 29:4 (1987): 236–43.

Gould-Davis, Nigel. "Rethinking the Role of Ideology in International Politics During the Cold War," *Journal of Cold War Studies* 1:1 (1999): 90–109.

Green, William C. "Human Rights and Detente," *Ukrainian Quarterly* 36:2 (1980): 138–49.

Grishchenko, A. I. and A. I. Stepanov. "Khel'sinki: Bor'ba Za Mir, Bezopasnost' i Sotrudnichestvo v Europe," *Voprosy Istorii* 10 (1985): 3–20.

Hanhimäki, Jussi. "'They Can Write it in Swahili': Kissinger, The Soviets, and the Helsinki Accords, 1973–1975," *Journal of Transatlantic Studies* 1:1 (2003): 37–58.

Hanson, Philip. "Economic Aspects of Helsinki," *International Affairs* 61:4 (Autumn 1985): 619–29.

Hartmann, Hauke. "US Human Rights Policy Under Carter and Reagan, 1977–1981," *Human Rights Quarterly* 23 (2001): 402–30.

Hass, Ernst B. "Why Collaborate?: Issue-linkage and International Regimes," *World Politics* 32 (April 1980): 357–405.

Hazewinkel, Harm J. "Ottawa 1985 – The Half-Way Meeting Recollections of a Participant," *OSCE ODHR Bulletin* 3:3 (Fall 1995): 40–6.

Helling, Lisa L. "U. S. Human Rights Policy Toward the Soviet Union and Eastern Europe During the Carter Administration," *Denver Journal of International Law and Policy* 9:1 (Winter 1980): 85–118.

Heneghan, Thomas E. "Human Rights in Eastern Europe," *World Today* 33:3 (1977): 90–100.

Hoffman, Stanley. "Will the Balance Balance at Home?" *Foreign Policy* 7 (Summer 1972): 60–86.

Holsti, K. J. "Bargaining Theory and Diplomatic Reality: The CSCE Negotiations," *Review of International Studies* 8:3 (1982): 159–70.

Horvath, Robert. "'The Solzhenitsyn Effect': East European Dissidents and Demise of the Revolutionary Privilege," *Human Rights Quarterly* 29 (2007): 879–907.

Horwitz, Jon and Mark Peffley. "Public Images of the Soviet Union: The Impact on Foreign Policy Attitudes," *The Journal of Politics* 52:1 (February 1990): 3–28.

Howard, Michael. "Helsinki Reconsidered: East–West Relations Two Years After the Final Act," *Round Table* 267 (1977): 241–8.

Hoyer, Steny. "The United States and Eastern Europe in the Next Four Years," *The Washington Quarterly* (Spring 1989): 171–81.

Jacoby, Tamar. "The Reagan Turnaround on Human Rights," *Foreign Affairs* 64:5 (1986): 1066–86.

Jarzabek, Wanda. "Home and Reality: Poland and the Conference on Security and Cooperation in Europe, 1964–1989," Cold War International History

Project, Working Paper Number 56, Woodrow Wilson International Center for Scholars.

Judt, Tony. "The Dilemmas of Dissidence: The Politics of Opposition in East-Central Europe," *East European Politics and Societies* 2:2 (1988): 185–240.

Kadnar, Milan. "Czechoslovakia Since Helsinki," *International Affairs* (USSR) 2 (1977): 74–8.

Kashlev, Yuri. "The CSCE in the Soviet Union's Politics," *International Affairs* (USSR) 7 (1992): 66–72.

Katzenstein, Peter J. "International Relations and Domestic Structures: Foreign Economic Policies of Advanced Industrial States," *International Organization* 30 (1976): 1–45.

Kelly, Sean. "Third Basket at Belgrade," *Foreign Service Journal* 54:9 (1977): 6–11, 23.

Keohane, Robert O. "The Demand for International Regimes," *International Organization* 36:2 (Spring 1982): 325–55.

Killham, Edward L. "The Madrid CSCE Conference," *World Affairs* 146:4 (1984): 340–57.

"The Madrid CSCE Conference: A Fourth Opinion," *American Foreign Policy Newsletter* 8:2 (April 1985): 1, 7–9.

Kirkpatrick, Jeane. "Dictators and Double Standards," *Commentary* (1979): 34–45.

Klotz, Audie. "Norms Reconstituting Interests: Global Racial Equality and U. S. Sanctions Against South Africa," *International Organization* 49:3 (Summer 1995): 451–78.

Koh, Harold Hongju. "Review: Why Do Nations Obey International Law?" *The Yale Law Journal* 196:8 (June 1997): 2599–659.

Kohl, Wilfrid L. "The Nixon-Kissinger Foreign Policy System and U. S. -European Relations: Patterns of Policy Making," *World Politics* 28:1 (October 1975): 1–43.

Korey, William. "Sin of Omission," *Foreign Policy* 39 (1980): 172–5.

"The Helsinki/Madrid Meeting," *The Washington Quarterly* 5:2 (Spring 1982).

"Challenge in Vienna: Making Helsinki Matter," *The New Leader* (August 11–25, 1986): 11–13.

"Helsinki, Human Rights, and the Gorbachev Style," *Ethics and International Affairs* 1 (1987): 113–33.

"The Jackson-Vanik Amendment in Perspective," *Soviet Jewish Affairs* 18:1 (1988): 29–47.

"The Legacy of Helsinki," *Reform Judaism* (Spring 1988): 8–9.

"The Unanticipated Consequences of Helsinki," *OSCE ODIHR Bulletin* 3:3 (Fall 1995): 8–14.

Kovrig, Bennett. "Western Approaches," *International Journal* 43:1 (1987–8): 35–62.

Kramer, Mark. "The Collapse of East European Communism and the Repercussions within the Soviet Union (Part 1)," *Journal of Cold War Studies* 5:4 (Fall 2003): 178–247.

"The Collapse of the Soviet Union (Part 2)," *Journal of Cold War Studies* 5:4 (Fall 2003): 3–42.

"The Collapse of East European Communism and the Repercussions within the Soviet Union (Part 2)," *Journal of Cold War Studies* 6:4 (Fall 2004): 3–64.

"The Collapse of East European Communism and the Repercussions within the Soviet Union (Part 3)," *Journal of Cold War Studies* 7:1 (Winter 2005): 3–96.

Krux, Ernst. "Revolution in Eastern Europe—Revolution in the West?" *Problems of Communism* 40 (May–June 1991): 1–13.

Kulish, V. M. "Na Strazhe Mira i Bezopasnosti Narodov," *Voprosy Istorii* 2 (1986): 41–57.

Kuran, Timur. "Now Out of Never: The Element of Surprise in the East European Revolution of 1989," *World Politics* 44:1 (October 1991): 7–48.

Laqueur, Walter. "The Issue of Human Rights," *Commentary* (May 1977): 29–35.

Laux, Jeanne Kirk. "CSCE: Symbol of the Search for East–West Co-operation," *International Perspectives* 5 (1974): 23–6.

László, Bruszt. "1989: The Negotiated Revolution in Hungary," *Social Research* 57:2 (Summer 1990): 365–87.

Lebedev, A. "Imperativy Khel'sinki," *Mirovaia Ekonomika i Mezhdunarodnye Otnosheniia* 8 (1985): 3–14.

Lipatti, Valentin. "The CSCE and Innovations in the Practice of Multilateral Diplomatic Negations," *International Social Science Journal* 44:2 (1992): 299–305.

Luers, William H. "Czechoslovakia: Road to Revolution," *Foreign Affairs* 69:2 (Spring 1990): 77–98.

Luxmoore, Jonathan. "And So to Vienna ... The CSCE Eleven Years On," *Contemporary Review* 249:1451 (1986): 302–9.

MacKinnon, Elaine. "Grasping at the Whirlwinds of Change: Transitional Leadership in Comparative Perspective. The Case Studies of Mikhail Gorbachev and F. W. de Klerk," *Canadian Journal of History* XLIII (Spring–Summer 2008): 69–107.

Maechling, Jr., Charles. "Human Rights Dehumanized," *Foreign Policy* 52 (Autumn 1983): 118–35.

Maresca, John J. "Ensuring CSCE Promises Are Kept," *ODIHR Bulletin* 3:3 (Fall 1995): 31–4.

"A Proposal for Helsinki Observers," *Atlantic Community Quarterly* 26 (1988): 249–54.

Mastny, Vojtech. "New History of Cold War Alliances," *Journal of Cold War Studies* 4:2 (2002): 55–84.

"The Soviet Non-Invasion of Poland in 1980–81 and the End of the Cold War," Cold War International History Project Working Paper Number 5, Woodrow Wilson International Center For Scholars.

"Europe in US–USSR Relations: A Topical Legacy," *Problems of Communism* XXXVII: 1 (Jan–Feb 1988): 16–29.

Maynard, Edwin S. "The Bureaucracy and Implementation of US Human Rights Policy," *Human Rights Quarterly* 11:2 (May 1989): 175–248.

Mazower, Mark. "The Strange Triumph of Human Rights, 1933–1950," *The Historical Journal* 47 (2004): 379–98.

Meissner, Boris. "The Soviet Concept of Coexistence and the European Security Conference," *Modern Age* 19:4 (Fall 1975): 364–74.

Meyer, David S. and Nancy Whittier. "Social Movement Spillover," *Social Problems* 41 (1994): 277–98.

Millar, T. B. "Helsinki, Belgrade, and Beyond," *Australian Outlook* 32:1 (1978): 16–23.

Molineu, Harold. "Negotiating Human Rights: The Helsinki Agreement," *World Affairs* 14 (Summer 1978): 24–39.

Nagy, J. "The Spirit of Helsinki," *The New Hungarian Quarterly* 17:64 (Winter 1976): 7–17.

Nathans, Benjamin. "The Dictatorship of Reason: Aleksandr Vol'Pin and the Idea of Rights under 'Developed Socialism,'" *Slavic Review* 66:4 (Winter 2007): 630–63.

Nowak, Jerzy M. and Stanislaw, Parzymies. "The Mediterranean Region and the CSCE Process," *Studies on International Relations* 14 (1980): 87–108.

Oslzly, Petr. "On Stage with the Velvet Revolution," *The Drama Review* 34:3 (Fall 1990): 97–108.

Patman, Robert G. "Some Reflections on Archie Brown and the End of the Cold War," *Cold War History* 7:3 (August 2007): 439–45.

Peeters, Yvo J. D. "Minority Provisions in the Helsinki-Process," *Plural Societies* 18:2–3 (1989): 95–119.

Pepper, David. "The Helsinki Legacy," *International Perspectives* (Jan.–Feb. 1987): 11–14.

Pflüger, Friedbert. "Human Rights Unbound: Carter's Human Rights Policy Reassessed," *Presidential Studies Quarterly* 19:4 (Fall 1989): 705–16.

Pierre, Andrew J. "The United States and the New Europe," *Current History* 89:550 (November 1990): 353–6, 391–2.

Podhoretz, Norman. "The Reagan Road to Détente," *Foreign Affairs* 63 (Winter 1984–5): 447–64.

Radio Free Europe Research. "Six Months After: The East European Response to Helsinki," *Atlantic Community Quarterly* 14:1 (Spring 1976): 59–65.

Rakhmaninov, Iu. "Evropa na Otvetstvennom Rubezhe," *Mirovaia Ekonomika i Mezhdunarodnye Otnosheniia* 8 (1982): 3–14.

Rand, Robert. "USSR Commitment to the CSCE Process in the Face of Western Criticism: Five Profitable Reasons," *Atlantic Community Quarterly* 20:2 (Summer 1982): 179–81.

Raymond, Gregory A. "Problems and Prospects in the Study of International Norms," *Mershon International Studies Review* 41:2 (November 1997): 205–45.

Rey, Marie-Pierre. "'Europe is our Common Home': A Study of Gorbachev's Diplomatic Concept," *Cold War History* 4:2 (January 2004): 33–65.

Ribuffo, Leo P. "Is Poland a Soviet Satellite?: Gerald Ford, the Sonnenfeldt Doctrine, and the Election of 1976," *Diplomatic History* 14 (Summer 1990): 385–403.

Richmond, Yale. "Cultural Exchange and the Cold War: How the Arts Influenced Policy," *The Journal of Arts Management, Law and Society* 35:3 (Fall 2005): 239–45.

Risse-Kappen, Thomas. "Ideas Do Not Float Freely: Transnational Coalitions, Domestic Structures, and the End of the Cold War," *International Organization* (Spring 1994): 185–214.

Robertson, A. H. "The Helsinki Agreement and Human Rights," *Notre Dame Lawyer* 53:34 (October 1977): 34–48.

Rotfeld, Adam Daniel. "The Conference on Security and Cooperation in Europe (its Conception, Realization, and Significance)," *Polish Western Affairs* 17:1 (1977): 26–63.

"Implementation of the CSCE Final Act and the Development of Détente in Europe," *Studies on International Relations* 8 (1977): 17–41.

"The Evolution of the Helsinki Process," *ODIHR Bulletin* 3:3 (Fall 1995): 3–37.

Roth, S. J. "From Madrid to Vienna: What Progress in the Helsinki Process?" *Soviet Jewish Affairs* 16:3 (1986): 3–16.

Rubenstein, Joshua. "The Enduring Voice of the Soviet Dissidents," *Columbia Journalism Review* (Sept/Oct 1978): 32–39.

Russell, Harold. "The Helsinki Declaration: Brobdingnag or Lilliput?" *American Journal of International Law* 70:2 (April 1976): 242–72.

Rychlowski, B. and J. Symonides. "Helsinki and After," *Polish Perspectives* 18:12 (December 1975): 9–15.

"European Security and Cooperation and the Concept of Peaceful Coexistence," *Studies on International Relations* 7 (1976): 17–34.

Schlager, Erika. "The Procedural Framework of the CSCE: From the Helsinki Consultations to the Paris Charter," *Human Rights Law Journal* 12:6 (July 12, 1991): 221–37.

Schmitz, David F. and Vanessa Walker, "Jimmy Carter and the Foreign Policy of Human Rights: The Development of a Post-Cold War Foreign Policy," *Diplomatic History* 28 (January 2004): 113–43.

Scrivner, Douglas G. "The Conference on Security and Cooperation in Europe: Implications for Soviet-American Détente," *Denver Journal of International Law and Policy* 6:1 (1976): 122–58.

Siekman, Rob. "The Linkage Between Peace and Security and Human Rights in the CSCE Process," *Helsinki Monitor* 5:1 (1994): 43–51.

Sherer, Albert W. Jr. "Helsinki's Child: Goldberg's Variation," *Foreign Policy* 39 (1980): 154–9.

Sherer, Carroll. "Breakdown at Belgrade," *The Washington Quarterly* 1:4 (1978): 80–4.

Sikkink, Kathryn. "Human Rights, Principled Issue-Networks, and Sovereignty in Latin America," *International Organization* 47 (1993): 411–41.

Skilling, H. Gordon. "Charter 77 and the Musical Underground," *Canadian Slavonic Papers* 22:1 (1980): 1–14.

"CSCE in Madrid," *Problems of Communism* (July–August 1981): 1–16.

Smith, Jackie. "Exploring Connections between Global Integration and Political Mobilization," *Journal of World-Systems Research* 10 (2004): 255–85.

Snyder, Sarah B. "'Jerry, Don't Go': Domestic Opposition to the 1975 Helsinki Final Act," *Journal of American Studies* 44:1 (February 2010): 67–81.

"The CSCE and the Atlantic Alliance: Forging a New Consensus in Madrid," *Journal of Transatlantic Studies* 8:1 (March 2010): 56–68.

"Through the Looking Glass: The Helsinki Final Act and the 1976 Election for President," *Diplomacy and Statecraft* 21:1 (March 2010): 87–106.

"The Foundation for Vienna: A Reassessment of the CSCE in the mid-1980s," *Cold War History* 10:4 (November 2010): 493–512.

Spiro, Elizabeth. "A Paradigm Shift in US Foreign Policy: From Self-Determination to Human Rights," *Worldview* 20:1–2 (1977): 42–7.

Stefan, Charles G. "The Drafting of the Helsinki Final Act: A Personal View of the CSCE's Geneva Phase (September 1973 until July 1975)," *Society for Historians of American Foreign Relations Newsletter* 31:2 (2000): 1–10.

Suri, Jeremi. "Explaining the End of the Cold War: A New Historical Consensus?" *Journal of Cold War Studies* 4:4 (Fall 2002): 60–92.

"Détente and Human Rights: American and West European Perspectives on International Change," *Cold War History* 8:4 (November 2008): 527–45.

Tabory, Mala. "The Vienna CSCE Concluding Document: Some General and Jewish Perspectives," *Soviet Jewish Affairs* 19:1 (1989): 3–18.

Tannenwald, Nina. "Ideas and Explanation: Advancing the Theoretical Agenda," *Journal of Cold War Studies* 7:2 (Spring 2005): 13–42.

Tannenwald, Nina and William C. Wohlforth. "Introduction: The Role of Ideas and the End of the Cold War," *Journal of Cold War Studies* 7:2 (Spring 2005): 3–12.

Tarrow, Sidney. "'Aiming at a Moving Target': Social Science and the Recent Rebellions in Eastern Europe," *PS: Political Science and Politics* 24:1 (March 1991): 12–20.

Thomas, Daniel C. "Boomerangs and Superpowers: International Norms, Transnational Networks and US Foreign Policy," *Cambridge Review of International Affairs* 15:1 (2002): 25–44.

"Human Rights Ideas, the Demise of Communism, and the End of the Cold War," *Journal of Cold War Studies* 7:2 (Spring 2005): 110–41.

Tismaneanu, Vladimir. "The Revolutions of 1989: Causes, Meanings, Consequences," *Contemporary European History* 18:3 (2009): 271–88.

Toogood, J. D. "Arms Control Negotiation: Two Approaches," *International Perspectives* (July–August 1983): 21–3.

Vogelgesang, Sandy. "Diplomacy of Human Rights," *International Studies Quarterly* 23:2 (June 1979): 216–45.

Vukadinovic, Radovan. "The Warsaw Pact and European Security and Cooperation, *Review of International Affairs* (Belgrade) 25: 579 (May 20, 1974): 23–5.

Wallander, Celeste A. "Western Policy and the Demise of the Soviet Union," *Journal of Cold War Studies* 5:4 (Fall 2003): 137–77.

Wallensteen, Peter. "American Soviet Détente: What Went Wrong?" *Journal of Peace Research* 22:1 (March 1985): 1–8.

Wohlforth, William C. "The End of the Cold War as a Hard Case for Ideas," *Journal of Cold War Studies* 7:2 (Spring 2005):165–73.

Yaroslavtsev, V. "Basis of European Security," *International Affairs* (USSR) 5 (May 1976): 13–20.

Yurev, N. "Towards a Europe of Security and Cooperation," *International Affairs* (USSR) 2 (February 1977): 19–28.

Zubok, Vladislav. "Gorbachev and the End of the Cold War: Perspectives on History and Personality," *Cold War History* 2:2 (January 2002): 61–100.

"The Soviet Union and Détente in the 1970s," *Cold War History* 8:4 (November 2008): 427–47.

Zuzowski, Robert. "The Origins of Open Organised Dissent in Today's Poland: KOR and Other Dissident Groups," *East European Quarterly* 25:1 (Spring 1991): 59–90.

Symposium: Human Rights and the Helsinki Accord: A Five-Year Road to Madrid, *Vanderbilt Journal of Transnational Law* 13:2–3 (Spring-Summer 1980).

Books

Memoirs

Adamishin, Anatoly and Richard Schifter. *Human Rights, Perestroika, and the End of the Cold War*. Washington: United States Institute of Peace Press, 2009.

Amal'rik, Andrei. *Notes of a Revolutionary*. trans. Guy Daniels. New York: Alfred A. Knopf, 1982.

Arbatov, G. A. *The System: An Insider's Life in Soviet Politics*. New York: Times Books, 1992.

Baker, James A. *The Politics of Diplomacy: Revolution, War, and Peace, 1989–1992*. New York: G. P. Putman's Sons, 1995.

Boldin, Valery. *Ten Years that Shook the World: The Gorbachev Era as Witnessed by His Chief of Staff*. New York: Basic Books, 1994.

Bonner, Elena. *Alone Together*. trans. Alexander Cook. New York: Alfred A. Knopf, 1986.

Braithwaite, Rodric. *Across the Moscow River: The World Turned Upside Down*. New Haven: Yale University Press, 2002.

Brzezinski, Zbigniew. *Power and Principle: Memoirs of the National Security Adviser, 1977–1981*. New York: Farrar, Straus and Giroux, 1983.

Bukovsky, Vladimir. *To Build a Castle – My Life as a Dissenter*. New York: The Viking Press, 1979.

Bush, George and Brent Scowcroft. *A World Transformed*. New York: Vintage Books, 1998.

Carter, Jimmy. *Keeping Faith: Memoirs of a President*. New York: Bantam Books, 1982.

White House Diary. New York: Farrar, Straus and Giroux, 2010.

Chalidze, Valery. *The Soviet Human Rights Movement: A Memoir*. New York: The American Jewish Committee, 1984.

Chernyaev, Anatoly. *My Six Years with Gorbachev*. University Park: Pennsylvania State University Press, 2000.

Clift, Denis A. *With Presidents to the Summit*. Fairfax: George Mason University Press, 1993.

Daniloff, Nicholas. *Two Lives, One Russia*. Boston: Houghton Mifflin Company, 1988.

Of Spies and Spokesmen: My Life as a Cold War Correspondent. Columbia: University of Missouri Press, 2008.

Drakulic, Slavenka. *How We Survived Communism and Even Laughed*. New York: Harper Perennial, 1993.

Dobrynin, Anatoly. *In Confidence: Moscow's Ambassador to America's Six Cold War Presidents*. New York: Random House, 1995.

Dubinin, Iu. V. *Vremia Peremen: Zapiski Posla v SshA*. Moscow: Aviarus-XXI, 2003.

Fascell, Dante B. *U. S. -Soviet Relations at the Crossroads: Congressman Dante Fascell Reflects on his Visit to the Kremlin*. Institute for Soviet and East European Studies, Graduate School of International Studies, University of Miami, 1987.

Fenwick, Millicent. *Speaking Up*. New York: Harper and Row, 1982.

Ford, Gerald R. *A Time to Heal*. New York: Harper and Row, 1979.

Gates, Robert M. *From the Shadows: The Ultimate Insider's Story of Five Presidents and How They Won the Cold War*. New York: Simon and Schuster, 1996.

Genscher, Hans-Dietrich. *Rebuilding a House Divided: A Memoir by the Architect of Germany's Reunification*. trans. Thomas Thornton. New York: Broadway Books, 1998.

Goldberg, Dorothy. *A Private View of a Public Life*. New York: Charterhouse, 1975.

Gorbachev, Mikhail. *Perestroika: New Thinking for Our Country and the World*. New York: Harper and Row, 1987.

Memoirs. New York: Doubleday, 1996.

Gorbachev: On My Country and the World. trans. George Shriver. New York: Columbia University Press, 2000.

Gorbachev, Mikhail and Zdeněk Mlynář. *Conversations with Gorbachev: On Perestroika, the Prague Spring, and the Crossroads of Socialism*. New York: Columbia University Press, 2003.

Grachev, Andrei S. *Final Days: The Inside Story of the Collapse of the Soviet Union*. trans. Margo Milne. Boulder: Westview Press, 1995.

Grigorenko, Petro G. *Memoirs*. trans. Thomas P. Whitney. New York: W. W. Norton and Company, 1982.

Gromyko, Andrei. *Memoirs*. New York: Doubleday, 1989.

Haig, Alexander M. Jr. *Caveat: Realism, Reagan, and Foreign Policy*. New York: MacMillan Publishing Company, 1984.

Haig, Alexander M. with Charles McCarry. *Inner Circles: How America Changed the World: A Memoir*. New York: Warner Books, 1992.

Hartmann, Robert T. *Palace Politics: An Inside Account of the Ford Years*. New York: McGraw-Hill, 1980.

Havel, Václav. *Disturbing the Peace: A Conversation with Karel Hvíždala*. trans. Paul Wilson. New York: Alfred A. Knopf, 1990.

To the Castle and Back. trans. Paul Wilson. New York: Alfred A. Knopf, 2007.

Hochman, Jiri, ed. and trans. *Hope Dies Last: The Autobiography of Alexander Dubcek*. New York: Kodansha International, 1993.

Hurd, Douglas. *The Search for Peace*. New York: Little, Brown and Company, 1997.

Hutchings, Robert L. *American Diplomacy and the End of the Cold War: An Insider's Account of US Diplomacy in Europe, 1989–1992.* Baltimore: The Johns Hopkins University Press, 1997.

Hyland, William. *Mortal Rivals: Superpower Relations from Nixon to Reagan.* New York: Random House, 1987.

Kalugin, Oleg. *Spymaster: My Thirty-two Years in Intelligence and Espionage Against the West.* New York: Basic Books, 2009.

Kampelman, Max M. *Entering New Worlds: The Memoirs of a Private Man in Public Life.* New York: HarperCollins, 1991.

Kissinger, Henry. *The White House Years.* Boston: Little, Brown, 1979.

Years of Upheaval. New York: Little Brown, 1982.

Years of Renewal. New York: Simon and Schuster, 1999.

Kovalev, A. *Azbuka Diplomatim.* Moscow: Interpraks, 1993.

Kristol, Irving. *Reflections of a Neoconservative: Looking Back, Looking Ahead.* New York: Basic Books, 1983.

Laber, Jeri. *The Courage of Strangers: Coming of Age with the Human Rights Movement.* New York: Public Affairs, 2002.

Ligachev, Yegor. *Inside the Gorbachev's Kremlin: The Memoirs of Yegor Ligachev.* trans. Catherine A. Fitzpatrick, Michele A. Berdy, and Dobrochna Dyrcz-Freeman. New York: Pantheon Books, 1993.

McRae, Rob. *Resistance and Revolution: Václav Havel's Czechoslovakia.* Ottawa: Carleton University Press, 1997.

Marchenko, Anatoly. *My Testimony.* trans. Michael Scammel. New York: Dell Publishing, 1969.

Maresca, John J. *To Helsinki: The Conference on Security and Cooperation in Europe, 1973–75.* rev. ed. Durham: Duke University Press, 1987.

Matlock, Jack Jr. *Autopsy of an Empire: The American Ambassador's Account of the Collapse of the Soviet Union.* New York: Random House, 1995.

Neier, Aryeh. *Taking Liberties: Four Decades in the Struggle for Rights.* New York: Public Affairs, 2003.

Nesson, Ron. *It Sure Looks Different From the Inside.* Chicago: Playboy Press, 1978.

Nixon, Richard. *RN: The Memoirs of Richard Nixon.* New York: Grosset & Dunlap, 1978.

In the Arena: A Memoir of Victory, Defeat, and Renewal. New York: Simon and Schuster, 1990.

Novak, Michael. *Taking Glasnost Seriously: Toward an Open Soviet Union.* Washington: American Enterprise for Public Policy Research, 1988.

Orlov, Yuri. *Dangerous Thoughts: Memoirs of a Russian Life.* trans. Thomas P. Whitney. New York: William Morrow and Company, 1991.

Owen, David. *Time to Declare.* London: Michael Joseph, 1991.

Pazchenko, Pavel. *My Years with Gorbachev and Shevardnadze: The Memoir of a Soviet Interpreter.* University Park: The Pennsylvania State University Press, 1997.

Powell, Jody. *The Other Side of the Story.* New York: Morrow, 1984.

Reagan, Ronald. *An American Life.* New York: Simon and Schuster, 1990.

Richmond, Yale. *Practicing Public Diplomacy: A Cold War Odyssey*. New York: Berghahn Books, 2008.

Rubbi, Antonio. *Incontri con Gorbaciov: I colloqui di Natta e Occhetto con il leader sovietico: giugno 1984-novembre 1989*. Rome: Editori Riuniti, 1990.

Sakharov, Andrei. *Alarm and Hope*. Efrem Yankelevich and Alfred Friendly Jr., ed. New York: Alfred A. Knopf, 1978.

Memoirs. trans. Richard Lourie. New York: Knopf, 1990.

Moscow and Beyond, 1986 to 1989. trans. Antonina Bouis. New York: Knopf, 1991.

Schmidt, Helmut. *Men and Powers: A Political Retrospective*. trans. Ruth Hein. New York: Random House, 1989.

Sevechenko, Arkady. *Breaking with Moscow*. New York: Alfred A. Knopf, 1985.

Sharansky, Natan. *Fear No Evil*. New York: Random House, 1988.

Shcharansky, Avital with Ilana Ben-Josef. *Next Year in Jerusalem*. trans. Stefani Hoffman. New York: William Morrow and Company, 1979.

Shevardnadze, Eduard. *The Future Belongs to Freedom*. trans. Catherine Fitzpatrick. London: Sinclair-Stevenson, 1991.

Shultz, George P. *Turmoil and Triumph: Diplomacy, Power, and the Victory of the American Ideal*. New York: Simon and Schuster, 1993.

Sukhodrev, V. M. *Iazyk moi – drug moi: Ot Khrushcheva do Gorbacheva*. Moscow: AST, 1999.

Taubman, William and Jane Taubman. *Moscow Spring*. New York: Summit Books, 1989.

Thatcher, Margaret. *The Downing Street Years, 1979–1990*. New York: Harper Perennial, 1993.

Vance, Cyrus. *Hard Choices: Four Critical Years in American Foreign Policy*. New York: Simon and Schuster, 1983.

Waldheim, Kurt. *In the Eye of the Storm: A Memoir*. Bethesda: Adler and Adler, 1986.

Walesa, Lech. *A Way of Hope: An Autobiography*. New York: Henry Holt and Company, 1987.

The Struggle and the Triumph: An Autobiography. New York: Arcade Publishing, 1992.

Weinberger, Caspar W. *In the Arena: A Memoir of the 20th Century*. Washington: Regnery Publishing, 2001.

Yakovlev, Alexander. *Sumerki*. Moscow: Materik, 2003.

Secondary Sources

Acimovic, Ljubivoje. *Problems of Security and Cooperation in Europe*. Rockville: Sijthoff and Noordhoff, 1981.

Adamishin, A., et al. *From Helsinki to Belgrade: The Soviet Union and the Implementation of the Final Act of the European Conference: Documents and Material*. Moscow: Progress Publishers, 1977.

Ahonen, Pertti. *After the Expulsion: West Germany and Eastern Europe, 1945–1990*. New York: Oxford University Press, 2003.

Alexeyeva, Ludmilla. *Soviet Dissent: Contemporary Movements for National, Religious, and Human Rights*. Middletown: Wesleyan University Press, 1985.

Alexeyeva, Ludmilla and Paul Goldberg. *The Thaw Generation: Coming of Age in the Post-Stalin Era*. Boston: Little, Brown, 1990.

Aminzade, Ronald R., et al., eds. *Silence and Voice in the Study of Contentious Politics*. Cambridge: Cambridge University Press, 2001.

Anderson, Carol. *Eyes Off the Prize: The United Nations and the African American Struggle for Human Rights, 1944–1955*. Cambridge: Cambridge University Press, 2003.

Anderson, Patrick. *Electing Jimmy Carter: The Campaign of 1976*. Baton Rouge: Louisiana State University Press, 1994.

Andren, Nils and Karl E. Birnbaum, eds. *Belgrade and Beyond: The CSCE Process in Perspective*. Rockville: Sijthoff & Noordhoff, December 1980.

Andrew, Christopher and Vasili Mitrokhin. *The Sword and the Shield: The Mitrokhin Archive and the Secret History of the KGB*. New York: Basic Books, 1999.

Ash, Timothy Garton. *The Uses of Adversity: Essays on the Fate of Central Europe*. New York: Random House, 1989.

 The Magic Lantern: The Revolution of '89 Witnessed in Warsaw, Budapest, Berlin and Prague. New York: Vintage Books, 1993.

 The Polish Revolution: Solidarity. 3rd ed. New Haven: Yale University Press, 2002.

Baehr, Peter R. and Monique Castermans-Holleman. *The Role of Human Rights in Foreign Policy*. 2nd ed. New York: Palgrave Macmillan, 2004.

Bange, Oliver and Gottfried Niedhart, eds. *Helsinki 1975 and the Transformation of Europe*. New York: Berghahn Books, 2008.

Ball, Alan M. *Imagining America: Influence and Images in Twentieth-Century Russia*. New York: Rowman & Littlefield, 2003.

Barker, Colin. *Festival of the Oppressed: Solidarity, Reform and Revolution in Poland, 1980–81*. Chicago: Bookmarks, 1986.

Batt, Judy. *Economic Reform and Political Change in Eastern Europe: A Comparison of the Czechoslovak and Hungarian Experiences*. New York: St. Martin's Press, 1988.

Beckerman, Gal. *When They Come For Us, We'll Be Gone: The Epic Struggle to Save Soviet Jewry*. New York: Houghton Mifflin Harcourt, 2010.

Berend, T. Ivan. *From the Soviet Bloc to the European Union: The Economic and Social Transformation of Central and Eastern Europe since 1973*. New York: Cambridge University Press, 2009.

Berg, Rolf and Adam-Daniel Rotfeld. *Building Security in Europe: Confidence-Building Measures and the CSCE*. New York: Institute for East–West Security Studies, 1986.

Bermeo, Nancy, ed. *Liberalization and Democratization: Change in the Soviet Union and Eastern Europe*. Baltimore: The Johns Hopkins University Press, 1992.

Bernhard, Michael H. *The Origins of Democratization in Poland: Workers, Intellectuals, and Oppositional Politics, 1976–1980.* New York: Columbia University Press, 1993.

Beschloss, Michael R. and Strobe Talbott. *At the Highest Levels: The Inside Story of the End of the Cold War.* Boston: Little, Brown and Company, 1993.

Birnbaum, Karl E., ed. *Beyond Détente: Prospects for East–West Cooperation and Security in Europe.* Leyden: A. W. Sijthoff-Leyden, 1976.

Confidence Building and East–West Relations. Vienna: Wilhelm Braumüller, 1983.

Bloed, A. and P. Van Dijk, eds. *Essays on Human Rights in the Helsinki Process.* Boston: Martinus Nijhoff, 1985.

The Human Dimension of the Helsinki Process: The Vienna Follow-up Meeting and its Aftermath. Boston: Martinus Nijhoff, 1991.

Bloed, A. ed. *From Helsinki to Vienna: Basic Documents of the Helsinki Process.* London: Martinus Nijhoff, 1990.

The Conference on Security and Cooperation in Europe: Analysis and Basic Documents, 1972–1993. London: Kluwer Academic Publishers, 1993.

Bloed, A. *The Challenges of Change: The Helsinki Summit of the CSCE and its Aftermath.* Boston: Martinus Nijhoff, 1994.

Borgwardt, Elizabeth. *A New Deal for the World: America's Vision for Human Rights.* Cambridge: Harvard University Press, 2005.

Bowker, Mike and Phil Williams. *Superpower Détente: A Reappraisal.* Newbury Park: SAGE Publications, 1988.

Bozo, Frédéric. *Mitterrand, The End of the Cold War and German Unification.* trans. Susan Emmanuel. New York: Berghahn Books, 2009.

Bozo, Frédéric, et al., eds. *Europe and the End of the Cold War: A Reappraisal.* New York: Routledge, 2008.

Bozóki, András, ed. *The Roundtable Talks of 1989: The Genesis of Hungarian Democracy: Analysis and Documents.* Budapest: Central European University Press, 2002.

Braun, Reiner, et al., eds. *Joseph Rotblat: Visionary for Peace.* Weinheim: Wiley-VCH, 2007.

Brezhnev, Leonid I. *To Uphold the Ideals of Helsinki – Security and Cooperation.* Moscow: Novosti Agency Publishing House, 1982.

Brinkley, Douglas, ed. *The Reagan Diaries.* New York: Harper Collins, 2007.

Brinton, William M. and Alan Rinzler, eds. *Without Force or Lies: Voices from the Revolution of Central Europe in 1989–90: Essays, Speeches, and Eyewitness Accounts.* San Francisco: Mercury House, 1990.

Brown, Archie. *The Gorbachev Factor.* New York: Oxford University Press, 1996.

Seven Years that Changed the World: Perestroika in Perspective. New York: Oxford University Press, 2007.

The Rise and Fall of Communism. New York: Harper Collins, 2009.

Brown, Archie, ed. *The Demise of Marxism-Leninism in Russia.* New York: Palgrave Macmillan, 2004.

Brown, J. F. *Surge to Freedom: The End of Communist Rule in Eastern Europe.* Durham: Duke University Press, 1991.

Brownlee, W. Elliot and Hugh Davis Graham, eds. *The Reagan Presidency: Pragmatic Conservatism and Its Legacies.* Lawrence: University of Kansas Press, 2003.

Brudny, Yitzhak. *Reinventing Russia: Russian Nationalism and the Soviet State.* Cambridge: Harvard University Press, 1998.

Brzezinski, Zbigniew. *The Grand Failure: The Birth and Death of Communism in the Twentieth Century.* New York: Charles Scribner's Sons, 1989.

Buergenthal, Thomas and Judith R. Hall, eds. *Human Rights, International Law and the Helsinki Accord.* Montclair: Allanheld, Osmun & Co. Publishers, 1977.

Bugajski, Janusz. *Czechoslovakia: Charter 77's Decade of Dissent.* New York: Praeger Publishers, 1987.

Bugajski, Janusz and Maxine Pollack. *East European Fault Lines: Dissent, Opposition, and Social Activism.* Boulder: Westview Press, 1989.

Buncher, Judith, F., ed. *Human Rights & American Diplomacy, 1975–77.* New York: Facts on File, 1977.

Burr, William, ed. *The Kissinger Transcripts: The Top-Secret Talks with Beijing and Moscow.* New York: The New Press, 1998.

Byers, R. B., Stephen Larrabee and Allen Lynch, eds. *Confidence-Building Measures and International Security.* New York: Westview Press, 1987.

Cannon, James. *Time and Chance: Gerald Ford's Appointment with History.* New York: HarperCollins Publishers, 1994.

Cannon, Lou. *President Reagan: The Role of a Lifetime.* rev. ed. New York: PublicAffairs, 2000.

Carroll, Peter. *It Seemed Like Nothing Happened: The Tragedy and Promise of America in the 1970s.* New York: Holt, Rinehart and Winston, 1982.

Castells, Manuel. *The Rise of the Network Society.* Oxford: Blackwell, 1996.

Chalidze, Valery. *To Defend These Rights: Human Rights and the Soviet Union.* New York: Random House, 1974.

Checkel, Jeffrey T. *Ideas and International Political Change: Soviet/Russian Behavior and the End of the Cold War.* New Haven: Yale University Press, 1997.

Clark, Ann Marie. *Diplomacy of a Conscience: Amnesty International and Changing Human Rights Norms.* Princeton: Princeton University Press, 2001.

Clifford, Bob, ed. *The International Struggle for New Human Rights.* Philadelphia: University of Pennsylvania Press, 2009.

Cohen, Stephen F. and Katrina Vanden Heuvel. *Voices of Glasnost: Interviewing Gorbachev's Reformers.* New York: W. W. Norton Company, 1989.

Colton, Timothy J. *The Dilemma of Reform in the Soviet Union.* New York: Council on Foreign Relations, 1986.

Crampton, R. J. *Eastern Europe and the Twentieth Century – And After.* 2nd ed. New York: Routledge, 1997.

Curry, Jane Leftwich, ed. *Dissent in Eastern Europe.* New York: Praeger, 1983.

Davies, Norman. *God's Playground: A History of Poland: Volume II.* rev. ed. New York: Columbia University Press, 2005.

Davy, Richard, ed. *European Détente: A Reappraisal.* London: SAGE for Royal Institute for International Affairs, 1992.

Dawisha, Karen. *Eastern Europe, Gorbachev, and Reform.* 2nd ed. New York: Cambridge University Press, 1990.

De Porte, A. W. *Europe and the Superpower Balance.* New York: Foreign Policy Association, 1979.

Deese, David A., ed. *The New Politics of American Foreign Policy.* New York: St. Martin's Press, 1994.

DeFrank, Thomas F. *Write It When I'm Gone: Remarkable Off-the-Record Conversations with Gerald R. Ford.* New York: G. P. Putnam's Sons, 2007.

Deighton, Anne and Gerard Bossuat, eds. *The EC/EU: A World Security Actor?* Paris: Soleb 2007.

della Porta, Donatella and Sidney Tarrow, eds. *Transnational Protest and Global Activism.* Lanham: Rowman and Littlefield, 2005.

Deutsch, Karl W., et al. *Political Community and the North Atlantic Area: International Organization in Light of Historical Experience.* Princeton: Princeton University Press, 1957.

Dobson, Alan P. *Anglo-American Relations in the Twentieth Century: Of Friendship, Conflict and the Rise and Decline of Superpowers.* New York: Routledge, 1995.

Drinan, Robert F. *The Mobilization of Shame: A World View of Human Rights.* New Haven: Yale University Press, 2001.

Dumbrell, John. *The Carter Presidency: A Re-evaluation.* New York: St. Martin's Press, 1993.

American Foreign Policy: Carter to Clinton. New York: St. Martin's Press, 1997.

A Special Relationship: Anglo-American from the Cold War to Iraq. 2nd ed. New York: Palgrave Macmillan, 2006.

Dunne, Tim and Nicholas J. Wheeler, eds. *Human Rights in Global Politics.* Cambridge: Cambridge University Press, 1999.

Dyson, Kenneth, ed. *European Détente: Case Studies of the Politics of East–West Relations.* London: Francis Pinter, 1986.

East, Roger and Jolyon Pontin. *Revolution and Change in Central and Eastern Europe.* rev. ed. London: Pinter Publishers, 1997.

Edsall, Thomas with Mary Edsall. *Chain Reaction: The Impact of Race, Rights, and Taxes on American Politics.* New York: Norton, 1991.

Ekiert, Grzegorz. *The State against Society: Political Crises and Their Aftermath in East Central Europe.* Princeton: Princeton University Press, 1996.

Ekiert, Grzegorz and Jan Kubik. *Rebellious Civil Society: Popular Protest and Democratic Consolidation in Poland, 1989–1993.* Ann Arbor: The University of Michigan Press, 1999.

Ehrman, John. *The Rise of Neoconservatism: Intellectuals in Foreign Affairs, 1945–1994.* New Haven: Yale University Press, 1995.

The Eighties: America in the Age of Reagan. New Haven: Yale University Press, 2005.

Engel, Jeffrey A., ed. *The Fall of the Berlin Wall: The Revolutionary Legacy of 1989.* New York: Oxford University Press, 2009.

English, Robert D. *Russia and the Idea of the West: Gorbachev, Intellectuals and the End of the Cold War.* New York: Columbia University Press, 2000.

Evangelista, Matthew. *Unarmed Forces: The Transnational Movement to End the Cold War*. New York: Cornell University Press, 1999.

Falk, Barbara J. *The Dilemmas of Dissidence in East-Central Europe: Citizen Intellectuals and Philosopher Kings*. New York: Central European University Press, 2003.

Ferraris, Luigi Vittorio, ed. *Report on a Negotiation: Helsinki-Geneva-Helsinki, 1972–1975*. trans. Marie-Claire Barber. Alphen ann den Rijn: Sijthoff & Noordhoff, 1979.

Finnemore, Martha. *National Interests in International Society*. Ithaca: Cornell University Press, 1996.

Firestone, Bernard J. and Alexej Ugrinsky, eds. *Gerald R. Ford and the Politics of Post-Watergate America*. 2 Vol. New York: Greenwood Press, 1992.

Fischer, Beth A. *The Reagan Reversal: Foreign Policy and the End of the Cold War*. Columbia: University of Missouri Press, 1997.

Fischer, Thomas. *Neutral Power in the CSCE: The N + N States and the Making of the Helsinki Accords 1975*. Baden-Baden: Nomos, 2009.

FitzGerald, Frances. *Way Out There in the Blue: Reagan, Star Wars, and the End of the Cold War*. New York: Simon & Schuster, 2000.

Foglesong, David S. *The American Mission and the "Evil Empire."* New York: Cambridge University Press, 2007.

Fosdick, Dorothy, ed. *Staying the Course: Henry M. Jackson and National Security*. Seattle: University of Washington Press, 1987.

Foot, Rosemary. *Rights Beyond Borders: The Global Community and the Struggle over Human Rights in China*. New York: Oxford University Press, 2000.

Franck, Thomas. *The Power of Legitimacy Among Nations*. New York: Oxford University Press, 1990.

Freeman, John. *Security and the CSCE Process: The Stockholm Conference and Beyond*. London: Macmillan Academic and Professional, 1991.

Fry, John. *The Helsinki Process: Negotiating Security and Cooperation in Europe*. Washington: National Defense University Press, 1993.

Gaddis, John Lewis. *The Cold War: A New History*. New York: Penguin Press, 2005.

Galtung, Johan, ed. *Cooperation in Europe*. New York: Humanities Press, 1979.

Garthoff, Raymond L. *Détente and Confrontation: American-Soviet Relations from Nixon to Reagan* rev. ed. Washington: Brookings Institution, 1994.

The Great Transition: American-Soviet Relations and the End of the Cold War. Washington,: Brookings Institution, 1994.

Gati, Charles. *The Bloc that Failed: Soviet-East European Relations in Transition*. Indianapolis: Indiana University Press, 1990.

George, Alexander L. Philip J. Farley, and Alexander Dallin, eds. *U. S. -Soviet Security Cooperation: Achievements, Failures, Lessons*. New York: Oxford University Press, 1988.

Gerstle, Gary and Steve Fraser, eds. *The Rise and Fall of the New Deal Order, 1930–1980*. Princeton: Princeton University Press, 1989.

Geseau, Frans A. M. Alting von, ed. *Uncertain Détente*. Alphen aan den Rijn: Sijthoff and Noordhoff, 1979.

Gilbert, Martin. *Shcharansky: Hero of Our Time*. New York: Viking, 1986.

Gilligan, Emma. *Defending Human Rights in Russia: Sergei Kovalyov, Dissident and Human Rights Commissioner, 1969–2003.* New York: Routledge, 2004.

Glad, Betty. *Jimmy Carter: In Search of the Great White House.* New York: W. W. Norton and Company, 1980.

An Outsider in the White House: Jimmy Carter, His Advisors, and the Making of American Foreign Policy. Ithaca: Cornell University Press, 2009.

Gladwell, Malcolm. *The Tipping Point: How Little Things Can Make a Big Difference.* Boston: Little, Brown and Company, 2000.

Glendon, Mary Ann. *A World Made New: Eleanor Roosevelt and the Universal Declaration of Human Rights.* New York: Random House, 2001.

Glenn, John K. *Framing Democracy: Civil Society and Civic Movements in Eastern Europe.* Stanford: Stanford University Press, 2001.

Goedde, Petra, William Hitchcock, and Akira Iriye, ed. *Human Rights in the Twentieth Century: An International History.* New York: Oxford University Press, 2011.

Goldberg, Paul. *The Final Act: The Dramatic, Revealing Story of the Moscow Helsinki Watch Group.* New York: Morrow, 1988.

Goodby, James E. *Europe Undivided: The New Logic of Peace in U. S. –Russian Relations.* Washington: United States Institute of Peace, 1998.

Griffith, William E. *The Superpowers and Regional Tensions.* Lexington: Lexington Books, 1982.

Haas, Ernst. *The Uniting of Europe: Political, Social, and Economic Forces, 1950–1957.* Stanford: Stanford University Press, 1958.

Hagihara, Nobutoshi, et al., eds. *Experiencing the Twentieth Century.* Tokyo: University of Tokyo Press, 1985.

Halliday, Fred. *The Making of the Second Cold War.* London: Verso, 1983.

Hanhimäki, Jussi. *The Flawed Architect: Henry Kissinger and American Foreign Policy.* New York: Oxford University Press, 2004.

Hargrove, Erwin C. *Jimmy Carter as President: Leadership and the Politics of the Public Good.* Baton Rouge: Louisiana State University Press, 1988.

Hasenclever, Andreas, Peter Mayer, and Volker Rittberger. *Theories of International Regimes.* Cambridge: Cambridge University Press, 1997.

Hayden, Jacqueline. *The Collapse of Communist Power in Poland: Strategic Misperceptions and Unanticipated Outcomes.* New York: Routledge, 2006.

Heiss, Mary Ann and S. Victor Papcosma, eds. *NATO and the Warsaw Pact: Intrabloc Conflicts.* Kent: The Kent State University Press, 2008.

Held, Joseph, ed. *The Columbia History of Eastern Europe in the 20th Century.* New York: Columbia University Press, 1992.

Heneka, A., et al., eds. *A Besieged Culture: Czechoslovakia Ten Years After Helsinki.* Stockholm: The Charta 77 Foundation, 1985.

Henkin, Louis. *The Age of Rights.* New York: Columbia University Press, 1990.

Heraclides, Alexis. *Security and Co-operation in Europe: The Human Dimension, 1972–1992.* Portland: Frank Cass, 1993.

Herrmann, R. K. *Perceptions and Behavior in Soviet Foreign Policy.* Pittsburgh: University of Pittsburgh Press, 1985

Herrman, Richard K. and Richard New Lebow, eds. *Ending the Cold War: Interpretations, Causation, and the Study of International Relations.* New York: Palgrave, 2004.

Hill, Dilys M., ed. *Human Rights and Foreign Policy: Principles and Practice.* New York: St. Martin's Press, 1989.

Hirschman, Albert O. *Exit, Voice, and Loyalty: Responses to Decline in Firms, Organizations, and States.* Cambridge: Harvard University Press, 1970.

Hitchcock, William I. *The Struggle for Europe: The Turbulent History of a Divided Continent, 1945 to the Present.* New York: Anchor Books, 2004.

Hoffmann, Stefan-Ludwig, ed. *Human Rights in the Twentieth Century.* New York: Cambridge University Press, 2010.

Hogan, Michael J., ed. *The End of the Cold War: Its Meanings and Implications.* New York: Cambridge University Press, 1992.

Horn, Gerd-Rainer and Padraic Kenney, eds. *Transnational Moments of Change: Europe 1945, 1968, 1989.* Boulder: Rowman and Littlefield, 2004.

Horvath, Robert. *The Legacy of Soviet Dissent: Dissidents, Democratisation and Radical Nationalism in Russia.* New York: RoutledgeCurzon, 2005.

Hosking, Geoffrey. *The Awakening of the Soviet Union.* rev. ed. Cambridge: Harvard University Press, 1991.

Hough, Jerry F. *Russia and the West: Gorbachev and the Politics of Reform.* New York: Simon and Schuster, 1988.

Hufton, E. Olwen, ed. *Historical Change and Human Rights: The Oxford Amnesty Lectures, 1994.* New York: Basic Books, 1995.

Hughes, Henry Stuart. *Sophisticated Rebels: The Political Culture of European Dissent, 1968–1987.* Cambridge: Harvard University Press, 1988.

Humphrey, John P. *Human Rights and the United Nations: A Great Adventure.* Dobbs Ferry: Transnational Publishers, 1984.

Ignatieff, Michael. *The Rights Revolution.* Toronto: Anasi, 2000.

Ignatieff, Michael, ed. *American Exceptionalism and Human Rights.* Princeton: Princeton University Press, 2005.

International Helsinki Federation for Human Rights. *On Speaking Terms: An Unprecedented Human Rights Mission to the Soviet Union, January 25–31, 1988.* Vienna: International Helsinki Federation for Human Rights, 1988.

Iriye, Akira. *Global Community: The Role of International Organizations in the Making of the Contemporary World.* Berkeley: University of California Press, 2002.

Isaacson, Walter. *Kissinger: A Biography.* New York: Simon and Schuster, 1992.

Jackson, Thomas F. *From Civil Rights to Human Rights: Martin Luther King, Jr. and the Struggle for Economic Justice.* Philadelphia: University of Pennsylvania Press, 2007.

Jarausch, Konrad H. *The Rush to German Unity.* New York: Oxford University Press, 1994.

Jennings, Jeremy and Anthony Kemp-Welch, eds. *Intellectuals in Politics: From the Dreyfus Affair to Salman Rushdie.* New York: Routledge, 1997.

Josselin, Daphné and William Wallace, eds. *Non-State Actors in World Politics.* New York: Palgrave, 2001.

Judt, Tony. *Postwar: A History of Europe Since 1945*. New York: Penguin Press, 2005.

Kaiser, Robert G. *Why Gorbachev Happened: His Triumphs and His Failure*. New York: Simon and Schuster, 1991.

Kashlev, Y. B. ed. *Khel'sinskii Protsess v Sovetskoi/Rossiiskoi Vneshnei Politike: 1975–2000*. Moscow: Diplomaticheskaia Akademiia MID RF, 2000.

Katzenstein, Peter J., ed. *The Culture of National Security: Norms and Identity in World Politics*. New York: Columbia University Press, 1996.

Kaufman, Burton Ira. *The Presidency of James Earl Carter, Jr*. Lawrence: University Press of Kansas, 1993.

Kaufman, Roberts G. *Henry M. Jackson: A Life in Politics*. Seattle: University of Washington Press, 2000.

Kaufman, Scott. *Plans Unraveled: The Foreign Policy of the Carter Administration*. Dekalb: Northern Illinois University Press, 2008.

Keane, John. *Václav Havel: A Political Tragedy in Six Acts*. New York: Basic Books, 2000.

Keck, Margaret and Kathryn Sikkink. *Activists Beyond Borders: Advocacy Networks in International Politics*. Ithaca: Cornell University Press, 1998.

Kennedy, Paul. *The Rise and Fall of the Great Powers*. New York: Vintage Books, 1989.

Kenney, Padraic. *A Carnival of Revolution: Central Europe 1989*. Princeton: Princeton University Press, 2002.

Keohane, Robert and Joseph S. Nye, Jr. eds. *Transnational Relations and World Politics*. Cambridge: Harvard University Press, 1971.

Khagram, Sanjeev, James V. Riker, and Kathryn Sikkink, eds. *Restructuring World Politics: Transnational Social Movements, Networks, and Norms*. Minneapolis: University of Minnesota Press, 2002.

King, Robert R. and Robert W. Dean, eds. *Eastern European Perspectives on European Security and Cooperation*. New York: Praeger, 1974.

Kissinger, Henry. *Diplomacy*. New York: Simon and Schuster, 1994.

Klaiber, Wolfgang, et al. *Era of Negotiations: European Security and Force Reductions*. Lexington: Lexington Books, 1973.

Klotz, Audie. *Norms in International Relations: The Struggle Against Apartheid*. Ithaca: Cornell University Press, 1995.

Knopf, Jeffrey W. *Domestic Society and International Cooperation: The Impact of Protest on US Arms Control Policy*. New York: Cambridge University Press, 1998.

Kommers, Donald P. and Gilburt D. Loescher, eds. *Human Rights and American Foreign Policy*. Notre Dame: University of Notre Dame Press, 1979.

Korey, William. *Human Rights and the Helsinki Accord*. No. 264. New York: Foreign Policy Association, 1983.

Korey, William. *The Promises We Keep: Human Rights, the Helsinki Process and American Foreign Policy*. New York: St. Martin's Press, 1993.

Kotkin, Stephen. *Armageddon Averted: The Soviet Collapse, 1970–2000*. New York: Oxford University Press, 2000.

Kotkin, Stephen. *Uncivil Society: 1989 and the Implosion of the Communist Establishment*. With a contribution by Jan T. Gross. New York: Modern Library, 2009.

Kotz, David with Fred Weir. *Revolution from Above: The Demise of the Soviet System*. New York: Routledge, 1997.

Kozlova, V. A. and C. V. Mironenko, eds. *Kramola: Inakomyslie v SSSR pri Khrushcheve u Brezhneve 1953–1982 gg*. Moscow: Materik, 2005.

Krehbiel, Carl. *Confidence- and Security-Building Measures in Europe: The Stockholm Conference*. New York: Praeger, 1989.

Kubik, Jan. *The Power of Symbols Against the Symbols of Power: The Rise of Solidarity and the Fall of State Socialism in Poland*. University Park: The Pennsylvania State University Press, 1994.

Kull, Stephen. *Burying Lenin: The Revolution in Soviet Ideology and Foreign Policy*. Boulder: Westview Press, 1992.

Lane, David. *The Rise and Fall of State Socialism: Industrial Society and the Socialist State*. Cambridge: Polity Press, 1996.

Lauren, Paul Gordon. *Evolution of International Human Rights*. Philadelphia: University of Pennsylvania Press, 2003.

Lawson, George. *Negotiated Revolutions: The Czech Republic, South Africa and Chile*. Burlington: Ashgate, 2005.

Lawson, George, Chris Armbruster, and Michael Cox, eds. *The Global 1989: Continuity and Change in World Politics, 1989–2009*. New York: Cambridge University Press, 2010.

Leatherman, Janie. *From Cold War to Democratic Peace: Third Parties, Peaceful Change, and the OSCE*. Syracuse: Syracuse University Press, 2003.

Leebaert, Derek, ed. *European Security: Prospects for the 1980s*. Lexington: Heath, 1979.

Leffler, Melvyn P. *For the Soul of Mankind: The United States, the Soviet Union and the Cold War*. New York: Hill and Wang, 2007.

Lehne, Stefan. *The Vienna Meeting of the Conference on Security and Cooperation in Europe, 1986–1989*. Boulder: Westview Press, 1991.

Lettow, Paul. *Ronald Reagan and his Quest to Abolish Nuclear Weapons*. New York: Random House, 2006.

Levesque, J. *The Enigma of 1989: The USSR and the Liberation of Eastern Europe*. Los Angeles: University of California Press, 1997.

Lichbach, Mark Irving and Alan S. Zuckerman, eds. *Comparative Politics: Rationality, Culture, and Structure*. New York: Cambridge University Press, 1997.

Lieber, Robert J., ed. *Eagle Rules?: Foreign Policy and American Primacy in the Twenty-first Century*. Upper Saddle River: Prentice Hall, 2002.

Lipski, Jan Józef. *KOR: A History of the Workers' Defense Committee in Poland, 1976–1981*. trans. Olga Amsterdamska and Gene M. Moore. Berkeley: University of California Press, 1985.

Logevall, Frederik and Andrew Preston, eds. *Nixon in the World: American Foreign Relations, 1969–1977*. New York: Oxford University Press, 2008.

Loth, Wilfried. *Overcoming the Cold War: A History of Détente, 1950–1991*. trans. Robert F. Hogg. New York: Palgrave, 2002.

Lourie, Richard. *Sakharov: A Biography*. Hanover: Brandeis University Press, 2002.

Lucas, Michael R. *The Western Alliance After INF: Redefining U. S. Policy Toward Europe and the Soviet Union*. Boulder: Lynne Reinner, 1990.

Lundestad, Geir and Odd Arne Westad, eds. *Beyond the Cold War: New Dimensions in International Relations*. New York: Scandinavian University Press, 1993.

Lynch, Allen, ed. *Building Security in Europe: Confidence-Building Measures and the CSCE*. New York: Institute for East–West Security Studies, 1986.

Maier, Charles S. *Dissolution: The Crisis of Communism and the End of East Germany*. Princeton: Princeton University Press, 1997.

Mann, James. *The Rebellion of Ronald Reagan: A History of the End of the Cold War*. New York: Viking, 2009.

Mastny, Vojtech, ed. *Helsinki, Human Rights, and European Security: Analysis and Documentation*. Durham: Duke University Press, 1986.

Mastny, Vojtech. *The Helsinki Process and the Reintegration of Europe, 1986–1991*. New York: Institute for East–West Security Studies, 1992.

Mastny, Vojtech and Malcolm Byrne, eds. *A Cardboard Castle?: An Inside History of the Warsaw Pact, 1955–1991*. New York: Central European University Press, 2005.

Matlock, Jack. *Reagan and Gorbachev: How the Cold War Ended*. New York: Random House, 2004.

McDermott, Kevin and Matthew Stibbe, eds. *Revolution and Resistance in Eastern Europe: Challenges to Communist Rule*. New York: Berg, 2006.

Mead, Walter Russell. *Special Providence: American Foreign Policy and How It Changed the World*. New York: Routledge, 2002.

Medvedev, Roy. *Andropov*. Moscow: Molodaya Gvardiya, 2006.

Melanson, Richard A. *American Foreign Policy Since the Vietnam War: The Search for Consensus from Nixon to Clinton*. 2nd ed. Armonk: M. E. Sharpe, 1996.

Mendelson, Sarah E. *Changing Course: Ideas, Politics, and the Soviet Withdrawal from Afghanistan*. Princeton: Princeton University Press, 1998.

Mendelson, Sarah E. and John K. Glenn, ed. *The Power and Limits of NGOs: A Critical Look at Building Democracy in Eastern Europe and Eurasia*. New York: Columbia University Press, 2002.

Meyer, Michael. *The Year That Changed the World: The Untold Story behind the Fall of the Berlin Wall*. New York: Scribner, 2009.

Möckli, Daniel. *European Foreign Policy During the Cold War: Heath, Brandt, Pompidou and the Dream of Political Unity*. New York: I. B. Tauris, 2009.

Moore, Jonathan and Janet Fraser, eds. *Campaign for President: The Managers Look at '76*. Cambridge: Balinger Publishing Company, 1977.

Mosckovskai Khel'sinskai Gruppa – Obshchestvo "Memorial." *Dokumenty Moskovskoi Khel'sinkskoi Gruppi, 1976–1982*. Moscow: Mosckovskai Khel'sinskai Gruppa, 2006.

Möttölä, Kari, ed. *Ten Years After Helsinki: The Making of the European Security Regime*. Boulder: Westview Press, 1986.

Mower, A. Glenn. *The United States, the United Nations, and Human Rights: the Eleanor Roosevelt and Jimmy Carter Eras*. Westport: Greenwood Press, 1979.

—— *Human Rights and American Foreign Policy: The Carter and Reagan Experiences*. New York: Greenwood Press, 1987.

Moyn, Samuel. *The Last Utopia: Human Rights in History*. Cambridge: Harvard University Press, 2010.

Muravchik, Joshua. *Uncertain Crusade: Jimmy Carter and the Dilemmas of Human Rights Policy*. Lanham: Hamilton Press, 1986.

Muskie, Edmund S., Kenneth Rush, and Kenneth W. Thompson, eds. *The President, the Congress and Foreign Policy*. Lanham: University Press of America, 1986.

Naimark, Norman M. *Fires of Hatred: Ethnic Cleansing in Twentieth-Century Europe*. Cambridge: Harvard University Press, 2001.

Nash, George H. *The Conservative Intellectual Movement in America Since 1945*. Wilmington: Intercollegiate Studies Institute, 1998.

Nelson, Keith T. *The Making of Détente: Soviet-American Relations in the Shadow of Vietnam*. Baltimore: Johns Hopkins University Press, 1995.

Neuhold, Hanspeter, ed. *CSCE: N+N Perspectives. The Process of the Conference on Security and Cooperation in Europe from the Viewpoint of the Neutral and Non-Aligned Participating States*. Laxengerb Papers No. 8. Vienna: Wilhelm Braumuller & Austrian Institute for International Affairs, 1987.

Newsom, David D., ed. *The Diplomacy of Human Rights*. Lanham: University Press of American for Institute for the Study of Diplomacy, Georgetown University, 1986.

Njølstad, Olav, ed. *The Last Decade of the Cold War: From Conflict Escalation to Conflict Transformation*. New York: Frank Cass Publishers, 2004.

Nuti, Leopoldo, ed. *The Crisis of Détente in Europe: From Helsinki to Gorbachev, 1975–1985*. New York: Routledge, 2009.

Nye, Joseph. *Soft Power: The Means to Success in World Politics*. New York: PublicAffairs, 2004.

Oberdorfer, Don. *From the Cold War to a New Era: The United States and the Soviet Union, 1983–1991*. Baltimore: Johns Hopkins University Press, 1998.

Osa, Maryjane. *Solidarity and Contention: Networks of Polish Opposition*. Minneapolis: University of Minnesota Press, 2003.

Ouimet, Matthew J. *The Rise and Fall of the Brezhnev Doctrine in Soviet Foreign Policy*. Chapel Hill: University of North Carolina Press, 2003.

Oye, Kenneth A., Robert Lieber, and Donald Rothchild, eds. *Eagle Resurgent?: The Reagan Era in American Foreign Policy*. Boston: Little Brown, 1983.

Paczkowski, Andrzej. *The Spring Will Be Ours: Poland and the Poles from Occupation to Freedom*. trans. Jane Cave. University Park: Pennsylvania State University Press, 2003.

Palmer, Michael. *The Prospects for a European Security Conference*. London: Chatham House, 1971.

Parchomenko, Walter. *Soviet Images of Dissidents and Nonconformists*. New York: Praeger, 1986.

Parmet, Herbert S. *George Bush: The Life of a Lone Star Yankee*. New York: Scribner, 1997.

Pienkos, Donald. *PNA: A Centennial History of the Polish National Alliance of the United States of North America*. New York: Columbia University Press, 1984.

———. *For Your Freedom Through Ours: Polish American Efforts on Poland's Behalf, 1863–1991*. New York: Columbia University Press, 1991.

Pleshakov, Constantine. *There Is No Freedom Without Bread!: 1989 and the Civil War That Brought Down Communism.* New York: Farrar, Straus and Giroux, 2009.

Power, Samantha. *"A Problem from Hell:" America and the Age of Genocide.* New York: Harper Perennial, 2002.

Power, Samantha and Graham Allison, eds. *Realizing Human Rights: Moving from Inspiration to Impact.* New York: St. Martin's Press, 2000.

Puddington, J. Arch. *Broadcasting Freedom: The Cold War Triumph of Radio Free Europe and Radio Liberty.* Lexington: University Press of Kentucky, 2000.

Rabben, Linda. *Fierce Legion of Friends: A History of Human Rights Campaigns and Campaigners.* Hyattsville: Quixote Center, 2002.

Ramet, Sabrina P. *Social Currents in Eastern Europe: The Sources and Consequences of the Great Transformation.* Durham: Duke University Press, 1995.

Richmond, Yale. *Cultural Exchange and The Cold War: Raising the Iron Curtain.* University Park: The Pennsylvania State University Press, 2003.

Risee, Hans-Peter, ed. *Since the Prague Spring: The Continuing Struggle for Human Rights in Czechoslovakia.* New York: Random House, 1979.

Risse, Thomas, et al. eds. *The Power of Human Rights: International Norms and Domestic Change.* New York: Cambridge University Press, 1999.

Risse-Kappen, Thomas, ed. *Bringing Transnational Relations Back In.* Cambridge: Cambridge University Press, 1995.

Robertson, Geoffrey. *Crimes Against Humanity: The Struggle for Global Justice.* 3rd ed. New York: The New Press, 2006.

Robinson, Herbert W. *Election Issues of 1976.* Washington: International Management Systems Corporation, 1976.

Romano, Angela. *From Détente in Europe to European Détente: How the West Shaped the Helsinki CSCE.* New York: P. I. E. Peter Lang, 2009.

Rosenberg, Emily. *Spreading the American Dream: American Economic & Cultural Expansion 1890–1945.* New York: Hill and Wang, 1982.

Rosati, Jerel. *The Carter Administration's Quest for Global Community: Beliefs and Their Impact on Behavior.* Columbia: University of South Carolina Press, 1987.

Rosenbaum, Herbert D. and Alexej Ugrinsky, eds. *Jimmy Carter: Foreign Policy and the Post-Presidential Years.* Westport: Greenwood Press, 1994.

Ross, Robert S. *Negotiating Cooperation: the United States and China, 1969–1989.* Stanford: Stanford University Press, 1995.

Rostagni, Carla Meneguzzi, ed. *The Helsinki Process: A Historical Reappraisal.* Padua: CEDAM, 2005.

Rotfeld, Adam Daniel. ed. *From Helsinki to Madrid: Conference on Security and Co-operation in Europe: Documents, 1973–1983.* Warsaw: Polish Institute of International Affairs, 1983.

Royal United Service Institute for Defence Studies, ed. *RUSI and Brassey's Defence Yearbook 1991.* London: Brassey's 1991.

Rubenstein, Joshua. *Soviet Dissidents: Their Struggle for Human Rights.* 2nd ed. Boston: Beacon Press, 1985.

Rubenstein, Joshua and Alexander Gribanov, eds. *The KGB File of Andrei Sakharov.* New Haven: Yale University Press, 2005.

Rubin, Barry M. and Elizabeth P. Spiro, ed. *Human Rights and U. S. Foreign Policy*. Boulder: Westview Press, 1979.

Ruggie, John G. *Constructing the World Polity: Essays on International Institutionalization*. London: Routledge, 1998.

Ryback, Timothy. *Rock Around the Bloc: A History of Rock Music in Eastern Europe and the Soviet Union*. New York: Oxford University Press, 1990.

Sarotte, Mary Elise. *Dealing with the Devil: East Germany, Détente, and Ostpolitik, 1969–1973*. Chapel Hill: University of North Carolina Press, 2001.
    1989: The Struggle to Create Post-Cold War Europe. Princeton: Princeton University Press, 2009.

Saxonberg, Steven. *The Fall: A Comparative Study of the End of Communism in Czechoslovakia, East Germany, Hungary and Poland*. Amsterdam: Harwood Academic Publishers, 2001.

Schapiro, Amy. *Millicent Fenwick: Her Way*. New Brunswick: Rutgers University Press, 2003.

Schell, Jonathan. *The Unconquerable World: Power, Nonviolence, and the Will of the People*. New York: Metropolitan Books, 2003.

Schlesinger, Arthur M., Jr. *The Imperial Presidency*. Boston: Houghton Mifflin, 1973.

Schoultz, Lars. *Human Rights and United States Policy toward Latin America*. Princeton: Princeton University Press, 1981.

Schulz, Matthias and Thomas A. Schwartz, eds. *The Strained Alliance: U.S. – European Relations from Nixon to Carter*. New York: Cambridge University Press, 2009.

Schweizer, Peter. *Victory: The Reagan Administration's Secret Strategy That Hastened the Collapse of the Soviet Union*. New York: The Atlantic Monthly Press, 1994.

Sebestyen, Victor. *Revolution 1989: The Fall of the Soviet Empire*. New York: Pantheon Books, 2009.

Sellars, Kristen. *The Rise and Rise of Human Rights*. London: Sutton Publishing, 2002.

Sewell, Bevan and Scott Lucas, eds. *Challenging US Foreign Policy: America and the World in the Long Twentieth Century*. London: Palgrave, 2011.

Sharp, Paul. *Thatcher's Diplomacy: The Revival of British Foreign Policy*. London: Macmillan Press, 1997.

Shulgan, Christopher. *The Soviet Ambassador: The Making of the Radial Behind Perestroika*. Toronto: McClelland and Stewart, 2008.

Sikkink, Kathryn. *Mixed Signals: U. S. Human Rights Policy and Latin America*. Ithaca: Cornell University Press, 2004.

Simpson, A. W. Brian. *Human Rights and the End of Empire: Britain and the Genesis of the European Convention*. New York: Oxford University Press, 2001.

Sizoo, Jan and Rudolf Th. Jurrjens. *CSCE Decision-Making: The Madrid Experience*. Boston: Martinus Nijhoff Publishers, 1984.

Skidmore, David. *Reversing Course: Carter's Foreign Policy, Domestic Politics, and the Failure of Reform*. Nashville: Vanderbilt University Press, 1996.

Skilling, H. Gordon. *Charter 77 and Human Rights in Czechoslovakia.* London: George Allen and Unwin, 1981.

Samizdat and an Independent Society in Central and Eastern Europe. London: Macmillan Press, 1989.

Skinner, Kiron K., ed. *Turning Points in Ending the Cold War.* Stanford: Hoover Institution Press, 2008.

Skinner, Kiron K., Annelise Anderson, and Martin Anderson, eds. *Reagan In His Own Hand: The Writings of Ronald Reagan that Reveal His Revolutionary Vision for America.* New York: Simon and Schuster, 2001.

Reagan: A Life In Letters. New York: Free Press, 2003.

Slaughter, Anne-Marie. *A New World Order.* Princeton: Princeton University Press, 2004.

Smith, Gaddis. *Morality, Reason and Power: American Diplomacy in the Carter Years.* New York: Hill and Wang, 1986.

Smith, Geoffrey. *Reagan and Thatcher.* London: Bodley Head, 1990.

Smith, Steve and Michael Clarke, eds. *Foreign Policy Implementation.* Boston: G. Allen & Unwin, 1985.

Sneh, Itai Nartzizenfield. *The Future Almost Arrived: How Jimmy Carter Failed to Change U. S. Foreign Policy.* New York: Peter Lang, 2008.

Sodaro, Michael J. *Moscow, Germany, and the West from Khrushchev to Gorbachev.* New York: Cornell University Press, 1990.

Solzhenitsyn, Alexander. *One Day in the Life of Ivan Denisovich.* trans. Gillon Aitken. New York: Farrar, Straus and Giroux, 1971.

Spencer, Robert, ed. *Canada and the Conference on Security and Co-operation in Europe.* Toronto: Centre for International Studies, University of Toronto, 1984.

Stanley, Timothy W. and Darnell M. Witt. *Detente Diplomacy: United States and European Security in the 1970's.* Cambridge: University Press of Cambridge, 1970.

Staniszkis, Jadwiga. *Poland's Self-Limiting Revolution.* Jan Gross, ed. Princeton: Princeton University Press, 1984.

Stebenne, David L. *Arthur J. Goldberg: New Deal Liberal.* New York: Oxford University Press, 1996.

Stent, Angela. *Russia and Germany Reborn: Unification, The Soviet Collapse, and the New Europe.* Princeton: Princeton University Press, 1999.

Stern, Paula. *Water's Edge: Domestic Politics and the Making of American Foreign Policy.* Westport: Greenwood Press, 1979.

Stokes, Gale. *The Walls Came Tumbling Down: The Collapse of Communism in Eastern Europe.* New York: Oxford University Press, 1993.

Strong, Robert A. *Working in the World: Jimmy Carter and the Making of American Foreign Policy.* Baton Rouge: Louisiana State University Press, 2000.

Sundelius, Bengt. *The Neutral Democracies and the New Cold War.* Boulder: Westview Press, 1987.

Suny, Ronald Grigor. *The Revenge of the Past: Nationalism, Revolution, and the Collapse of the Soviet Union.* Stanford: Stanford University Press, 1993.

Sussman, Leonard R. ed. *Three Years at the East–West Divide: The Words of U.S. Ambassador Max M. Kampelman at the Madrid Conference on Security and Human Rights.* New York: Freedom House, 1983.

Tarrow, Sidney. *Power in Movement: Social Movements and Contentious Politics.* 2nd ed. New York: Cambridge University Press, 1998.
The New Transnational Activism. Cambridge: Cambridge University Press, 2005.
Thomas, Daniel C. *The Helsinki Effect: International Norms, Human Rights, and the Demise of Communism.* Princeton: Princeton University Press, 2001.
Thompson, Kenneth W. ed. *Reagan Presidency: Ten Intimate Perspectives.* Lanham: University Press of America, 1993.
Tökés, Rudolf L. *Hungary's Negotiated Revolution: Economic Reform, Social Change, and Political Succession, 1957–1990.* New York: Cambridge University Press, 2004.
Torpey, John C. *Intellectuals, Socialism, and Dissent.* Minneapolis: University of Minnesota Press, 1995.
Traugott, Mark, ed. *Repertoires and Cycles of Collective Action.* Durham: Duke University Press, 1995.
Troy, Gil. *Morning in America: How Ronald Reagan Invented the 1980s.* Princeton: Princeton University Press, 2005.
Van Oudenaren, John. *Détente in Europe: The Soviet Union and the West since 1953.* Durham: Duke University Press, 1991.
Verba, Lesya and Bohdan Yasen, eds. *The Human Rights Movement in Ukraine: Documents of the Ukrainian Helsinki Group, 1976–1980.* Washington: Smolosky Publishers, 1980.
Vladislav, Jan, ed. *Václav Havel: Living in Truth.* Boston: Faber and Faber, 1986.
Wasserstrom, Jeffrey N., Lynn Hunt, and Marilyn Young, ed. *Human Rights and Revolutions.* Lanham: Rowman & Littlefield, 2000.
Wenger, Andreas, Christian Nuenlist, and Anna Locher, eds. *Transforming NATO in the Cold War: Challenges Beyond Deterrence in the 1960s.* New York: Routledge, 2007.
Wenger, Andreas, Vojtech Mastny, and Christian Nuenlist, eds. *Origins of the European Security System: The Helsinki Process Revisited, 1965–75.* New York: Routledge, 2008.
Weigel, George. *The Final Revolution: The Resistance Church and the Collapse of Communism.* New York: Oxford University Press, 1992.
Wells, Samuel J. Jr., ed. *The Helsinki Process and the Future of Europe.* Washington: The Wilson Center Press, 1990.
Westad, Odd Arne, ed. *The Fall of Détente: Soviet-American Relations During the Carter Years.* Boston: Scandinavian University Press, 1997.
Reviewing the Cold War: Approaches, Interpretations, Theory. London: Frank Cass, 1998.
Westad, Odd Arne and Poul Villaume, eds. *Perforating the Iron Curtain: European Détente, Transatlantic Relations, and the Cold War, 1965–1985.* Copenhagen: Museum Tusculanum Press, 2009.
Whelan, Joseph G. *Soviet Diplomacy and Negotiation Behavior: Emerging New Context for U. S. Diplomacy.* Washington: Congressional Research Service, 1979.
Wills, Garry. *Reagan's America: Innocents at Home.* rev. ed. New York: Penguin Books, 2000.

Witcover, Jules. *Marathon: The Pursuit of the Presidency, 1972–1976.* New York: Viking Press, 1977.

Wohlforth, William, ed. *Cold War Endgame: Oral History, Analysis, Debates.* University Park: Pennsylvania State University Press, 2003.

Yurchak, Alexei. *Everything Was Forever, Until It Was No More: The Last Soviet Generation.* Princeton: Princeton University Press, 2006.

Zagladin, Vadim. *To Restructure and Humanize International Relations.* Moscow: Novosti Press Agency Publishing House, 1989.

Zelikow, Philip and Condoleezza Rice. *Germany Unified and Europe Transformed.* Cambridge: Harvard University Press, 1995.

Zubok, Vladislav. *A Failed Empire: The Soviet Union and the Cold War from Stalin to Gorbachev.* Chapel Hill: University of North Carolina Press, 2007.

Index

CPSIA information can be obtained
at www.ICGtesting.com
Printed in the USA
LVOW12s1945151216
517433LV00002B/192/P